The World Is Our Stage

The Global Rhetorical Presidency and the Cold War

ALLISON M. PRASCH

The University of Chicago Press
Chicago and London

The University of Chicago Press, Chicago 60637
The University of Chicago Press, Ltd., London
© 2023 by The University of Chicago
All rights reserved. No part of this book may be used or reproduced in any manner
whatsoever without written permission, except in the case of brief quotations in
critical articles and reviews. For more information, contact the University of Chicago
Press, 1427 E. 60th St., Chicago, IL 60637.
Published 2023
Printed in the United States of America

32 31 30 29 28 27 26 25 24 23   1 2 3 4 5

ISBN-13: 978-0-226-82365-2 (cloth)
ISBN-13: 978-0-226-82366-9 (paper)
ISBN-13: 978-0-226-82364-5 (e-book)
DOI: https://doi.org/10.7208/chicago/9780226823645.001.0001

Library of Congress Cataloging-in-Publication Data

Names: Prasch, Allison M., author.
Title: The world is our stage : the global rhetorical presidency and the Cold War /
    Allison M. Prasch.
Description: Chicago : The University of Chicago Press, 2023. | Includes
    bibliographical references and index.
Identifiers: LCCN 2022020540 | ISBN 9780226823652 (cloth) | ISBN 9780226823669
    (paperback) | ISBN 9780226823645 (ebook)
Subjects: LCSH: Rhetoric—Political aspects—United States—History—20th century.
    | Presidents—United States—Influence. | Cold War. | BISAC: LANGUAGE ARTS &
    DISCIPLINES / Rhetoric | POLITICAL SCIENCE / International Relations / Diplomacy
Classification: LCC P301.5.P67 P73 2023 | DDC 808—dc23/eng/20220601
LC record available at https://lccn.loc.gov/2022020540

♾ This paper meets the requirements of ANSI/NISO Z39.48-1992 (Permanence
of Paper).

To Jason, Oliver, and Lucy—
my apodeixis *of grace*

All the world's a stage.

WILLIAM SHAKESPEARE, *As You Like It*

The image of America that exists in other people's minds is of fundamental importance, *not* because we have a sentimental, infantile craving to be "loved" (though perhaps we do) but for a far more tangible reason: the *actions* of other people, in a great variety of unpredictable future situations, are likely to be greatly influenced by what they think about us. . . . We want them to regard us as "good guys" *in our role on the world stage* and in our relation *to them*.

"Aspects of the American Image That Matter Most," US Information Agency, 1960

Contents

Illustrations

Introduction

Six minutes before 2:00 a.m. on July 15, 1948, Harry S. Truman spoke to the crowd assembled inside the Philadelphia Convention Hall on the third night of the Democratic National Convention. The man who many considered an accidental president after Franklin Delano Roosevelt's sudden death in April 1945 had survived a contentious delegate vote to secure the formal nomination of the Democratic Party for president of the United States.[1] The root cause of the conflict had been Truman's civil rights legislation program, which Southern Democrats argued was a direct assault on states' rights.[2] In his acceptance speech that "set the convention on fire," according to one *New York Times* reporter, Truman tacitly acknowledged the party split.[3] There had been "differences of opinion," he said, "and that is the democratic way." But now, he argued, it was "time for us to get together and beat the common enemy"—namely, the Republican Party. And yet, even as he implored voters to reject the "party of special interest," Truman did stress one area of common ground. "The record on foreign policy of the Democratic party is that the United States has been turned away permanently from isolationism, and we have converted the greatest and best of the Republicans to our viewpoint on that subject," he said. In fact, Truman continued, it was time for the United States "to accept its full responsibility for leadership in international affairs," noting that the country's "foreign policy should be the policy of the whole Nation and not the policy of one party or the other. Partisanship should stop at the water's edge."[4]

Prominent Republicans agreed. Two months later, US senator Arthur Vandenberg spoke to the Michigan State Republican Convention in Detroit. With the US presidential election between Truman and New York governor Thomas E. Dewey just five weeks away, Vandenberg, the powerful chair of the Senate Foreign Relations Committee, promised that, at least in foreign affairs, Republicans would also "halt politics at the water's edge." The postwar international situation was too consequential for the US government to be divided by partisan politics, he acknowledged—and Vandenberg soon had the opportunity to make good on his promise.[5] In a Lincoln Day Dinner speech two weeks after Truman's inauguration, Vandenberg reaffirmed his belief that nonpartisanship was essential in US foreign policy. "It will be a sad hour for the Republic if we ever desert the fundamental concept that politics shall stop at the water's edge," he said. All US elected officials, regardless of party affiliation, had a duty "to put their country first," Vandenberg concluded. "Those who don't will serve neither their country nor their party."[6] This oft-repeated declaration that politics should "stop at the water's edge" encapsulates the view held by many US political officials at the dawn of the Cold War. If the United States was to rally the "Free World" against the growing threat of Soviet communism, the nation needed to present a confident, unified image to the global public.

Throughout the Cold War, US officials directed enormous time, attention, and financial resources to portraying American superiority, prestige, and global hegemony to audiences at home and abroad. This campaign extended to all areas of American life, including political ideology, civil rights, cultural production, science, technology, and gender equity. Regardless of area or focus, however, the aim was to present a robust vision of the United States as the rightful "Leader of the Free World." US presidents played a crucial role in this image making, arguing that US democracy was preferable and ultimately superior to totalitarian rule. In the end, their goal was to convince the US public to embrace American values of democracy and individualism and to persuade a global, transnational audience to rally together against the threat of Soviet communism.

This book examines a critical yet understudied element of this rhetorical campaign: how US presidents utilized their physical travel beyond the nation's own borders to constitute, define, and even limit the boundaries of the "Free World" global imaginary. Where both Republicans and Democrats agreed that internal political squabbles should "stop at the water's edge" so as not to undermine US foreign policy initiatives, American chief executives came to rely on carefully orchestrated trips *beyond* the water's edge as a powerful symbolic weapon in their Cold War campaign. In fact, US presidents and their advisors saw these acts of going global as a mechanism by which they could accentuate American power and prestige in the minds of an international audience and persuade the US public that the United States was the preeminent actor on the Cold War world stage.[7]

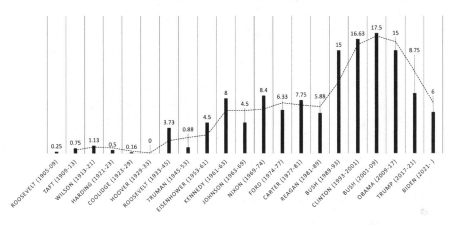

FIGURE O.1. Travels of the US president (1906–2021). This graph depicts the average number of international visits US presidents made to other countries per year while in office (beginning with Theodore Roosevelt's second term). Source: US Department of State Office of the Historian, with supplemental details for 2020–21 obtained from reporting by CNN, the *New York Times*, and the *Washington Post*.

Ever since Theodore Roosevelt's travel to the Panama Canal Zone in 1906, chief executives have used their international travels to portray the United States as preeminent in the global order. A careful examination of this practice reveals a deliberate rhetorical strategy that emerged as the United States sought to expand its geopolitical, military, and ideological influence beyond the nation's own shores. These tours reflect a larger pattern of US presidential rhetoric that developed during the twentieth century, what I call the global rhetorical presidency. The global rhetorical presidency examines how US presidents have used their rhetoric abroad to address and constitute a broad international audience; expand the president's power in foreign affairs; extend the United States' military, political, and psychological influence in various geopolitical regions and nation-states; and elevate the nation's image abroad. Although there are numerous instances of how US presidents utilized the global rhetorical presidency prior to 1945, the practice evolved to become a powerful form of public diplomacy during the Cold War (figure o.1).[8]

As chief executives sought to elevate US prestige and solidify American leadership of the "Free World" after the Second World War, the act of going global became much more intentional, premeditated, and rhetorically significant. As rhetorical actors on the Cold War world stage, US presidents used their physical travel to and rhetoric in specific places and regions to articulate and accentuate the boundaries of American influence. These tours symbolized an extension of US democratic values beyond the nation's own shores and suggested that virtues of self-determination, individual political participation, and free choice could—and should—be applied to the rest of the world. Although the ideological borders of this global order were created and sustained through language, this Cold War stage was also roped off and demarcated through the movement of the presidential body. Where the president went—or chose not to go—communicated volumes about what certain places or regions meant and how they functioned within a Cold War world. These movements delineated places or locales central to US foreign policy while also elevating new spaces in the "Free World" global imaginary. Multiple administrations also considered how images and live recordings of the president's rhetoric in place could reach audiences around the world. This intentional media coverage of these international tours enabled the president's rhetoric abroad—be it through photographs, radio broadcasts, newsreel footage, or live television—to extend beyond the local into the global as US presidents used their location to argue for a specific way of being and acting in the Cold War world. Ultimately, the deliberate planning, construction, placement, and circulation of these tours resulted in a vivid, dramatic enactment of US foreign policy for all the world to see.

To understand the historical context from which these campaigns emerged, one must first consider the relationship between presidential speech, US foreign policy, and the rhetorical construction of American global dominance. I use the rest of this introductory chapter to establish this contextual backdrop and set the stage for the scenes that follow.

US Presidential Rhetoric and the Language of American Global Dominance

Throughout history, US presidents have used their rhetorical appeals to exert power, extend influence, persuade audiences to adopt a specific view of the world, and rally the citizenry around a shared set of values or ideals. The words and actions of American chief executives define national identity, mediate mourning in times of tragedy, promote unity, commemorate significant events, and provide direction for moving forward in uncertain times. As democratically elected representatives of the citizenry, US presidents speak to the people, for the people, and about the people—or, at least, one should expect them to do as much. They craft a vision of the US public and use their bully pulpit "to promote the *idea* of an American people *to* the American people."[9] They are the nation's "interpreter-in-chief." They tell "us stories about ourselves, and in so doing . . . [tell] us what sort of people we are, how we are constituted as a community."[10] These rhetorical appeals—most often directed to the US public—have played a substantial role in shaping a national narrative about who the people believe they are and who they want to be.

The shared language of an overarching storyline or myth is foundational to rhetorics of US foreign policy. Myth, what Richard Slotkin has defined as those "stories drawn from a society's history" that "symboliz[e] that society's ideology" and "dramatiz[e] its moral consciousness," describes how individuals understand and make sense of communal norms, expectations, values, and ideals within and in relation to an overarching national narrative.[11] During the Cold War, US politicians relied on mythic language to portray the United States as uniquely qualified to protect, defend, and fight for individual rights and liberties—at least, for some—at home and abroad. But this narrative did not begin with the Cold War. It was the natural continuation of a deeply ingrained national story that positioned the United States as the rightful leader and epicenter of the globe.

The very idea of US "foreign policy" is itself a rhetorical construction. It describes the posture the country adopts toward and in relation to foreign "others"—those nations, groups, or communities of people deemed "outside" the bounds of the United States' imagined community.[12] This point is crucial for understanding how chief executives have crafted and deployed a language of American hegemony throughout history.[13] Although these postures evolved as the nation moved from a fledgling republic trying to prove itself to the self-proclaimed "Leader of the Free World," a consistent theme throughout this story is how US presidents used their rhetoric to position the United States as preeminent in their relationship toward foreign "others" and, in so doing, reaffirmed a shared sense of national unity—or identification—around which the US public could rally. In time, US presidents would market this image to global audiences to elevate US democracy and self-government as the ideal to which all others should aspire.

From the very beginning, the mythic language of American exceptionalism offered an alluring vision that positioned the United States of America as elevated and set apart. It is a story older than the nation itself. In a speech delivered before setting foot in the "New World" in 1630, Puritan leader John Winthrop famously described the Massachusetts Bay Colony as a "city on a hill." Having escaped the clutches of immorality and godlessness in Europe, Winthrop told his compatriots, they now had a moral duty to live as distinct and set apart from the rest of the world.[14] Although Winthrop's initial vision described one colony among many, the mythic narrative of a people carrying out a divinely inspired "errand into the wilderness" continued to reverberate throughout discourses in the pre-Revolutionary British colonies.[15] Implied throughout this discourse was the assumed right of European colonists to tame and occupy what they saw as "empty" land. This narrative, however, erased the presence of Indigenous people and communities living throughout North America. By describing the continent as a "wilderness," early colonizers discursively constituted the "New World" as one ready and waiting for conquest.[16]

After the Revolutionary War and the British surrender at Yorktown, thirteen individual colonies assembled to form the United States of America, a move that set rhetorical and geographical boundaries for who was included in—and excluded from—this new nation. The Articles of Confederation and the US Constitution intimated that rights of citizenship were limited to white, property-owning men. These documents also established the geographical parameters of the United States to encompass thirteen states on the eastern portion of the North American continent. Knowing full well that a wide expanse of land lay to the nation's western border, US politicians set the stage for westward expansion and the creation of, in Thomas Jefferson's words, an "empire for liberty." In fact, Jefferson argued that the nation would be distinct and set apart because "no constitution was ever before so well calculated as ours for extensive empire & self government."[17] But if the United States was to become the nation Jefferson and others envisioned, more land would certainly be needed. US politicians paid almost no heed to the fact that the Indigenous tribes living throughout the thirteen new states and beyond the United States' western border constituted sovereign nations. Instead, because they stood in the way of a rapidly expanding American empire, their displacement was essential.

Across the Atlantic, however, Europe's monarchies posed a grave threat to the infant republic. In his "Farewell Address" in 1796, Washington advised that the United States should have "as little political connection as possible" with other nations, cautioning that relationships with foreign governments would pollute the purity of the American experiment.[18] Washington's caution against developing diplomatic ties with other countries also reflected the bitter infighting between Federalists and Republicans on the issue of France. To many, including Thomas Jefferson, the French Revolution was an extension of the American Revolution and, as historian Jon Meacham explains, "to be for the French Revolution was to be a republican and a friend to liberty; to be against it, or to have reservations about it, was to be a monarchist and a traitor to freedom."[19] And yet, as president, Jefferson also would declare that the United States should avoid "entangling alliances" across the Atlantic and focus on so-called domestic affairs, even when such "internal" matters included the seizure of Indigenous lands.[20]

Throughout the nineteenth century, US presidents and other political officials would avoid direct involvement with European powers even as they made deliberate attempts to extend their "empire for liberty" across North America to the Pacific Ocean.[21] The insatiable desire to conquer the "wilderness" and extend US hegemony across the continent was a driving force behind Thomas Jefferson's purchase of the Louisiana Territory from France in 1803, the Lewis and Clark expeditions from 1803 to 1806, and the migration of thousands of pioneers to establish homesteads beyond the Mississippi. For many white Americans, this occupation of land became synonymous with individual success and personal freedom. A recurring theme was the idea that a country's sovereignty and influence extended only as far as nation's furthest geographical boundary line. If the new nation was to succeed, it needed to take up space—and defend the land they claimed as their own. In his 1823 annual message, James Monroe declared the "American continents" off-limits from European colonization and stated that the United States would "consider any attempt [by another nation] to extend their system to any portion of this hemisphere as dangerous to our peace and safety."[22] Although Monroe directed this pronouncement toward Russia and other European powers, the doctrine quickly became what historian Walter A. MacDougall has called a "venerated tradition of U.S. foreign policy," one that later US presidents used to justify the annexation of Texas, California, Cuba, Puerto Rico, and Guam.[23]

The impulse behind the United States' deliberate seizure and occupation of Indigenous land was linked, unsurprisingly, to the belief that North America was open, empty, and awaiting civilization. The westward spread of white settlers and US military troops during the nineteenth century represented the physical, embodied expansion of an American empire that would extend from sea to shining sea. In 1839, writer John O'Sullivan suggested that the formation of the United States marked the "beginning of a new history, the formation and progress of an untried political system, which separates us from the past and connects us with the future only." In fact, he predicted that the United States was destined to be *the great nation* of futurity" and had access to the "expansive future [as] our arena, and for our history. We are entering on its untrodden space."[24] The future, he implied, was theirs for the taking. O'Sullivan would extend this idea of empty, untrodden space awaiting American expansion and development six years later, when he argued in favor of the annexation of Texas. It was, he declared, the nation's "manifest destiny to overspread the continent allotted by Providence for the free development of our multiplying millions."[25] Great Britain and France had done the same, O'Sullivan reminded his readers. Expansion was simply what empires did.

All this changed at the beginning of the twentieth century, when US presidents redirected impulses of annexation, westward expansion, manifest destiny, settler colonialism, and capitalism to the rest of the world. This deliberate shift from so-called domestic concerns to the global arena was, in many ways, a continuation of the insatiable drive to conquer the "American frontier."[26] Frederick Jackson Turner famously argued that the conquering of the final frontier marked a significant moment in US history, a history that had "been in large degree the history of the colonization of the Great West."[27] In fact, Turner suggested that this desire to conquer the wilderness represented a core trait of the American identity, explaining that over time settlers began to "transform the wilderness" so that it resembled "not the old Europe" but "a new product that is American."[28] But with the conquest of the "American frontier" now complete, the desire to conquer land demanded "a wider field for its exercise"—a field that extended beyond the shores of North America to the rest of the world.[29] The impulse to tame, civilize, and democratize a global wilderness was a primary motivation behind the Spanish-American War— and the first real desire of a US president to travel overseas.

Cloaking US impulses of imperialism and global hegemony in a rhetoric of democracy and individual choice, US presidents positioned the United States as the defender and arbiter of the democratic world. This deliberate, calculated turn to expanding American influence overseas also extended the borders of the nation's imagined community and sense of self. Although US citizens still understood themselves as distinctly separate—even set apart— from the rest for the world, they also began to see the potential for American democracy to take root in other places such as Puerto Rico and Cuba. So it was that the United States went to war against Spain in 1898 under the pretenses of helping the Cuban people liberate themselves from Spanish rule. Under this logic, military intervention in the region aligned with the United States' manifest destiny, its divinely appointed mission to spread democracy to the rest of the world. As Frederick Jackson Turner, who predicted the need for a "wider field" for American territorial advancement, later wrote: "It is not strange that we find the United States again involved in world-politics. Having completed the conquest of the wilderness, and having consolidated our interests, we are beginning to consider the relations of democracy and empire."[30]

It is no accident that US presidents began to consider going global at the exact moment that they began to intervene in the affairs of other counties through military force. In July 1901, after the United States assumed control of the Philippines, Puerto Rico, Guam, and Cuba following its victory over Spain, McKinley suggested that he would visit Cuba during his second term. If some "sort of tradition had been established" against presidential travel abroad, McKinley said, it was because the nation did not "have the foreign affairs that it has today."[31] Because Cuba was now an American protectorate, the president hoped a visit there would "be a step made on a path which would allow the President to leave the soil of the United States."[32] McKinley's hope to visit Cuba never materialized; he was assassinated less than two months later. It was his successor who would finish what McKinley started and become the first US president to travel outside the United States while in office.

Theodore Roosevelt set sail for the Panama Canal Zone not just because he could, but also because earlier US presidents had paved the way. Indeed, the only reason the United States was involved in building the Panama Canal was because of an earlier declaration of US hegemony: the Monroe Doctrine and its various extensions. But where the initial policy was designed to prevent European nations from further colonization in the Americas, Roosevelt argued that doctrine made room for US intervention against governments they deemed problematic. "No independent nation in America need have the slightest fear of aggression from the United States," Roosevelt wrote, as long as it "maintain[ed] order within its own borders and . . . discharge[d] its just obligations to foreigners."[33] The implication, nonetheless, was that if any southern neighbor did not "maintain order" at home, "outside influence" from the United States would be warranted and justified. Through his extension of the Monroe Doctrine to Central America, Theodore Roosevelt set the stage for US military intervention in the affairs of other nation-states in the Americas, including Panama. When the Columbian government refused to ratify a treaty granting the United States exclusive rights to complete the Panamanian isthmus project, the president told advisors that he would be "delighted" to hear of a revolt on the isthmus, indirectly encouraged French military leader Phillipe Bunau-Varilla to lead the charge, and directed US warships to the region to deter any Colombian military response. After a successful uprising by Panamanians on November 3, the US government recognized the new Republic of Panama on November 6, 1903. Just two weeks later, Panama and the United States signed an agreement that would allow the United States to oversee the canal project and act as a sovereign power in the zone.[34] So invested was Roosevelt in the project's success that when criticism of the project threatened to halt its progress, the president sailed to Panama to take stock of the situation himself and, in so doing, became the first US president to travel beyond the United States' borders while in office.[35]

Theodore Roosevelt's inauguration of the global rhetorical presidency is instructive in at least two ways. First, although the president's stated goal was to "see how the ditch [was] getting along" and address widespread criticism of project mismanagement, the visit also allowed Roosevelt to see—and be seen in—the Panama Canal Zone and relay this knowledge back to Congress and the US public.[36] One defining feature of this rhetorical practice is how multiple administrations utilized changes in communication technology to present a robust, confident image of the American chief executive—and, by extension, the United States—as *the* central actor in global affairs. When Theodore Roosevelt became the first sitting US president to travel outside the United States, he ensured that journalists traveling with him captured images of his movements throughout the Panama Canal Zone. These photographs were reprinted alongside Roosevelt's formal report to the US Congress, marking the first instance photographs were published in the official *Congressional Record*. These images also were reproduced in the *New York Times* to ensure that the US public could witness their president traveling beyond the nation's own borders.[37] Going global quickly became a mechanism for displaying American power, influence, and prestige to audiences at home and abroad.

Roosevelt's visit to the Panama Canal Zone also demonstrates how the US president's movements on the world stage embody key foreign policy commitments and display these initiatives to the public. Where earlier US military actions in the isthmus were planned and executed behind the scenes, Roosevelt's trip was widely reported, photographed, and circulated to audiences at home and abroad. Numerous images of Roosevelt's movements throughout the Panama Canal Zone and transcripts of his public speeches in the region contributed to an overarching narrative of rugged individualism, exceptionalism, and US prestige. The president's written report to Congress also relied upon visual images and the president's own personal experience. The transmission and circulation of this message to Congress, the US public, and a wider international audience also transcended national borders to bolster a vision of the United States as a global world power. This combination of Roosevelt's written message, images of the Panama Canal Zone, and the president's own embodied experience in the region produced a compelling multimedia object of presidential rhetoric, a message that accomplished, according to one advisor, "what no other utterance could have done."[38] The global rhetorical presidency had begun.[39]

US presidents also used the act of going global to expand their foreign policy powers and to extend their rhetorical influence in the affairs of other nation-states.[40] Twelve years after Theodore Roosevelt inaugurated the global rhetorical presidency, Woodrow Wilson became the first US president to cross the Atlantic while in office. Under Wilson's leadership, Americans had grown more accustomed to the idea that the United States should take an active role in the world. As Europe's monarchies collapsed with the onset of world war in 1914, Wilson held fast to his belief that US democracy offered the surest solution to a world in turmoil. In a speech to the League to Enforce Peace on May 27, 1916, Wilson told his audience that they could no longer afford to consider themselves "mere disconnected lookers-on." Instead, the president said, the nation needed to acknowledge that they were "participants, whether we would or not, in the life of the world. The interests of all nations are our own also. We are partners with the rest. What affects mankind is inevitably our affairs as well as the affairs of the nations of Europe and Asia."[41] When the United States entered the war in April 1917, Wilson famously declared that the United States' task was to make the world "safe for democracy."[42] For Wilson, US involvement overseas was a moral mandate. Only the United States could lead the way to a permanent and lasting peace.

The president capitalized on this view of the United States as a global leader—and his own position as diplomat in chief—as the Great War drew to a close. Wilson insisted that he play a major role in postwar negotiations at Versailles and positioned himself as an emissary who could help shepherd Europe and the rest of the world into a new era. In his 1918 annual message to the US Congress just before his departure, the president declared that it was his "paramount duty to go" and provide his "personal counsel" to the other nations involved in the negotiations. "It is highly desirable that I should give it," Wilson said, because the "peace settlements which are now to be agreed upon are of transcendent importance both to us and to the rest of the world."[43] It was only natural, he concluded, that the American chief executive occupy a central place in discussions that would shape the global balance of power. Before the formal conference began at Versailles, Wilson traveled to Great Britain, France, and Italy to meet with various political leaders and speak to cheering crowds. According to one historian, Wilson "became the focus of all the pent-up emotions generated at the war's end. To the common people, longing for permanent peace, he alone appeared to have the key."[44] Even Secretary of State Robert Lansing, who had been critical of Wilson's visit, changed his mind and wrote: "There can be no doubt of the wisdom of his coming to Europe and of the effect it will have on the acceptance of our program."[45] Ultimately, however, Wilson failed to convince the US Congress or the American people to support his vision for the postwar world, one in which the United States would adopt the preeminent role.

Wilson's decision to attend the Paris Peace Conference was the most significant extension of the global rhetorical presidency since Theodore Roosevelt's trip to the Panama Canal Zone in 1906. It was an explicitly rhetorical act, a tour designed to showcase American power and prestige at the end of a world war and to elevate Wilson's foreign policy leadership on the world stage. Dedicated to bolstering his own reputation as leader of an international coalition along with the United States' position as a global power, Wilson understood that going global at this pivotal moment would allow him to speak directly to international audiences about his plan for the postwar world while also presenting himself as a global leader to the US public watching at home. Wilson's decision to attend the Paris Peace Conference also can be read as a way to overstep the bounds of Congress and mobilize domestic and international public opinion for his League of Nations.[46] Unfortunately for Wilson, these attempts would backfire. Republican members of Congress resented Wilson's decision to speak for the nation at the Versailles Conference and waged a concerted campaign to defeat the president's plan when he returned to the United States. It is notable that one of their chief criticisms was that Wilson acted as if he and he alone were responsible for US foreign policy— and not Congress. Although Wilson attempted to bolster public support for his plan by speaking to audiences at home and abroad, these attempts ultimately failed. In Wilson's case, going global served as fodder for Republican accusations that the president was usurping their constitutional prerogative to enact foreign policy. Where Wilson saw his visit to the Paris Peace Conference as a chance to reassert—and expand—presidential power in foreign affairs, members of Congress deemed it presumptuous and vain.[47]

The two decades between the end of the Great War in 1919 and Germany's invasion of Poland in 1939 were formative in how US presidents and the American public understood their role within and relationship to the rest of the world. As Susan Schulten argues, the postwar changing geopolitical landscape in Europe led to an expanding "geographical imagination" in the United States, one that stressed the economic, commercial, and political interdependence of nation-states.[48] And yet, the failure of Wilson's Fourteen Points—what isolationist Senate Republicans considered a major victory for US foreign policy—also led to a deliberate inward turn. During the 1920 presidential campaign, Warren G. Harding promised to return the country to "normalcy," a normalcy that meant, as Richard J. Ellis notes, "pulling back from Europe" and "an end to heroic crusades and sharp partisan divisions."[49] Despite this public distaste for anything and anyone across the Atlantic, US officials continued to expand their imperialist reach in Central and South America through the military occupations of Nicaragua, Haiti, and the Dominican Republic.[50] In other cases, the United States quietly supported the rise of various dictators in Nicaragua, Guatemala, El Salvador, Honduras, the Dominican Republic, and Cuba.[51] After the stock market crash in October

1929, the nation increased its inward focus as millions of citizens struggled to survive the Great Depression. Many believed US involvement in the Great War was to blame for the current economic crisis. As David M. Kennedy explains, "So far from being redeemed from American intervention, Europe swiftly slid back into its historic vices of authoritarianism and armed rivalry, while America slid back into its historic attitude of isolationism."[52] But when Franklin Delano Roosevelt was elected president in November 1932, he attempted to bridge the gap between his internationalist bent and the nation's isolationist stance. The nation—and the world—would never be the same.

As president, Franklin Delano Roosevelt used both his public statements and his physical travel to help the American people to see—both metaphorically and literally—their connection to the rest of the world.[53] In his first inaugural address, the president stated that "in the field of world policy," the United States would adopt "the policy of the good neighbor—the neighbor who resolutely respects himself and, because he does so, respects the rights of others."[54] This "Good Neighbor" initiative shaped the Roosevelt administration's foreign policy during the 1930s and set the stage for US hegemonic advances in South America in the years to come. Shortly after his reelection in 1936, FDR traveled to South America and delivered a speech to the Brazilian legislature in Rio de Janeiro. "No nation can live entirely to itself," he said. "We are showing in international relations what we have long known in private relations—that good neighbors make a good community."[55] Of course, Roosevelt's "Good Neighbor" policy was more than a policy of friendly neighborliness toward South American nations. Instead, it was an imperialist move, one the president used to elevate the United States' power and position on the global stage. As Mary E. Stuckey observes, FDR believed that "American values were universal and could be appropriately generalized to the entire world."[56] Thus, even as Roosevelt increased the power of the executive at home and abroad, he also envisioned "the role of the United States as both hemispheric and managerial—it was to be first among equals in a tiered system of global administration."[57] These policies, first articulated by FDR, would influence later interactions between the United States and South America during the Cold War.

Although Roosevelt did much to expand the US public's consciousness of their role in the world during the 1930s, the preeminence of an American national imaginary ended with the onset of the Second World War. A global conflict that undermined "the normality and self-contained coziness of the modern nation-state," writes Manfred Steger, "the [Second] World War served as a crucial catalyst for the birth of the global era," for it "helped to open the dominant national imaginary to penetration by new ideas and practices taking the entire globe as their frame of reference."[58] However, many Americans still rejected the idea of US involvement in the fight against Nazi Germany. Between 1939 and 1941, FDR struggled to convince the citizenry that their fate was interwoven with the survival of Europe. Staunch isolationists, many of whom were members of the "America First" movement, argued that the United States should focus its energies on domestic concerns and that Europeans should be left to deal with their own mess. Roosevelt, however, argued that the nation had a moral duty to defend the cause of freedom around the world. In his 1941 State of the Union message, Roosevelt emphasized the United States' commitment to supporting European democracies in their fight against Nazi aggression. "We Americans are vitally concerned in your defense of freedom," he declared, promising that the nation would exert all its energies to "give you the strength to regain and maintain a free world."[59] Later that year, Roosevelt argued that the very survival of the American "way of life" was dependent on the country's ability to defend "a free society."[60] In his "Fireside Chat" delivered two days after Pearl Harbor, Roosevelt described the world situation as inextricably linked. "All the continents of the world, and all the oceans," he said, were now "one gigantic battlefield."[61] To those members of his audience still embracing the spirit of isolationism, the president's argument was simple: the United States could either take a leading role in the fight against Nazi Germany or it would be strangled by Hitler's forces encircling the globe.

In time, the US public rallied around FDR's vision. The United States' entry into the Second World War became a unifying factor for much of the US public, especially because Nazi tyranny posed a direct threat to the American "way of life." After the Allied victory in the Second World War and the gradual Soviet military expansion throughout Eastern Europe, the United States' commitment to protecting the "Free World" shifted to account for a new foe: the spread of Soviet communism at home and abroad.

US Presidential Rhetoric on the Cold War World Stage

The Cold War now occupies a mythic status in the American national imaginary. Often portrayed by the US government as a struggle between good and evil, democracy and communism, individual freedom and totalitarian rule, it became a political drama enacted by heroes united against villains in an epic battle for civilization, a geopolitical race between two superpowers to determine who would control specific countries, borders, and territories. Where the two world wars were fought with tanks, bombs, and military force, the Cold War became a symbolic contest of words, images, and propaganda campaigns. These conflicts spread beyond the boundaries of national identity as countries aligned themselves ideologically and politically with the United States or the Soviet Union. Ultimately, it was a global contest of prestige, a question of which country, ideology, and "way of life" would emerge as triumphant on the world stage.[62]

As the United States asserted its position as the "Leader of the Free World" after the Second World War, the act of going global emerged as a deliberate rhetorical strategy to symbolize the rapid expansion of American influence abroad. As I will detail in the case studies that follow, the specific tactics of this rhetorical strategy shifted over time to capitalize on changes in media technology and transportation and to address the ever-evolving nature of US foreign policy in an increasingly globalized world. Here, however, I consider how key terms such as "Cold War," "Iron Curtain," and "Free World" demarcated the symbolic boundaries of the Cold War world stage. Where mythic narratives of American exceptionalism, westward expansion, the frontier, and manifest destiny shaped the national consciousness during the nineteenth and early twentieth centuries, these spatialized metaphors expanded the United States' global reach.

During the Cold War, the president's physical travel to and through various spaces and regions became a specific means by which the US government could shape, shift, and extend the contours of this Cold War global imaginary—and, by extension, the way the US public understood the nation's metaphorical place or position in the postwar world. By framing the "Cold War" as an ideological struggle over two opposing "ways of life," US presidents presented the conflict as one dominated by an underlying division between the "Free World" and the "Soviet World." In this mythic framework, the Cold War was a contest over core democratic ideals such as freedom, capitalism, individual choice, and self-government. This rhetorically constituted drama invited audiences to imagine themselves as part of a larger Cold War rhetorical vision, actors in a "world divided into democratic free peoples and Communist enslaved peoples."[63] Even as these mythic narratives provided evidentiary support for US global dominance, they also constituted metaphorical spaces and regions to and through which US presidents could travel and reassert American leadership on the Cold War world stage.

The very idea of a "cold war" was a rhetorical creation, a linguistic move that constituted the contours and communities that would define the second half of the twentieth century. Unlike the "hot" war the United States had just fought against Germany, Italy, and Japan, this new "cold" war set the stage for a contest between two ideologies and "ways of life." The phrase was first used by George Orwell in October 1945 to describe "the kind of world-view, the kind of beliefs, and the social structure that would probably prevail in a State which was at once *unconquerable* and in a permanent state of 'cold war' with its neighbours."[64] But it was in September 1947 that influential syndicated columnist and public opinion expert Walter Lippmann popularized the phrase for a set of essays for the *New York Herald Tribune* entitled "The Cold War." These articles, which were compiled and published in book form later that year, solidified the idea of the US-Soviet conflict as a "cold war" between two superpowers, two competing adversaries, and two incompatible "ways of life."[65] As Lynn Boyd Hinds and Theodore Otto Windt have argued, Lippmann's popularization of the "cold war" metaphor soon became "accepted as the definitive description" of the global state of affairs and "encouraged the militarization of U.S. foreign response and the hunt for subversives on the domestic side."[66]

The rhetorical construction of a "cold war" between the United States and the Soviet Union was bolstered by another vivid metaphor: the descent of the "Iron Curtain." Although the term was first introduced by British prime minister Winston Churchill in a telegram to Harry S. Truman on May 12, 1945, it came into public circulation after a speech Churchill delivered at Westminster College in Fulton, Missouri, on March 5, 1946.[67] The former British prime minister described the "present position in Europe" as a continent threatened from within. Drawing on metaphors of light and darkness, Churchill noted that "a shadow has fallen upon the scenes so lately lighted by the Allied victory. Nobody knows what Soviet Russia and its Communist international organisation intends to do in the immediate future, or what are the limits, if any, to their expansive and proselytizing tendencies." Despite the hope and light brought by the Allied liberation of Germany and other European countries, Churchill said, the rapidly expanding Soviet presence in the region threatened to undermine the victory that had just been won. "From Stettin in the Baltic to Trieste in the Adriatic, an iron curtain has descended across the Continent," Churchill declared. "Behind that line lie all the capitals of the ancient states of Central and Eastern Europe. Warsaw, Berlin, Prague, Vienna, Budapest, Belgrade, Bucharest and Sofia, all these famous cities and the populations around them lie in what I must call the Soviet sphere." The rhetorical construction of this imaginary boundary line created two distinct "spheres": those peoples and nations who lived behind the "Iron Curtain" in darkness and totalitarian rule and those who existed outside of it, free from Soviet domination. The spatial elements of this metaphor must not be overlooked. By partitioning off the European continent with a vivid yet imaginary dividing line, Churchill created a sharp separation between "the west and the east," between those countries who supported "the cause of freedom and democracy" and those who aligned themselves with Soviet Union.[68] Ultimately, this "Iron Curtain" metaphor contributed to a larger cohesive narrative that made sense of an increasingly polarized world.

Rife with ideological and spatial connotations, the "Free World" quickly became a way to envision the United States as an institutional, hegemonic force leading other democracies against Soviet encroachment. Although the idea of the "free world" was used in earlier diplomatic contexts, it took on particular significance during the Cold War to describe a globe divided between the "Free World" and the "Communist World."[69] In his "Truman Doctrine" speech to the US Congress in March 1947, Harry S. Truman defined the current world situation as a competition between two "alternative ways of life," explaining that the "free people of the world look to us for support in maintaining their freedoms. If we falter in our leadership, we may endanger the peace of the world—and we shall surely endanger the welfare of this Nation."[70] The only choice, Truman argued, was for the United States to answer the call of duty and send economic aid to Greece and Turkey, two European nations under dire threat of a Soviet takeover. The next year, British economist Barbara Ward used the phrase "leader of the free world" to describe the United States' rapidly increasing global influence. In an essay published in the *New York Times*, Ward noted that the Western powers had remarkable assets in their symbolic struggle against the Soviet Union. "At the top of the ledger stands the United States, unchallenged in economic power, almost alone in the post-war years in its position to create surplus wealth, potentially the political leader of the free world."[71] The phrase quickly caught on. In 1952, the Democratic National Convention used the phrase in their party platform, noting that the nation had "strengthened its national defenses against the menace of Soviet aggression" and lauded policies such as the Truman Doctrine, the Marshall Plan, and the North Atlantic Treaty as "landmarks of America's progress in mobilizing the strength of the free world to keep the peace."[72] This descriptor would only grow in prominence under the Eisenhower administration, where, as I detail in chapter 3, it became a commonplace descriptor for those who aligned themselves with US global leadership.

This rhetorical construction of a "Free World," of course, also underscored the sharp division between those peoples and nations who would not or could not align themselves with democratic principles. Importantly, this symbolic global landscape was demarcated not by physical or geopolitical borders, but through ideological constructs that were constituted, imagined, and described through rhetorical means. By portraying itself as an impassioned defender of democracies around the world, the United States also reaffirmed its role as the leader and epicenter of the "Free World" global imaginary. As chief executives and other governmental officials faced the urgent task of enlarging the United States' role in the Cold War world, they proactively deployed the president's physical travel to and presence in foreign countries as a way to demarcate US influence on the global stage. An overarching theme throughout these depictions was the spatial, geographical, and ideological divisions between the United States and the Soviet Union—and, by extension, the "Free World" and the "Communist World." This divisional language also extended the mythic notion of America as "set apart" or distinct from the rest of the world. But where earlier mythic narratives suggested that that the nation should stand as an example to other nations, these mental or metaphorical lines now defined those who stood with the United States (the "West") and those who stood against them.

Through the deployment and circulation of vivid ideological and spatial metaphors such as the "Cold War," the "Iron Curtain," and the "Free World," US politicians and other public officials rhetorically inscribed the contours of the Cold War world stage. These now-mythic descriptions of a bipolar world neatly divided between freedom-loving democracies and totalitarian-embracing political regimes also established particular stages for rhetorical action, spaces that gave way to particular scenes or moments within a larger global conflict. Here and in the pages that follow, I deliberately invoke the stage metaphor and other related terms to describe the various encounters I examine in this book, for US officials designed individual acts of going global to create a metaphorical and literal stage from which chief executives could perform their role as the "Leader of the Free World."

To elevate their leadership role in foreign affairs, US presidents and other political officials spent enormous time and energy designing rhetorical backdrops—scenes—that aligned with the administration's foreign policy priorities. Scene setting, therefore, played a crucial role in the composition of a Cold War drama unfolding across time and space. As Kenneth Burke argues, humans are symbol-using animals who act—speak, move, protest, mourn, celebrate—in the world. There is, after all, "implicit in the quality of a scene the quality of the action that is to take place within it," Burke writes. "When the curtain rises to disclose a given stage-set, this stage-set contains, simultaneously, implicitly, all that the narrative is to draw out as a sequence, explicitly."[73] The location of these scenes, and how these stages were set, also displayed motive and intention. As actors in a Cold War drama, US presidents often referred their audiences back to earlier rhetorical acts and scenic backdrops that had contributed to the growth of US power and prestige. They deployed their words, images, movements, and physical travel to construct a platform from which they spoke to the nation and the world. The boundaries or contours of this metaphorical and literal stage were roped off, drawn, and demarcated by the body of the US president. As a dramatic encounter between the US president and an international public, the global rhetorical presidency was a traveling roadshow, an opportunity for the chief executive to see and be seen before audiences at home and abroad. As this practice developed and expanded over time, it became a powerful way to underscore US leadership of the "Free World" and American dominance on the global stage.

But even as US officials sought to display particular scenes and images to a global audience, they also used these image events to obscure other political realities. The selection and privileging of particular actors, spaces, and narratives both reflected the administration's priorities and deflected attention from less-than-ideal parts of the story—such as the dark underbelly of US racism, imperialism, and clandestine military campaigns around the world. In the chapters that follow, I also consider what voices and stories were obscured or ignored in the tidy narrative of the "Free World" united against the "Soviet Bloc." Because this book is a study of US presidential rhetoric during the Cold War, I attend most closely to archival materials from five presidential libraries and the records of executive agencies housed at the National Archives and Records Administration. However, I make the explicit choice to complicate this president-centric story by broadening my research to include voices and stories from historically Black newspapers and journalists, surveys of international public opinion, declassified intelligence reports, and new accounts that seek to deepen and extend our understanding of this period in history. Doing so reveals how the global rhetorical presidency operated on multiple levels, simultaneously featuring the positive elements of American global leadership while obscuring the limits of what this "Free World" offered to millions of Americans and a larger international public during the Cold War.

*

This book examines the various means by which US presidents used their rhetoric abroad to create and sustain a vision of the United States as the leader and epicenter of the Cold War global imaginary. My aim in this project is neither to provide a comprehensive history of the Cold War nor to outline an exhaustive history of each administration or event that appears in the chapters that follow. Rather, my goal is to demonstrate how and why the global rhetorical presidency developed as a persuasive strategy during the second half of the twentieth century and the means by which it did so. Where this introductory chapter established the historical context for these deliberate acts of going global, I use the next chapter to outline the concept

of the global rhetorical presidency and detail how this theoretical and ana-
lytical perspective enlarges and extends our understanding of US presidential rhetoric, foreign policy, and public diplomacy. Readers should approach
chapter 1 as a framework to understand how I read the historical examples
that follow. Chapters 2 through 6 draw on extensive archival research from
five US presidential libraries and the records of the US State Department and
the US Information Agency (USIA) to examine five representative moments
that demonstrate how the global rhetorical presidency evolved during the
Cold War: Harry S. Truman's 1945 participation in the Potsdam Conference,
Dwight D. Eisenhower's 1959–60 "Good Will" tours, John F. Kennedy's 1963
visit to West Berlin, Richard Nixon's "Opening to China" in 1971–72, and Ronald Reagan's 1984 commemoration of D-day in Normandy. These individual
case studies proceed chronologically and consider the specificities of individual moments in time while also asking how the global rhetorical presidency developed throughout the Cold War. I deliberately have selected these
five case studies to demonstrate how multiple presidential administrations
and other US government agencies designed these global tours as dynamic,
multifaceted persuasive campaigns—communicative encounters that were
simultaneously verbal and visual, mediated and circulated, enacted by bodies
within particular spatial and geopolitical locations and addressed to audiences at home and abroad. In the final chapter, I conclude by considering how
this historical practice contributed to our current conceptions of US foreign
policy rhetorics in the twenty-first century. Ultimately, this book argues that
US presidents took their rhetoric abroad in their attempt to create and sustain a very particular version of the Cold War world, one that positioned the
United States as the preeminent leader of the twentieth-century global order.

The Global Rhetorical Presidency

All rhetorical action is situational, developed in response to the needs or exigencies of a particular moment in time and space. It is a contingent exercise, one shaped and constrained by its historical circumstances and also created as a response to those circumstances. It is both a product of and a contributor to its context. The implication of this perspective is that scholars must attend to the radical specificity of each rhetorical act while also tracing how these individual moments contribute to overarching patterns of discourse that emerge throughout history and over time. Such an approach attends to the microhistories of individual rhetorical encounters ("deep" or synchronic history) even as it considers how these specific cases contribute to a broader macrohistory ("linear" or diachronic history) of a particular era.[1]

Throughout this book, I trace how individual administrations used the act of going global to address specific foreign policy challenges they encountered—and, at times, created—while also examining how each instance of presidential travel overseas responded to previous instances and shaped future iterations of the practice. In the case studies that follow, I demonstrate how the presidential act of going global operated as a persuasive force throughout the Cold War, one designed to bolster US power and elevate national prestige to audiences at home and abroad.[2] In this chapter, however, I outline the overarching framework that shapes the analyses to come: the global rhetorical presidency. Drawing on relevant scholarship from rhetoric, political science, and other related disciplines, I outline the theoretical and methodological considerations that inform this approach and detail how five specific elements or foci—body, place, image, audience, and circulation—constitute the presidential act of going global. Before turning to this discussion, however, it is important to note what I mean by theory and method here and throughout the rest of the book.

Theory means different things to different academic disciplines. I use the term theory to describe a framework or set of considerations that inform and define a study of the global rhetorical presidency. Crucially, however, this framework arises from my reading and analysis of thousands of archival documents, audiovisual recordings, newspaper reports, public opinion surveys, and other historical artifacts. Although a theory of the global rhetorical presidency allows the critic to anticipate a particular form of rhetorical action, it also reflects those recurring patterns or strategies that typify the presidential act of going global. Theory, in other words, is something that emerges from a careful, sustained study of "the particulars of the case—the local circumstances that frame and motivate the work and the unique blend of formal and material elements that constitute its substance." My aim in this book, therefore, is to demonstrate how a theory of the global rhetorical presidency emerges from "an understanding of the particular" and a careful study of those "abstract principles . . . [that] are instantiated and individuated within the texture of the actual discourse."³ To develop a theory of the global rhetorical presidency is not an exercise in prescribing or determining what all US presidents do when they speak on the global stage. Instead, a careful reading of the historical record reveals consistent themes or patterns that emerged over time, across administrations, and in response to a variety of historical and political exigencies. While the particulars of the immediate moment change, a number of patterns remain consistent. A theory of the global rhetorical presidency attends to these recurring patterns and offers a way of reading and analyzing the act of going global.

If theory describes a way of seeing, viewing, or understanding rhetorical action, method outlines the steps one takes to get there. As a rhetorical historian who studies US presidential discourse, I seek to understand the methods employed by various administrations to create and sustain a particular vision of the Cold War world. To uncover and recover this historical narrative, I rely on critical methods of archival research, oral history, close textual analysis, fieldwork, and surveys of public opinion. During my research, I uncovered five constituent elements of the global rhetorical presidency that recur throughout history and over time: body, place, image, audience, and circulation. As I detail in the pages to come, multiple presidential administrations, the State Department, and the USIA (among many others) deliberately incorporated verbal, visual, spatial, mediated, and embodied elements into these global tours. To be clear: I am not reading new disciplinary trends into or on top of the story of US presidential rhetoric during the Cold War. Instead, I show how multiple administrations made a concerted effort to capitalize on these multiple dimensions of going global. For them, the potential success of speaking overseas was dependent upon strategies of placement, visuality, embodiment, and the mediation and circulation of rhetorical "texts"— including, and perhaps most importantly—the travel of the presidential body to spaces and regions throughout the globe.

The global rhetorical presidency is not confined to talk or text. It is a dynamic, multifaceted discursive act, a communicative encounter that is verbal and visual, mediated and circulated, enacted by bodies within a particular spatial and/or geopolitical location and addressed to a multitude of audiences. Although the proponents of the original rhetorical presidency thesis often defined "going public" or "speaking to the people" as a primarily verbal exchange between speaker and audience, I take a much wider view of how rhetoric operates.[4] I approach rhetoric as a means of symbolic action, a mode of creating, defining, sustaining, and at times undermining shared political and social realities. It is a means of directing the attention, identifying with a particular audience (and dividing oneself from another), and creating terministic screens that privilege some facts while concealing others from public view. At the same time, specific rhetorical acts (or actions) also work symbolically—they "speak" or communicate, even when words are absent. The concept of the global rhetorical presidency also expands our scholarly focus not just outside national borders, but also beyond spoken oratory and toward a more global or comprehensive nature of the rhetorical act.

With this extended definition of presidential rhetoric in mind, I use the rest of this chapter to outline a theory of the global rhetorical presidency—a way of seeing, assessing, uncovering, and recovering how US presidents used their physical presence abroad to invite identification, create division, constitute communities real and imagined, and cast a robust vision for US leadership on the world stage.

Defining the Global Rhetorical Presidency

The global rhetorical presidency describes how US presidents use their rhetoric abroad to extend the United States' military, political, and psychological influence in various geopolitical regions and nation-states, expand presidential power in foreign affairs, and elevate the United States' image and position on the world stage.[5] This concept builds on the initial rhetorical presidency thesis and yet extends this perspective to account for presidential rhetoric directed to a global or transnational audience. In its original formulation, political scientists argued that "popular or mass rhetoric" had become one of the "principal tools in attempting to govern the nation," a move that under-mined constitutionally mandated workings between the executive and legis-lative branches of the US government. Instead of deliberating with Congress, chief executives relied on the "active and continuous presidential leadership of public opinion" to accomplish political goals.[6] At the heart of these studies was the focus on—and concern over—how targeted appeals to the US public changed the constitutional norms of governance.

Forty years later, the rhetorical presidency thesis remains a prominent fixture in studies of the US presidency and the subject of spirited academic debate in several important domains. Many scholars have interrogated how direct appeals to the US public have changed constitutional norms, public expectations, and the institution of the presidency as a whole.[7] Others have countered the idea that direct presidential address began with Theodore Roosevelt or Woodrow Wilson, offering valuable studies that expand our understanding of presidential communication during the eighteenth and nineteenth centuries.[8] Within the field of speech communication, some have argued that the linking of "rhetoric" with "the presidency" implied a nega-tive function; that is, the view that a president's invocation of speech was in-herently dangerous not just for the institution of the presidency, but for the very foundations of US government. Rhetoricians argued that this thesis, at its best, missed important political and communal functions of presidential speech and, at its worst, denigrated the very nature of rhetorical discourse.[9] In response, scholars of speech communication revisited questions of audience, effects on public opinion, genres of presidential rhetoric, critical methods for analyzing the discourse of chief executives, and the ethics of using speech to persuade publics. Numerous essays and book-length studies also analyzed the rhetorical strategies of individual US presidents, the historical legacies of single speeches, and recurring themes or foci within presidential discourse. This impressive and continually expanding body of work makes plain that presidential rhetoric wields tremendous power, whether for good or ill.[10] The primary concern for many of these studies, however, is how US presidents spoke to, for, and about the US public. After all, if the rhetorical presidency was about "going public" or "speaking to the people" to achieve public sup-port for particular policy initiatives, this audience needed to have a vested interest—or a vote—in the issues at hand.[11]

The global rhetorical presidency enlarges its focus from a domestic, US-centric audience and questions of institutional change to describe when, where, why, and how US presidents took their rhetoric abroad. It is no ac-cident that US presidents began to exert their presence on the global stage at the exact moment that the nation began to expand its leadership—and dominance—in international affairs. Thus, where the original rhetorical presidency model primarily was concerned with institutional change, the global rhetorical presidency reveals how US presidents and their administrations intentionally designed particular international visits to extend their power materially and symbolically in foreign affairs and to elevate the image of the United States to audiences at home and abroad. Extending the rhetorical presidency model to the international arena reveals how the act of going global worked not just to persuade publics, but to symbolically expand the image of the US president and the United States in an increasing era of globalization.

Stressing the *global* aspect of these rhetorical appeals underscores the potential for presidential rhetoric abroad to constitute, strengthen, contribute to, and even undermine geopolitical, economic, and transnational relations between nation-states, relations that are dynamic and ever-changing. It is not simply that chief executives leave the borders of the nation. Instead, as presidents extend their rhetoric from the domestic arena to the world stage, they themselves engage in the process of global integration, or globalization, for, as Raka Shome and Radha S. Hegde argue, globalization "produces a state of culture in transnational motion—flows of people, trade, communication, ideas, technologies, finance, social movements, cross border movements, and more."[12] The movement of the presidential body establishes a network of relationships between the United States and other nations. The media coverage of these presidential tours produces a flow of images, newsreel footage, sound bites, and live cable coverage. Presidential speeches delivered before, during, and after the visits are reproduced and circulated within the United States and around the world. Such instances of presidential rhetoric contribute to what Manfred Steger has termed the "global imaginary," a network of peoples and nation-states who see themselves as connected across space and time through their mutual identification as members of a global community.[13] Presidential movements abroad can constitute or renew geopolitical networks of interconnectivity, alliances that elevate the United States' leadership role on the world stage. There can, however, be a problematic aspect to these tours, for they reveal how presidential rhetoric in and movement between nations, borders, and audiences can "produce complex planes of exclusion and inclusion, empowerment and disempowerment."[14] The global rhetorical presidency has always functioned as a strategy for including some and not others, for marking some countries as worthy of mention while obscuring others from view. In fact, as the United States exerted ideological, military, and geopolitical force in other countries, the travel of the presidential body symbolized the extension of US imperialism throughout the globe. Any study of the global rhetorical presidency, therefore, must also emphasize the power relations always already embedded in these tours.

Of course, US presidents do not need to travel abroad to address an international audience. The near-constant barrage of sound bites, tweets, images, and textual fragments from the US president make it easier than ever to follow the words and actions of the American chief executive.[15] And yet, the concept of the global rhetorical presidency focuses on specific instances where chief executives move beyond the nation's borders to capture public attention and asks what this physical travel symbolizes within its broader historical and geopolitical contexts. This emphasis on a more diverse public also does not mean that domestic rhetorical appeals have disappeared. To the contrary, going global offers chief executives a powerful, tangible way to showcase the merits of US international involvement and the sheer force of American power and prestige to audiences watching at home. But as I detail in the chapters that follow, tracing the rise of the global rhetorical presidency reveals the inherent connection between the bodily movements of the chief executive and the deliberate extension of US hegemony during the Cold War. Attending to moments of personal direct contact between the US president and the global public reveals one important way chief executives trumpeted the tenets of US democracy for all the world to see.

Examining the global nature of the rhetorical presidency also emphasizes a wider scope of address and the numerous audiences involved. Proponents of the original rhetorical presidency thesis focused on how US presidents used their public speech to "go over" the heads of Congress to speak to the American people to gain support for their policy initiatives. In this model, the constitutionally mandated audience (Congress) was bypassed in favor of the American electorate. However, in the years immediately following the initial rhetorical presidency thesis, some gestured toward an "international presidency," noting that overseas travel allowed chief executives to "appear presidential," "thoroughly [exploit] their opportunities for publicity at home," and address "a global audience."[16] More recently, scholars have considered how US presidents craft messages for an international public.[17] The global rhetorical presidency contributes to this growing body of literature by detailing how and why US presidents use their spoken oratory and the physical act of international travel to symbolically expand the image of the US president and the United States in an increasing era of globalization. Rather than merely going public, US presidents utilize the act of going global to elevate the image of the nation—and of themselves—to audiences at home and abroad. Tracing the history of this practice reveals how going global emerged as a deliberate rhetorical strategy designed to amplify the United States' role in the Cold War world. Importantly, however, these rhetorical campaigns also were designed to appeal to US political officials and the American people. Stressing the global does not exclude the domestic. It calls for a more nuanced analysis of how audiences were addressed, invoked, constituted, and rendered mute—often all at the same time. This view rejects the idea of the rhetorical encounter as a unidirectional exchange between speaker and receiver and instead asks how addressing one audience might reach another.

The global rhetorical presidency interrogates how US presidents deployed the constellation and coalescence of five constituent elements or tactics—body, place, image, audience, and circulation—to present an image of American power and global leadership, one that extended to audiences foreign and domestic. Specific examples of these constituent elements will emerge in the chapters that follow. Here, however, I detail how these five individual elements enable and contribute to a robust reading of presidential rhetoric on the world stage.

Presidential Bodies and the Body Politic

The US president is a rhetorical actor, a body that speaks, moves, and performs on the world stage. Although scholars of presidential rhetoric most often analyze the constitutive, definitional power of "deeds done in words," attending to the embodied dimensions of these rhetorical acts reveals a richer, more nuanced understanding of how chief executives address publics through both word and deed.[18] US presidents speak, move, and perform as individuals in service of an institution. Elected or reelected every four years by the citizenry, they are but temporary custodians of the Executive Office of the President. Individuals come and go, but the institution remains. However, the individual actions of US presidents contribute to its institutional character. The decisions and policies of one chief executive influence, shape, and condition the next, even as the decisions of past presidents influence future ones. US presidential rhetoric, therefore, is always speech or embodied action that represents both an individual—the current occupant of the White House—and the institution of the US presidency. This dual nature of the individual/institution points to the cumulative, constantly evolving nature of presidential rhetoric. The words and actions of one individual contribute to the public's expectation of what presidential rhetoric looks like, how it sounds, where it happens, and why it matters.[19]

The body of the US president also represents the body politic. It provides what Kenneth Burke might call the ideal synecdoche, where the part can represent the whole and the whole the part.[20] Even as US presidents speak to, for, and about the people, their bodies also index and display communal norms and ideals, functioning as what Christa J. Olson has identified in other contexts as "embodiable topoi." Where topoi represent "nodes of social value and common sense that provide places of return for convening arguments across changing circumstances," embodiable topoi reference and contain commonly held values of the larger body politic.[21] Because US presidents electorally represent the US public, their bodies can "reproduce . . . the 'contradictory, collective passions and convictions that constitute a people' through a corporeal common sense."[22] They are, in other words, bodies that speak—even when words are absent.

Reading presidential bodies as rhetorical also requires critics to account for what these bodies and actions limit, privilege, conceal, gloss, overlook, and exclude. The presence or absence of particular bodies in the White House communicates much about important national issues such as ability, race, gender, and sexuality within the larger body politic. For example, Franklin D. Roosevelt went to enormous lengths to conceal his paralysis from the public eye because of concerns that it would weaken his presidential image and thus limit his ability to lead the nation.[23] Barack Obama's election as the first Black president of a country once governed by individuals who owned enslaved persons was deeply symbolic.[24] Similarly, the United States' proclivity for male chief executives reveals, as Kristina Horn Sheeler and Karrin Vasby Anderson have deftly noted, "the intransigent sexism that continues to constrain women in presidential politics."[25] Indeed, for many supporters of Hillary Clinton in the 2016 presidential contest, it was a particularly cruel irony that the nation's first viable female candidate was defeated by a man who boasted about his sexual conquests. This is also why Vice President Kamala Harris's election as the first woman and Black and South Asian woman in the Executive Office of the President was significant—and long overdue. Former South Bend mayor (and now secretary of transportation) Pete Buttigieg's run for the 2020 Democratic presidential nomination garnered important discussions of what it might mean to nominate the first openly gay presidential candidate. In short, the body of the president—and what that body does or does not represent—speaks volumes about the current state of the nation.

During the Cold War, the presidential body functioned as the locus of American power abroad. This image of US global leadership was particularly linked with masculinity, strength, and vitality. After FDR's death, Harry S. Truman's ascendence to the presidency provided a vivid contrast to Roosevelt's often immobile body, with many press reports noting his energy and alacrity. As the supreme commander of the Allied forces in Europe, Dwight

D. Eisenhower embodied the Allied victory in the Second World War. Later Cold War presidents sought to portray themselves as active, strong, and confident. As able bodies who moved beyond the United States, US presidents offered a vivid portrait of American leadership abroad. These images—made visible to the US public and a global audience through newsreel footage, print photographs, and live television—displayed a triumphant touring diplomat being welcomed by audiences around the world. As the following chapters will demonstrate, the presidential body always was the focal point of these tours, a living, breathing display of the United States' status as the "Leader of the Free World."

Place and Space

Because the presidential body operates as a symbol of the nation, its travel in and through space to a designated place or location directs attention, elevates position, constitutes and communicates power differentials, and establishes geopolitical relations between the United States and the rest of the world. The global rhetorical presidency examines what a president's bodily presence in a particular *place* or location communicates about the United States' relationship to other countries and regions in the larger *space* of the Cold War global imaginary.

Scholars often approach space as fluid, open, and constituted by a complex set of social and political relations that condition and even govern certain ways of being and acting in the world. Place describes a geographic point on a map, a location that often functions as a storehouse of political symbols and cultural memories. Space and place are always interconnected, however, for, as Yi-Fu Tuan writes, "if we think of space as that which allows movement, then place is pause; each pause in movement makes it possible for location to be transformed into place."[26] Here and in the chapters that follow, I build on these definitions to uncover how US presidents reflected and relied on multiple iterations of space and place in their acts of going global.

Although the concept of space might suggest a neutral, ethereal quality—the air surrounding a more important place or location—it constitutes, conditions, and constrains power relations that take root and flourish within its domain. Space plays a crucial role in the "production, organization, and distribution of cultural power," argues Raka Shome. It is "not merely a backdrop . . . against which the communication of cultural politics occurs." Instead, space "functions as a technology—a means and medium—of power that is socially constituted through material relations that enable the communication of specific politics."[27] The global rhetorical presidency asks how the movement and travel of chief executives produce and maintain hierarchies of geopolitical, economic, and social power relations between the United States and the rest of the world.

US presidents contributed to hierarchies through their rhetorical construction of imagined—but very real—spatial divisions between the "Free World" and the "Soviet Bloc," the "First World" and the "Third World," and the "West" and the "East." US presidents, political officials, and journalists deployed these spatial descriptors to define the contours of the Cold War geopolitical structure. These rhetorical moves also contributed to a robust vision of what a "Free World" global imaginary entailed. Here and throughout this book, I draw on the work of Benedict Anderson, Charles Taylor, and Manfred Steger to examine how chief executives and other political officials used the presidential act of going global to constitute a shared image or vision of the world.[28] Although the concept of a "Free World" could not be defined by physical borders or spatial boundaries, US presidents used their rhetoric abroad to outline and expand those people who were included—and, importantly, excluded—from this imagined community. Going global allowed chief executives to constitute a web of geopolitical relations between nations and peoples who aligned themselves with the "West." These international tours contributed to a US-centric and US-dominated Cold War global imaginary, a vision of the world that positioned the United States as a central figure in and leader of the twentieth-century world order.

Like space, the idea of place contains a multitude of meanings. The global rhetorical presidency accounts for four distinct yet interwoven elements: place as location, place as storehouse, place as connectivity, and place as station. In its most basic sense, place describes a point or position within some larger space or terrain. It specifies a spot one can see, locate, find, and identify. Approaching place as location stresses its geographical or topographical dimensions, such as the coordinates of West Berlin and the city's relative proximity to other markers or spaces. Place can also function as a storehouse or container of shared values, memories, and ideals. It can provide "bountiful aegis—active protective support—to what it locates."[29] This second aspect— place as storehouse—prioritizes the idea that multiple (and, at times, competing) histories, memories, objects, people, or ideals can reside, be housed, or develop in place.[30] The third dimension of place—place as connectivity— considers what individual places symbolize and asks how the links and connections between multiple places coalesce to form a larger whole. Although it may be demarcated by borders or territorial boundaries, place often is defined by its relationship to other spaces or regions. Places are linked together—or separated by—social, political, and ideological relationships and represent "a particular moment in those networks of social relations and understandings."[31] Finally, considering place as station underscores the metaphorical position one can occupy in relationship to others. It asks what place a country or region occupies in the global order and considers how that imagined station is discursively constituted. This last element connotes a hegemonic, imperialist reading of the world order, a perspective that is vital for understanding global power relations between nation-states.

During the Cold War, US presidents used their physical travel to specific locales to demarcate these places as meaningful and significant for US foreign policy. But it is not merely the location of these visits that matters. The very movement—or circulation—of the presidential body from one location to the next transformed these places of pause into nodes within a much larger geopolitical network of connectivity. This rhetoric in *place* quickly extended beyond its physical situatedness within spatial and geographical borders into the broader *space* of the Cold War global imaginary. The president, the White House, the US State Department, and other governmental agencies saw the place of address not merely as a means of invention, but as a physical symbol of US power and prestige during the Cold War—one the president could activate and amplify simply because he was there. The deliberate movement of the presidential body beyond the United States' own borders created a geopolitical network of nation-states who aligned themselves with the United States: a "Free World" global imaginary. US presidents made a deliberate effort to cross territorial, ideological, and spatial boundaries—oceans, continents, geographical borders, the "Iron Curtain," "Red China," and more—through the act of going global. In so doing, they physically and symbolically linked the United States with the rest of the "Free World" and asserted American power and prestige—or the nation's "place" in the world—on the global stage.[32]

Images of the Nation

The global rhetorical presidency asks how the strategic deployment of visual images—newsreels, still photographs, live television coverage, and artistic renderings of the president's presence abroad—contributed to a robust vision of American power and prestige. Attending to image emphasizes the crucial role visuality played in these Cold War public diplomacy campaigns.[33] These global rhetorical encounters were intended to make the US president—and, by extension, the nation as a whole—visible, tangible, relatable, and easily transmittable to audiences at home and abroad. Throughout this book, I detail how US presidents maintained a vigorous image of American power and prestige through careful, calculated visual documentation of their global tours.

Chief executives did not just describe their hopes for a democratic world. They made this vision accessible and recognizable by deliberately planning, arranging, and deploying images of them speaking about and enacting this democratic vision of the world in front of international audiences. These were image events, "deliberately staged spectacles designed to attract the attention of the mass media" and to reach a "wide audience" through the circulation of "persuasive images."[34] The image of the US president traveling abroad and speaking on the global stage transcended any barrier of language or translation. If international audiences could experience the American president in the flesh or see images of cheering crowds welcoming the presidential motorcade in countries around the world, they also could imagine the United States as the "Leader of the Free World." But these image events were not limited to a global audience. They also were designed to portray a vivid picture of active, engaged American leadership to US citizens watching at home.

Even as US presidents deployed strategies of active language and vivid description to create a shared vision of the "Free World," they also relied on the physical images of them traveling abroad to help US citizens and the global community imagine a broader network of nations connected by shared democratic ideals. In the chapters that follow, I consider how the president's own words interacted with and built upon visual images that were intentionally staged, mediated, and circulated to audiences at home and abroad. Doing so aligns with Cara Finnegan and Jennifer L. Jones Barbour's call to "adapt our critical practices to the challenges of the visual" so that we might have a "richer sense of the forms and functions of rhetoric as well as a deep understanding of the historical role of visuality in public culture."[35] I consider multiple types of images, including the actual physical encounters international audiences had with the traveling US president as well as images of these tours that were mediated and circulated through newsreel footage, still photographs, and live news coverage. Multiple administrations invested significant time and energy to ensure that audiences would *see* the person of the president in these particular places—and witness a choreographed spectacle of international acclaim. By considering the verbal and visual dimensions of the global rhetorical presidency, this study demonstrates the central role rhetorical vision and visual rhetoric played in the act of going global.

Audience

Even as the global rhetorical presidency interrogates the multifaceted nature of presidential speech, it also examines the various strategies and tactics US presidents deployed to address audiences at home and around the world.

Where the original rhetorical presidency thesis directed its primary attention to how "going public" shifted institutional norms, extending this perspective to the international arena requires critical attention to how US presidents attempted to reach a global, transnational audience. As I will demonstrate in the chapters to come, Cold War chief executives deployed a rhetoric of shared identification to constitute an audience who saw themselves as part of the "Free World"—an identity diametrically opposed to Soviet communism. Kenneth Burke famously argued that rhetoric's defining term should be identification, not persuasion, and called rhetoricians to consider how individuals use language as symbolic action to emphasize similarities between speaker and audience. By focusing on what individuals had in common, rhetoric would encourage "the audience to identify itself with the speaker's interests," thus allowing the speaker to "establish rapport between [themselves] and [their] audience."[36] Identification, of course, also suggests division, for to identify oneself with one group or community requires a separation or distancing from something or someone else. US presidents frequently drew on strategies of identification and division to create a shared identity around which all free-loving nations could rally. A critical part of this strategy was their physical travel to and presence in other countries. It was one thing to speak to or about another country or group from US soil. It was quite another to expend time, effort, and financial resources to appear physically among the global public and speak to them on their home turf.

But even as US presidents traveled overseas, they also used these tours to underscore the importance of American global leadership to a US public watching at home. They frequently would address this domestic audience before traveling abroad to outline their specific goals and objectives. Upon their return, chief executives would often deliver a report to the US public, summarizing key events, experiences, and conversations with their foreign counterparts. These domestic reports allowed the president to establish the geopolitical context for why this place or location mattered to the overall interests of the United States. In this way, US presidents presented themselves as emissaries of the American people and as the preeminent actor in global affairs.

Circulation

The global rhetorical presidency approaches the physical travel of the presidential body as a deliberate rhetorical choice, one motivated by an attempt to move or circulate particular texts through time and space. Attending to circulation demonstrates how the various "texts" associated with a president's travel abroad—speeches, images, newsreel footage, cable news coverage, live Twitter feeds—move through space and time to address multiple audiences. Although Michael Warner's influential work on publics and counterpublics privileged the circulation of linguistic discourse (e.g., written or spoken texts), other discursive artifacts such as bodies and images also circulate to address publics.[37] As Catherine Chaput observes, "rhetorical circulation implies that some element moves throughout material and discursive spaces to connect the differently situated moments comprising its organic whole."[38] In this vein, Cara A. Finnegan and Jiyeon Kang argue that studies of rhetorical circulation must examine the individual and collective histories embedded in the continual "re-presentation" and "mediation" of the artifact at hand. Scholars, they contend, must "avoid untenable distinctions between images and texts focusing not on individual types of discourse, but on their movement in a scene of circulation."[39] Attending to the movement and placement of rhetorical artifacts within a "scene of circulation" shifts our attention beyond the question of *which* texts circulate to a consideration of *where* texts circulate, *how* they reach those spaces, and *why* they pause in some places and not others. This perspective also considers how a circulating text or image related to the president's rhetoric abroad links these individual encounters to a larger body of discourse—namely, rhetorics of American exceptionalism, imperialism, and influence on the world stage. Each and every place a text—a speech, an image, a body moving through space—pauses within this "scene of circulation" became another symbolic node within this larger nationalistic narrative.

Extending the oral, visual, aural, spatial, and sensory dimensions of this scene was of paramount importance. The White House, the US Department of State, the USIA, and other governmental entities designed these international tours to be seen, heard, and experienced by a global audience—and the circulation of the entirety of the presidential rhetorical act was a crucial element of these coordinated propaganda campaigns. This deliberate focus on the circulation of presidential performance builds on a robust conversation about how technological advances have altered the norms of presidential speech.[40] While this book does not attempt to offer a media history of the Cold War, it does consider how various administrations harnessed the technological powers available to them to showcase the presence of the president (and, by extension, the prominence of the United States) on the metaphorical and literal world stage.

The means by which these texts moved across space and time was a critical aspect of the Cold War campaigns I examine in the following chapters.

Where the original rhetorical presidency thesis saw the rise of mass media as just one motivating factor behind the need to "go public," chief executives and various administrations harnessed technological changes to expand their power, increase their visibility, and elevate the image of the United States around the world. A primary way this was accomplished was through the deliberate transmission and circulation of the entirety of the presidential rhetorical act—the physical, spatial, geopolitical, visual, and verbal aspects of presidential performance overseas. Where audiences once experienced presidential performance through written newspaper accounts, the rise of radio and television during the first half of the twentieth century significantly expanded the integral relationship between those "texts on a page" and what the audience could see, hear, and witness in real time.[41] These images of the presidential rhetorical act—be it through print journalism, live news coverage, or the Internet—have become part of the text itself.[42] In this reading, presidential rhetoric extends beyond talk or text and must include the entirety of the rhetorical act—the verbal, the visual, the spatial, the geopolitical, and the mediation and circulation of presidential performance.

Within a Cold War rhetorical context, it was not guaranteed that an image of the president or an audio recording of a rally in West Berlin would be captured by members of the live audience. Instead, the White House, the US State Department, and other government officials understood the importance of circulation to their rhetorical campaigns. Even if the US president delivered a brilliant address before a cheering crowd in a foreign capital city that symbolized US values and moral resolve, this performance would do little for the US public at home or the rest of the "Free World." For this campaign to be effective, various pieces or artifacts from the event needed to be sent—or circulated—around the world. And as the body of the US president traveled outside the borders of the United States and throughout the world, it symbolized an extension of US influence, power, and prestige into various "spheres of influence"—those spaces and regions the United States saw as siding with them during the Cold War struggle between democracy and communism.

*

The concept of a global rhetorical presidency provides a way of seeing, viewing, and understanding how presidential rhetoric abroad works in and through the deployment of body, place, image, audience, and circulation. Attending to these five constituent elements, regardless of time period, helps scholars trace how various administrations used the act of going global to reach, identify with, and at times persuade audiences at home and abroad.

And yet, as I detailed in the introductory chapter, the specific dynamics of each iteration of the global rhetorical presidency will change or shift due to its historical and political contexts. It is to these varied, multilayered contextual dynamics that I now turn to demonstrate how the act of going global developed, extended, and transformed US presidential rhetoric during the Cold War.

Truman at Potsdam

The present conference projects him into the world spotlight. Those who know him closest predict that he will emerge from the meeting as a world leader. Not even the lengthy shadow of the late and highly honored Franklin Roosevelt will obliterate Harry Truman's worth, they say.

ROBERT G. NIXON, *Washington Post*, July 22, 1945[1]

Harry S. Truman is easy to miss. Sandwiched between two presidential giants, Franklin Delano Roosevelt and Dwight David Eisenhower, the thirty-third president of the United States was underestimated, overlooked, and frequently compared to the four-term luminary whose death made him president and the five-star general who succeeded him. Devoid of family money or military accolades, Truman even lacked a proper middle name.[2] But on April 12, 1945, after serving only eighty-two days as vice president, he ascended to the presidency and inherited a slate of impossible problems—many he knew nothing about.[3] Despite his rapidly declining health, Roosevelt had sidelined his new vice president from any substantive discussions of foreign policy—including the US government's top-secret development of the atomic bomb.[4] Roosevelt's death came at a pivotal moment. American, British, and Russian military forces were closing in on Berlin, the capital of the Third Reich. US scientists were completing their final tests on the atomic bomb in Los Alamos, New Mexico. And in Washington, US officials wondered if Truman was even up to the task. As Charles Bohlen recalled, "We in the State Department shared the concern of all Americans whether the 'Little Man from Missouri' could rise to the occasion."[5] Even Truman had his own doubts, writing just hours after assuming office that he was "very much shocked" and feared "what reaction the country would have to the death of a man whom they all practically worshiped."[6]

Between April and August 1945, Truman would make numerous decisions that would shape the postwar world. Some, such as his choice to drop the atomic bomb, had immediate and obvious ramifications. On August 6, the US military detonated sixteen kilotons of uranium over Hiroshima, killing approximately 140,000 people. Three days later, US aircraft dropped twenty-one kilotons of plutonium on Nagasaki, killing approximately 73,000 citizens.[7] The Japanese Imperial Army surrendered to US military forces shortly thereafter. The long-term ramifications of other diplomatic agreements would surface over time.[8] Although Stalin committed to hold "free and fair elections" in Poland, this ambiguous phrase left much open to interpretation—and misrepresentation.[9] And while the "Big Three" agreed on permanent zones of occupation in Berlin and greater Germany, military officials could not reach an agreement on routes of access into Berlin—a problem that would resurface during the Soviet blockade of Berlin in 1948.[10] Although much did happen behind the scenes at Potsdam, the most important elements of the story are the ones that were reported, mediated, and circulated to an audience wondering whether the new US president could hold his own on the global stage and, if so, what position the United States would take in a postwar world.

Understanding how the global rhetorical presidency evolved and expanded as a powerful mechanism of US foreign policy during the Cold War requires a reassessment of the Potsdam Conference—a scene that encapsulates the end of a global military conflict and the beginning of an ideological one. In fact, this conference was significant for reasons far beyond determining spheres of influence in Eastern Europe or settling the question of German reparations. Potsdam provided the place and the moment for Truman to assert US dominance on the global stage. This chapter details how the president's travel to and participation in the Potsdam Conference represents a pivotal moment in American image making and stage setting at the dawn of the Cold War. Where studies of Potsdam most often focus on the behind-the-scenes negotiations that were obscured from public view, I attend to the public-facing aspects of this tour to demonstrate how Truman's participation in the Potsdam Conference was experienced, reported, and received by the general public.[11] Unlike the two previous "Big Three" conferences at Tehran and Yalta, which were "tightly held secrets," this one was "known to the whole world."[12] In the pages that follow, I examine how Truman's travel to and physical presence in Potsdam portrayed a confident, victorious image of a US president—and, by extension, a nation—willing and able to adopt a position of global leadership in the postwar world. This robust vision of American power and prestige was communicated through numerous press reports, newsreel footage, photographic images, public statements, and a presidential victory lap through a decimated Berlin.

In 1945 (and, indeed, for many years later), ordinary citizens would not be privy to the details of the conference debates or occupy a spot at a private dinner between Truman, Churchill, and Stalin. They could, however, watch newsreel footage of President Truman cruising across the Atlantic on the USS

Augusta, encounter images of a ruined Berlin on the pages of prominent news magazines, and read journalistic accounts of the president's drive through the former Nazi capital. They could listen to Truman's remarks at the flag-raising ceremony in the American sector of Berlin via radio and newsreel. Images of Truman sitting between Attlee and Stalin splashed across the pages of the nation's most prominent newspapers and magazines, elevating Truman's presidential image and leadership of the "Big Three" alliance in the minds of the US public. When he returned home, Truman delivered a radio address to the nation in which he declared that the United States had "emerged from this war [as] the most powerful nation in the world—the most powerful nation, perhaps, in all history" because of its commitment to defending "the worth and the dignity of man" against the tyrannical rule.[13] Where Roosevelt had used similar language to justify US involvement in the Second World War, Truman's declaration was both retrospective and forward looking. It established a context for American global leadership and elevated the United States as the natural, rightful defender of the "Free World," a position the president would later codify as the "Truman Doctrine" in March 1947.

This form of public engagement was possible due to technological affordances of radio, newsreel footage, and the ability to transmit photographic images across the Atlantic. At Potsdam, Truman enacted the presidential role through his bodily movements in and through space—and the relative ease with which he did so. This was a sharp departure from his predecessor. In a *Life* editorial commemorating Truman's first one hundred days in office, the magazine observed that "in the previous 12 years Americans had become accustomed to pictures of a President who could not walk unaided and who, by tacit agreement, was photographed only in certain conventional poses. Now they began seeing pictures of Truman against many backgrounds, doing many things." In fact, the editors noted, as "the cameras clicked [as] Truman moved through epochal events and routine duties with the same quiet calm. . . . In 100 days the man who was a Missouri farmer until he was 33 mastered the toughest job in the world—the business of being U.S. President."[14] These images of Truman performing the presidential role reassured a US public wondering whether or not their new president was capable of his new post. And, where images of Roosevelt were carefully staged and controlled, Truman seemed to be everywhere, all at once, eager and ready to tackle the issues facing the country and the world.

This chapter also establishes the historical context for how and why the global rhetorical presidency garnered such persuasive force in the decades to come. Where later chapters detail how multiple administrations designed their global tours with the explicit goal of capturing public attention, this chapter traces the organic development of Truman's visit to Potsdam. Although this tour was a natural progression of previous wartime Allied conferences—one that Truman sought to continue after FDR's death—it also provided Truman the opportunity to demonstrate his presidential leadership and credibility to audiences at home and abroad. In the immediate moment, Truman's decisions reflected his desire to enact Roosevelt's foreign policy vision for a postwar world. He made decisions in response to the needs of the particular moment with the information available to him. He was, as William E. Leuchtenberg has argued, speaking and acting in the shadow of FDR.[15] But at Potsdam, Truman physically and symbolically stepped into the role Roosevelt had long occupied as the leader of the "Big Three"—and he made it his own.

To Potsdam

Truman went to Potsdam keenly aware of his inexperience but determined to act in the nation's best interests. "How I hate this trip!" he recorded in his diary as he set sail for Europe. "But I have to make it—win, lose, or draw— and we must win." Indeed, Truman accepted his journey to Potsdam as part of the job. "I'm not working for any interest but the Republic of the United States," he continued. "I [am] giving nothing away except to save starving people and even then I hope we can only help them to help themselves."[16] For Truman, however, the postwar journey to Berlin also accomplished another crucial goal: it provided him with the opportunity to step—both literally and symbolically—into his role as leader of the "Big Three" alliance. Franklin Delano Roosevelt was a tough act to follow. As Charles E. Bohlen, who served as FDR's interpreter at the Tehran and Yalta conferences, later recalled, "It was inevitable to compare him [Truman] with Roosevelt and inevitable that the unknown President should suffer in comparison with the fallen giant."[17] Many believed the man who never wanted to be president was ill prepared for the task. At Potsdam, however, Truman's public appearances and statements contributed to a significant shift in how the US public viewed both his leadership capabilities and the nation's ability to lead on the postwar world stage.

During the weeks leading up to Truman's departure, numerous commentators suggested that Truman's performance at Potsdam would serve not only as the president's first real test of leadership, but also an indication of how the United States would act in the postwar world. Anne O'Hare McCormick, one of the *New York Times* reporters sent to cover the Potsdam Conference, described Truman as "the man from Missouri emerging full-panoplied on the international stage. He is the average American raised to the nth power in the democratic drama and cast for the leading part in one of the momentous passages in history."[18] Calling Truman's performance at Potsdam the "first major test of his statesmanship," the *Los Angeles Times* noted that a "waiting world not forgetful of the tragic mistakes of a quarter of a century ago hopes and prays for the best."[19] And the *Chicago Daily Tribune* suggested that the president "probably will not attempt to be Mr. Roosevelt at Berlin. If he knows that the meeting with Stalin and Churchill is a test of his talents he does not betray anxiety. . . . Certainly everybody in this country hopes that Mr. Truman qualifies for the work before him. We'd all like to have him come home with the appropriate smile on his face—and not inside the other fellow."[20]

One of Truman's major challenges at home was how to navigate varying public attitudes about the United States' role in the postwar world. Should the nation return to its prewar pattern of isolationism, or should it step into a position of world leadership? This was by no means a foregone conclusion. As historian Tony Judt argues, "The United States in 1945 and for some time to come seriously expected to extricate itself from Europe as soon as possible, and was thus understandably keen to put in place a workable settlement that would not require American presence or supervision."[21] There was also the extreme naïveté and innocence of the US public's understanding of Stalin and his intentions for Eastern Europe. By the summer of 1945, three in four Americans surveyed believed that the United States should take an "active part" in an international organization of countries dedicated to preventing another war. Even more telling, 63 percent of respondents reported that the United States would "have the most influence in world affairs" after the war.[22] Although the US public had grown accustomed to the idea of American leadership abroad, it was up to Truman to dictate exactly what this meant in practical terms.

As the new US president struggled to ascertain how to lead the nation out of world war, Truman fielded incessant demands from British prime minister Winston Churchill that the United States take a firm stance against Soviet expansion in Europe—and exert his leadership of the "Big Three" alliance. It was imperative, Churchill said, that the Allies meet in person at the soonest possible moment. "I am profoundly concerned about the European situation," he telegraphed to Truman just days after the Soviet army conquered Berlin. "An Iron Curtain is drawn down upon their front. We do not know what is going on behind."[23] Stalin had selected the location of the previous two conferences of the "Big Three," both of which took place on Russian soil.[24] This time, Churchill was adamant that discussions must occur within an American or British sphere of influence. "We should not rendezvous at any place within the present Russian military zone," Churchill telegraphed to Truman. "Twice running we have come to meet him."[25] Instead, Churchill believed that holding the conference within British or American occupation zones would allow them to assert influence over the key issues of the conference. Stalin suggested meeting in the "area of Berlin," provided they could find a location appropriate to house all corresponding delegations. Truman agreed, and Churchill followed suit.[26]

Although all three leaders agreed to meet in the "vicinity of Berlin," Stalin selected the exact spot: Potsdam, a suburb twenty-two miles southwest of Berlin and within the Soviet zone of occupation. On the surface, this location seemed convenient because portions of the city remained intact after Allied bombing raids and mass destruction during the Battle of Berlin and the weeks that followed. Located in a lovely lake district with old stone houses and summer villas, it featured "a large proportion of usable houses suitable for their occupation" and the grand Cecilienhof Palace for the conference's major sessions.[27] But Potsdam offered more than convenience. The city was itself an enduring symbol in German historical memory. It was here, in Potsdam, that Frederick the Great built his summer palace, plotted his Prussian military campaigns, and was buried on church grounds. It was here that the newly elected chancellor of Germany, Adolf Hitler, orchestrated a "Day of Potsdam" to open a new session of the Reichstag in the Garrison Church.[28] It was here that ousted German president Paul von Hindenburg delivered a short speech surrendering control of the government. As historian Charles Mee would later observe, "Potsdam was a memorial to the beginnings of Prussian militarism, the end of German military might, and the continuous struggle in peace and war for power. Potsdam was an appropriate setting for the aims of all three leaders who met to confirm, though only Stalin knew it."[29]

At the time, Truman responded to these early debates over where the conference would happen and who would select its location as a bothersome aside, the campaign of an unrelenting and telegraph-happy prime minister desperate to be needed and liked. The president was determined to avoid any impression that he and Churchill were "ganging up" on Stalin.[30] Letting the Soviet premier select the exact meeting location seemed to make sense, especially since the Russian zone of occupation encompassed the only inhabitable parts of the city—and certainly the only areas that could accommodate the diplomatic personnel, security details, and press that would accompany the three heads of state. Fighting over conference real estate seemed to be the least of Truman's concerns.

As the president prepared to sail across the Atlantic, press reports focused their attention on three overarching concerns: how Truman would perform at the Potsdam Conference, what role the United States would take in the postwar world, and what the "shape of Europe" would look like following the meeting of the "Big Three." Reporters frequently equated Truman's performance in Potsdam as a determining factor in his ability to lead the United States—and the global democratic order in the postwar world. *Time* suggested that a pressing concern of the upcoming conference would be the "relation between the Big Three themselves—the countries as well as the men. Franklin Roosevelt had gained some fame at previous Big Three meetings as the mediator between the other two. . . . Harry Truman, in no position to fill such a role, seemed determined that all three of the Big Three should talk and bargain on an equal footing."[31] Maintaining this "equal footing," of course, would allow Truman to demonstrate his own capabilities on the world stage and to use his position to advocate for US interests. The *New York Times* noted that Truman's assumption of "the international lead taken by Mr. Roosevelt . . . demonstrated his own capacity for prompt and direct approach to difficult problems." It was clear, the paper opined, that Truman had "no intention of narrowing the American role to that of 'mediator' in international affairs." Instead, his actions demonstrated "that this country is ready to play the positive part in making world policy that its power and vital interests dictate."[32] Going global was a deliberate hegemonic move.

Truman's appearance at Potsdam also allowed the new president to display his credibility to the rest of the world. The *New York Herald Tribune* asserted that "the most important result of Mr. Truman's probationary period is that he went to Potsdam with the respect and confidence of a nation united, as seldom before, on the essentials of foreign policy." In fact, the paper continued, Truman had earned the right to "speak for the United States in Potsdam with the concentrated will and purpose of this country to support his endeavors. And that is no small triumph."[33] As the *Los Angeles Times* put it, the president saw "his role not simply as a mediator between two powerful allies but as a spokesman for a nation which is seeking to arrange a world structure in which its technological leadership and democratic ideals will have a greater play than ever before."[34] As these reports make plain, Truman's participation in the conference allowed him to assume his role as national spokesperson on the world stage. The president of the United States traveled to the origin of Nazi tyranny to orchestrate German atonement and European recovery. In so doing, Truman also positioned the United States as the geopolitical leader and epicenter of the postwar global order. Although the phrase "Leader of the Free World" would not become a common refrain until 1948, this is exactly what Truman's presence in place espoused.

A second overarching theme was the question of what role the United States would take in the postwar world. Many US press accounts predicted that the United States would lead the world in the new postwar reality, and Truman was identified as a central player. "The United States is in [a] position to give direction to world policy," wrote Anne O'Hare McCormick. "In this enterprise Mr. Truman is in some respects more representative of emerging America than Mr. Roosevelt was. He typifies the forward-looking mind of the Middle West, the region in which national policy is made and broken, and he mixes with a Rooseveltian and Wilsonian recognition of the necessity of international cooperation a little of that native suspicion of foreigners which Stalin should understand."[35] The question, McCormick noted, was if the president—and, by extension, the country—would learn from past history. Although there were many Americans who wanted to get out of Europe as quickly as possible, to do so would be a mistake. "The war is not over; the most difficult and dangerous phase is just beginning," she argued. "To leave that phase to others to handle, to withdraw the visual evidence of American power while the Continent is bristling with armed force, open and hidden, is to shirk responsibility at a critical moment and betray millions who put their trust in us. Worst of all, it is to waste the lives and incalculable treasure we have spent in this battlefield and to repeat the fatal mistake of 1919."[36] These explicit references to Wilson and the Versailles Conference provided a jarring reminder of the high price the United States paid in retreating from Europe so quickly. In this framing, only the United States had the military power, economic resources, and courage to finish the job. It was, in fact, the nation's "responsibility" to "millions who put their trust in us" and to those who gave their lives in the Second World War. American leadership on the world stage was, in effect, a moral mandate.

Other reports stressed the stark contrast between US democracy and Soviet rule and suggested that these competing ideologies would shape the Potsdam discussions—and the future of the postwar world. *Washington Post* reporter Barnet Nover observed that Russia had become a dominant global force and had "established [in Eastern and southeastern Europe] something resembling an international feudal system." The United States' policy at Potsdam, he wrote, should be to "seek with all the power we have to break down the present system of international feudalism that has been developing in Europe. . . . Not being ourselves interested in securing any sphere of interest in Europe[,] we are in the best position to work for a free, democratic and united Europe."[37] According to the *Chicago Daily Tribune*, "Americans these days are asking themselves what they wish Mr. Truman to bring back from Potsdam. . . . The one-worlders have been assuring us for a generation that the moral force of America in a concert of nations can reform the world." In fact, the paper concluded, the "Big Three" Conference was an important test of whether the "moral force" of American leadership could in fact "reform the world."[38]

Finally, there was the question of what shape of Europe would take following the Potsdam Conference. The spatial and physical references to geopolitical realities pervade the news coverage, and many noted the connection between the present realities in Berlin and future possibility of a Europe removed of war. There was a hope that being in Berlin—and seeing all the destruction that war had wrought—would motivate Truman, Churchill, and Stalin to craft a new vision for the future. In an incredibly prescient commentary, Anne O'Hare McCormick wrote: "It is clear to the blindest that drawing a line across the Continent and dividing enemy territory into four uncoordinated zones of occupation is to perpetuate the disintegration not of Germany alone but of Europe, and to intensify the economic, political, social and moral strains which will make impossible the peace we have all fought to win."[39] Indeed, she noted, "the final irony of the war would be to create two Europes in the process of fashioning one world. It would be even more ironical if it turned out that the civilization of Europe had been destroyed in the process of saving it."[40] And yet, according to some political commentators, there was cause for hope. As James Reston of the *New York Times* observed: "The bright side of all of this is that, by the force of our arms and the military collaboration of our Allies, we find ourselves for the second time in a generation in a position of leadership in the world. We have, moreover, shown from time to time a great capacity for making policy when the urgency of events forced us to tackle that task."[41] Now was the time for Truman and the United States to exercise this leadership once again—and to avoid the mistakes of 1919 at Versailles.

As these newspaper reports make plain, the Potsdam Conference was about much more than German reparations or determining new zones of occupation. Important as these questions were, and as much as they would contribute to the coming Cold War conflict, Truman's initial performance on the global stage was a physical, embodied display of American power, influence, and prestige. Eager to demonstrate credibility as an international statesman, the president agreed to Stalin's choice of location and refused to meet privately with Churchill before the conference began to avoid any appearance of "ganging up" on Stalin.[42] He wanted to start both relationships on equal footing, in Potsdam. A place of national triumph and tragedy, it was here that the Allies would carve up the country as retribution and determine the literal and symbolic shape of the postwar world.

Arrival

On July 15, after eight days at sea, the USS *Augusta* docked in Antwerp, Belgium. General Eisenhower was there to welcome the new president. Truman's motorcade drove south to an airfield in Brussels, where he boarded the presidential aircraft, *The Sacred Cow*—the same one FDR used to attend the summits at Tehran and Yalta.[43] The president's plane touched down at Gatow airfield outside Berlin that afternoon. "It was the first time in history that an American President had visited Berlin," noted the *Chicago Daily Tribune*. "Mr. Truman, in fact, is the first American chief executive to set foot on German soil."[44] After a brief arrival ceremony, Truman drove ten miles through Soviet-controlled territory to the American headquarters in Babelsberg.[45] Universal Newsreels featured footage of the president speeding along the autobahn toward Potsdam, greeted by an American military division lining the road.[46] The president took up residence at Two Kaiser Strasse, a three-story, yellow home on Lake Griebnitz, that would come to be known as the "Little White House" during Truman's stay in Potsdam. As Raymond Daniell of the *New York Times* described it for readers, "This summer resort area, once popular with Nazi stars of the stage and screen, has been almost completely depopulated of Germans to furnish the security essential for the Big Three. The American and British groups are housed in little territorial islands well within the Soviet zone in Greater Berlin."[47]

Despite these readily available details about Truman's arrival in Potsdam, the actual conference proceedings remained a tightly guarded secret. In fact, the "Big Three" leaders agreed that, like at Tehran and Yalta, no newspaper reporters or camera crews would be allowed on the grounds.[48] Correspondents sent to cover the conference from around the world were barred from the "forbidden zone"—the area surrounding the Cecilienhof Palace and the American, British, and Russian compounds.[49] Photographers, however, were given an escorted tour of the grounds and buildings of the main compound and invited to take pictures of the proceedings.[50] The apparent reasoning behind this decision was that newspaper correspondents could not be trusted with the sensitive nature of internal deliberations, where photographers could only capture images of the scene. These images, however, became a powerful visual medium through which the US public saw and experienced the president's performance overseas. Although print journalists were understandably frustrated with this limited access, it also encouraged the media to focus their attention on what was available to them: the sights and sounds of Berlin, the president's rare public statement on the raising of the flag, and images of the "Big Three" leaders together for what would be the final Allied conference.

Ultimately, the privileging of these texts and images—and their widespread circulation to the US public watching at home—portrayed Truman as a credible, capable leader ready to represent the nation on the world stage.

"Absolute Ruin"

The president began his visit as any tourist on vacation might—with a sightseeing expedition of the region.[51] On July 16, after meeting British prime minister Winston Churchill for the first time and still waiting for Soviet premier Joseph Stalin to arrive, Truman set out on a driving tour of Berlin. The president decided to make the trip at the urging of Fred Canfil, one of Truman's fellow soldiers in his World War I outfit, who had just returned from a tour of his own. In fact, conference attendees were invited to participate in tours of "Berlin and [the] vicinity" that were "scheduled twice daily at 0900 and 1400 hours." One simply had to pick up the phone and make a reservation.[52] The president's driving tour, however, was a bit more formal. Donned in a blue suit and a gray hat and accompanied by Secretary of State James Byrnes and Admiral William D. Leahy, the president left his compound at 3:30 p.m. The British prime minister soon followed in his own motorcade. "Emerging separately from behind the wall of secrecy and the thousands of crack American, British and Russian troops guarding the Kaiser Wilhelm Palace," noted the *New York Times*, "Messrs. Truman and Churchill, each with his retinue of advisers and high military chiefs, traveled through the wreckage of Berlin."[53] On his way to the city center, the president reviewed the Second Armored (Hell on Wheels) Division lined up on the autobahn between Potsdam and Berlin. This was an overwhelming display of American military power, one that would be portrayed to US audiences via print journalism and newsreel footage in the days and weeks to come. The United States had defeated its greatest adversary, and now the US public could see their victorious commander in chief tour the wreckage on their behalf. The president's party proceeded toward Berlin, entering the city from the southwest. The scene was one of absolute destruction. "Not a single building in this district remains," reported one British officer of the area Truman encountered. "[No] shops, flats, [or] hotels. The world famous Adlon Hotel is a complete ruin. . . . The damage has to be seen to be believed, words cannot describe the destruction"[54] (figures 2.1 and 2.2).

Truman's motorcade passed the destroyed Berlin radio center and shattered government buildings before turning onto the Charlottenburger Chaussee, which the *Los Angeles Times* described as a "broad avenue leading through the once beautiful Tiergarten, which is now littered with crashed

FIGURE 2.1. President Harry S. Truman on a driving tour of Berlin, July 16, 1945. Photograph by the US Army Signal Corps. Courtesy of the Harry S. Truman Library and Museum. Accession Number: 64-375.

planes, fire-blackened smashed tanks[,] and parks of once magnificent trees transformed into ugly stumps by shellfire."[55] The motorcade reached the Brandenburg Gate, a famous symbol of German history that marked the entrance to the Russian zone of occupation. As Truman's car drove under the Brandenburg Gate, Colonel General Alexander V. Gorbatoff, the Soviet commander of the region, saluted the president.[56] A report printed in the *Los Angeles Times* described the scene: "Russian flags were prominent on top of the

FIGURE 2.2. President Truman's motorcade passes the Royal Palace, July 16, 1945. Photograph by the US Bureau of Aeronautics. Courtesy of the Harry S. Truman Library and Museum. Accession Number: 63-1454-44.

battered, bombed-out buildings and the President passed between two huge signs, on one side the street showing the new Big Three, on the other showing the old Big Three including the late President Roosevelt."[57]

Truman later recalled the "absolute ruin" in Berlin. "Hitler's folly," the president wrote in his diary later that day. "He overreached himself by trying to take in too much territory. He had no morals and his people backed him up. Never did I see a more sorrowful sight, nor witness retribution to the nth degree." These images would stay with Truman and resurface in his radio address to the American people on August 9. "The most sorrowful part of the situation is the deluded Hitlerian populace. We saw old men, old women, young women, children from tots to teens carrying packs, pushing carts, pulling carts, evidently ejected by their conquerors and carrying what they could of their belongings to nowhere in particular."[58] The president's tour, however, was of little interest to the German populace, reported the *New York Times*. "Berliners paid little notice as the procession drove past the wreckage of the Reichstag, past the breadlines and under giant photographs of the President, Mr. Churchill and Generalissimo Stalin, put up in the Russian section of the capital."[59] After driving by the Reichstag, which had been burned by the Nazis in 1933, Truman's car turned around and drove down Unter den Linden to the Reich Chancellery, the site of many of Hitler's speeches. There, the *Los Angeles Times* reported, the president "looked up at the jagged remains of the balcony on which Hitler used to make his ranting speeches." The president commented to reporters, "It's a terrible thing, but they brought it upon themselves. It's just a demonstration of what can happen when a man overreaches himself."[60] Declining to inspect the interior of Hitler's headquarters, the president made his way back to Potsdam. Churchill, however, arrived at the Reich Chancellery ten minutes later and eagerly toured the abandoned site.[61] Later that evening, the president recorded his reaction to the scene. "I thought of Carthage, Baalbek, Jerusalem, Rome, Atlantis, Peking, Babylon, Nineveh; Scipio, Rameses II, Titus, Herman, Sherman, Jenghis Kahn, Alexander the Great. But Hitler only destroyed Stalingrad—and Berlin. I hope for some sort of peace—but I fear that machines are ahead of morals by some centuries and when morals catch up perhaps there'll be no reason for any of it."[62]

Even as print journalists narrated the details of Truman's tour of a decimated Berlin, various news outlets also provided photographs and live camera shots of the wreckage in Berlin. *Time* published two photos from Berlin in its July 16 issue: one featuring a towering portrait of Stalin at the city entrance and another of German women conscripted by the Russians to clean up the city.[63] The scene of destruction was made even more vivid one week later, when *Life* published a nine-page photographic essay of Berlin's ruins. The images revealed a city devastated by air raids and Soviet occupation.[64] Readers were exposed to massive portraits of Stalin and photos of the "Big Three" throughout the city. There "were even portraits of the Big Three," *Life* reported, "the old trio with the American President who had died, the new one with the American President who was on his way to Berlin." Readers also encountered images of the destroyed Reichstag, Gestapo headquarters, German women cleaning up destruction, the Adlon Hotel, Joseph Goebbels's mansion, and Hitler's Reich Chancellery. One photograph showed the Brandenburg Gate reflected in a pool of dirty water and sewage. "On May 2," the magazine noted, "when the Russians captured Berlin, they marched thousands of German prisoners through the gate."[65]

Newsreels also provided footage of Truman driving along the autobahn, saluting US troops lining the route from Potsdam to Berlin, and touring the decimated city. In one such Paramount Newsreel story, the narrator explained to the audience: "The President utilizes the extra time with a motor tour of the bombed-out ruins of Berlin. Under the famous Brandenburg Gate and along street after street of utter devastation, they are silent testimony to the accuracy of American precision bombing."[66] Similarly, Pathé News narrated the president's arrival by plane, declaring: "The American President Comes to Germany." The footage then showed Truman's motorcade driving through the streets of Berlin with this description: "An army convoy takes the president from the airport for a brief tour of shattered Berlin. Harry Truman sees with his own eyes the destruction brought upon the once-arrogant capital of Germany. An object lesson to aggressors of the future taught by united free men."[67] Collectively, these news reports reinforced the significance of Truman's tour of Berlin and allowed the US public to see firsthand what damage had been done to Nazi Germany.

This deliberate movement and travel of the presidential body—and what this body could do—also portrayed the United States as strong, healthy, and capable of leading the postwar global order. The rhetorical construction of physical capability—and the concealment of any disability—was particularly relevant at this moment, for Truman's predecessor, Franklin D. Roosevelt, worked to conceal his paralysis from public view and used metaphors of vigor, strength, and perseverance to construct his presidential ethos. Indeed, as Amos Kiewe and Davis W. Houck argue, FDR "emphasized a visual rhetoric that drew attention to his ostensibly healthy body" and "used the spoken word to portray his own health, while denigrating the health of his opponents."[68] Truman, however, had no such need. News accounts often referenced his intellectual curiosity, quick wit, and overall vigor. The implication, of course, was that Truman's able body replaced FDR's war-weary one. At Potsdam, the strength and health of the nation was encapsulated by the vigorous "Missouri farmer" who drove through the streets of a decimated Berlin as a conquering hero.[69]

"We . . . Raise the Flag of Victory"

Where images of the traveling presidential body amid the ruins of Berlin symbolized the Allied victory over Nazi Germany, the president also made a rare public appearance to articulate the position the United States would take in the postwar world.[70] After three days of formal meetings and informal socializing with Stalin and Churchill, Truman "emerged from the secrecy-fenced Potsdam compound of the Big Three meeting" to participate in a flag-raising ceremony over the American zone of occupation in Berlin. The president, reported *Time*, "had a ceremonial job to do in Berlin, and he evidently relished doing it."[71] The event, which was separate from the Potsdam Conference, took

FIGURE 2.3. President Truman at a flag-raising ceremony over US military headquarters in Berlin, July 20, 1945. Photograph by the US Army Signal Corps. Courtesy of the Harry S. Truman Library and Museum. Accession Number: 63-1455-47.

place in what had once been the German Air Force headquarters. In a speech less than two minutes in length, Truman "made the biggest international news of the week"[72] (figure 2.3).

The president's remarks were notable for several reasons, the first of which being that he even delivered them at all. From the beginning, "Big Three" leaders had agreed to keep the negotiations secret until the conclusion of the conference. "It must have taken a considerable amount of courage and conviction on the part of a country boy from Missouri to stand up in public and tell where he and his country stood in the midst of the debates that are going on regarding which part of Germany shall become part of Poland, how the rest of Germany is to be divided up and who is to control the Dardanelles," wrote Tania Long of the *New York Times*. "President Truman, like Mr. Stalin and Mr. Churchill, is bound by agreement not to give the people of the world the slightest idea of what they are talking about, what problems lie before them or how they are getting on with their grave business until their meeting is finished and the final communiqué is issued."[73] And yet, in a very brief address, Truman tipped his hand.

General Eisenhower, officers and Men: This is an historic occasion. We have conclusively proven that a free people can successfully look after the affairs of the world. We are here today to raise the flag of victory over the capital of our greatest adversary. In doing that, we must remember that in raising that flag we are raising it in the name of the people of the United States, who are looking forward to a better world, a peaceful world, a world in which all the people will have an opportunity to enjoy the good things of life, and not just a few at the top. Let us not forget that we are fighting for peace, and for the welfare of mankind. We are not fighting for conquest. There is not one piece of territory, or one thing of a monetary nature that we want out of this war. We want peace and prosperity for the world as a whole. We want to see the time come when we can do the things in peace that we have been unable to do in war. If we can put this tremendous machine of ours, which has made this victory possible, to work for peace we can look forward to the greatest age in the history of mankind. That is what we propose to do.[74]

With this statement, Truman articulated at least three important themes that would come to dominate the United States' postwar consciousness—and, ultimately, the nation's Cold War policy for years to come.

First, Truman underscored the significance of this moment in relationship to time and place. The nation had "conclusively proven that a free people can successfully look after the affairs of the world." Now, in Berlin, they had gathered to "raise the flag of victory over the capital of our greatest adversary." In so doing, they were raising it on behalf of the "people of the United States," who eagerly anticipated a "better world, a peaceful world, a world in which all the people will have an opportunity to enjoy the good things in life, and not just a few at the top."[75] Here, the president described the war effort as encapsulating the central ideals of the United States: liberty and justice for all. This had been, he argued, a fight undertaken for all of humanity. And yet, as several Black newspaper correspondents later noted, there was a good deal of hypocrisy found in Truman's remarks, for this vision of liberty did not extend to minority groups living in the United States. Such a commitment, if issued in the United States, would have "brought howls unending from the majority electorate and their fascist-minded representatives in the sacred halls of Congress," wrote William A. Fowlkes in the *Atlanta Daily World*.[76] It was one thing for the president to denounce prejudice from the former capital of Nazi Germany. And yet, as the *Chicago Defender* noted, Truman's statement bore little significance for his home country. "Is race hate to be rooted out of Germany but left to grow wild and flourishing in America?"[77] The inconsistency between word and deed was nothing short of appalling.

The president also used his brief statement to remind his audience of the

United States' national mission. The country, he said, was "fighting for peace, and for the welfare of mankind," not "for conquest." The nation had no desire to occupy more territory or control other governments—unlike, perhaps, his contemporaries at the "Big Three" meeting. Instead, their stated desire was to secure "peace and prosperity for the world as a whole."[78] The president's explicit emphasis on the moral dimensions of this war reinforced the nation's commitment to ensuring that all peoples could determine their own destiny. "His statement that the ideals for which the United States was fighting came as a refreshing affirmation of the principles for which the war was fought before it lost its ideological character with victory clearly in sight," noted Tania Long of the *New York Times*. There was some indication that Truman desired the speech to be broadcast to individuals around the world, for, as Long noted, the president "made it clear in words that could not be misunderstood even in the sloppiest translation that the United States had gone to war only because it loved peace and that, however great the temptations, it would not sow the seeds of another and perhaps disastrous conflict by taking a neighbor's pasture or insisting on a monetary tribute."[79] And yet, as W. E. B. DuBois noted in an editorial published in the *Chicago Defender*, this policy of no occupation did not square with the US occupation of various islands and nations in the Pacific. "We have outposts ranging over thousands of miles which can be turned into fortresses to dominate the Pacific ocean, and enable us to point our guns toward the heart of Asia and the domination of the yellow race," DuBois wrote. "The time is coming, and it is not far away, when somebody has got to explain just where the United States stands in the matter of colonial imperialism."[80]

Finally, Truman used his speech to describe the nation as a force for good. As a "free people" that could "successfully look after the affairs of the world," he said, the American people had "conclusively proven" that democracy could triumph over tyranny. This image of the nation on a democratic crusade suggested that Truman would continue Roosevelt's interventionist policies and adopt a position of world leadership in the postwar world. "Europeans cannot help wondering whether this new voice of America that they hear speaking is only an echo of the Wilsonian past or whether Main Street has become more cosmopolitan in the years between the two wars," reported the *New York Times*.[81] Would the United States retreat to its prewar isolationist impulses? Or, under Truman, would it continue the policy of active engagement overseas? Truman would answer this question more fully in his August 9 radio address to the nation, but his flag-raising speech in Berlin offered an important clue. In fact, many read the speech as an early expression of what policies the United States would adopt in the postwar world. As the *New York Herald Tri-*

bune opined, the United States desired "a world which is healthy—politically and economically. . . . The danger to the United States from a sick world has been amply demonstrated." Rather than adopting the isolationist stance that defined US foreign policy after the Great War, Truman's brief remarks suggested that he would adopt a different approach. "This danger cannot be averted by putting a sanitary cordon around the country, no matter how far distant the quarantine signs may be placed," the paper continued. "The only answer is to work with other nations to strike at infection wherever it may appear."[82] Drawing on metaphors of sickness and disease, this striking passage anticipated and perhaps even contributed to "communism as cancer" metaphors that would emerge just several years later to describe the Soviet threat to the United States.[83] "America's vital interest lies in amicable and equitable arrangement of the affairs of a troubled continent," the editorial continued. "The main point is the recognition of the American goal in world affairs and of her unique position. . . . And the American position, if utilized skillfully and courageously, can be of great advantage in advancing the common goal of men of good will everywhere."[84] This was the stance Truman would take when he returned from Potsdam and in the Cold War years to follow.

The president's public appearance at the flag-raising ceremony became the prominent news story out of Berlin for several days. Images of the event were printed in prominent US newspapers and magazines. Clips of the speech were featured on newsreels.[85] One Universal Newsreel report dated July 23, 1945, featured footage of Truman speaking at the flag-raising ceremony. The commentator noted: "Over the old German barracks in Berlin, the stars and stripes fly in victory. This historic banner has flown over much captured territory: Casablanca, Algiers, Rome, and Berlin. Let us pray it will not be long before it flies over Tokyo."[86] This narrative reinforced an image of the United States as a conquering hero, ready and willing to liberate peoples from political oppression. In another Paramount Newsreel clip, the commentator noted that "from a cobblestone barrack square in Berlin, the outside world gets its first big uplift from the scene of the conference. . . . The President, with characteristic plain talk, restates America's simple, easy-to-understand war aims."[87] These images and newsreels allowed the US public to witness a formal military victory speech in the capital of their former adversary. More broadly, they also positioned the US president—and the nation—as a liberating force, the natural defender of peoples who wished to be free.

Although brief, Truman's speech was incredibly important because it was the first time he spoke publicly since the start of the Potsdam Conference. His words reinforced the idea that the United States would assume an active role on the world stage. He not only articulated the US victory over Nazi

Germany; he linked this victory to a larger national commitment to pursuing peace and justice. This moment, he argued, proved that "a free people can successfully look after the affairs of the world." Despite the uncomfortable truth that this "free people" referred to some—not all—Americans, Truman's proclamation set the stage for the United States' self-appointed role as international referee and arbiter of the "Free World."

The "No. 1 Seat"

Perhaps the most widely photographed and circulated image from the Potsdam Conference was a deliberate recreation of an earlier scene: the "Big Three" seated side by side.[88] Circulating images of Roosevelt, Churchill, and Stalin quickly became the dominant visual artifact after previous Allied wartime conferences. In November 1943, the three heads of state posed on the veranda of the Soviet embassy in Tehran. The American president occupied the center seat, a chair that was itself slightly elevated above the other two. Looking off into the distance, his expression displayed an air of calm confidence and visionary statesmanship. He was the clear leader of the "Big Three." Seated to Roosevelt's right—but appearing in the left side of the photograph—the Russian premier appeared slightly out of focus but was the only one looking directly at the camera. This positioning made Stalin appear on the same level as FDR. Their shoulder height was almost exactly parallel. It was only Roosevelt's cleanly tailored dark suit that gave him the edge over Stalin's military dress. The British prime minister appeared on the right hand of the frame and was seated to Roosevelt's left. Stalin and Roosevelt appeared tall and erect, but Churchill looked shorter, chubbier, and decidedly more comfortable in his velvet easy chair, with his hat in hand (figure 2.4).

Just over a year later, in February 1945, the "Big Three" met again in Yalta. Still occupying the middle seat, the American president looked haggard, with deep circles under his eyes, shoulders slumped under a dark overcoat, and a cigarette in his left hand. The British prime minister appeared on the left side of the frame, a position that from this angle made him appear the most prominent of the three. The lighting of the image accentuated his bald head as he gazed off to his left. The Soviet premier seemed to almost disappear in the right side of the image, his face shaded by his military cap. Where the photograph from Tehran portrayed Roosevelt with an air of confidence and charisma, the Yalta image depicted a president wearied by war—and weakened by an illness he tried to obscure from public view.[89] And yet, these corresponding images suggested a continuity of global leadership, three global superpowers united against fascism across time and place (figure 2.5).

FIGURE 2.4. Soviet premier Joseph Stalin, President Franklin D. Roosevelt, and British prime minister Winston Churchill at the "Big Three" Conference in Tehran, Iran, November 29, 1943. Courtesy of the Franklin D. Roosevelt Presidential Library and Museum. Photo ID: 48-22:3715(107).

FIGURE 2.5. British prime minister Winston Churchill, President Franklin D. Roosevelt, and Soviet premier Joseph Stalin at the "Big Three" Conference in Yalta, USSR, February 9, 1945. Courtesy of the Franklin D. Roosevelt Presidential Library and Museum. Photo ID: 48-22:3659(69).

After Roosevelt's untimely death, Truman had to convince the US public—
and the rest of the watching world—that he could fill the void the thirty-second
president had left. Images of Truman's participation in the Potsdam Conference played an essential role in this broader image campaign. Indeed, the new
chief executive many considered accidental understood the persuasive power
of these photographs—and the fact that his position in the image spoke louder
than words. With specific details of conference negotiations embargoed and reporters itching to find available content, pictures of the "Big Three" in Potsdam
dominated the news coverage in the United States. Several images mirrored
the earlier "Big Three" portraits taken at Tehran and Yalta, photos captured
with the specific aim of presenting "a show of unity so that people around the
world would gain the impression that the negotiations were going well."[90] During the conference, Truman followed Roosevelt's example and deliberately positioned himself between Stalin and Churchill (and, after Churchill's defeat in
the British elections, Clement Attlee) for these official portraits. Several official
photographers from the US Army Signal Corps reported that "President Truman is running the Big Three show all by himself from what we can see." They
continued: "When the big shots appear for pictures[,] the President marches to
the center chair, sits down and invites Churchill or Attlee and Stalin to sit on either side. Churchill sort of shied off when we took the first pictures. Stalin had
an eye on the middle seat when Attlee returned as Prime Minister and we took
the new group. But Mr. Truman never batted an eye—just motioned to his colleagues to hustle along and pose, then hurried back to discussions after we shot
the scenes."[91] Images of Truman seated between the British prime minister and
the Soviet premier not only reinforced the president's central leadership role
at the conference, but they also visually encapsulated the symbolic transfer of
power between Roosevelt and Truman (figure 2.6).

Images of the "Big Three" at Potsdam appeared in some of the most prominent periodicals in the United States, including *Time*, *Life*, the *New York Herald Tribune*, the *Chicago Daily Tribune*, and the *Atlanta Daily World*.[92] These
images also were featured on newsreel coverage of the Potsdam Conference's
conclusion.[93] Collectively, these photographs provided a striking visual display of continuity in the midst of chaos. Roosevelt's premature death created a void in the "Big Three" alliance, a void that was both physical and
symbolic. Moreover, the loss of the FDR's wartime leadership was a source
of deep concern for US political officials, the American public, and many
others around the world. Truman's presence in the "number 1" seat offered
visible, tangible proof that the United States had every intention of leading on the global stage—and that the new president was up to the task. The
placement of Truman between the Soviet premier and the British prime min-

FIGURE 2.6. British prime minister Winston Churchill, President Harry S. Truman, and Soviet premier Joseph Stalin at the "Big Three" Conference in Potsdam, Germany, July 25, 1945. Photograph by the US Bureau of Aeronautics. Courtesy of the Harry S. Truman Library and Museum. Accession Number: 63-79.

ister stood as a physical, embodied symbol of Truman's elevation to the role of president of the United States and the "Leader of the Free World." He was symbolically and literally replacing Roosevelt as the central, mediating figure in these discussions, a pivotal link between Great Britain and the Soviet Union. Moreover, these images portrayed Truman as jovial, healthy, and well rested—a striking contrast to earlier visual depictions of Roosevelt at Yalta and Tehran. Where the late president appeared burdened by the demands of world war, his successor displayed youthful energy and enthusiasm. Explicit or not, comparisons between images of Truman with Stalin and Churchill/ Attlee and Roosevelt with Stalin and Churchill were inevitable—and, in this case, helped Truman position himself as leader and central figure of the "Big Three" alliance (figure 2.7).[94]

There was one particular image, however, that received laudatory news coverage not because of its subjects, but rather for its technological advancement: the first color photograph ever transmitted via radio (figure 2.8).[95] One of the final images transmitted out of Potsdam was a color-saturated image of Clement Attlee, Harry S. Truman, and Joseph Stalin seated on the grounds

FIGURE 2.7. British prime minister Winston Churchill, President Harry S. Truman, and Soviet premier Joseph Stalin shake hands at the Potsdam Conference, July 23, 1945. Pictorial Press Ltd./Alamy Stock Photo. Image ID: HRFP5F.

of the Cecilienhof Palace. Where the general public was accustomed to see-ing black-and-white images of the "Big Three" from earlier conferences, this image portrayed three leaders in living color. In some outlets, this image was accompanied by articles detailing the technological advancements that made this color image possible. For example, the *Philadelphia Inquirer* printed the color image alongside a graphic detailing a three-plate one-shot camera. They were reproducing this image, the paper wrote, "in the interest of giving its readers the benefit of all the latest methods devised by science for the rapid transmission of public information." This photo "represents a resolute step toward mastery of a chain of highly complicated processes," the paper noted, one that had been accomplished by the US Army Signal Corps Pictorial Service.[96] The weekly magazine *Collier's* highlighted the speed and relative ease, publishing this description below the color reproduction: "Light a cigarette. Smoke it down, not too fast. That's about how long it took to transmit this color photograph from Berlin direct to Washington. . . . Black-and-white telephotos are a common occurrence by now, but radioed color photos—let's call them telechromes—are a new development in news coverage."[97]

The fanfare associated with this particular color image reveals a press and a public increasingly aware of advances in communication technology. Even as these journalistic accounts focused on the mechanics of transmitting a color photograph, they also reflected a significant shift in how the president could be seen, envisioned, and displayed to US audiences and the global public. Prior to this photograph of the "Big Three" at Potsdam, all previous images of the US president traveling abroad appeared in hues of black, white, and gray—completely devoid of color. To a public accustomed to such portrayals, the introduction of a vivid image of the US president holding court on the international stage made American leadership abroad visible, accessible,

FIGURE 2.8. British prime minister Clement R. Attlee, President Harry S. Truman, and Soviet premier Joseph Stalin at the "Big Three" Conference in Potsdam, Germany, August 1, 1945. Photograph by the US Army Signal Corps. Courtesy of the Library of Congress.

tangible, imaginable, and closer to "real life" than ever before. In the years to come, US officials harnessed other newfound media technologies such as live television feeds and cable news to portray the presence of the president on the world stage to audiences at home and abroad.

A "Heart-to-Heart Talk with the People"

Truman's performance at Potsdam—and the media coverage surrounding it—positioned the president as the natural heir to Roosevelt's legacy and a reputable leader well prepared to tackle the challenges of a postwar world.[98] But where news reports and images of Truman in Berlin and the president's speech at the flag-raising ceremony reinforced the president's leadership role, the president's August 9 radio address to the US public offered the clearest demonstration of the president's rhetorical leadership. In fact, it was in this speech that Truman described the United States' defense of democracy in postwar Europe as a moral mandate, a theme that would reverberate throughout the rest of the Cold War. After his performance at Potsdam, Truman had both the stature and the confidence to define the meaning of the Second World War for his audience and to cast a vision of what that meaning signified for the future of US foreign policy. In this radio address to the US public, Truman offered a moral framework to make sense of what the United States had fought for, what they had fought against, and how they would direct similar energies in the postwar world.

"My fellow Americans," Truman began, "I have just returned from Berlin, the city from which the Germans intended to rule the world. It is a ghost city. The buildings are in ruins, its economy and its people are in ruins." Here, Truman spoke to an audience who had encountered these images via newspaper coverage and newsreel footage. The president's words of vivid description supplemented what they had already seen. The president went on to describe the images he saw in the streets during his driving tour of Berlin. "German women and children and old men were wandering over the highways, returning to bombed-out homes or leaving bombed out cities, searching for food and shelter." This narrative depicted human individuals in need of basic necessities such as food, water, and shelter—people just like them. "War has indeed come home to Germany and to the German people. It has come home in all the frightfulness with which the German leaders started and waged it," he said. This firsthand experience, the president noted, made him deeply grateful that the United States had been spared similar destruction. "How glad I am to be home again," he exclaimed. "And how grateful to Almighty God that this land of ours has been spared!" As these initial comments demonstrate, Truman's personal experience in Berlin conditioned his own understanding of this postwar moment. "We can never permit any aggressor in the future to be clever enough to divide us or strong enough to defeat us," he said. This vow of "never again" would becoming a rallying cry for the future. To millions of Americans who had lost husbands, sons, fathers, and brothers, the vivid imagery of European destruction coupled with their own personal experience offered a powerful argument against future war—one supported by both reason and emotion.

Toward the end of his speech, Truman returned to the vivid imagery of suffering citizens throughout Europe. "Europe today is hungry," he said. "I am not talking about Germans. I am talking about the people of the countries which were overrun and devastated by the Germans, and particularly about the people of Western Europe. Many of them lack clothes and fuel and tools and shelter and raw materials. They lack the means to restore their cities and their factories." Truman warned that as the winter came, "distress will increase. Unless we do what we can to help, we may lose next winter what we won at such terrible cost last spring." To a citizenry well aware of the sacrifices required during the most recent war, the idea of "losing" what so many had fought and died to obtain would have been unfathomable. But Truman went further, describing in detail what it might mean if the United States retreated from its moral and military positions across the Atlantic. "If we let Europe grow cold and hungry, we may lose some of the foundations of order on which the hope for worldwide peace must rest. We must help to the limits of our strength. And we will." Here, Truman framed US economic aid as a natural progression of US military action during the Second World War. The only way to preserve the victories over totalitarian rule the country just secured, Truman argued, was to support the well-being of Europe's most vulnerable. Here, the president painted a vivid, compelling portrait of suffering citizens who, through no fault of their own, lacked basic necessities to survive. These were the real victims of the war, and the ones most vulnerable to succumb to another totalitarian regime. In contrast, Truman depicted the United States as willing, able, and morally compelled to adopt the role of protector and benefactor.

To conclude, the president offered a clear mandate that would dictate US foreign policy throughout the Cold War. This was a vision inspired by past historical lessons, the moral clarity of the present moment, and a hope for a better, more peaceful future. "Our victory in Europe was more than a victory of arms," Truman told his audience. He defined the Allied triumph over Nazi Germany as "a victory of one way of life over another. . . . A victory of an ideal founded on the rights of the common man, on the dignity of the human being, on the conception of the State as the servant—and not the master—of its people." Here, Truman's usage of the phrase "way of life" was strategic. Wilson had used the phrase in 1917 when asking Congress for a declaration of war. The nation was fighting "for the rights of nations great and small and the privilege of men everywhere to choose their way of life and of obedience," Wilson had declared. "The world must be made safe for democracy."[99] Franklin D. Roosevelt also invoked this phrase to warn of those who would undermine a "democratic way life" or attempt "to impose their way of life on other nations."[100] In those rhetorical contexts, "way of life" was always linked in some way to the United States' responsibility to act on behalf of individuals whose political rights were being threatened by active war. In Truman's usage, the phrase described a "way of life" able to defeat Nazi Germany and any other ideology that threatened individual liberty. It was a "way of life" that extended beyond the tumult of war, a prospect available to all—and one that the United States should defend at home and abroad.

This "victory of one way of life over another" came with great responsibility, Truman argued. The United States had "emerged from this war the most powerful nation in the world—the most powerful nation, perhaps, in all history." This power, he said, came not from military might or technological advances but from a new realization of the United States' moral strength and leadership. The war had revealed a

> new thing—the thing which we had not known—the thing we have learned now and should never forget, is this: that a society of self-governing men is more powerful, more enduring, more creative than any other kind of society, however disciplined, however centralized. We know now that the basic proposition of the worth and dignity of man is not a sentimental aspiration or a vain hope or a piece of rhetoric. It is the strongest, most creative force now present in this world.

Here, the president described "the basic proposition of the worth and dignity of man" as a force that could be used not only in war, but in peacetime. "Now let us use that force and all our resources and all our skills in the great cause of a just and lasting peace!"[101] Strengthened by their past victories and motivated by their common beliefs, Truman argued that this power of self-governance and democratic leadership would allow the United States to position itself as the "Leader of the Free World."

Public Reception

Contemporary news reports and citizen letters from the historical record reveal just how important this negotiation of presidential image and global leadership at Potsdam was to the general US public. A fascinating feature of many of these accounts is their emphasis on how Truman navigated the complexities of honoring his predecessor's wishes while also offering his own vision for the future of US foreign policy in the postwar world. For example, the *New York Herald Tribune* observed that "President Truman's greatest single contribution to the international problem" was how he had "managed to de-personalize and to institutionalize the organs of co-operation and creative action which Roosevelt, Churchill and Stalin developed as individual leaders." Where the original "Big Three" personalities embodied the Allied wartime alliance, Truman was "modest in depicting himself as an agent of the United States and its constitutional authorities rather than as a 'leader' on his own account" in the negotiations at Potsdam.[102] Although FDR advocated for American influence on the global stage, Truman reinterpreted this impulse for the realities of the postwar world. In so doing, the new president shifted the locus of US foreign policy beyond Roosevelt's shadow.

Press reports also noted the US public's wide approval of Truman's performance at Potsdam—and how the president's confident approach allayed their secret fears. In a lengthy article analyzing the role Truman played at Potsdam, syndicated columnist Roscoe Drummond admitted that US citizens drew "a sigh of relief when they contemplate the significant and successful role which Truman played at the Berlin Conference." Drummond noted that Truman, like Roosevelt, believed that "the only way the United States can keep out of war is to help keep war from breaking out anywhere in the world, and he has acted to put American power behind that policy." However, Drummond suggested that Truman's major victory was his decision to position himself not as an individual leader, as Roosevelt had often done, but "as the voice of the whole American people." In fact, he suggested that Truman's performance at Potsdam was possible because he was "given—through the unity of the American people in foreign policy—a power of attorney such as no President had previously enjoyed. President Truman's strength as a world figure is the strength of American democracy."[103] Although there were mixed reactions to the policy implications of the agreements reached at Potsdam, there was widespread agreement that the new president had proved himself on the international stage and solidified the United States' leadership role in the postwar world.

Ordinary citizens agreed. Upon Truman's return from Potsdam, people from around the country wrote to the president to express their confidence in his world leadership. Wat Arnold, a member of Congress from Kirksville, Missouri, wrote to the president on August 4: "You are doing a fine job as representative of the America people and I congratulate you most heartily."[104]

One of the president's own advisors, Herbert Baynard Swope from New York, told Truman in a letter dated August 6: "Your work in Berlin removed any lingering doubt as to your capacity to function in your high office. You did a fine job. I feel a sense of pride in your record."[105] J. C. Nichols from Kansas City, Missouri, wrote: "From all I can hear and learn I believe you did a grand job at the Potsdam conference. . . . I have absolute confidence in the fine results you are achieving for our country."[106] Commenting on the news of Russia's declaration of war on Japan, George H. Hodges and Frank Hodges of Olathe, Kansas, wrote: "Biggest man in the world today you brought home bacon from Berlin[:] Russia declares war on Japan."[107] That same day, C. Conner Makin of Jacksonville, Florida, wrote in enthusiastic support: "You did a wonderful job Sir. Your great buddy Roosevelt smiles upon you."[108] The president's performance was even lauded by members of the Republican Party. C. H. Bryson, the chairman of the Republicans for Roosevelt League in Columbus, Ohio, telegraphed on August 8: "The results of your Potsdam conference are heartily approved by our associates by all apparently except hard boiled reactionaries you have settled all doubts as to where you stand on the common man's prayers you are now securely our own."[109]

To many Americans and military service members, however, the Potsdam Conference only underscored the inconsistencies between the United States' democratic zeal abroad and the bitter ironies of racial injustice at home. Black periodicals highlighted the inherent contradictions between fighting for freedom abroad when such opportunities did not exist for many US citizens. The *Chicago Defender* reminded readers that it was "an old diplomatic axiom that representatives abroad should not sign anything they would not support at home," and suggested that "the paradox at Potsdam was that the President of the United States signed a document making democrats and republicans of ex-Nazis, while at home he cannot get democrats and republicans to make first-class citizens of Negroes." If Truman indicated at Potsdam that he "realizes that racism is too dangerous a disease to be unchecked and that it is not immune to forceful, direct action," why would he not take similar steps at home? "Slowly we are being maneuvered into a position where we have outfaced and outfought everyone's race prejudice except our own."[110] The *Pittsburgh Courier* declared that Black Americans were determined "to march forward to final freedom and equality. They know that their enemies in this country, powerful though they may be, are fearful of their determination to be full citizens, else they would not resort to such desperate tactics in a vain effort to hold them back. . . . All the Goebbels-like lies that the tortured minds of Dixie demagogues can concoct cannot stop them, ever."[111] This inherent contradiction between the purported ideal of "liberty and justice for all" and overt racist policies such as segregation, Jim Crow, redlining, the deliberate exclusion of Black veterans from the GI Bill, and many other indignities would continue throughout the rest of the Cold War.

Conclusion

Harry S. Truman's elevation to the US presidency and his subsequent performance at the Potsdam Conference encapsulates a monumental shift in US foreign policy—and not for the reason one might expect. To be sure, the conference negotiations did accomplish several important objectives, such as Stalin's agreement to join in the war against Japan. Other items on the agenda, such as the question of Polish sovereignty and a detailed plan for governing the various sectors of Berlin, were never formalized and would contribute to the deterioration of the US-Soviet relationship in the weeks and months to come. In fact, some of the conference participants attributed little permanent significance to the Potsdam negotiations, noting that Stalin had no intention of ceding territory or political influence in Eastern Europe.[112] Why, then, this focus on a meeting of hesitant wartime allies who would quickly become arch enemies? What is the significance of Truman's performance at Potsdam for the global rhetorical presidency?

The overarching argument of this chapter is that going to Potsdam allowed the new president to step into the void left by Roosevelt and prove to the US public and the rest of the world that he was qualified for the job. As a towering presence in American political life during the Great Depression and the Second World War, FDR did more than articulate the United States' relationship to the rest of the world. He embodied and defined it. With virtually no experience in international affairs, Truman ascended to the presidency at an extreme disadvantage. Although relations between the United States and the Soviet Union rapidly deteriorated soon after the third and final "Big Three" meeting, Truman's presence in Potsdam bolstered something else: his stature and credibility as president of the United States. In this instance, going global offered the surest way to reinforce Truman's credibility and leadership role in foreign affairs. Importantly, however, the president's personal experience in Berlin—what he saw, what he heard, what he experienced through his presence in place—also shaped his vision for America's position on the global stage.

To a nation beginning to see itself as the protector and defender of the "Free World," the next few years offered several opportunities to step into such a role. The first occurred just six months after the conclusion of the Potsdam Conference. In an election-eve speech to the Russian Politburo,

Soviet premier Joseph Stalin declared Soviet communism to be altogether superior to US democracy, a statement some influential American diplomats said amounted to a declaration of war.[113] In his now famous "Long Telegram," State Department analyst George Kennan argued that the Soviets were intent on dismantling the United States' democratic way of life. "If Soviet power is to be secure," he wrote, the Russians believed "that it is desirable and necessary that the internal harmony of our society be disrupted, our traditional way of life be destroyed, [and] the international authority of our state be broken." Ultimately, Kennan concluded, the "Soviets are still by far the weaker force. Thus, their success will really depend on [the] degree of cohesion, firmness and vigor which [the] Western World can muster. And this is [the] factor which it is within our power to influence."[114] Although Kennan's telegram did not immediately change US foreign policy toward the Soviets, it put the Truman administration on alert and, as Denise M. Bostdorff argues, "planted the seeds for such a change."[115]

To those who were skeptical of the need for US global leadership, additional evidence quickly mounted. After the British government informed the United States it could no longer continue sending military and economic aid to Greece to ward off communist-backed factions, Truman decided to intervene. In a March 12, 1947, address to Congress, the president outlined what would become known as the Truman Doctrine, stating that "at the present moment in world history nearly every nation must choose between alternative ways of life. . . . The free people of the world look to us for support in maintaining their freedoms. If we falter in our leadership, we may endanger the peace of the world—and we shall surely endanger the welfare of this Nation."[116] This clear description of alternative "ways of life" and the need for US defense of "the free people of the world" was a natural progression of the arguments Truman made on his return from Potsdam. The vision he presented to the American people in his August 9, 1945, address prepared them to support future military and economic aid to other nations struggling to maintain a democratic "way of life." If the nation wanted to honor the sacrifices made during the Second World War, US support for other "free people of the world" was the only option.

Truman's visit to Berlin also set the stage for what would become a dramatic flashpoint in the Cold War global imaginary: the symbolic status of the city of Berlin. The movement of his presidential body to and through Berlin inaugurated the process of shifting the city's symbolism from the capital of Nazi Germany to a space where Western democracy could flourish. To be sure, events such as the Berlin Airlift in 1948–49 and East Germany's construction of the Berlin Wall in 1961 contributed to this shift, a subject I will take up in chapter 4. However, Truman's decision to cite his own personal experiences in Berlin as evidence for US leadership on the global stage elevated Berlin and its citizens as individuals in desperate need of reeducation, reform, and renewal. And, as Truman argued in his victory speech in Berlin, the Allied victory in Berlin conclusively proved "that a free people can successfully look after the affairs of the world."[117] This moral imperative of protecting and defending freedom and democracy on the world stage, a commitment that would dominate Cold War discourse for the next fifty years, emerged from the wreckage Truman encountered in Berlin.

3

Eisenhower and the "Good Will" Tours

If we are to carry our democratic concepts into the international sphere, we have to be just as concerned about seeking and gaining popular approval abroad for our international behavior as we are diligent in seeking it at home for our domestic actions. If we honestly believe in the principle of government by consent of the governed[,] we should constantly try to speak and act and explain our actions in such a way as to command the greatest possible consent and approval abroad, at least in respect to matters affecting people abroad.

USIA, 1960[1]

Dwight D. Eisenhower was a brilliant military strategist, both on and off the battlefield. If Franklin Delano Roosevelt shepherded the nation through the Second World War and Harry S. Truman presided over the final diplomatic negotiations to end the conflict, Dwight D. Eisenhower symbolized the United States' military triumph over the Axis powers. As the supreme commander of the Allied Expeditionary Force in Europe, General Eisenhower planned Operation Overlord (colloquially known as D-day) and led the Allied forces to victory. When he returned to the United States for a visit in June 1945, the general was hailed as a conquering hero by four million New Yorkers who cheered his open car procession through the city. One month later, when then president Truman arrived in Germany to attend the Potsdam Conference, Eisenhower was the first one to welcome him to the former capital of the Third Reich.[2] "At this moment of triumph," writes historian William I. Hitchcock, Eisenhower was "the world's best-known and most-respected soldier. He embodied America's victory over fascism and Nazism."[3] And seven years later, in November 1952, the US public elected this Republican war hero to the US presidency amid a number of international crises. Although Truman had positioned the United States as a triumphant victor in a battle between two "ways of life" at the end of the Potsdam Conference, he would spend the rest of his presidency trying to figure out exactly what this new role meant for the nation in foreign affairs. The decisions Truman made set the stage for another prominent Cold War actor, the president who more than any other would establish the global rhetorical presidency as an offensive weapon in the battle for global public opinion.

Eisenhower assumed office at a moment of critical importance, one surrounded by global events that threatened American prestige and international leadership at the dawn of the Cold War. In August 1949, the Soviet Union detonated its first atomic bomb, an indication that the United States no longer had a monopoly on nuclear weapons. In October 1949, Mao Tse-tung and the Communist Party of China established the People's Republic of China (PRC) after a four-year civil war against Chinese nationalists led by Chiang Kai-shek. This "loss" of what many began to call "Red China" sent shock waves throughout the United States and its pro-democratic allies. In fact, US officials warned that this communist victory in Asia might soon spread to other countries, particularly after the PRC signed a treaty with the Soviet Union in February 1950. This fear was only further confirmed in June 1950, when the North Korean People's Army crossed the boundary between the Soviet-backed Democratic People's Republic of Korea and the US-backed Republic of Korea (ROK). Although Stalin's desire for European domination was well known, these military moves into Asia increased the fear of a growing communist state. The "attack on Korea," Truman declared when announcing his decision to send US troops to the region on June 27, 1950, made it "plain beyond all doubt that communism has passed beyond the use of subversion to conquer independent nations and will now use armed invasion and war."[4] But two years later, with criticism of the Truman administration's handling of the Korean War at an all-time high, Eisenhower told the public that, if elected, he would "go to Korea" and assess the situation himself.[5]

Dwight D. Eisenhower was the man for the moment. He was the candidate with enough military training and wartime experience to lead the nation in a new type of war, an ideological struggle to win over the hearts and minds of millions. But where the United States fought Nazi Germany with tanks, bombs, aircraft carriers, and millions of soldiers, this new type of war required an altogether different strategy, one designed to demonstrate the superiority of the American democratic "way of life" over Soviet communism. Under Eisenhower's direction, US officials reimagined how to tell the nation's story to the rest of the world. To do so, they repackaged strategies of wartime propaganda into peacetime "public information" campaigns directed to audiences foreign and domestic. Through the creation of various intergovernmental agencies including the USIA and the Operations Coordinating Board, the Eisenhower administration sought to defend US democratic ideals across the airwaves, newsreels, and printed page.[6] And, by the end of his second term, Eisenhower would solidify the global rhetorical presidency as a calculated form of public diplomacy, a Cold War maneuver that all future presidents would use to their advantage.

This chapter examines how the Eisenhower administration strategically deployed the physical travel and circulation of the presidential body as an embodied weapon in a Cold War crusade designed to portray the United States as preeminent on the global stage.[7] Between December 1959 and June 1960, Eisenhower embarked on three "missions of peace and good will" spanning countries in Europe, South America, Asia, North Africa, and the Middle East.[8] The president and other US officials devoted enormous time and attention to orchestrating global tours that would simultaneously project a positive image of the United States abroad and help the US public see their president as a global emissary for peace, a powerful yet benevolent friend who could help lead the world in a moment of grave peril. Although many international leaders clamored for a presidential stop, the specific locations and regions included in—and excluded from—Eisenhower's "Good Will" tours reveal a complex web of geopolitical relational networks. It was not just a question of what Eisenhower would say on these tours, but *where* he would speak, *who* he could address, *when* he would go there, and *how* these performances would reach a global audience. As he traveled outside, beyond, and between borders, boundaries, regions, and nation-states, Eisenhower's bodily movement became its own rhetorical performance.

After considering the general, overarching rationale behind these tours and detailing how they established the global rhetorical presidency as a deliberate mode of Cold War foreign policy engagement, I examine how the Eisenhower administration designed the president's visit to South America (what US officials referred to as "Operation Amigo") as a way to extend US influence in the region, counteract a growing communist presence in Cuba, and mobilize global public opinion in support of the United States. I focus my attention on "Operation Amigo" for two specific reasons. First, the movement of Eisenhower's body in South America was designed to take up material and symbolic space in the Western Hemisphere, a region both the United States and the Soviet Union eyed for ideological expansion. Second, this specific tour also provides a striking example of how a president's global movements can articulate and extend key tenets of US foreign policy, even when their words obscure or deny such policies. Although Eisenhower publicly affirmed the United States' policy of nonintervention in Cuba during his tour of South America, officials back in Washington used the president's absence to prepare various scenarios for military action against Cuba. In fact, Eisenhower's presence in the region quickly became a means of directing attention to "democracies" and deflecting attention from those who had "given in" to the Soviets—particularly, Cuba.

This chapter also details the pivotal role Eisenhower played in establishing the global rhetorical presidency as a symbolic weapon in the Cold War. As I will show, Eisenhower and other administration officials designed these visits to increase presidential power in foreign affairs, elevate the image and prestige of the United States, and mobilize global public opinion. In the end, the "Good Will" tours amounted to something of a traveling propaganda show designed to proclaim the superiority of the American "way of life" to audiences around the world. Having commanded the Cold War from his Washington headquarters for most of his presidency, Eisenhower used his final year in office to travel to the front lines himself.

Eisenhower, Global Public Opinion, and the Creation of the "Good Will" Tours

From the earliest days of the Eisenhower administration, US officials deployed the circulation of words, images, visuals, newsreels, and other artifacts as deliberate weapons in their campaign to elevate the United States' image to audiences at home and abroad. Where physical bodies or military tanks would be blocked by walls or barbed wire, words and images could flow freely across geographical borders and spatial boundaries, whether imagined or real. In June 1953, the President's Committee on International Information Activities (also known as the Jackson Committee) recommended that the goal for all future "information activities" should be to "persuade foreign peoples that it lies in their own interest to take actions which are also consistent with the national objectives of the United States" and "harmonize wherever possible the personal and national self-interest of foreigners with the national objectives of the United States."[9] In fact, the administration quickly recognized that targeted public diplomacy campaigns to global, transnational publics might very well determine the outcome of the ideological struggle between democracy and communism. As George V. Allen, the director of the USIA predicted, "the eventual outcome of the struggle between the Communist world system and the free society, assuming general war can be avoided, will depend in considerable degree on the extent we are able to influence the attitudes of people."[10] Whatever military superiority the United States had, administration officials stressed that actively shaping international public opinion was in fact the best weapon in their arsenal.

The struggle to win the hearts and minds of the international public was a critical mechanism of US foreign policy—one almost as old as the nation itself. "Since Benjamin Franklin went to Paris after the signing of the Declaration of Independence," noted one internal memorandum, "the United States has been engaged in efforts to communicate its policies and objectives abroad. But today, because of the growing importance of public opinion, rapid technological developments . . . and the omnipresence of the massive Soviet propaganda apparatus, the problem of communication is more urgent and more complex than ever before."[11] To address this "problem," officials underscored the importance of crafting and circulating messages to an international audience. "These American communications to other peoples, flowing life [like] rivers into a reservoir of world communications, define a special basin of America's international relations. As they carry through the filters of other nations' accepted values and media, they become the chief sources of the American image to those peoples."[12] As these internal memoranda make plain, each and every episode of "American communications" overseas offered the opportunity to shape the "American image" on the world stage. To defend against the "omnipresence of the massive Soviet propaganda apparatus," US officials created their own public diplomacy campaigns to reach a global, transnational audience.

As a crucial mechanism of US foreign policy discourse, these public information campaigns were directed to audiences behind the "Iron Curtain" and to those living outside of the Soviet Bloc. Although there was a temptation to "immediately think also of how many words can be poured behind the Iron Curtain," read one strategy memo from July 1959, US officials stressed that public diplomacy should be aimed toward so-called neutral countries and even pro-US government allies. "Public opinion is like the air waves over which thoughts are often transmitted—there are no geographical boundaries," the memorandum continued. "Influence exerted inside Great Britain or France can be as important in relation to opinion behind the Iron Curtain as if it were directed alone to the countries within the Soviet orbit."[13] Elevating US prestige in the minds of international audiences was the surest way to guarantee "neutral" audiences would identify themselves with the "Free World." This was to be a rhetorical arms race, a campaign to rally global public opinion around the United States—and against the Soviet Union.

Eisenhower's "Good Will" tours emerged out of this desire to mobilize international public opinion and elevate the image of the United States at home and abroad. However, there were at least two other motivations behind these diplomatic missions. First, administration officials suggested that these global tours would enable the president to assert more leadership in foreign affairs and even "go over" the heads of Congress. In a memorandum written just weeks after a sweeping Democratic victory in the 1958 midterm elections, White House press secretary James C. Hagerty suggested that although the "conduct of foreign affairs is exclusively the responsibility of the President," there were "some politicians—particularly in the Congress, but more particularly in the Senate—who are trying to muscle their way into this area—deliberately to weaken the responsibility of the president." In Hagerty's estimation, senators such as Lyndon Johnson, Hubert Humphrey, John F. Kennedy, Mike Mansfield, and Albert Gore Sr. were "trying to give the public the impression that they are the great statesmen and diplomats. They should be slapped down hard—whenever they try—for political purposes—to encroach on the President's prerogatives. There is no one in the world who can speak for America like the President." The best way to respond to such gross overreaches of political leadership, Hagerty concluded, was for the president to "personally participate more in foreign affairs and the campaign for peace. By 'personally,' I mean trips by the President outside the United States."[14] Hagerty told Eisenhower that a deliberately planned and highly publicized world tour would allow the president to remind the American people, members of Congress, and a wider global audience of his leadership role in the Cold War world. The White House press secretary also provided a list of potential countries and regions that the president might visit. Countries and regions on the list included India, Pakistan, the Philippines, Formosa, Japan, the ROK, South America, Europe, Russia, Africa, and the Near East.[15] In the months that followed, Eisenhower made plans to visit every spot on this list and completed trips to every nation or region except Russia and Japan between December 1959 and June 1960.

A second and related motivation for the "Good Will" tours was Eisenhower's belief that these international tours would solidify his presidential legacy as he neared the end of his second term. The president was explicit about this goal, writing in his autobiography that he "began seriously to consider the feasibility of a personal visit to the Mediterranean area and the Middle East" in September 1959. "How, I wondered, could I make the best use of this remaining time for the benefit of the United States? I realized that internationally I enjoyed a measure of good will. . . . [that] might be put to some use," Eisenhower recalled. "Possibly a trip or a series of trips to visit representative regions of the Free World might be a means of doing so."[16] To be sure, Eisenhower did enjoy widespread popularity overseas due in large part to his service as supreme commander of the Allied Expeditionary Force during World War II. Noting that "presidents do not ordinarily travel far and wide," Eisenhower recalled his hope that "such an ambitious and dramatic venture, unprecedented in peacetime, would . . . assure all the people I could reach of the sincerity of our search for peace and our desire to be helpful." Such a trip would also "raise the morale of struggling and underprivileged peoples, to enhance the confidence in the value of friendship with the United States, and to give them assurance of their own security and chance for progress."[17] Here, Eisenhower emphasized his desire to engage in personal diplomacy with a global audience and to remind them of the United States' desire for peace and friendship. At the same time, however, Eisenhower noted the strategic, even calculated purpose behind his visits to "neutral" nations like India. "My present-day purpose was not tourism. It was an obvious fact that the Free World should do everything possible to make certain that India—an announced neutral in the polarized power struggle—should never be allowed, with its 400 million people, to fall within the Communist orbit."[18] To the White House and the State Department, nothing was more important than presenting a strong, vigorous, paternal image of the United States to a global audience—and Eisenhower's "Good Will" tours were designed to do just that.

The president departed for his first "Good Will" tour on December 3, 1959. In a private letter on the eve of the president's departure, Central Intelligence Agency (CIA) director Allen Dulles told Eisenhower that his trip would "mark an important milestone in the development of our foreign policy" and would have "the deep influence in impressing the peoples of the countries you visit that their hopes lie with the West under American leadership."[19] In his address to the American people upon his departure in December 1959, Eisenhower told his audience that he intended "to promote a better understanding of America and to learn more of our friends abroad." His goal, the president explained, was "to make widely known America's deepest desire—a world in which all nations may prosper in freedom, justice, and peace, unmolested and unafraid."[20] Here, Eisenhower emphasized the United States' commitment to helping individual countries to assert their own political sovereignty instead of being swallowed up by the Soviet Union (figure 3.1).

Eisenhower's three-week journey to Italy, Turkey, Pakistan, Afghanistan, India, Iran, Greece, Tunisia, France, Spain, and Morocco was, by many accounts, a remarkable success. Press reports both within the United States and around the world heralded Eisenhower's widespread popularity as evidence that the United States was making some gains in the propaganda campaign against the Soviet Union. In a report sent back to US secretary of state Christian A. Herter for a cabinet meeting during Eisenhower's trip, a staffer wrote that "it seems to us that [the] trip so far is achieving our objectives. Public reception and acclaim have been spectacular, growing in crescendo, as the President passed through Ankara, Karachi, Kabul and reaching unexpected volume and enthusiasm in New Delhi."[21] Upon Eisenhower's return to the United States just two days before Christmas, the *New York Times* opined: "Surely no other individual from any country going around the world today could have received a tribute comparable to the popular acclaim which greeted Mr. Eisenhower. Peace on earth is obviously what everybody wants."[22] The president's touring roadshow had begun.

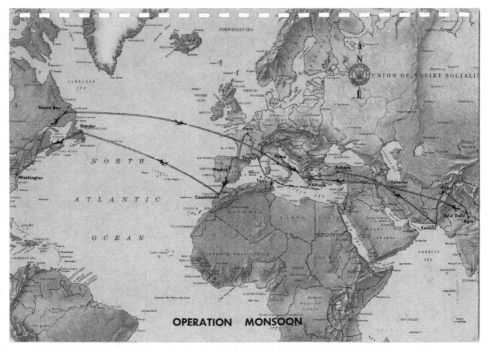

OPERATION MONSOON

FIGURE 3.1. Internal White House map depicting President Eisenhower's route for "Operation Monsoon." Records of William P. Draper, Naval Aide to the President. Courtesy of the Dwight D. Eisenhower Presidential Library and Museum.

"Operation Amigo"

Two months later, on February 22, 1960, Dwight D. Eisenhower departed for a ten-day "Good Will" tour of Brazil, Uruguay, Argentina, Chile, and Puerto Rico. Code-named "Operation Amigo," the trip was designed to reaffirm the United States' friendship with its southern neighbors and to extend the nation's geopolitical influence in Latin America. In his remarks to the US public the day before his departure, the president described the connections between the United States and South America in terms that were friendly and familial, noting that the purpose of his trip was to "learn more about our friends to the south" and to remind his hosts that the United States' "interest in our sister Republics is of longstanding, and of deep affection." At the same time, Eisenhower acknowledged that "even among close comrades, friendships too often seem to be taken for granted. We must not give our neighbors of Latin America cause to believe this about us."[23] But even as Eisenhower described the trip in terms of "peace and friendship," the president and other US officials saw this tour as a way to extend US political and ideological

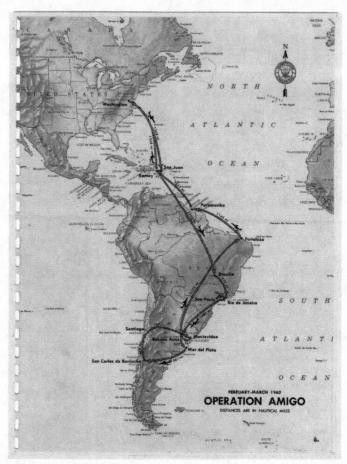

FIGURE 3.2. Internal White House map depicting President Eisenhower's route for "Operation Amigo." Records of William P. Draper, Naval Aide to the President. Courtesy of the Dwight D. Eisenhower Presidential Library and Museum.

influence in the region and to counteract a growing Soviet presence in Cuba (figure 3.2).

While on the surface the president's second "Good Will" tour was designed to highlight "peace and friendship" between the United States and South America, this descriptor only further revealed the paternalistic overtones of these tours.[24] Indeed, the idea for the trip arose from Eisenhower's observation that "the Latin American countries felt somewhat neglected" from his first "Good Will" trip in December 1959. As a result, Eisenhower floated the idea of a trip to Brazil, Columbia, or "some other South American country where it was thought useful."[25] Although the White House portrayed this visit as another "Good Will" tour, it was by far the most condescending of the bunch. Where Eisenhower's tours to Europe in December 1959 and Asia in June 1960 were described as meetings between equal partners, internal descriptions of the president's South American tour displayed what might be described as paternalistic paranoia.[26] "We are going to have more and more trouble in Latin America," reported one internal memorandum. "The Communist apparatus there is very strong now, and it has learned how to take advantage of local discontent."[27] This phrasing suggested that the Latin American public had little to no political agency. They were mere pawns in a geopolitical game of chess between two superpowers locked in a Cold War contest for global dominance.

Indeed, one of the main objectives of "Operation Amigo" was to "defend" the United States' southern neighbors from Soviet expansion and interference—a goal supported with ample historical precedent under the Monroe Doctrine and its various iterations. As noted in the book's introductory chapter, this ultimatum against European interference in the Western Hemisphere quickly evolved to support US military action that would prevent such attempts. Franklin D. Roosevelt's "Good Neighbor" policy was a containment strategy of its own, for it ensured that the United States could keep a friendly but watchful eye on its southern neighbors. Even the Rio Pact, which guaranteed that all republics in the Western Hemisphere would aid one another against acts of aggression, did not stop US clandestine military operations in Guatemala, Chile, Grenada, Nicaragua, Brazil, and, of course, Cuba.[28] Although publicly the Eisenhower administration championed the ability of individual countries to choose their way of life, privately they saw "Operation Amigo" as a way to exert "friendly" influence in their own backyard and align "neutral" countries with US foreign policy interests in the hemisphere and around the world. Eisenhower's tour of South America was a deliberate strategy in this broader diplomatic counteroffensive, an embodied extension of the Monroe Doctrine enacted by the president himself.

To explicate how the Eisenhower administration designed the president's bodily movement through space as an attempt to extend US influence on the global stage and to displace Soviet influence in Latin America, I approach "Operation Amigo" as a multifaceted, multilayered rhetorical encounter that developed over time, in place, and under the shadow of a growing communist presence in Cuba. As I attend to the president's central role in this touring Cold War drama, I also consider how other US political actors curated the scenic dimensions of the trip so that audiences around the world could experience Eisenhower's rhetoric in place. The complexities of this tour, therefore, require a different organizational structure. Rather than approaching this trip chronologically, I detail how the Eisenhower administration sought to display US prestige and global hegemony through the strategic circulation of four elements: body, place, image, and text. In the analysis that follows, I consider how these elements moved in and throughout various spaces and detail how US governmental agencies and media outlets transmitted—or circulated—various textual and audiovisual fragments of "Operation Amigo" to audiences around the world. The persuasive elements of this tour extended far beyond Eisenhower's spoken oratory. Instead, the movement and circulation of the president's body—and the words, images, newsreel footage, and geographical representations attached to Eisenhower's travel through South America—became the preeminent "text" or persuasive artifact. It was not simply Eisenhower's words that took up space. His embodied presence within and movement between specific regions—and the media artifacts that captured this circulation—reminded US and international audiences that the president of the United States (and, by extension, the United States) occupied a central leadership role on the global stage.

DUELING BODIES, DUELING NATIONS

The decision to travel to South America reflected decades of US foreign policy, and specifically the belief that Latin America was a space or region in need of US intervention and support. There is a lengthy history connecting US imperialism and foreign policy with the forcible seizure of land and clandestine US intervention in Latin America. This pattern continued to shape how the Eisenhower administration conceptualized the importance of the region in Cold War geopolitics. The movement of Eisenhower's presidential body throughout the globe was seen as a deliberate persuasive strategy, one that not only enabled the US government to extend American hegemony in the region but also offered a way to counteract the deliberate movements of another body: Soviet premier Nikita Khrushchev.

During the summer of 1959, Eisenhower and Khrushchev agreed to hold reciprocal visits in their respective countries. The Soviet premier would visit the United States in the fall, and the president would visit Moscow that winter or the following spring. After the announcement, Karl H. Harr, a special assistant to the president and vice chair of the Operations Coordinating Board, wrote that these visits were "undoubtedly creating a considerable aura of expectancy throughout the world that some dramatic new turns in international affairs are occurring, or are in the offing." Such expectancy, Harr noted, offered "a favorable climate within which to try some relatively bold overtures in areas, such as Asia and the Middle East, where positions have been somewhat static."[29] Khrushchev arrived in Washington, DC, on September 15, 1959, and spent two weeks touring the nation, making stops in New York, California, Iowa, and Pennsylvania before spending several days in talks with Eisenhower at Camp David. Throughout his visit, the Soviet premier delivered twenty-three speeches or public statements, including an address to the American people that was broadcast live over radio and television on September 27.[30] Two recurring themes dominated Khrushchev's discourse: his call for "peaceful coexistence" and "peace and friendship" between the Soviet Union and the United States. For example, in a brief speech upon his arrival in Washington, DC, Khrushchev stated his hopes for the trip: "We have come to you with an open heart and with good intentions. The Soviet people want to live in peace and friendship with the American people."[31] Two months later, Eisenhower would appropriate similar phrases to describe his first "Good Will" mission abroad.

After the Soviet premier's visit to the United States in September 1959, Khrushchev visited the PRC and several countries in South Asia. US officials cautioned that the widespread media coverage of the tour boosted Khrushchev's image abroad. "In Europe and Latin America," noted one CIA memorandum, "the visit of the Soviet Premier to the US and the peaceful tone of Soviet pronouncements have tended to raise Khrushchev's stature and increase the respectability of Soviet policies."[32] Other high-ranking Soviet officials also made visits to Central and South America. These not-so-subtle overtures included a visit by Soviet first deputy premier Anastas Mikoyan to Mexico; a one-month tour of a Czech parliamentary delegation throughout Columbia, Venezuela, Bolivia, Mexico, Peru, and Brazil; and a Soviet presence at the National Congress of the Cuban Confederation of Workers, the principle labor organization in the island nation. Such visits, predicted the CIA, were designed to use the "more relaxed international atmosphere to develop closer relations with Latin America."[33] Eisenhower's tour of South America was designed to provide a symbolic counterpunch to these visits and Khrushchev's other world tours.

By the time Eisenhower departed for his South American tour, various press reports noted that the doing and making of Cold War foreign policy took on performative dimensions. "The homebody type of a statesman is out of fashion," wrote the New York Times. "Mr. Eisenhower in Brazil, Argentina, Chile and Uruguay; Mr. Khrushchev in India, Burma, Indonesia, Afghanistan—such are the diplomatic battle lines that the air age has made possible. . . . The job calls for a personal appearance . . . [and] the bulk of the work is being done in the public eye."[34] These public campaigns to "neutral" countries suggested that their "immediate targets were the underdeveloped areas in which [heads of state] were touring. But both were aiming their messages at the entire world."[35] In fact, as reporter Daniel Schorr noted, this "jet-borne popularity contest" represented "highly competitive salesmanship on behalf of the countries and systems the leaders symbolize" designed to "[alter] the balance of world public opinion."[36] International press reports also identified the symbolic significance of these dueling tours. One Dutch periodical described them as "part of the 'third undeclared World War' for the underdeveloped nations, and they will decide the fate of the world."[37] In Yugoslavia, US Embassy officials reported that the pro-Soviet *Politika*, the newspaper with the largest circulation in Yugoslavia, depicted Eisenhower as "a worried leader anxiously seeking to reassure his impatient Latin American neighbors with 'kind words' and 'general promises,' while Khrushchev, dynamic defender of the underdeveloped countries, is shown as the 'herald of peace,' generously providing steel plants and other help, 'all the more valuable since it consists of capital goods and not merely consumer products.'"[38] In Turkey, US officials noted that local reports compared Eisenhower's visit to South America with Khrushchev's simultaneous tour of South Asia and "generally found them to be based on similar motivation—to win or hold the sympathy of uncommitted nations."[39]

Journalistic reports also portrayed the president's bodily movement as a symbolic, rhetorical act, one that demarcated the boundaries of American influence on the Cold War world map. On February 28, the *New York Times* printed a world map comparing the "Travels of the Big-Two Leaders."[40] With the capitals of the United States and the Soviet Union prominently marked, the graphic depicted Eisenhower's trips to Europe, Asia, and South America and Khrushchev's visits to Washington, the PRC, and the capital of Indonesia, Jakarta. The competing directional lines did not cross each other, implying that the physical movements of the two leaders had claimed and now occupied distinct psychological and geographical regions through their international travels. The corresponding text also reinforced the apparent mission of these visits. The paper highlighted Khrushchev's trip to "Communist China on [the] occasion of regime's tenth anniversary, presumably to explain Soviet policy after his United States trip" and described the Soviet leader's "eighteen-day tour of South Asia" as an attempt "to mend Soviet fences in nations at odds with Communist China." Eisenhower's trips, however, were directed at "discuss[ing] Western policy," "reassur[ing] allies before meeting with Khrushchev," and emphasizing themes of "goodwill." It is also notable that this image visually divided the globe between the United States and the Soviet Union—and did not call out the physical presence of Great Britain. Where the "Big Three" global powers dominated the international scene during the Second World War and the immediate postwar period, this depiction underscored the increasingly bipolar nature of Cold War world. In another similar portrayal, *Time* printed a visual depiction of the president's "Southern Swing" in its March 7, 1960, issue.[41] The image, which positioned the viewer at the southernmost tip of South America looking north toward Washington, displayed Eisenhower's route with bright red directional arrows. The graphic also printed the specific locations (both city and country) where the president would stop and the dates of his visits. It was difficult to miss the island nation of Cuba just south of Washington. Although Eisenhower would not stop there, his physical proximity to the regime was noticeable. These two images (among others) highlighted the symbolic significance of Eisenhower's physical travel in South America and around the globe. The visual depiction of Eisenhower's bodily movement between various places roped off the stage where "Operation Amigo" would unfold. By marking the specific places the president would stop, these images also portrayed particular scenes of address, places of pause within the president's embodied movements in and through South America.

SPHERES OF INFLUENCE

Even as the physical travel and movement of Eisenhower and Khrushchev depicted a competition of global superpowers intent on world domination, these movements also sketched the boundaries of what many might consider the spheres of influence assigned to the United States and Soviet Union at this moment during the Cold War. The travel of Eisenhower's presidential body to South America also underscored the region's significance for US interests. Given the continent's proximity to the United States, US officials worried that any communist presence in the region would threaten US hegemony and undermine pro-democratic governments. Because of this, the administration used Eisenhower's physical travel to particular *places* or locations throughout South America to bolster pro-democratic sentiment, extend US psychological dominance, and counteract communist advances in Cuba. As the closest ideological battlefield to the United States, South America was a pivotal *space* to be conquered.

From the earliest planning stages of the tour, US officials approached "Operation Amigo" as a way to signal the administration's renewed attention to US-Latin American relations. "There has been some criticism in this country and in Latin America that the United States has given a higher priority to other parts of the world and has paid too little attention to the needs and desires of its close neighbors," one confidential State Department memorandum noted just before Eisenhower's tour. "The forthcoming trip should do much to dispel that belief and to provide a dramatic stimulus to establish closer United States relations with the countries to be visited and other countries of Latin America."[42] The ultimate goal for these advances, however, was to ensure that South American nations would align themselves with the United States—and deliberately against Soviet communism. More often than not, the Eisenhower administration adopted a paternalistic, condescending tone toward the region, privately characterizing South America as a space in desperate need of US economic assistance and political leadership. In public statements, private correspondence, secret memoranda, and visual depictions of the trip, the region was almost always characterized as secondary to the United States and in dire need of American economic intervention and political leadership. This is, of course, unsurprising, as it reflects a long history of US imperialism in the Southern Hemisphere. And yet, it is important to note that the Eisenhower administration had something to gain by depicting its southern neighbors as underdeveloped: political power and dominance over so-called neutral countries in the Cold War struggle between US democracy and Soviet communism. In the words of one State Department memorandum, Eisenhower's visit to the region would demonstrate "the interest which the United States has in assisting the peoples of Latin America to meet their aspirations for higher living standards, increased economic development, and democratic, representative governments."[43] However genuine some of this "interest" might have been, it was always linked to the United States' quest for global dominance and ideological superiority.

At the same time, US officials carefully planned Eisenhower's itinerary to include specific countries that either demonstrated an ongoing commitment to democratic values or that could benefit from a not-so-subtle reminder of their strategic importance to the United States. In a memorandum circulated to foreign service posts around the world, US secretary of state Christian A. Herter explained the rationale behind the president's itinerary. Eisenhower's visit to Brazil would emphasize a "special regard for Brazil's economic and political importance in the Americas" and "provide a needed psychological impulse to improvement in United States–Brazilian relations." In Argentina, the president's visit would "increase the prestige of the Argentine Government" and was "designed to point up the present warmth of Argentine–United States relations" in contrast to the "often strained and even hostile relations which existed during the Peron regime." Eisenhower's stop in Chile would reward the country for "plac[ing] itself firmly on the side of the West" and its long-standing commitment to "a democratic, free enterprise system." Finally, Uruguay was deemed "particular[ly] suitable for a Presidential visit" because of its "unique record of democratic stability, its long tradition of friendship with the United States and with its neighbors, and its devotion to Free World interests."[44] This internal yet widely circulated rationale gestured toward the White House's real intentions for "Operation Amigo." Of the four countries Eisenhower would visit, three had ongoing diplomatic relations with the Soviet Union: Argentina, Brazil, and Uruguay. Chile, in contrast, broke formal ties with the USSR in 1947.[45] The president's presence in these specific countries, therefore, was designed to symbolize US interest in and relationship to the region. From this perspective, the administration's code name for the president's tour, "Operation Amigo," seems particularly apt.

There were two other places, however, that played a significant role in the president's tour of Latin America: Puerto Rico and Cuba. Although Eisenhower stopped in one and ignored the other (publicly, at least), circulating discourses about both places reveal just how important this geopolitical region was to the Eisenhower administration—and how determined they were to combat Soviet encroachment. Although not an official part of the "Operation Amigo" trip itinerary, Eisenhower's stop in Puerto Rico was a prelude to the rest of the tour. What originated as a simple refueling stop evolved into a strategic display of "what can be done in a free society."[46] For US officials, Puerto Rico demonstrated the powerful potential of individual political agency. The island, which William McKinley seized in the aftermath of the Spanish-American War, was a US territory for fifty-four years before Puerto Ricans voted to become a commonwealth in 1952.[47] As the White House formalized Eisenhower's trip itinerary, some Puerto Rican officials clamored for an official visit. Puerto Rican undersecretary of state Arturo Morales Carrion argued that a presidential stop would refute Soviet attempts "to play up the idea that, as far as the United States is concerned, Puerto Rico is an exploited colony and a base for nuclear weapons."[48] Roy Rubottom, the US assistant secretary of state for Latin American affairs, concurred, telling the president a formal visit to Puerto Rico "would help demonstrate to the people of Latin America the large degree of autonomy and the democracy Puerto Rico enjoys. It should help provide a counter to the Communist propaganda."[49] After some internal debate, the president and his advisors agreed. In his brief arrival remarks in San Juan, Eisenhower elevated Puerto Rico as an example of "a proud, free, self-governing Commonwealth, joined to the United States by her own choice" and praised its "program of development—rooted in self-confidence, self-help and self-achievement." Puerto Rico, he said, offered a "record of achievement in which many other people around the globe have found hope and inspiration."[50]

Despite Eisenhower's rosy description of Puerto Rico's political evolution, not everyone agreed. "It is perfectly true that Puerto Ricans have themselves chosen the commonwealth status and that they are equally free to choose independence or to ask for statehood if they want it," opined the *New York Times*. And yet, this was "not the general belief in Latin America. One cannot be precise, but certainly a great segment of opinion all over the hemisphere rates Puerto Rico as the equivalent of a colony of the United States and Puerto Ricans as North American stooges."[51] But to Eisenhower and other US officials, the president's stop in Puerto Rico featured a promising, inspiring example of self-government—one that offered a powerful antidote to the political evolution of another island contemporary: Cuba.

Although Eisenhower did not speak publicly about Cuba during his visit to South America, the archival record reveals just how central the issue was for US officials before, during, and after "Operation Amigo." After Fidel Castro's rise to power in 1959, the administration took overt and covert steps to combat the rising influence of "international communism" in Cuba and the surrounding region. In November 1959, a secret memorandum entitled "Current Basic United States Policy towards Cuba" called for "actions, policies and statements designed to emphasize throughout Latin America the United States concepts of genuine representative democracy, sound economic development, nonintervention, and inter-American solidarity within the free world."[52] Eisenhower's tour through South America represented a critical part of this strategy. Although Eisenhower would not stop in Cuba, the movement and circulation of the president's body over, around, and alongside the island was designed to symbolize and extend US hegemony in the region.

Multiple news reports read "Operation Amigo" as a way to combat rising trends of communism and socialism in the region, including Cuba. Eisenhower's challenge, Walter Lippmann predicted, was to convince "our American neighbors and the world outside that we are not the enemies but are indeed the friends of [the] liberating, democratic, and progressive movements of our age."[53] Diplomatic posts also reported the widespread belief that Eisenhower's trip was designed to counteract the rise of Cuba. According to one report from the US embassy in Turkey, "the Castro revolution in Cuba and recent Mikoyan trips to the area are viewed as causing the United States considerable uneasiness and as compelling it to reassess its Latin American policies. The president's trip to Latin America is pictured as a defensive action to these events."[54] US officials in Moscow relayed the commentary of one Russian journalist who accompanied Khrushchev to the United States in September 1959. The "timing of [Eisenhower's South American] visit [was] 'not accidental,'" this journalist wrote, "and [its] purpose was 'to try disperse anti-American feeling' stimulated . . . by [the] Cuban revolutionary 'example' and [the] widespread economic ills" in the region.[55] In Warsaw, a newspaper editorial suggested that the "aim of [Eisenhower's South American] trip was to isolate Cuba from continent."[56] US diplomats stationed in Cuba reported that the government-run news media "violently condemned [the] tour." Where "Fidel [was depicted] as leader of masses . . . Eisenhower [was seen as] upholding imperialism."[57] Overall, these officials reported, Cuban public opinion reflected the "belief [that the] President's trip [was] inspired by deteriorating Cuba-American relation[s]. Radical Castro supporters express belief [that] it [is] another effort [to] isolate Cuba."[58] These "radical" supporters were in fact correct.

At the time, some of these reactions may have seemed a bit conspiratorial. Was Eisenhower's visit to South America *really* about Cuba—or did it just make a good story for a public worried about Castro's rise to power? Both assessments are accurate. Although it was impossible for journalists or embassy officials writing in 1960 to know the inner workings of the White House intelligence working groups, these descriptions of motive and intent are strikingly accurate. In fact, the now-declassified archival record reveals just how much of a deflection strategy Eisenhower's visit to South America really was. Weeks before the president embarked on "Operation Amigo," the National Security Council (NSC) began discussing under what circumstances the United States would—or should—intervene militarily in Cuba. Questions included if the US should intervene "now, later, never, covertly, overtly, alone or with others? If we do intervene, what are we going to try to do—defend American lives and property, set up a new regime, or what?"[59] Another key question was "What is our strategic interest as distinguished from our psychological interest in Cuba? What difference does it make if we lose Cuba?" There were also discussions as to whether the United States should "reaffirm the *Monroe Doctrine* and tell the Communists to keep their hands off Latin America."[60] This was the context under which Eisenhower went to South America.

During the president's South American tour, various US military officials and White House senior advisors debated what next steps the president should take in Cuba.[61] After the president's return from South America, the NSC discussed the Cuban situation at length. According to the official record of the meeting, the president commented that "every effort should be made to influence the other members of the Organization of American States to recognize the dangers involved in the Cuban situation and support action with respect to them."[62] On March 17, Secretary of State Christian Herter informed the president that the State Department, CIA, and the USIA were engaged in public diplomacy campaigns in Latin America to ensure broad public support for any US action in Cuba.[63] "Operation Amigo," therefore, also functioned as a strategic means of deflection from the covert actions by the Eisenhower administration to prepare for a US-backed coup. While the global public saw images of a triumphant American president espousing themes of "peace and friendship" throughout the hemisphere, behind the scenes his administration was contemplating military action in Cuba, a plan that would ultimately culminate in the Bay of Pigs fiasco under the newly inaugurated John F. Kennedy.

IMAGES OF THE NATION

A motivating factor behind Eisenhower's "Good Will" tours was the desire to create, circulate, and maintain a very particular image of the US president and the nation to audiences at home and abroad. Even as the administration sought to elevate national prestige, it also used these tours to remind the US public of Eisenhower's widespread international popularity and the superiority of the democratic "way of life." However deliberate the movement of Eisenhower's body to and through specific places was, it would have little real significance if it did not reach its intended audience: the global public. Because "Operation Amigo" was designed as a strategic public relations campaign, it mattered just as much what audiences would see and hear of Eisenhower's presence in place and how these images and sound bites would circulate around the world (figures 3.3, 3.4, and 3.5).

Rapid advances in media technology played a crucial role in the creation and circulation of these images. The advent of transatlantic cable meant that the three major news networks—CBS, NBC, and ABC—could provide same-day coverage of the president's overseas travel. "Never before," Craig Allen argues, "not even in the earlier years of the Eisenhower presidency, could such a calculation have been made, due to technical constraints in overseas communications. The United States may have trailed the USSR in rocket technology, but in the late 1950s American capabilities in the television field were opening unprecedented possibilities." Eisenhower's global tours provided the perfect opportunity for networks to showcase their "technological and logistical magic," and the White House reaped the benefit of widespread international coverage.[64] This television coverage could transport the US public to faraway places from the comfort of their living rooms, with Eisenhower as their tour guide. At the same time, US officials worked tirelessly to ensure that images of the president's stops in Latin America would capture Eisenhower being greeted by adoring fans throughout the region.

To ensure that images and audiovisual footage of "Operation Amigo" reached the widest possible audience, the White House issued clear instructions to journalists who would travel with the president and to US embassy

FIGURE 3.3. President Dwight D. Eisenhower in Brazil during his "Good Will" tour of South America, February 23–26, 1960. Courtesy of Arquivo Nacional Collection (Brazilian National Archives). Accession Number: BR_RJANRIO_PH_0_FOT_20292_290.

FIGURE 3.4. President Dwight D. Eisenhower's motorcade drives through Montevideo, Uruguay, during his "Good Will" tour of South America, March 2–3, 1960. Photograph by Francisco Bonfiglio. Courtesy of US Embassy Montevideo.

FIGURE 3.5. President Dwight D. Eisenhower in Brazil during his "Good Will" tour of South America, February 23–26, 1960. The sign reads "Welcome Ike—Ambassador of Peace and Cooperation." Courtesy of the Dwight D. Eisenhower Presidential Library and Museum. Accession Number: 73-807-2.

staff and USIA representatives stationed in South America. In early February, White House press secretary James Hagerty sent specific instructions to US embassies in Argentina, Brazil, Chile, and Uruguay detailing how they could achieve "good press coverage of [the] visit." He warned embassy officials to reserve space for camera operators and photographers from outlets including AP, UPI, *Life*, NBC, CBS, Telenews, Fox-Movietone, and various international press organizations. He placed specific emphasis on ensuring that photo trucks and press buses were "available to cover receptions by people along [the] route to wherever the President is staying." The goal was to capture images of jubilant crowds lining the president's motorcade route, and Hagerty told officials to make sure that the press could "see and report on the reception afforded the President by the people in any particular city." Although various formal protocols and security restrictions might make this difficult,

Hagerty told the embassy staff that "it should be explained that these are the men who will report the reception accorded the president to the world, and if they are so far back that they cannot see or hear what is going on, then their stories will lack the reporting of the warmth of the reception and will be detrimental both to the nation concerned and to the United States."[65] The emphasis here, of course, was the paramount importance of circulating images to audiences around the world.

Importantly, however, these plans for circulating the image of the president to audiences at home and abroad were not limited to photographers and journalists. In the weeks leading up to "Operation Amigo," Abbott Washburn, the deputy director of the USIA, submitted the agency's plans for projecting the president's South American tour to a global public. The agency's role, Washburn wrote, was "to project the image of the President's personality to our audience overseas who will not have the opportunity to see him and hear him in person" and "to sustain the impact of the trip after it is over" through films that would be distributed to posts around the world.[66] The USIA also took an active role in preparing US embassies and global media outlets to cover the president's visit and thus depict vivid, emotional imagery of the president's widespread popularity in South America and to underscore his stature as the "Leader of the Free World." Ultimately, the goal was to provide "evidence of [an] emotional response in such key countries as Brazil, Argentina, and Chile [which would] do more than anything else to bring home the symbolism of the visit to other Latin Americans."[67] By carefully staging, capturing, and circulating these images to a global audience, US officials portrayed a powerful, protective, wildly popular US president who appeared as the rightful "Leader of the Free World."

EXTENDING THE MONROE DOCTRINE
TO THE COLD WAR WORLD

Up to this point, I have focused my attention on the nonverbal elements of Eisenhower's tour. I have done so intentionally so as to demonstrate how the administration designed "Operation Amigo" as a dynamic, multifaceted rhetorical act. However, the president's public remarks also played an important role. Throughout his tour of South America, the president delivered formal speeches, informal remarks, and toasts throughout Brazil, Argentina, Chile, Uruguay, and the Commonwealth of Puerto Rico. Although all of them contributed to the multifaceted dimensions of "Operation Amigo," it was Eisenhower's address before a joint session of the Brazilian Congress that amounted to a major declaration of US foreign policy in the region. Where Eisenhower's physical travel to and through particular locations symbolized the United States' presence in the region, the president's speech at the Tiradentes Palace in Rio de Janeiro on February 24 articulated the deliberate extension of US foreign policy. In other words, the symbolic significance of Eisenhower's physical travel to South America was amplified and extended through the president's formal address to the Brazilian Congress. Together, this compilation of body/place/text embodied the message Eisenhower would deliver: his extension of the Monroe Doctrine for the Cold War moment.

It is no accident that this declaration came during Eisenhower's major speech in Brazil. In fact, this timing and location reveals the administration's desire to stroke Brazil's ego while also asserting the United States' right to intervene in the region. In a State Department memorandum circulated to "all American diplomatic posts," Secretary of State Christian A. Herter noted that "because of its great size, strategic location, prominent role in inter-American affairs and long tradition of close cooperation with the United States, and the fact that relations with Brazil cooled in 1959, the visit to Brazil has special significance."[68] The Brazilian government also held fast to the "belief that Brazil will soon become a world power and ought to be consulted by the United States in important United States foreign policy matters not directly related to United States–Brazilian relations."[69] A confidential USIA report stressed Brazil's desire "to be a 'great' power" and pursue any policy that would "support Brazil's claim of being the voice of the less developed Latin American countries." In fact, the agency noted, "Brazil's preoccupation with its position as leader of Latin America is reflected in a sense of strong nationalism" often equated with patriotism by many Brazilians. Perhaps even more concerning to the Eisenhower administration, the report noted that "the Brazilian attitude toward Communism tends to be ambivalent," a fact further demonstrated by the recent trade agreement between the USSR and Brazil "envisioning total trade of $200,000,000 over a three year period."[70] Thus, when Eisenhower spoke to a nation determined to represent the continent and be "the voice of the less developed Latin American countries," he told them exactly what they should say to their neighbors—and then he said it for them.

The president and his advisors designed an address that played directly into Brazil's desire for geopolitical influence. To begin, the president described the speech as one not designed just for a Brazilian audience, but to everyone living in the Western Hemisphere. He directed his remarks to "the governments and peoples of all the Western Hemisphere nations as an expression of hope from the millions of my country to the millions who constitute Latin America." He was speaking here on behalf of the entire US citizenry to a global audience. Eisenhower stated that if he could, he would "travel to the largest cities and the remotest villages of all the Americas" to discuss the "awesome responsibilities" they all shared at this moment in history. It was fitting, he said, that he should make these statements "here, at the beginning of my present journey, for you of Brazil and we of the United States have always worked together for the spiritual unity and material advancement of the hemisphere. If it were physically possible for us to do so, I am sure we would speak with a single voice to all our neighbors of this vast continent." In other words, Eisenhower's speech not only amounted to a declaration of US policy; it suggested that Brazil would take the same approach. This metaphor of "one voice" was a consistent theme throughout the speech, one Eisenhower used to reemphasize a shared unity and purpose. Moreover, it suggested that regardless of language or nationality, these democratic values could extend to the rest of the world.

Throughout the speech, the president frequently drew on the collective, constitutive "we" to emphasize the shared values that connected both countries across space and time. Eisenhower listed three areas of shared responsibility: responsibility to the interests of their own citizens, responsibility to the well-being of their hemispheric neighbors, and responsibility to the peace of the rest of the world. In the first realm, that of one's home country, Eisenhower declared that both nations "would emphasize that heavy reliance must be placed upon the creative talents of the people themselves, with government a helpful partner." Ideals of individual responsibility, free enterprise, and self-determination were the ultimate goal. This was an ongoing theme throughout all of Eisenhower's public statements, so much so that one could read the president's remarks as a paternalistic scolding of children who could not take care of themselves. But, because Eisenhower argued that the United States and Brazil spoke with "one voice," then surely Brazilians could adopt a similar leadership role in their own hemisphere. If Latin Americans really wanted to lead, the president inferred, self-help was the place to start.

The second realm of responsibility was a shared concern for hemispheric interests. "We, Brazil and the United States, hold the common, burning conviction that relations among these sister nations must be characterized by mutual respect, juridical equality, independence, respect for each human being, regardless of his race, creed, or color, and a willingness to help one another promote the well-being of all our peoples." Here, Eisenhower defined what relationships between nation-states should look like in moral terms. The president also acknowledged that "we," both the United States and Brazil, "do not wish to impose our particular form of democracy upon one another," but instead hoped that "the nations of the hemisphere will each, according to its own genius and aspiration, develop and sustain free government." The structure and composition of such governments were up to individual initiative and ability. Again, this descriptor smacked of condescension; the United States and Brazil were the ones to refrain from "impos[ing]" their "form of democracy," but clearly there was only one right choice to make.

Finally, Eisenhower turned his attention to "the third responsibility which we may speak of in common voice—that which involves the larger world." Today, he said, it was the "imperative responsibility of every statesman—of yours, of ours, of all countries" to "strive ceaselessly, honestly, and effectively for peace today." Themes of responsibility and doing one's duty abounded. Peace, it seemed, should be their ultimate goal—but peace could only be achieved through one particular structure of government. In the "same moment of this great crisis," the president said, "we face anew decisions involving tyranny or freedom, totalitarianism or democracy." Here Eisenhower underscored the divide between East and West as a stark contrast between two "ways of life." And yet, the president continued, "our shared view on this issue is so eloquent and clear that any words of mine would not be enlightening." In other words: the United States and Brazil were so aligned, so likeminded, so similar in their influence over their respective continents, that the American president had no need to explain the stakes of these "decisions." To underscore the point, Eisenhower described the divide in spiritual terms, noting that "in contrast to our adherence to a philosophy of common sonship [sic], of human dignity, and moral law, millions now live in an environment permeated with a philosophy which denies the existence of God." In this telling, true freedom could be found in Judeo-Christian values. Atheism—not a belief in God—was a form of oppression. Of course, the president continued, both countries upheld the right of the individual to choose their system of government, even if that meant they would "return to that unenlightened system of tyranny, if they so wish. We should feel a great sorrow for them, but we would respect their right to choose such a system. Here is the key to our policy—the right to choose." But if this right to choose was denied, Eisenhower declared that "we—you of Brazil and we of the United States—would consider it intervention in the internal affairs of an American State if any power, whether by invasion, coercion, or subversion, succeeded in denying freedom of choice to the people of any of our sister Republics."[71] An intervention of this sort would be considered an attack on the hemisphere, the Organization of American States, and the principles laid out in the Rio Pact. The unstated implication, of course, was that the communist "takeover" of Cuba was a Soviet attack on the hemisphere. By this logic, Cuban citizens had been denied their "right to choose" their system of government. Surely, if given the choice, they would oust Castro from power.

Throughout his speech, Eisenhower rhetorically constructed Brazil as the hemispheric leader they longed to be. In this masterful stroke of political flattery, the president told his audience exactly what they wanted to hear so he could convince them to do exactly what he wanted them to do. By stressing the idea that both the United States and Brazil shared the common responsibilities in their national, hemispheric, and global contexts, Eisenhower invited Brazilians to see themselves as a global leader and subtly reinforced the idea that the United States (and the Organization of American States) would be justified in responding to "intervention" in Cuba by communists. The American president was here to convince the Brazilian legislature—and the rest of his South American audience—that the clandestine operations being planned at that very moment in the White House and the US Department of State were natural, warranted, and justified.

US officials in Brazil reported a positive response to the president's speech and, more broadly, Eisenhower's visit. One report from Sao Paulo expressed the widespread belief that "the visit of the President of the United States will without doubt enhance continental unity." Some even saw Eisenhower's presence as evidence that the United States' relationship with South America had progressed "a long way from the famous 'big stick' of the first Roosevelt as well as from 'dollar diplomacy,' and even from the ideal and fraternal formula of the policy of the 'Good Neighbor' of the second Roosevelt." Of particular importance to this progression was the president's decision to move beyond "the routine of a press conference" and instead "speak to the people in a 'coast to coast televised hookup'" for, as one report noted, "millions of television viewers here [in Rio de Janeiro] and in Sao Paulo watched and heard the congressional address."[72]

Although Eisenhower would deliver many other speeches throughout the tour, his speech in Brazil offered the most explicit definition of US policy for Latin America: a justification of extending the Monroe Doctrine to include any attempts by communist forces to infiltrate the Western Hemisphere. The importance of this declaration was noted both in the United States and around the world. Although the idea of "no outside interference in the Western hemisphere has been a basic tenet of United States foreign policy since the Monroe Doctrine of 1823," wrote the *New York Times*, "the chief threat today comes in a form never contemplated by the Monroe Doctrine. It is a threat of the spread of Communist doctrine aided by propaganda originating in Moscow." The implication here, of course, was that this was a cold war to be fought not through military means, but through strategies of propaganda. Any attempt to infiltrate the Western Hemisphere should be resisted—strongly.[73] This "contemporary interpretation of the Monroe Doctrine"—what the *New*

York Times described as the United States' opposition to "the extension of the Communist system to any country of this hemisphere"—was striking and would pave the way for future covert US actions in South America. Even though the president offered the caveat that each country had "the right to choose," the paper explained: "the obvious implication [was] that a hemispheric nation could only go Communist 'by invasion, coercion or subversion.'" Clearly, the president's emphasis on "democracy as well as free choice" suggested that "no democratic country or movement would commit the suicide of turning Communist."[74]

However, other international news reports rightly noted the inherent US imperialism embedded any further extension of the Monroe Doctrine. In one Yugoslavian newspaper, an editorial noted that Eisenhower's "extension" of the Monroe Doctrine would "undoubtedly give rise to anxiety with a majority of the Latin American public" since such an "elastic formula . . . could provide once more for one-sided intervention of the United States on the American continent." It was clear, this correspondent wrote, that the "reestablishment of elements of the Monroe Doctrine is in direct connection with strained American-Cuban relations."[75] In Turkey, US officials noted that reports critical of the United States often "rehearsed the history of U.S.-Latin American relations [by] mentioning the Monroe Doctrine and then sweeping through a century or so to the oft-repeated charges that the United States in recent years has been prone to disregard the popular aspirations of Latin America and to support dictators as the expedient way to forestall communism in the area."[76]

Themes of US interference in South America continued to dominate international press coverage even after Eisenhower returned to the United States. One editorial from the Mexican periodical *Novedades* suggested that Eisenhower's visit demonstrated "beyond doubt that America takes its place in world scene and sets the bases for its future aggrandizement."[77] In Paris, news reports commented on the "jealousy and resentment felt by many South Americans towards [their] more prosperous Northern neighbor" and warned of the "growth of neutralism in [the] area, with L[atin] A[merican] countries using economic gestures of [the] Soviet Union in attempt to play the West against East."[78] The London *Times* wrote that Eisenhower's visit was intended "to dispel Latin Americans' deepest rancor, which is that the United States takes them for granted." In fact, the paper continued, South Americans believed that "Washington, in advocating Pan-Americanism and a common stand against Communism, thinks of Latin America only as a rivet in the shield of her own defences and has provided nothing like the same help which she has given elsewhere to enable these countries to build up their own defences against poverty and political upheaval."[79] These reports made plain that the president's trip, although publicly described as a way to reaffirm the United States' commitment to the region, was in reality motivated by Cold War self-interest.

Perhaps the most poignant description of this power imbalance between the United States and Latin American countries was expressed in a confidential aide-mémoire delivered to Secretary of State Christian Herter by the Brazilian foreign minister. The memorandum, which was intended for Eisenhower himself, demanded that the United States provide economic support in exchange for Brazil's help in combating "neutralist" trends among underdeveloped countries. The economic divides between "North" and "South," the memo stated, were even more dangerous than divisions between East and West. It seemed "expedient to draw the attention of the Government of the United States to the danger which is outlined in the shape of a 'North v. South' antagonism throughout the world, an antagonism as sharp as, if not sharper than, that which divides the Western world from the Eastern along a meridian represented by the so-called 'Iron curtain.'" There was "instinctive solidarity, more powerful than any political combination and fatal to the Western cause" in underdeveloped nations, the memorandum continued. "The Fact that such an attitude may propagate itself—and has indeed already done so—to the American Continent, has been proved by the recent Cuban proposal to convene in Havana a world Conference of under-industrialized countries, with the attendance of Afro-Asian States."[80] In the view of this Brazilian foreign minister, the Cold War battle lines extended far beyond the division between the United States and the Soviet Union. Instead, the gaping economic disparities between developed nations and the developing concept of the Third World demonstrated yet another fissure in the Cold War geopolitical landscape—a divide that continues to this day.

Public Reception

Tracing the movement of Eisenhower's body between various locales and the circulation of texts and images connected to these travels also reveals how the administration designed these deliberately situated rhetorical acts to garner public attention in the United States and around the world. The president's travel to and through South America did more than link the United States with its southern neighbors. The intentional movement and circulation of the presidential body was in itself a campaign to transmit US ideology overseas and mobilize global public opinion in support of the United States.

Indeed, the Eisenhower White House and State Department paid close attention to international journalistic accounts of "Operation Amigo." After Eisenhower's return, the secretary of state told the president that "Latin American press coverage on your tour of South America emphasized the benefit to hemisphere relations through first-hand knowledge of the area gained by you as Chief Executive of the United States." In fact, he continued, "editorial treatment, particularly in the four countries visited, viewed your tour as a demonstration of renewed interest in Latin America by the United States and greater importance placed by the United States by its relations with the area."[81] This impact on global public opinion extended beyond the places Eisenhower visited.[82] For example, press reports from Venezuela described Eisenhower's trip "as new evidence of increasing interest of US in Latin America and lauded it as a good sign. Others felt moral effects would be of considerable importance for future development of mutual friendship."[83] The general public reaction in the Dominican Republic was "generally favorable," US officials noted, and most comments "made to embassy officers indicate [their belief that the] trip shows extreme interest in problems of hemisphere."[84] In Peru, Eisenhower's tour "received considerable publicity in local press," and journalists "warmly applauded the trip and expressed [the] opinion that it would greatly benefit hemisphere relations, would go a long way toward making [the] US more conscious of and sympathetic to Latin America's problems and aspirations, and would focus attention on [the] need for greater assistance."[85] These reports reveal the symbolic significance various countries assigned to the president's travel through South America, particularly their newfound belief that their voice actually mattered. Eisenhower's physical presence in the region—and the circulation of various images and texts attached to his visit—played an important role in cultivating this view.

News reports throughout the United States also emphasized the importance of this trip for hemispheric relations and global politics. Tad Szulc of the *New York Times* wrote that the visit "proved that with genuine United States interest and understanding of Latin America's psychology and problems—and above all, with sincere United States attention for the region—there can be ample room for far-reaching and mutually profitable cooperation of the North and South."[86] *Time* noted that "in the warmth of the uproarious welcome for the *norteamericano* President, old animosities and old suspicions melted perceptibly. These were the same Latinos whose envy of their prosperous northern cousins has festered for a century, who bitterly recall the bygone days of *Yanqui* imperialism, and who just as bitterly accuse the U.S. of neglecting them and leaving them to their own destiny."[87] Other media outlets, however, took a less positive approach. "When the United States undertakes to play the rich uncle to everybody in sight," wrote the *Chicago Daily Tribune*, "it immediately exposes itself to the risk of being accused of discriminating in favor of this nation or that, or of one class against another. . . . When the

United States, through foreign aid, assumes a global job of trying to uplift peoples, it is jockeyed into a position where it seems to be accepting responsibility for all their misfortunes."[88]

On the issue of Cuba, press reports noted that the president's "untiring reaffirmation of United States respect for the principle of non-intervention in the hemisphere" was a relief to many concerned about "the possibility of drastic moves in Cuba." In fact, the president's remarks "took the thunder out of charges by Communist and other anti-United States groups that the principal purpose of the Presidential voyage was to win support for 'intervention' against the regime of Premier Fidel Castro."[89] Robert Hartmann of the *Los Angeles Times* noted that in his report to the US public upon his return, "President Eisenhower tonight warned the world—and inferentially the Communists in Cuba—that the United States will not permit a tyrannical form of government to be imposed upon any American nation 'from outside or with outside support, by force, threat or subversion.'"[90] There was, however, still cause for alarm about what might happen in Cuba in the weeks and months to come. "U.S. citizens were not able to take their full pleasure from Mr. Eisenhower's goodwill triumphs because in their minds Castro brooded over every glorious scene," noted one editorial.[91] In fact, another reporter argued that "what must be generally realized is that Cuba is no longer an isolated case of trouble in Latin America but rather the main, largest and most active center of organized opposition to the United States, with ramifications extending throughout the continent."[92]

Although the official administration archives from the Eisenhower White House and the State Department feature numerous accounts from international news outlets and US-based journalists, reporting from prominent African American newspapers across the country is noticeably absent. These accounts, however, offer an important corrective to the mythic narrative offered by many mainstream US newspapers who described the president's tour of Latin America as a triumphant success. In contrast, Black journalists rightly noted the striking contradictions between the president's promotion of a democratic "way of life" to audiences abroad even as US citizens did not enjoy these same rights in their home country. "While Eisenhower basks in the sun of South America and helps leaders of those countries outline programs of peace," noted the *Chicago Defender*, "racial violence is spreading like fire here in his own country as Negroes and whites take part in sit-down demonstrations throughout the south."[93] Two months later, the same paper called out Eisenhower's deliberate inaction in response to these sit-in protests. "Again at a critical moment in the history of race relations in America, the leadership from the White House has faltered," the paper wrote. "Presumably the President is waiting for a massacre, for the spilling of Negro blood before raising his little magistral finger. Yet he went all over South America, in Argentina, Brazil, Chile and Uruguay preaching on the virtues of democracy and how well the experiment is working in the United States."[94]

Perhaps the most poignant and painful assessment came from an anonymous Black physician on the eve of Eisenhower's South American tour. The letter, which was written to the *Los Angeles Times*, described the physician's reaction to statements from US politicians who wondered how they might develop a foreign policy that would "sell America to our neighbors."

> I feel sorry for those Americans engaged in the task of making America appear good in the eyes of foreigners, because they have failed to do the one thing that would accomplish this end. It is simply to clean house here. How, in heaven's name, can anyone go and preach democracy to anybody when there are Negroes who cannot even vote in their own country? When a court of law still upholds the perpetrators of injustice and fails to properly deal out the punishment deserved?. . . . Until the brave one appears who will state these facts and face up to them with strength and conviction we are liable not to gain any real ground in our foreign policy program, but must be content with the shouts and applause of the mobs which greet our caravans in various parts of the world and who are always willing to accepts the gifts of Santa Claus.

And with that, the anonymous author signed the letter: "Negro Physician, Los Angeles."[95]

Conclusion—and a Cautionary Tale

Eisenhower's visit to South America—and, indeed, his other "Good Will" tours—solidified the global rhetorical presidency as a key diplomatic strategy during the Cold War. "World travel has become an important arm of diplomacy," wrote *New York Times* correspondent C. L. Sulzberger on the eve of "Operation Amigo."[96] The circulation of the presidential body to various places and regions extended US hegemony in ways that were both material and symbolic. Its deliberate movement to—and, importantly, its absence from—particular spaces and regions functioned as a physical manifestation of US interest, investment, and ideological dominance. Unnerved by the growing Soviet influence in Cuba and its appeal in South America, the president and his advisors designed this second "Good Will" tour to showcase the superiority of democratic ideals on the world stage. As Eisenhower traveled from the United States to South America and moved within and between Brazil, Argentina, Chile, and Uruguay, the circulation of his presidential body accomplished at least four objectives. First, it countered a growing communist presence in the region, particularly in the island nation of Cuba. Second, it offered a symbolic counterpunch to the worldwide travels of Soviet premier Nikita Khrushchev and other Soviet officials in Latin America and the rest of the world, tours the Eisenhower administration saw as a direct threat to their campaign for winning global public opinion. Third, it suggested to political leaders in Argentina, Brazil, Chile, and Uruguay that they had seats at the proverbial Cold War bargaining table, even if this perception was not a reality. Finally, it represented the extension of key aspects of the Monroe Doctrine to meet the needs of the Cold War moment. In this instance, the cliché rings true: Eisenhower's actions—and the circulation of his presidential body—spoke louder than his words.

And yet, if the global rhetorical presidency can elevate the national image on the world stage, it also can deliver swift international humiliation—a fact made unmistakably plain by Eisenhower's final "Good Will" tour of Asia in June 1960. Mere days before the president was to visit Tokyo, the government of Japan—and one of the United States' closest allies in Asia—abruptly canceled Eisenhower's visit due to student demonstrations that were organized, at least according to the administration, by communists. Eisenhower learned of the decision during a public rally at Manila's Luneta Park. According to one reporter on the scene, the president's "face told the story: his mouth turned down; his eyes, framed with crowfoot lines, squinted. Then he shook his head and pursed his lips" before "mouthing a single, soundless word."[97] In his memoirs, Eisenhower recalled his disappointment: "Viewed from any angle, this was a Communist victory. . . . I resolved that upon my return I would try to use the Japanese incident as one device to help explain to the American people once more what we were up against in dealing with international Communism"[98] (figure 3.6).

Public reaction was swift, incredulous, and unsparing. The New York Times noted that the incident "caused chagrin and vague disquiet in much of official Washington. . . . The feeling was general that something was fundamentally wrong if the President of the United States could be prevented by the violent actions of a small minority from visiting a friendly ally."[99] Senator J. William Fulbright, chairman of the Senate Foreign Relations Committee, stated that the cancellation "hurts our prestige" and Senate Majority Leader Lyndon B. Johnson, who would enter the 1960 presidential campaign in July, went so far as to question the effectiveness of the president's foreign policy. "It is evident that this is a time to re-examine our polices and to determine whether they are effective in penetrating the walls which the Communists seek to build between men."[100] As New York Times correspondent C. L. Sulzberger wrote, "the United States has suffered a major blow to its prestige as a result of the inept

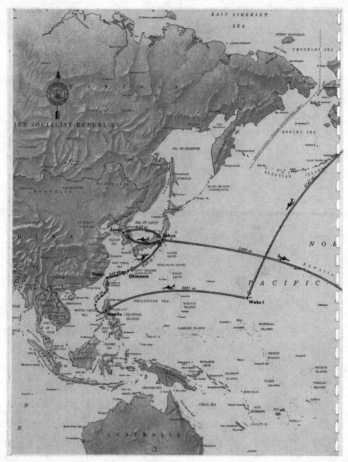

FIGURE 3.6A. Internal White House map depicting President Eisenhower's route for "Operation Cosmos." Records of William P. Draper, Naval Aide to the President. Courtesy of the Dwight D. Eisenhower Presidential Library and Museum.

handling of President Eisenhower's proposed journey to Japan. . . . We have lost considerable face in the Orient, where face counts most."[101]

Behind the scenes, administration officials closely monitored how American allies and enemies responded. Diplomats stationed at US embassies and consulates around the world submitted detailed reports to the State Department.[102] In a summary memo to Eisenhower, Herter explained that most press reports in Western Europe "interpreted [the] cancellation [of the] Tokyo visit as [a] communist propaganda triumph and [a] very serious blow [to] US and Japanese prestige." In London, the *Times* called the cancellation the "biggest blow [to the] prestige [of a] US President since [the] war." Press in West Germany, Austria, Switzerland, and Italy "claimed summit collapse

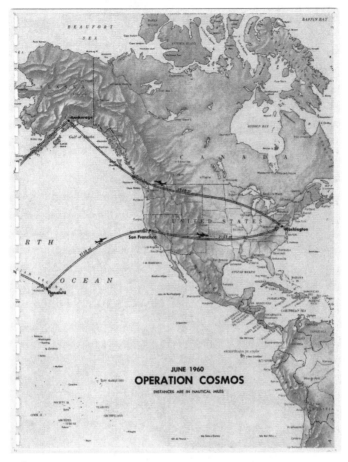

JUNE 1960
OPERATION COSMOS
DISTANCES ARE IN NAUTICAL MILES

FIGURE 3.6B.

and cancellation reflected lack [of] effective US leadership." Newspaper editors in India and Indonesia "agreed cancellation [was a] severe defeat for [the] US in Asia," and news commentators in Taiwan, Vietnam, Korea, the Philippines, and Australia noted their concern over "Japanese inability [to] control riots and [a] possible Japanese drift to neutralism."[103] To those nations who aligned themselves with the Soviet Union, however, the events in Japan were cause for celebration. In Moscow, commentators "stressed role [of] Japanese communists in cancellation, predicted fall of Kishi government, [and the] destruction [of the] US-Japanese alliance."[104] The Chinese communist press described the president as the "vicious wolf Eisenhower" and the "biggest enemy of the Chinese and Asian people and the peace-loving people of the world" who had embarked on a "nine-day robber's tour of the Far East." Nikita Khrushchev also commented on the trip cancellation, calling it a "public slap in the face. As the saying goes: you reap what you sow . . . the Japanese People slammed the door in the face of an unwelcome guest."[105] Communists around the world, Herter concluded, were "jubilant over [the] cancellation."[106] The shock and dismay expressed by US politicians, press commentary, and even the president himself highlights the deep angst over how this incident would influence the United States' image abroad and its self-proclaimed status as the "Leader of the Free World."

Even as major US newspapers noted their shock and grave concern, Black periodicals around the country rightly noted the disconnect between the United States' self-appointed position as the "Leader of the Free World" and the realities of civil rights abuses for millions of Americans living within the nation's own borders. Some of these reports focused their comments on what the country should do to ensure that other nations—particularly those in the Global South—did not succumb to Soviet influence. "The black peoples of Africa are on the rise," wrote the *Atlanta Daily World*. "No less than eight nations have gained their independence this year. Communist Russia is contending for their friendship and we must not allow their loyalties to turn in that direction." Reiterating the idea that the United States needed to set an example for the rest of the world, the paper suggested that "since they [citizens of African nations] are black and brown, the black and brown people of this nation must be treated with dignity and equality; all vestiges of second class citizenship must be removed from America—speedily."[107] The *Chicago Defender* called the trip cancellation "another humiliating defeat," noting somewhat dryly that if "Eisenhower could have had a triumphal entry in the Japanese capital, he would have been hailed as the 'Great White Father,' as the greatest force for peace and goodwill that has ever penetrated the Far East."[108]

It was the *Los Angeles Sentinel*, however, that offered the most prescient commentary on the Japan visit cancellation. The paper wrote that the president should learn "a valuable lesson in public relations." Eisenhower, the paper continued, had "failed miserably to convince outsiders of American sincerity" and should thus "make a fresh start by assessing some of the reasons for the rejection." Chief among these was widespread racism and bigotry around the United States. "To put it bluntly, too many 'red-blooded' Americans hate Negroes because of their color, Jews and Catholics because of their religion, and Mexicans and Orientals because of their national backgrounds. This dedication to hatred cannot be hidden from the rest of the world." What, then, should the country do? The paper offered this concrete suggestion:

We could clean up our own backyard. A starting point would be for a presidential mission to go to some of the "under-developed" (both mentally and morally) areas of the South and demand of its leaders a greater respect for our laws, institutions, and the rights of all mankind. . . . The selling job, then, must begin at home before it is spread abroad. Otherwise our acceptance in other lands will continue to be somewhat less than cordial.[109]

Here the paper underscored the supreme irony of Eisenhower's visits. Although the president could undertake a domestic "mission" to "'under-developed' areas of the South" and provide moral leadership for civil rights at home, Eisenhower was concerned primarily with foreign public opinion. Eager to champion democratic values on the world stage, Eisenhower—and many other US presidents—continued to deny them to US citizens. A cruel paradox, indeed.

But despite the abysmal failure of the president's final "Good Will" tour to Asia, US officials maintained that presidential rhetoric abroad was a powerful weapon in their Cold War arsenal—and a strategy that would extend beyond the Eisenhower administration. In August 1960, the Sprague Committee issued a report suggesting that the president needed to take a more active role in the formation and education of US public opinion. Although "Congress has long been opposed to organized efforts of the Executive Branch to forge a direct link with U.S. public opinion" and had "always reacted sharply against efforts by the Executive Branch to organize strong informational programs beamed at a domestic audience," there were benefits to be had for speaking directly with the people. The challenge, the report continued, was for the president to find "an acceptable balance between his urgent need to inform and instruct the people, and his respect for the prerogatives of Congress." However, the report predicted that "the problems of the coming decade will require, in the national interest, the most vigorous approach by the President to his responsibility for measuring, educating and leading public opinion in foreign affairs."[110] This recommendation seems to be linked directly to the success of Eisenhower's "Good Will" tour. As a June 1960 memorandum explained, the president's overseas trips "had significant impact abroad," and "USIA public opinion polls indicate[d] a rising trend in foreign estimation of America's prestige and desire for peace, coinciding with the period immediately following the trips."[111]

Weeks before Eisenhower left office, the President's Committee on Information Activities Abroad published its final report and offered recommendations for the next decade. In its executive summary, the committee predicted that the "eventual outcome of the struggle" between the United States and the Soviet Union would "depend in considerable degree on the extent we are able to influence the attitudes of people."[112] The committee's ultimate concern was with maintaining "our general prestige in the world and our image as a dynamic and progressive society" because the "understanding [of foreign leaders] will influence political and social developments within their countries and ultimately their international orientation."[113] One of the most effective ways to increase the United States' "general prestige in the world," the committee concluded, was through the president's decision to go global. "Visits to other countries by the President or the Secretary of State can have extraordinary political and psychological value," they wrote. "To the extent possible they should be planned and managed in ways which will increase and prolong their favorable impact on local leaders and populations."[114] All future Cold War US presidents would follow this advice—beginning with Eisenhower's successor, John F. Kennedy.

4

Kennedy in West Berlin

West Berlin is a lighthouse of freedom in a dark totalitarian sea. It demonstrates the material superiorities of a free society which allows and encourages individual initiative. More important, it is a shining model of political, intellectual, and spiritual freedom in which individual liberties are assured and the people choose those who govern them. . . . All peoples throughout the globe who enjoy or aspire to freedom, including the captive peoples of the Communist empires, have a vital interest in the preservation of freedom—of self-determination—in West Berlin. In defending Free Berlin we defend not only Bonn, Paris, London, Oslo, Ottawa, Washington, Kansas City, Boise, but, in fact, every citizen in the North Atlantic community. Equally we defend New Delhi, Kuala Lumpur, Tokyo, Lagos, Tunis, Cairo, Rio de Janeiro, Montevideo, and every other city and village and people who wish to be free.

US DEPARTMENT OF STATE, August 1961[1]

The story of John F. Kennedy's unfinished presidency is one influenced, shaped, and defined by place—the places he visited, the places he ignored, the places he promised the country would go, and, above all, the central place he believed the United States should occupy on the world stage. Consider some of the most the iconic moments of Kennedy's one thousand days: the Bay of Pigs, the Vienna Summit, the Cuban Missile Crisis, Vietnam, Birmingham, Berlin, and his pledge to go to the moon. Embedded within each of these spatiotemporal moments is the question of US prestige during the Cold War. In fact, all of these examples reflect Kennedy's belief that the United States should and would remain preeminent on the world stage.

Even as a presidential candidate, Kennedy positioned the United States as the epicenter and arbiter of global affairs. When he announced his intention to seek the Democratic nomination for president of the United States on January 2, 1960, Kennedy described the presidency as "the most powerful office in the Free World," for "in it [were] centered the hopes of the globe around us for freedom and a more secure life." It was the sun around which the rest of the "Free World" revolved. In fact, Kennedy defined his political experience and rhetorical authority in relation to the places he had been, noting that he had "toured every state in the Union" in the past forty months and had "traveled in every nearly continent and country—from Leningrad to Saigon, from Bucharest to Lima" in the "last 20 years." Through his travels across the country and around the globe, Kennedy explained, he had "developed an image of

America as fulfilling a noble and historic role as the defender of freedom in a time of maximum peril—and of the American people as confident, courageous and persevering. It is with this image that I begin this campaign."[2] This mythic image of America's role in the world characterized Kennedy's foreign policy both during the 1960 presidential campaign and throughout his time in office.

There is one place, however, that looms large throughout this narrative: the city of West Berlin. As I detailed in chapter 2, Berlin's symbolic status on the Cold War world stage began even before the Second World War ended. It was here that Harry S. Truman celebrated the victory of the democratic "way of life" and declared that the United States had "conclusively proven that a free people can successfully look after the affairs of the world."[3] It was here that the leaders of the "Big Three" agreed to divide up the former Nazi capital into four zones of occupation—a temporary agreement that would soon become permanent. And it was here that a city once synonymous with Hitler's Third Reich could evolve into a symbol of democratic resolve. More than any other location, the city of West Berlin would come to occupy a mythic status in the American Cold War consciousness. It functioned as both stage and scene, a place where the global rhetorical presidency could be enacted across time, space, and multiple administrations. And it was John F. Kennedy who solidified the city's iconic status in the Cold War global imaginary through his famous "Ich bin ein Berliner" declaration on June 26, 1963.[4]

Well into the twenty-first century, Kennedy's visit to West Berlin remains an iconic moment in US presidential history. Images of Kennedy peering over the Berlin Wall, visiting Checkpoint Charlie, and speaking to a million West Berliners packed into the Rudolph Wilde Platz underscore the stark divide between East and West during the Cold War. The text of the president's address continues to fascinate. Part of this is due to popular lore, such as the humorous but inaccurate story that Kennedy had declared himself to be a jelly doughnut. Scholarly accounts of Kennedy's visit to Berlin, however, note the historical and rhetorical significance of the president's visit. German historian Andreas Daum examines the careful staging and drama of the president's tour within its larger Cold War context, arguing that "symbolic politics, performative action, and emotions [were] constitutive for transatlantic and especially German-American relations."[5] Robert Dallek writes that Kennedy's European tour was a "grand triumph of public diplomacy."[6] Ted Sorenson, one of the president's speechwriters, recalled that Kennedy received "the most overwhelming reception of his career" during his visit to West Berlin.[7] In his analysis of Kennedy's address, John M. Murphy argues that "from the opening stanza, the President of the United States as president became one with West

Berlin and the rest of the speech amplified that status."[8] Through his rhetoric
of identification in West Berlin, write Isabel Fay and Jim A. Kuypers, Kennedy "helped lay the foundation for Germany's cultural identification with
the West" and created "a triumphant moment for the United States against the
Soviet interest."[9] With all this fanfare, then, why another scholarly examination of Kennedy's visit to West Berlin?

Where many earlier studies attend to the rhetorical flourishes of the "Ich
bin ein Berliner" declaration or the implications of the president's tour within
in a Cold War historical frame, in this chapter I turn my attention to an obvious but understudied dimension of Kennedy's visit: the role of place itself.
Because Kennedy's famous identification with Berliners is now legendary,
it is tempting to gloss over what Berlin symbolized in the Cold War global
imaginary prior to 1963 and how these rhetorical histories were embedded in
the actual location of the president's address. Where Truman used his performance at Potsdam to display his presidential ethos and Eisenhower's movement through South America functioned as an embodied counteroffensive
to an increasing Soviet presence in the region, Kennedy took the ideological contest between democracy and communism to the front lines of Cold
War by going to West Berlin himself. Beginning in 1945, the city took on a
mythic status in the ideological contest between the United States and the
Soviet Union. It was here, in Berlin, that the ideals of democracy were under
siege, surrounded on all sides by Soviet encroachment. And it was here, in
Berlin, that the United States stood resolute in its commitment to defend a
democratic "way of life." I detail how Kennedy's visit to West Berlin elevated
this "defended island of freedom" in the Cold War global imaginary while
also highlighting the United States' role in defending it from a tidal wave
of communist oppression.[10] This chapter, then, offers not only an account of
Kennedy's legendary "Ich bin ein Berliner" address, but also details how the
city functioned as a consummate rhetorical resource throughout the Cold
War. In fact, I go so far as to argue that the mythic qualities of Kennedy's
speech are due as much to the placement of the address as they are to Kennedy's rhetorical skill.

This explicit focus on Kennedy's deployment of West Berlin also underscores the central role of place in the global rhetorical presidency. As I noted
in chapter 1, going global not only activates the symbolic resonances of particular locations, but it also enables US presidents to create networks of geopolitical association and identification between the United States and other
nations. Such was the case with Kennedy's visit to West Berlin. As "a small
island of free men in the midst of communist territory," the city occupied
a mythic status in the Cold War global imaginary.[11] But the city represented

more than a point on a map. It also functioned as a storehouse of memory, a container of past histories and future possibilities. The rhetorical history of the city itself became a powerful rhetorical resource, one that Kennedy activated and reappropriated for his own purposes. Drawing on the city's physical location and the histories embedded in place, Kennedy described the city and its citizens as inextricably linked to the rest of the "Free World." West Berlin thus became a central node in the Cold War global imaginary, operating as what Doreen Massey might call "a particular articulation of those relations, a particular moment in those networks of social relations and understandings."[12] Through his travel to and presence in the city, Kennedy embodied and physically displayed the connections between West Berlin and the rest of the "Free World." In turn, Kennedy's performance established a rhetorical precedent for future US presidents, constituting West Berlin as its own place of return, a site commonly shared and well known and yet ripe for rhetorical (re)appropriation.

"Berlin Has Become a Symbol": The Postwar Period

The city of West Berlin, perhaps more than any other place during the Cold War, stood as a physical and metaphorical symbol of the ideological struggle between democracy and communism.[13] In what was often a Cold War clash of words and ideology, the dividing line between East and West Berlin made the conflict physically visible and geographically locatable. As US Air Force military historian Royce E. Eckwright explained, "it was only in Berlin that the world's two great nuclear powers—the United States and the Soviet Union— met like flint and steel in a tinder box. Berlin was the only geographical point in the world where military forces and political commitments of the United States and the Soviet Union were locked continuously in a direct confrontation."[14] Before Kennedy even set foot in West Berlin, the city occupied a mythic status in the Cold War global imaginary. But to understand why the president was able to activate this symbolism through his rhetoric in place, it is important to trace how West Berlin became a symbol of "Free World" moral resolve prior to Kennedy's visit in June 1963.

The very existence of West Berlin was a result of Germany's defeat after the Second World War. During their negotiations at Potsdam, the "Big Three" designated Berlin as the capital of Germany and divided the city into four zones of occupation.[15] Located more than one hundred miles east of the boundary between East and West Germany, the city was surrounded by Soviet-occupied territory. Although Berlin was divided between the United States, Great Britain, France, and the Soviet Union, the Potsdam agreements did not determine access rights for US, British, and French troops behind East German lines.[16] This seemingly small fact set up a full-scale confrontation between the United States, Great Britain, and the Soviet Union in what would become known as the "Berlin Airlift." On June 24, 1948, Soviet troops halted road and rail traffic between the Western occupation zones and the city of Berlin, in effect cutting off the Western sections—and 2.5 million people—from food, water, fuel, and medical supplies. Four days later, President Truman ordered a full-scale military operation to supply the necessary food and fuel to keep the city's inhabitants alive. Over the next thirteen months, the US-British airlift transported more than two million tons of food, coal, and other supplies to the city of Berlin.[17]

In the early years of the Cold War, the Berlin Airlift came to symbolize the strength and resilience of freedom-loving citizens living behind enemy lines and the moral resolve of the United States. Just three weeks after the airlift began, *Washington Post* reporter John G. Norris interviewed military chiefs on the situation in Berlin. Their feeling, he wrote, was that "Berlin has become the symbol of American determination. . . . The fact that the odds are against us makes victory in the 'cold' war all the more important. Firmness when our position is weak will have greater effect on western Europe than if it were strong."[18] Other US officials described West Berlin as a symbol not just because of where it was located, but also due to the memories it housed. They also knew that US actions in the besieged city would influence the battle for global public opinion. In this view, West Berlin was a symbol of *American determination*. Edward T. Lilly, a specialist in psychological operations in the Truman administration, explained that although Berlin itself was "strategically unimportant" from a military perspective, it held immense political and psychological weight. "Berlin has become a symbol," Lilly wrote in a report titled "Political Objectives in Berlin." "We have ostensibly promised to protect and guard the Germans in our zone. They and we realize that in case of a 'hot war' our protection is impossible. However, until that war arrives, they and Western Europe, even the world, expect that we will not abandon them." If the United States were to withdraw troops from Berlin, "the loss of political face . . . would increase Russian political prestige throughout the world and seriously jeopardize America's political position in Europe and Asia. Even though withdrawal might be justified on purely military grounds, such action would be interpreted as a political defeat for America and a victory for Russia."[19]

The city's symbolic status continued to increase after the Berlin Airlift, particularly after the Four Powers divided their German zones of occupation into two sectors. Areas governed by the United States, Great Britain, and

France formed the Federal Republic of Germany (FRG), or West Germany. Soviet territory became the German Democratic Republic (GDR), or East Germany. The city of Berlin, however, was still divided by the Four Powers. American, British, and French citizens lived and worked freely throughout the city.[20] But because the city was located deep inside East Germany, Berlin was the pro-democracy thorn GDR officials were determined to remove for good. By the time Kennedy took office in January 1961, the issue of Berlin loomed large. In November 1958, Nikita Khrushchev had demanded that the Western powers sign a peace treaty with East Germany and withdraw their military presence from Berlin within six months. Through back-channel negotiations, Eisenhower convinced Khrushchev to stand down until they could negotiate in person. But after the Soviet downing of the U-2 plane in May 1960, tensions escalated between the two superpowers. Still, Khrushchev seemed content to wait until a new administration took office in January 1961.

As a presidential candidate, Kennedy forcefully defended West Berlin's sovereignty, arguing that the city's right to existence encapsulated the larger Cold War struggle. At a campaign stop in Milwaukee in March 1960, he described West Berlin as "a small island of free men in the midst of communist territory," one sustained by "the courage and vitality of its people" and "reinforced by our own determination that Berlin shall—and must—remain free." Later on in the speech, Kennedy reasserted West Berlin's symbolic status. "Berlin is important as a symbol—as perhaps the chief symbol of the free world's determination not to yield to Russian threats and Russian pressure." But Kennedy did not stop there; instead, he linked US interests to Berlin's fate, arguing that "the protection of the freedom of Berlin is the surest protection of our own freedom." In fact, he said, for much of the world Berlin was "the touchstone of American determination—the measure of our dedication to freedom. It is this belief which makes the cause of Berlin the cause of free men everywhere."[21] Here, Kennedy held up the city as the living, breathing embodiment of "American determination" against Soviet oppression. And early in his presidency, Kennedy would have the opportunity to make good on his promise.

"An Island of Freedom in a Communist Sea": The Berlin Crisis

As much as Berlin symbolized US commitment to protecting and defending democracy during the Cold War, it was also the issue over which Kennedy and Khrushchev came to verbal blows in their first meeting at the Vienna Summit.[22] In June 1961, the US president and the Soviet premier met to discuss a variety of subjects related to US-Soviet relations, including Cuba, Laos, a ban on nuclear testing, and German reunification.[23] But it was the issue of Berlin that caused the greatest disagreement between the two leaders, a rift that would continue throughout the summer of 1961 and ultimately led to Khrushchev's order to build the Berlin Wall in August. Reemphasizing demands he first made in 1958, Khrushchev told Kennedy that he intended to sign a peace treaty with East Germany that would permanently establish the division between East and West Germany and cut off all Western access to areas inside the East German zone—including the city of West Berlin.[24] When Kennedy stated emphatically that the United States would not abandon its commitment to West Berlin and denounced Khrushchev's attempt to "disturb the balance of power" in Europe, Khrushchev was incensed.[25] In their final meeting, the president attempted to smooth things over by telling Khrushchev that he "would not present him with a situation so deeply involving our national interest"—the United States' long-standing commitment to Berlin—and again emphasized "the difference between a peace treaty and the rights of access to Berlin."[26] The Soviet leader replied that if the United States maintained its right of access to West Berlin following the signed peace treaty (thus violating East German borders), "force would be met by force."[27] Kennedy responded by telling Khrushchev that his statements left him no other option but to tell British prime minister Harold Macmillan that the Soviet Union gave him a choice between "accepting the Soviet action on Berlin or having a face-to-face confrontation."[28] Khrushchev then put the option in Kennedy's hands: "I want peace," he said, slamming his hand down on the table. "But if you want war, that is your problem." The meeting ended with Khrushchev telling Kennedy, "War will take place only if the U.S. imposes it on the U.S.S.R. It is up to the U.S. to decide whether there will be war or peace."[29] The Soviets gave the US delegation an aide-mémoire that demanded a German settlement within six months. The Berlin Crisis had begun.[30]

On July 25, Kennedy delivered a televised address to an audience of fifty million viewers to outline the official US policy on West Berlin.[31] The president had delivered earlier reports to the US public on his meeting with Khrushchev in a June 6 televised speech[32] and a June 28 press conference,[33] but this speech was designed, in the words of Kennedy speechwriter Ted Sorenson, to "explain the nature of the Berlin issue, our rights, obligations and objectives from which we will not back down an inch" and to "make clear our intent to defend Berlin at all costs."[34] In the address, Kennedy summarized the developments since his return from meeting with Khrushchev and reiterated Berlin's importance to US foreign policy. Throughout the speech, Kennedy used the qualifier "West" to describe the city seventeen times, a strategic choice designed to communicate the idea that, as Frederick Kempe notes, "the Soviets were free to do what they wanted with the city's eastern portion as long as they didn't touch the western part."[35] Although the "immediate threat to free men is in West Berlin," Kennedy argued, he cautioned that this "isolated outpost is not an isolated problem. . . . We face a challenge in our own hemisphere, and indeed wherever else the freedom of human beings is at stake."[36] The Soviet challenge to US rights in West Berlin was not limited to the German capital. Instead, it represented a physical and metaphorical outpost of freedom surrounded by totalitarianism.

To help his audience understand Berlin's geopolitical significance to the "Free World," Kennedy displayed an image of divided Germany on the television screen. "This map makes very [clear] the problem that we face," he said. The live feed then transitioned to a close-up image of the map, and the president oriented his audience to what they saw. "The white is West Germany—the East is the area controlled by the Soviet Union, and as you can see from the chart, West Berlin is 110 miles within the area which the Soviets now dominate—which is immediately controlled by the so-called East German regime." Here, Kennedy invited his audience to inhabit the boundaries he had just reinforced. After this orientation, the live shot returned to Kennedy in the Oval Office. The president defended the United States' right to be in West Berlin as stemming from "our victory over Nazi Germany." More importantly, however, he noted that the nation would remain in West Berlin to affirm its "commitment to sustain—defend, if need be—the opportunity for more than two million people to determine their own future and choose their own way of life." Like Truman and Eisenhower before him, Kennedy reinforced the paramount importance of the individual ability to freely choose a "way of life." He continued:

> For West Berlin lying exposed 110 miles inside East Germany, surrounded by Soviet troops and close to Soviet supply lines, has many roles. It is more than a showcase of liberty, a symbol, an island of freedom in a Communist sea. It is even more than a link with the Free World, a beacon of hope behind the Iron Curtain, an escape hatch for refugees. West Berlin is all of that. But above all it has now become—as never before—the great testing place of Western courage and will, a focal point where our solemn commitments stretching back over the years since 1945, and Soviet ambitions now meet in basic confrontation.[37]

In this passage, the president described the city in geographic and symbolic language. West Berlin's geographical situatedness—its place as location—was inherently symbolic. Behind the "East German regime," the city was also a "showcase of liberty," a "symbol," "an island of freedom in a communist sea," "a beacon of hope behind the Iron Curtain," and "the great testing place of

Western courage and will." These characterizations of West Berlin reinforced the city's status as a geographic location behind enemy lines and a metaphorical representation of the ideological war being waged between the United States and the Soviet Union. As a physical location ("an island of freedom in a Communist sea"), a storehouse of memory and history (a "focal point" of US "solemn commitments . . . since 1945"), and a "link with the Free World," the city encapsulated the stakes of the Cold War contest.

What was once a symbolic dividing line between East and West soon became a permanent fixture in the Cold War global consciousness. Just after midnight on August 13, 1961, the Soviet Union closed the border between West and East Berlin. Later that morning, East German soldiers drilled holes for concrete pillars and strung barbed wire across the boundary line. The Berlin Wall began to take shape, physically dividing the city.[38] Despite his earlier rhetoric lauding West Berlin as a "symbol" for the rest of the world, Kennedy remained silent on the matter for eight straight days.[39] Three hundred thousand West Berliners protested in front of the City Hall of West Berlin holding signs that read "Betrayed by the West" and "The West is Doing a Second Munich."[40] Willy Brandt, the mayor of West Berlin, told the crowd that "Berlin expects more than words. It expects political action."[41] Eventually, Kennedy sent Vice President Lyndon B. Johnson and General Lucius Clay—the beloved US commander of the Berlin airlift twelve years earlier—as his representatives to West Berlin. The presence of US officials mattered more than words. The vice president hailed West Berlin as a "fortress of the free" and "home of the brave," clearly echoing the famous words from the United States' national anthem.[42] In an address to the West German Parliament, Johnson said, "To the survival and to the creative future of this city we Americans have pledged, in effect, what our ancestors pledged in forming the United States: 'Our lives, our fortunes and our sacred honor.'"[43] But according to *New York Times* correspondent Sydney Gruson, "the Vice President said nothing essentially new." What really mattered to West Berliners, Gruson wrote, was Johnson's "presence as a tangible expression of the link that sustains them."[44] Brandt echoed similar sentiments years later, writing, "The fact that the vice president was there in West Berlin . . . was a most effective way of counteracting this feeling of uncertainty which was spreading during these days following August 13."[45]

These personal diplomatic overtures continued, offering a vivid demonstration of the United States' commitment to West Berlin. In February 1962, Kennedy's brother and attorney general Robert Kennedy traveled to West Berlin and spoke to a crowd of 150,000 gathered in front of City Hall. Another one hundred thousand lined the streets to greet him.[46] "You are our brothers," he told the crowd. In fact, the attorney general declared that "an attack on West Berlin is an attack on Chicago, New York, Paris, [and] London," a statement that reportedly garnered the loudest cheers from the crowd.[47] The *New York Times* explained that RFK's "visit was a symbol of the United States' commitment to West Berlin, an especially powerful symbol because he is the President's brother. Such symbols are important to the West Berliners in their mood of apprehension about the Communist threat."[48] For West Berliners (and the watching world), the presence of US officials in the besieged city offered physical proof of the United States' commitment to defending West Berlin from the threat of communism. This commitment, however, was crystalized by President Kennedy's visit to West Berlin on June 26, 1963.

"To See and Be Seen": Planning Kennedy's Visit to West Berlin

If the global rhetorical presidency examines how US presidents use their rhetoric abroad to bolster US prestige and the image of the president on the world stage, Kennedy's visit to West Berlin is a textbook case.[49] Indeed, the Kennedy administration outlined three specific goals for the president's visit to West Berlin: (1) reaffirm US commitment to maintaining and defending a free West Berlin; (2) offer a psychological boost to West Berliners; and (3) demonstrate Kennedy's status as world leader by using his physical presence in West Berlin to counteract Khrushchev's frequent visits to East Germany. Throughout the planning stages of this trip, US officials continually stressed the rhetorical significance of witnessing the US president drive through the streets of West Berlin. *Seeing* Kennedy present in West Berlin, a city encapsulating a rich history of American determination and commitment, would underscore the United States' resolve to protect and defend democracy, no matter the cost.

TO GO OR NOT TO GO

Kennedy's visit to West Berlin, now iconic, initially was perceived to be a risky undertaking. While many officials in both the United States and West Germany recognized the symbolic significance of a presidential visit to West Berlin, others cautioned that it could escalate already-tense relations between the United States and the Soviet Union. In early February 1963, E. Allan Lightner, chief of the US Berlin Mission, reported a conversation he had with the mayor of West Berlin. To Brandt, a presidential visit to West Berlin "would have the positive effect of underscoring Western solidarity re: Berlin and basic Western policy objectives," he reportedly asserted. The mayor also cautioned that if the president decided not to visit the city, West Berliners would "draw unfavorable comparison with recent Khrushchev visits to East

Berlin, as well as broader and unwarranted political conclusions."[50] This direct comparison between Khrushchev and Kennedy continued through February and March, and West German officials frequently cited personal visits
by Khrushchev to East Berlin as evidence that Kennedy should indeed visit
West Berlin. If the Soviet premier had gone to East Germany multiple times,
the logic went, shouldn't the president of the United States make a similar
trip? Socialist Democratic Party vice chairman Herbert Wehner was em-
phatic that it was "of utmost importance that [the president] also visit Berlin"
and "thought it a mistake to show undue restraint about seeking to influence
German policy in the Atlantic-Community sense." In fact, Wehner argued,
Kennedy "should present himself to the Germans as the leader of the nation
wielding the real power in the Alliance. It should be demonstrated 'who is
cook and who is waiter' (*wer ist Koch und wer ist Kellner*)."[51] Newspapers in
West Germany and West Berlin itself also expressed a similar sentiment. *Bild
Zeitung* declared that a visit by President Kennedy to Berlin would "demonstrate to the Kremlin that the Americans will act in Berlin with the same determination they showed in Cuba." Papers throughout West Berlin warned
of "serious repercussions if the President leaves Berlin out of his itinerary,"
adding that a most convincing argument of US advocates of the Berlin visit
is the fact that Khrushchev visited East Berlin six times; the last time was
in 1963."[52]

Within the US State Department, various officials strongly supported
a presidential stop in West Berlin and recognized the city's importance in
the broader Cold War geopolitical landscape. By going there personally, the
president would offer tangible proof of his own commitment to the city—and
those East Germans who desperately wished to be free. State Department official William Brubeck emphasized that the first objective of Kennedy's trip to
West Germany "should be to bring about a demonstration of popular support
for the President personally—a support which exists without question—and
for US-German relations in the Atlantic framework." Furthermore, Brubeck
stressed: "*He must visit Berlin. . . .* We should make it clear from the outset
that it is the President's intention to go to West Berlin."[53] In another State
Department memorandum, an anonymous official listed eleven bullet points
in support of a presidential trip to the German capital. The "best reason" for
a visit, the memo began, was articulated by Brandt in a letter to President
Kennedy on March 12: "Your visit to [this] outpost of freedom would become
demonstration of unity of Western community that could not be overlooked
anywhere in world." Moreover, Kennedy's visit to the city would provide "a
tremendous boost to morale of West Berliners as well as to East Berliners
and East and West Germans." This emphasis on boosting public morale went

beyond a simple foreign policy statement. It would also elevate Kennedy's foreign policy stature on the global stage and provide a symbolic antidote to Khrushchev's frequent trips to East Berlin:

> Khrushchev has visited East Berlin several times, as recently as January. No US President has visited Berlin since Truman went to Potsdam. This makes it appear that Soviets are much more interested in Berlin than is US. As Marguerite Higgins [a longtime foreign correspondent for the *New York Herald Tribune*] said, "If Kennedy does not show his face in the free part of Berlin after Khrushchev had himself praised in the enslaved part of Berlin—what will the world, and particularly the Kremlin, think of Western determination."[54]

Kennedy's reputation as a world leader—and US prestige—was at stake. These internal discussions and circulating memoranda culminated in the White House's official decision that Kennedy would stop in West Berlin during his visit to the FRG.

SYMBOLIC GOALS FOR KENNEDY'S PRESENCE IN PLACE

The first goal of Kennedy's visit was to reassure West Berliners (and the rest of the world) that the United States was committed to defending their city from Soviet encroachment, and US officials saw the president's physical presence in the city as a powerful testament to this fact. Edward R. Murrow, the director of the USIA, described a presidential visit to Berlin as a "weapon" that could "sustain morale in Berlin or underscore our negotiating position."[55] Murrow's deputy, Thomas C. Sorenson (the brother of Kennedy speechwriter Ted Sorenson), told National Security Advisor McGeorge Bundy that the goal of the president's trip was "to foster a better and more sympathetic understanding of U.S. policy regarding Europe. It needs to be done now; the President is the only one who can do it, and he can do it more effectively in Europe than here."[56] Although the president had sent the vice president and the attorney general to West Berlin in 1961 and 1962, nothing could replace the symbolic power of Kennedy's own presence in the besieged city. Just before Kennedy left for Europe, a State Department official reminded him that "we should never forget that the United States is the leader of the Atlantic world and that the great mass of Europeans look to America—and specifically to you, as President—for guidance and direction." Because of this fact, Kennedy needed to make "a special effort" to identify with the German people because they were "closest to the firing line. Berlin is a Soviet hostage, and the German people know that their only defense is the American strength and commitment."[57]

A second major goal for the visit was to use Kennedy's physical presence in Berlin to provide a "psychological lift" to West Berliners who stood on the front lines of the Cold War.[58] Where Truman's participation the Potsdam Conference had been designed for a US audience unsure of the new president's ability to lead, Kennedy's presence in West Berlin was directed to Berliners themselves as a way to bolster their confidence in the United States' commitment to their cause. The US Berlin Mission and the White House structured the president's day around events that would enable the largest number of people to see him in the flesh. One State Department official noted that "it would be desirable for him to spend as much of the day as possible driving around West Berlin by automobile in order to be seen by the maximum number of West Berliners throughout the city and to see for himself the actual situation in West Berlin, including of course the Wall."[59] For the site of Kennedy's major address of the day, US officials in Berlin selected Rathaus Schöneberg, West Berlin's City Hall. This space would allow for "maximum (preferably record) public attendance," which officials estimated at three hundred thousand people packed into the square, and thus was appropriate for a "public rally."[60]

This emphasis on being "seen" was of crucial importance. In a telegram to Secretary of State Dean Rusk dated May 1, the US Berlin Mission underscored the symbolic aspects of Kennedy's trip both for West Berlin citizens and the rest of the watching world:

> While US-Berlin solidarity [is] already well known, its reaffirmation in impressive and personalized form on June 26 seems likely to produce [an] advantageous political impression internationally and to give Berliners themselves [a] helpful . . . psychological lift. Therefore, we especially [are] interested in maximum (preferably record) public attendance. While there [is] little doubt Berliners will wish [to] turn out in record numbers to see, hear and cheer [the] president, it [is] necessary [that a] program be arranged to make it possible for them to do so.[61]

Kennedy's physical presence in Berlin would reaffirm his commitment to the city—and all it symbolized—in a particularly "impressive and personal form," one that the US Berlin Mission hoped would boost public morale and demonstrate to the rest of the world just how popular the US president was to these West Berliners.

Finally, Kennedy's trip offered the opportunity to create a symbolic antidote to Khrushchev's many visits to East Berlin and, more importantly, a chance for the president to reassert himself as the leader of the Western alliance. The US Berlin Mission emphasized the "Symbolic and Qualitative

Aspects" of the president's trip, noting that "careful attention should be given [to] certain qualitative aspects of President's Program, such as appearances at important symbolic sites and participation in significant representative actions."[62] Chief among these "sites" would be Kennedy's visit to the Berlin Wall. During the White House advance trip in May, Brandt expressed his opposition to a presidential stop because he felt it underscored Ulbricht's victory over West Berlin. But White House officials overruled him, explaining that

> from [a] public relations viewpoint in US, it [is] necessary [that the] president visit Checkpoint Charlie. This site has been and could become again [a] focal point of direct confrontation between Soviet and US forces. . . . Failure of [the] President [to] visit [the] checkpoint could elicit criticism from American correspondents [and would be] detrimental to [the] objective of achieving maximum worldwide impact of presidential visit.[63]

The White House's insistence that Kennedy stop at Checkpoint Charlie suggests that they saw the president's presence in this particular location— and the visual images of him at the East-West border—as a significant part of his visit.

TO BIRMINGHAM OR BERLIN

If place provides a stage, scene, and site of collective memory on which chief executives enact the global rhetorical presidency, such locations also can deflect or redirect attention from other spaces of contestation. Indeed, the story of Kennedy's visit to West Berlin must be understood within the context of another crucial site: Birmingham, Alabama. Beginning in April 1963, the Southern Christian Leadership Conference initiated the Birmingham Campaign, a set of strategic marches, protests, and sit-ins throughout the city. Although the campaign garnered national and international attention from the very beginning, the events of May 3 forever changed the narrative about civil rights in the United States. When over one thousand African American children and teenagers skipped school to march in the "Children's Crusade," Eugene "Bull" Connor ordered local officials to use high-pressure fire hoses, police dogs, and billy clubs to stop the demonstrations. Photographs of state-sanctioned violence against Black schoolchildren— particularly those taken by Charles Moore and subsequently published in *Life* magazine on May 17—sparked widespread outrage at home and abroad. The realities of segregation and Jim Crow were made visible to American citizens and the rest of the world, causing many to ask how proponents of a "Free World" democratic system could deny basic rights to its own citi-

zens.[64] Describing the Birmingham Campaign as an "image event," Davi
Johnson argues that Dr. Martin Luther King Jr. was "a strategic visual rhetor
who chose Birmingham as a staging ground" where he could "*make visible*
the injustice of segregation for groups of individuals (white moderates) who
did not regularly experience or even witness the evils of racism firsthand."
These images from Birmingham, Johnson writes, "pierce[d] the conscience
of white moderates in the context of Cold War concern about global perceptions of America and Americans."[65]

Contemporaneous news accounts from Black periodicals and international newspapers underscore this contradiction. As the *Chicago Defender*
noted, the events unfolding in Birmingham and elsewhere were "an American crisis one hundred years in the making," one that "jolted the nation with
the frightening suddenness of a volcano many believed would never erupt.
The floodtide of protest marches, demonstrations, violence, threats and court
action against racial segregation seemed ready to burst the dam that had held
since the Civil War." The paper went further, explicitly linking the realities of
domestic racial terror to what many white US citizens understood as global
Cold War crises. "For Americans," opined the *Defender*, this moment represented "a new kind of crisis. Instead of Havana, Moscow, or Berlin, the places
involved were—in many instances—their hometowns. Birmingham, Jackson,
Greensboro, Raleigh, Tallahassee, Philadelphia, New York. All figured in the
crisis which stemmed from the 'sugar-coated' segregation of the North to fla-
grant civil rights violations in the south."[66] In East Berlin, the *Berliner Zeitung*
declared that after Birmingham "the attention of the world has been called
to the barbaric relations in the U.S.A. through the courageous actions for
justice of the hand-cuffed, oppressed, exploited, and insulted American Negro population." Similarly, the Portuguese newspaper *Novidades* wrote that
"despite proclaiming itself a land of freedom, [the United States] has never
succeeded in doing away with the shame of racial segregation."[67] Even Willy
Brandt could not avoid the issue. In a press interview in Saint Louis, Missouri,
just two weeks before he would welcome Kennedy to West Berlin, he admitted that he felt "sorry" for the United States because, "in addition to other
burdens this country has . . . in world freedom . . . it also has to deal with this
(racial) problem."[68]

As the debate continued, some politicians and public figures suggested
that Kennedy should shift his attention to federal civil rights legislation at
home. US senator Barry Goldwater (R-AZ) argued that "with Cuba still a
burning issue in America, with problems here at home—economic and racial—he has no business being out of the White House even to go to Camp
David. He belongs there to run the country." Senator Hugh Scott (R-PA)

stated: "I'd rather see him go to Birmingham than to Berlin just now."[69] In a June 4 syndicated column, Walter Lippmann argued that Kennedy "need[ed] to have mastered the crisis in American national life before he can speak with self-confidence on the cause of democracy in world affairs."[70] The *New York Times* editorial page agreed the next day, writing that it was "unfortunate that [the president] will be away in Europe at a crucial stage in the mobilization of national opinion in support of a strong [federal] program" on civil rights. "The fatefulness of the debate over civil rights makes it a critical time to stay" at home, the paper concluded.[71]

Even after Kennedy's June 11, 1963, televised speech to the nation on civil rights, the Kennedy White House debated whether or not the president should cancel his trip to Europe.[72] Behind the scenes, Kennedy himself was especially worried about the optics of a trip. "You asked me last night why you should go to Europe—in view of the objections expressed by Mr. Lippmann, the N.Y. Times and others—and what you can accomplish in Germany," wrote one NSC staffer to Kennedy. If the president decided to stay at home, the "public and governmental reaction in West Berlin and West Germany would be one of shock, disbelief and profound disillusionment." Kennedy was on the verge of "achieving an East-West détente, or even an acceptable Berlin arrangement," and canceling the visit would have disastrous effects.[73]

In the end, Kennedy decided to go forward with the trip, arguing that a bold articulation of "Free World" leadership was needed. Less than two months after images from the Birmingham Children's Crusade shocked the nation and the world, Kennedy would offer an alternative image event, a carefully staged media spectacle designed to display American power and superiority to audiences at home and abroad. According to Kennedy senior advisor and speechwriter Theodore Sorenson, the president had "reached a point where he felt perhaps it would be better to divert attention from civil rights for a while" because "legislation was going to take a long time." The trip, Sorenson explained, "was one of these events which helped divert the attention of the nation (as well as his own)."[74] This idea of diverting attention from Birmingham to Berlin is further substantiated by *New York Times* writer Carroll Kilpatrick. Citing senior administration officials, Kilpatrick explained that Kennedy believed canceling the trip would be "abandon[ing] his role as a leader in a most critical time" and noted that White House officials "insist[ed] that it is immensely important for the President to speak to and be seen by the people of Italy and Germany at this time."[75] The unspoken premise here, of course, was that Kennedy's presence was required at a "most critical time" abroad—but not at a moment of racial crisis at home. The president's trip to West Berlin became, quite literally, a strategic means of deflection or distraction from very real issues of racial violence, segregation, and white supremacy at home. The nation and the world had witnessed firsthand the state-sanctioned acts of violence against Black Americans through images circulated around the world. By going to Berlin, Kennedy would offer a more flattering image of the United States: the triumph of American power and prestige on the Cold War world stage.

BROADCASTING BERLIN

To ensure that audiences in Berlin, the United States, and around the world could witness Kennedy's triumphal procession through the besieged city, news networks and US officials orchestrated a deliberate media campaign designed to feature the president's popularity and capture the vivid images of Berliners' uproarious welcome for the American president.

The US Berlin Mission made every possible effort to accommodate the press during the president's visit, which one internal assessment predicted at "approximately 400 newsmen, and possibly more."[76] Elevated platforms were built so that Kennedy could look into East Berlin at the Brandenburg Gate and Checkpoint Charlie—and so that the president would "be elevated above the crowd for the benefit of photographers and the Berliners." Arrangements were made for a designated pickup spot where camera crews could bring television footage "for immediate shipment to the United States" to be aired immediately upon return. In the United States, the president's trip would be covered by the three television networks (ABC, CBS, and NBC) with "at least 22 special reports varying from 15 minutes to an hour." The *New York Times* wrote that US public could expect "from one to three special TV reports daily in evening hours. Picture coverage will be relayed here by the Telestar II and Relay communications satellites and televised the day the events occur."[77] Throughout Western Europe, reported the *Los Angeles Times*, citizens could watch a "a seven-hour step-by-step telecast of his motor tour through [West Berlin] as it is beamed within range of more than 25 million television receivers in 12 countries."[78] In fact, it would be "the subject of the longest live transmission ever made by West German television."[79]

US officials in West Berlin also made sure that West Berliners—and their East German neighbors—would see and hear as much of the president's visit as possible. Loudspeakers would be set up in the Rudolph Wilde Platz to "carry live [radio] coverage of the President's city tour prior to his arrival at the City Hall."[80] Later State Department accounts would report family groups gathering in homes around the city to watch the president's tour unfold in real time. On the other side of the Berlin Wall, East Germans made arrangements to downplay the president's visit. According to a CIA report from inside East Berlin, building wardens were instructed to monitor their apartment buildings and news-jamming stations were installed to combat live radio and television coverage of Kennedy across the Berlin Wall. Party organizations, trade unions, and youth organizations planned rallies to prevent people from listening to the coverage. This CIA report also confirmed that "an as yet unidentified 'very high personality' from Moscow (but in no event Khrushchev) is expected to come to East Berlin. The presence of this personage and a visit on his part to the wall are designed to counter the propaganda effects of the Kennedy visit."[81] In fact, however, Khrushchev could not pass up an opportunity to deliver his own propaganda counterpunch to distract from Kennedy's visit. But that would be getting ahead of the story.

In its final press briefing prior to the president's departure for Europe, the White House underscored Kennedy's status as a foreign policy leader and emphasized the persuasive effect of Kennedy's physical presence would have in Europe and, specifically, West Berlin. McGeorge Bundy told the press that Kennedy's stop in the city would be "one of the most important elements of the trip." He said:

> I think those of you who have been there would agree that to see and be seen in Berlin is something different from most travels, and that there is a real advantage to both parties in knowing whom they have to deal with. The President of the United States has been the man who is speaking for the country, whose will and determination has been essential to the freedom of Berlin for a long time, and the courage and spirit of the Berliners has been equally essential to the policy of the West. That confrontation will not only be in the immediate sense a dramatic one, but I think in the wider sense a useful one to all concerned.[82]

These comments, uttered by a senior administration official who had direct knowledge of the trip's purpose, demonstrate the importance of Kennedy's physical presence in West Berlin for the occupants of the besieged city, the American people, the larger watching world, and even the president himself. Bundy underscored Kennedy's rhetorical authority and ethos as linked to place, characterizing the president's commitment to Berlin as evidence of American resolve. In turn, the "courage and spirit of the Berliners" was a core element of the foreign policy of "the West." Going to Berlin, therefore, was simply an expression of ongoing US commitments, but one that would allow the president "to see and be seen in Berlin." Although Bundy could not have anticipated the full events of the June 26 visit and the emotional impact the wall would have on the president, he accurately predicted that the interaction between Kennedy and West Berliners would be "a dramatic one"—an exchange that numerous presidents after Kennedy would try to recreate.

June 26, 1963

John F. Kennedy's triumphant procession through the streets of Berlin was a sight to behold—and millions throughout the city and around the world did, in real time. After touching down at 9:45 a.m. local time in Air Force One, the president's motorcade began a tour of the city.[83] Waving, cheering crowds lined his motorcade route, at times ten to twelve persons deep.[84] "Thousands of them tried to touch his hand," reported the *Chicago Tribune*. "He was showered with flowers and confetti."[85] White House officials later said it was the largest reception Kennedy ever had.[86] "More than a million West Berliners gave Mr. Kennedy the greatest spontaneous welcome in the memory of the former German capital," summarized the *Christian Science Monitor*. "The Associated Press quoted old-timers as saying that not even Hitler with his famous parades, had brought out the people the way the American President did. The screaming, cheering, flag-waving, confetti-tossing welcome exceeded the mammoth reception West German crowds gave Mr. Kennedy earlier this week."[87] The widespread euphoria extended to the other side of the Berlin Wall for, as one *Chicago Tribune* correspondent stationed in East Berlin reported, "the more the West Berlin crowd cheered, the happier were the faces of the crowd in the east"[88] (figure 4.1).

The president made several stops along the motorcade route before arriving at West Berlin's City Hall, pauses that allowed audiences watching via television to see as he saw in Berlin. At the Brandenburg Gate (Brandenburger Tor), Kennedy mounted a raised platform to look over the Berlin Wall into the eastern portion of the city. Communist officials had draped red cloth and an East German flag between the arches to prevent Kennedy from gazing down the Unter Den Liden, one of the city's former grand boulevards. The president was handed a bouquet of flowers thrown over the wall from East Berlin with a note asking that it be given to the president.[89] A dozen East German soldiers watched from their own checkpoint, about forty yards inside the communist sector,[90] and "a small group of East Berliners beyond the gate waved and cheered him."[91] Kennedy confidant Ken O'Donnell (who was on the trip with the president) recalled that Kennedy "was carried away by the

FIGURE 4.1. President John F. Kennedy's motorcade drives past the Victory Column in West Berlin, June 26, 1963. Photograph by Cecil Stoughton, White House Photographs. Courtesy of the John F. Kennedy Presidential Library and Museum. Accession Number: ST-C230-27-63.

courage of the West Berliners, and shocked by the sight of the Berlin Wall."[92] White House advisor Arthur M. Schlesinger later wrote that Kennedy's personal encounter with the Berlin Wall "shocked and appalled the President, and he was still angry when he came out of the city hall and faced the seething crowd in the Rudolph Wilde Platz, compressed into a single excited, impassioned mass."[93]

Kennedy's own physical experience at the wall—and the images of his stops at several iconic points—became a powerful visual argument against the communist state. Just before Kennedy left for Europe, one reporter asked if there was "any particular advantage in the President of the United States being seen and seeing or peering over the Wall?" In response, McGeorge Bundy replied that he could not "imagine the President of the United States going to Berlin without looking at the wall, which is so large and tragic a fact in that city's current situation."[94] The juxtaposition of the "Leader of the Free World" in front of the Berlin Wall, a concrete barrier preventing individuals from choosing their "way of life," was a vivid demonstration of the stark contrast between democracy and totalitarian rule. To those Berliners watching the tour via television, Kennedy's visit to Berlin Wall reminded them that the American president had experienced this dividing line personally. To those US citizens watching at home, the president's presence at these iconic points brought them quite literally before their eyes. Just as Truman's driving tour of a decimated Berlin in 1945 made the horrors of war vividly real, Kennedy's bodily travel to, around, and through the divided city reminded the watching world of the limits Soviets wanted to place on freedom not just in Germany, but around the globe (figure 4.2).

The president's motorcade departed from Checkpoint Charlie and made its way to West Berlin's City Hall. The surrounding Rudolph Wilde Platz was filled to capacity with bodies "packed so closely together that those who fainted just slumped or were held in a sort of standing position until help came. Many persons had been standing in the square for several hours in raincoats because of the threatening skies."[95] Loudspeakers were set up to project the president's speech beyond the plaza, and East Berliners tuned in over television to see images of Kennedy parading through the streets. "Young and old, mothers with babies, workers in overalls, crippled war veterans and women with tears streaming down their faces all looked to the President as the symbol of their freedom," wrote *Washington Post* reporter Robert H. Estabrook.[96] By the time Kennedy strode to the podium in front of the cheering, waving crowd chanting "Ken-Ne-Dy," his presence in West Berlin had already elevated the city.

FIGURE 4.2. President John F. Kennedy at Checkpoint Charlie along the Berlin Wall in West Berlin, June 26, 1963. Photograph by Robert Knudson, White House Photographs. Courtesy of the John F. Kennedy Presidential Library and Museum. Accession Number: KN-C29210.

"Ich bin ein Berliner"

The most iconic and well-known aspect of Kennedy's visit to Berlin was his declaration that he, too, was a citizen of Berlin. Although this statement is the subject of popular lore (particularly the incorrect assertion that the president mistakenly declared himself to be a "jelly doughnut"), a closer look at the archival record underscores that the place of Kennedy's address was more than a stage or scenic backdrop. Instead, the president's presence in Berlin and his symbolic identification with Berliners spoke louder than words. And yet, these words mattered. Understanding the rhetorical power of "Ich bin ein Berliner" requires an analysis of Kennedy's text delivered in place and how the place functioned as text. Kennedy's declaration was not extemporaneous or the product of emotion. It was carefully practiced and planned before the president left the United States. "Ich bin ein Berliner" was a deliberate rhetorical move, one that linked the president of the United States with the place of his address—and the citizens who embodied what Berlin had come to symbolize in the "Free World" global imaginary (figure 4.3).

From the very beginning, US officials saw the president's oratorical text as interwoven with the place of his address. In a May 3 memorandum, USIA official Morrill Cody noted that a statement by the president "on German soil" would be particularly persuasive in reaffirming the United States' leadership of the Atlantic Alliance and "underlin[ing] the sacrifices made by the United States for Germany and our other European partners." Because Germans "continue to feel the need for acceptance by their erstwhile enemies and present-day allies," Cody recommended that the president "should welcome the Germans fully into the camp of civilized peoples defending freedom."[97] Making this declaration on German soil would allow Kennedy to reaffirm the United States' commitment to Berliners and the nation's belief that Germany was an important part of the "Free World."

The earliest drafts of Kennedy's speech outside West Berlin's City Hall (Rathaus Schöneberg) underscored the city's significance on the Cold War

FIGURE 4.3. President John F. Kennedy speaks at the Rudolph Wilde Platz in West Berlin, June 26, 1963. Photograph by Robert Knudson, White House Photographs. Courtesy of the John F. Kennedy Presidential Library and Museum. Accession Number: KN-C29248.

global stage and emphasized its symbolism for the United States. "The name Berlin has unique significance for Americans and evokes strong and vivid associations," one draft compiled by the US Berlin Mission began. "Fate seems to have chosen this city to become in many ways a mirror and symbol of our world today, a microcosm reflecting its hopes and fears, its progress and its problems, its unity as well as its division." However, what made Berlin "a synonym for the indomitable courage of free men," the speech draft read, was its people: "Your stand, your accomplishments, and the important role you continue to play in the persistent quest for German reunification in peace and freedom have made you an inspiration to the American people and to free men everywhere."[98] Kennedy advisor and speechwriter Theodore Sorenson took these remarks and crafted the president's speeches for Europe—including Kennedy's remarks at the Rudolph Wilde Platz. Sorenson drafted a fine speech—an emotional, stirring address that cited historical milestones such as the Berlin Airlift and the 1961 Berlin Crisis to remind the audience why West Berlin was so important to the United States. Kennedy would also praise the courage of West Berliners, telling them that while the "story of West Berlin is many stories—valor, danger, honor, determination, unity, and hardship," it was, "above all . . . the story of achievement." In his conclusion, the president would reassure West Berliners: "You are not merely the object of our admiration—you are partners in the common purpose. . . . And I tell you once again that your liberty is ours, and your defense our own."[99]

Kennedy, however, wanted to communicate these ideas in a more personal way. In fact, "Ich bin ein Berliner" was the president's own rhetorical invention. Five days before Kennedy left for Europe, he met with three people to work on his speech: Robert H. Lochner, his interpreter for the trip; Margarete Plischke, a language instructor at the State Department; and McGeorge Bundy, his national security advisor.[100] It was during this June 18 meeting that Kennedy and Bundy brainstormed several phrases for his arrival speech in Berlin and his remarks at City Hall. During these discussions, Kennedy added the phrase "I am a Berliner" himself.[101] The Kennedy archives contain just one document referencing this meeting, but one that proves that the president's declaration of "Ich bin ein Berliner" was not hastily written up just hours before the speech or delivered extemporaneously as is sometimes claimed. A typed document entitled "Berlin" features German phonetic spelling of the following sentences in English: "I am proud to be in free Berlin, the city which is a shining symbol, not only for Europe but for the whole world. Your courage and your perseverance have made the words 'I am a Berliner' a proud declaration." Below the side-by-side translations in German and English, the secretarial note reads: "These translations are somewhat literal. The German is a very good free translation of what the President wrote on Tuesday, June 18."[102] Because a copy of this document is found both in the President's Office Files (collected by Evelyn Lincoln, the president's personal secretary) and the National Security Files at the Kennedy Library, it is likely that Mrs. Lincoln typed up the handwritten notations after the meeting and sent a copy to Bundy's office. However, these lines never made it into the notecards prepared for the president to use in Berlin.

This omission explains why numerous White House officials and later historians report that Kennedy wrote out "Civis Romanus sum [I am a citizen of Rome]," "Ich bin ein Berliner [I am a citizen of Berlin]," and "Lass' sie nach Berlin kommen [Let them come to Berlin]" on his notecards on the flight from Bonn to Berlin on the morning of June 26. More than likely, the president reviewed his prepared remarks and, noticing that they did not contain the phrases he and Bundy had written on June 18, decided to write them out himself.[103] "When we were arriving in Berlin," White House advisor Ken O'Donnell later recalled, "he said to me, 'What was the proud boast of the Romans—Civis Romanus sum? Send Bundy up here. He'll know how to say it in German.' When Bundy translated the phrase into 'Ich bin ein Berliner,' the President said, as he wrote it down, 'Now tell me how to say in German, "Let them come to Berlin."'"[104] It makes sense that the president would have asked specifically for Bundy, since he was familiar with the June 18 exchange. Brandt also recalled practicing the phrase with Kennedy just before his speech: "My own contribution to the speech was that before he went out—he was at my office of the city hall—he tried to get a reasonable pronunciation of the sentence, 'Ich bin ein Berliner.' Well, it was a moving thing. And he worked hard at it, at the pronunciation."[105]

As these archival materials and firsthand accounts demonstrate, the president played a crucial role in the development of this speech and personally supplied the "Ich bin ein Berliner" declaration. Charting the evolution of this speech from the US Berlin Mission's initial draft, Sorenson's rewrite, and Kennedy's own edits reveals the important role this speech would play in the White House's overall goals for the trip. Moreover, the president's description of West Berlin as a "shining symbol" and his personal identification with Berliners showcases how the city and its people offered a potent rhetorical resource. In his remarks, the president would identify himself with the Berliners—and all that the city symbolized—even as he held up Berlin as proof of the failures of communism. The place of Kennedy's speech, therefore, was more than a simple backdrop or geographical location; it was a material means of persuasion.

"I am proud to come to this city," Kennedy began. He thanked his two

hosts, West Berlin mayor Willy Brandt and German chancellor Konrad Adenauer, for their leadership and commitment to "democracy and freedom and
progress." The president made it clear that he was here as a guest of the German people, to learn from them and identify himself with them, rather than
speak to them as president of the United States. Even as Kennedy acknowledged the service these men had rendered to West Berliners and the cause of
freedom worldwide, he also gestured toward the symbolic significance "this
city" held "throughout the world."

After these introductory remarks, the president fully departed from the
script Sorenson had prepared and turned instead to the lines he had written a
week earlier and practiced with Bundy on their descent into West Berlin that
morning. "Two thousand years ago the proudest boast was 'civis Romanus
sum' ['I am a citizen of Rome']. Today, in the world of freedom, the proudest boast is 'Ich bin ein Berliner' ['I am a citizen of Berlin']." With these two
sentences, Kennedy advanced arguments that would structure the rest of his
speech. First, he equated West Berliners with Roman citizens twenty centuries earlier. In the ancient world, Roman citizenship was highly coveted, a
status that provided legal rights and military protection by the most powerful
empire in the world. When Kennedy equated Roman citizenship with Berlin
citizenship, he argued that being a Berliner supplied the most cherished identity "in the world of freedom." To an audience who just eighteen years earlier
had been members of the Third Reich under Adolf Hitler, this was no small
shift. In fact, recall the USIA's recommendation that Kennedy use his public
statements to "welcome the Germans fully into the camp of civilized peoples
defending freedom."[106] By equating his current audience—Berliners—with
Roman citizens, the president suggested that this tiny landlocked city in the
middle of communist-controlled East Germany held the same celebrated status as the Roman Empire two thousand years earlier.

The president furthered his identification with Berliners through his sentence construction and verb usage in the phrase, "Ich bin ein Berliner"—a
statement that received much popular press coverage for years after Kennedy's trip to West Berlin. Because German grammatical rules do not require an
indefinite article (ein) before the verbs sein (to be), bleiben (to remain), and
werden (to become), some popular press outlets in Germany and the United
States (including the New York Times and Newsweek) later reported that Kennedy's audience interpreted this statement as "I am a jelly doughnut" because
of a cream-filled pastry some called a Berliner.[107] However, Kennedy used
the phrase ein Berliner metaphorically as a "symbolic expression of solidarity
with West Berlin, with America's Berlin. It was a rhetorical intensification
of a symbolic common identity linking Americans and Berliners."[108] Iden-

tification is, as Kenneth Burke observes, the recognition of shared interests, principles, and ideologies between two parties.[109] In this particular instance, Kennedy aligned himself, the United States, and the "world of freedom" with citizens of Berlin and their shared struggle to defend democracy against the spread of Soviet communism. Although much of this struggle was metaphorical and ideological in nature, the citizens of West Berlin were foot soldiers on the front lines of the Cold War.

Continuing his extemporaneous performance in front of the roaring crowd, the president offered a striking juxtaposition of the differences between democracy and communism and reinforced a crucial point: the best way to see the evils of the Soviet system was to visit Berlin in person.

> There are many people in the world who really don't understand, or say they don't, what is the great issue between the free world and the Communist world. Let them come to Berlin. There are some who say that communism is the wave of the future. Let them come to Berlin. And there are some who say in Europe and elsewhere we can work with the Communists. Let them come to Berlin. And there are even a few who say that it is true that communism is an evil system, but it permits us to make economic progress. *Lass' sie nach Berlin kommen*. Let them come to Berlin.

In this passage, the president told his audience again and again that the city of Berlin itself offered sufficient evidence to refute arguments for appeasement or détente. The succession of four separate "There are . . ." statements offered specific arguments in support of (or deference toward) Soviet communism followed by the same response: "Let them come to Berlin." This combination of repetition and parallelism amplified the absurdity of an indifferent attitude toward communism even as it revealed one piece of evidence powerful enough to refute all claims in support of communism: the city of West Berlin itself. On four separate occasions—the last spoken first in German and then in English—the president supplied the city of West Berlin as his most powerful form of evidence. "This city" offered physical proof of the stark differences between democracy and communism.

The president continued by speaking to Berliners on behalf of the US public. "I want to say, on behalf of my countrymen, who live many miles away on the other side of the Atlantic, who are far distant from you, that they take the greatest pride that they have been able to share with you, even from a distance, the story of the last 18 years." In this sentence, Kennedy singled out the US public's relationship with citizens of West Berlin. The deictic pronoun "you" was a form of direct address, singling out each and every member of his audience. Although US citizens were "far distant" from West Berliners and separated by continents and the Atlantic Ocean, Kennedy argued that the United States and the city of Berlin were linked metaphorically, relationally, and ideologically. A shared commitment to individual liberty transcended time and space. "I know of no town, no city, that has been besieged for 18 years that still lives with the vitality and the force, and the hope and the determination of the city of West Berlin," he said. Here, Kennedy elevated "the city of West Berlin" as a model for the rest of the world. He continued: "You live in a defended island of freedom, but your life is part of the main," the president stated. This was a clear reference to John Donne's meditation, "No man is an island, entire of itself, every man is a piece of the continent, a part of the main."[110] Here, the president implied that citizens of Berlin and the city itself were linked to the larger "Free World." This metaphor also described the city of West Berlin as "a defended island of freedom" standing tall and proud in the midst of a communist sea.

Kennedy built off this individual and collective identity when he asked his audience to look beyond their immediate spatial and temporal present and toward a brighter future:

> So let me ask you, as I close, to lift your eyes beyond the dangers of today, to the hopes of tomorrow, beyond the freedom merely of this city of Berlin, or your country of Germany, to the advance of freedom everywhere, beyond the wall to the day of peace with justice, beyond yourselves and ourselves to all mankind.

This passage offered a stylistic counterpart to the "There are some. . . . Let them come to Berlin" repetition at the beginning of Kennedy's address. Where Kennedy had used that progression to shift the focus from abstract arguments to the immediate physical situation, the president now used references to space and time to extend his argument from the local to the global. Each grouping or phrase moved beyond the immediate to the imaginary. This stylistic device of *gradatio* suggested a spatial and temporal progression toward the ultimate goal: a city, country, and world united and finally free from communism. These four groupings also underscored the link between West Berliners' lived experience and the symbolic work their struggle accomplished for the rest of the world. "Lift your eyes" suggested a deliberate looking up and beyond from one thing and toward another. Although their immediate physical situation offered powerful evidence for the evils of communist rule, the president asked his audience to look toward and hope for what they could not see. This also reminded the audience of their symbolic status for the rest of the world—and that their struggle was not in vain. In fact, their daily experiences accomplished important rhetorical work on the "front lines" of the ideological Cold War. The "dangers of today" would be eclipsed by the "hopes of tomorrow." Attaining freedom for "this city of Berlin" and "your country of Germany" would also contribute to the "advance of freedom everywhere." Looking "beyond the wall" and toward "the day of peace with justice" encouraged West Berliners to aspire for more than their individual freedom—this was a struggle for "all mankind."

Kennedy continued this gradual progression from specific to general when he said, "Freedom is indivisible, and when one man is enslaved, all are not free. When all are free, then we can look forward to that day when this city will be joined as one and this country and this great Continent of Europe in a peaceful and hopeful globe." He proceeded from one to many, suggesting that the limitation of freedom anywhere threatened freedom everywhere. This causal argument suggested that the limitation of freedom anywhere threatened freedom everywhere. But when "all" were free—including the East Berliners watching Kennedy on television on the other side of the wall—West Berliners, US citizens, and all freedom-loving nations could anticipate the reunification of Berlin, Germany, and Europe. Kennedy predicted that when "that day"—a temporal moment hoped for but not seen—finally arrived, "the people of West Berlin can take sober satisfaction in the fact that they were in the front lines for almost two decades." This language yet again constructed West Berlin as the final outpost of freedom on the "front lines" of the Cold War battlefield. Their bravery and sacrifice, the president intimated, would not go unrecognized or unrewarded. They were the true soldiers of the Cold War.

In the final sentence of his address, the president returned to his opening declaration that the proudest boast in the world of freedom was to be called a citizen of Berlin. "All free men, wherever they may live, are citizens of Berlin, and, therefore, as a free man, I take pride in the words 'Ich bin ein Berliner.'" From the moment Kennedy uttered this line, it became the most celebrated line of his entire address. It is important to stress here that the president did not base his status as a "free man" upon his US citizenship or position as president of the United States. Instead, Kennedy suggested that his affiliation with the "Free World" was possible because he, too, identified as a citizen of Berlin.

The crowd's immediate reaction was electric. Arthur M. Schlesinger later wrote that the crowd "shook itself and rose and roared like an animal. . . . The hysteria spread almost visibly through the square. Kennedy was first exhilarated, then disturbed; he felt, as he remarked on his return, that if he had said, 'March to the wall—tear it down,' his listeners would have marched."[111] Sorenson called Kennedy's speech in West Berlin "one of his best, and most remembered—a speech designed to salute the citizens of West Berlin for their

courage and patience in peacefully maintaining an island of freedom amid
a sea of Communist military and political power."[112] White House advisor
Ken O'Donnell later suggested that the president's personal interaction with
West Berliners and his own personal encounter with the Berlin Wall had
a profound effect on his address outside West Berlin's City Hall. "Kennedy
could not prevent himself from saying what his heart wanted him to say,"
O'Donnell wrote. "He was carried away by the courage of the West Berliners,
and shocked by the sight of the Berlin Wall that he had seen that morning,
and he had to tell the people how he felt about them."[113] Moved as he was by
the West Berliners and his personal encounter with the wall, Kennedy's extemporaneous performance also caused a bit of a scramble as White House
advisors tried to backtrack his disparaging remarks about the Soviet Union.
As Sorenson later recalled, Bundy told him they "need[ed] to correct the
tenor of the speech, particularly its reference to the West's inability to work
with the Communists, weeks before negotiations were to begin in Moscow
on the nuclear test ban treaty." To do this, Bundy and Sorenson "inserted new
material into his afternoon speech to students at the Free University of Berlin,
talking about the winds of change blowing over the Iron Curtain and the rest
of the world."[114]

After a lunch at City Hall and his speech at the Free University, Kennedy
made one more stop at the US military headquarters in West Berlin before
proceeding to the airport. "Plans to give the American President a fitting reception were carefully laid, but the high-spirited warmth of the crowds was
not on the program," reported the *New York Times*. "As the Presidential plane
rose from Tegel Airport Wednesday evening, [Chancellor] Adenauer was
heard to murmur, 'The response of the German people—I was amazed.'"[115]
Aboard Air Force One en route to Ireland, the president "was glowing from
his reception," Sorenson later recalled. "It would make Americans recognize
that their efforts and risks had been appreciated, he said." Kennedy also said
that he would leave a note for his successor "to be opened at the time of some
discouragement": "Go to Germany." As he told Sorenson, "We'll never have
another day like this one as long as we live."[116]

Public Response

In the days and weeks after Kennedy's visit to West Berlin, numerous government officials, press outlets, and public opinion surveys described the president's performance as a remarkable success. This success was due in no small
part to how Kennedy and other US officials deployed the city of West Berlin

as the president's most powerful piece of evidence. In this instance, place really was everything.

To West Berliners, Kennedy's physical presence in the city underscored its symbolic significance for the rest of the Free World. The American president had traveled behind enemy lines to demonstrate the United States' solidarity with them. As Brandt wrote to Kennedy, "You will have seen yourself how much this occasion meant to my fellow-citizens and to myself and how intense are the feelings of gratitude and of confidence in you that found expression during that memorable day."[117] In his memoir years later, Brandt offered this further reflection: "The Berliners fêted him as something more than a powerful friend and guarantor of their freedom. Their homage contained an element of gratitude towards a former enemy who was demonstrating to the Germans that the West's foremost power had made its peace with them—that they had rejoined the family of nations."[118] US ambassador to Germany George McGhee reported that a "good part of [the] Fed[eral] Rep[ublic of Germany] spent June 26 watching television of President's visit to Berlin. Events were rebroadcast and summarized on TV and radio and some persons viewed or listened [a] second or even third time."[119] According to one estimate, "more than 7-1/2 million television sets brought [the] personality of [the] president and [the] effect of his dynamic expressions of assurance and guarantees of freedom" into homes throughout the city. However, it was hard to estimate the number of viewers, McGhee explained, because there were "large numbers of guests who were invited into private homes to watch president's tour and because of thousands more who stood in television salesrooms throughout Federal Republic and West Berlin in watching with almost hypnotic fascination."[120]

The president's identification of himself—and the United States—with Berlin and its citizens dominated press accounts of the trip. "Women and even men wept as the chief executive of the world's most powerful free nation told them that the proudest thing he could say is 'I am a Berliner,'" wrote two reporters who were present in the crowd. "The effect of his words was electric. He spoke the language Berliners understood."[121] The US embassy in Bonn reported that the German press "rejoiced at fact that president had personally identified himself with Berlin."[122] *Deutsche Zeitung*, a German newspaper in Cologne, wrote that "President Kennedy's symbolic words '*Ich bin ein Berliner*' opened a new chapter of German-American relations."[123] Writing from the US Consul in Munich, one State Department official noted that Kennedy's visit represented a "watershed in German-American relations." A major reason for this dramatic shift was the personal encounter between the president of the United States and the German citizenry. "He has left behind

deeper impressions than many visitors who entered in person or family circles," noted one editorial published in *Abendzeitung*. "He entered the houses
of most Germans only through newspapers, radio, and television, and still he
dramatically touched our lives."[124] According to Robert H. Estabrook of the
Washington Post, "the response in Berlin was far more than [simple applause],
and no one who witnessed it will soon forget it. This was the outpouring of
a whole people, who have learned something about war and the meaning of
freedom. Mr. Kennedy was a symbol."[125]

   To the larger watching world, Kennedy's visit—and the enthusiastic reaction he received from West Berliners—demonstrated a clear political triumph
for the "Free World." In Copenhagen, US officials detailed the widespread
press treatment of the president's trip to West Berlin, specifically noting the
widespread featuring of images depicting Kennedy's visit to the Brandenburg
Gate and touring the streets with German political officials.[126] The US embassy
in Ankara reported that the Turkish press stressed the "psychological impact
of [the] president's visit to Germany and West Berlin" and "viewed it as [a]
valuable success for [the] Atlantic community and Free World."[127] In Portu-
gal, US embassy officials reported that Kennedy's trip received "extensive and
complimentary coverage from Lisbon press," which emphasized "explosive
popular enthusiasm for President and US and have shown in graphic detail
[the] high degree [of] German-American good will generated by [the] visit."
According to editorials published in the Lisbon press, the visit "strengthened
[W]estern unity and underlined [the] significance of [the] Atlantic community." Moreover, these accounts noted that the president's "hard words" on
communism provided "needed clarity" to the US position.[128]

   And yet, perhaps the most compelling argument for analyzing Kennedy's presence in West Berlin as a Cold War psychological campaign was the
response it generated from the Soviet premier himself. Two days after the
American president's triumphal procession through the streets of West Berlin, Nikita Khrushchev made a trip to the other half of the city. Although the
publicly stated reason for the trip was the occasion of East German leader
Walter Ulbricht's seventieth birthday, it was designed as a clear countermove
to Kennedy's visit to West Berlin.[129] As Murrey Mardner of the *Washington
Post* observed, "Both leaders, grappling with challenges to their programs
on either side of the Berlin Wall, are trying to exhibit vitality, cohesion and
forward momentum in their own spheres of influence."[130] East German officials asked Western correspondents to report the "triumphal drive" of Khrushchev in East Berlin but, as Larry Rue of the *Chicago Tribune* explained, "to
those who had witnessed the overwhelming reception of President Kennedy
by West Berliners Wednesday, Khrushchev's welcome in East Berlin today

did not even attain the level of an anti-climax."[131] In a special report from East Berlin, *Washington Post* correspondent Katharine Clark reported that although Khrushchev "did his Communist best to match the recent Kennedy visit to West Berlin . . . he failed." Because the "intensity of Mr. Kennedy's understanding of [Berliners'] emotional feelings over the plight of their city surprised many observers and infuriated the East German Communists," the Soviet premier's visit "was intended to give them a psychological lift. But while his arrival pleased Communist [leaders] it obviously did not impress Berliners of either East or West."[132] Khrushchev's immediate attempt to counteract the president's triumph in West Berlin offers the best evidence for its rhetorical effectiveness. During a cold war waged with words and images as symbolic weapons, Kennedy's presidential presence in place was a direct assault on the "front lines"—a battle that Khrushchev could not afford to lose.[133]

Conclusion

John F. Kennedy's visit to West Berlin on June 26, 1963, stands as a remarkable example of how chief executives use the global rhetorical presidency to activate the power of place—and, at the same time, how US presidents deployed the symbolism of place to address and constitute a Cold War global imaginary. To be sure, the president's oratorical performance at the Rudolph Wilde Platz was memorable and gripping, but to focus exclusively on Kennedy's verbal address is to miss a crucial aspect of the story. In fact, it was Kennedy's deliberate *place*ment—and the way the president deployed the symbolism of West Berlin as a rhetorical resource—that made all the difference. Going to Berlin also offered the president a chance to bolster his presidential ethos and foreign policy acumen on the world stage. "The President was seen as wholly successful in projecting his own image as that of a spirited, young and determined leader whose personal warmth and emotional qualities had previously been underestimated," explained a USIA report of European responses to the president's trip. "He was widely credited for having brought American feelings and intentions closer to the understanding of most West Europeans."[134] A public opinion survey in West Germany reported that 61 percent of respondents named Kennedy as "the political leader in the world as a whole" in whom West Germans had "the greatest confidence in the area of maintaining world peace." Eleven months earlier, only 14 percent selected Kennedy in the same question. Although the report was careful to avoid causal claims, it did note that "the very large shift of opinion on such a trend question suggests very strongly that much of the change is attributable to the visit."[135]

One of the most striking results of the president's tour of West Berlin is

how Kennedy's presence in place harnessed the memories and histories embedded in that location and, in so doing, established the city as a symbolic
"place of return" for future US presidents.[136] By going to Berlin, the president
tapped into these symbolic dimensions and further elevated the city as an
icon of democratic possibility. As Christa J. Olson writes, "commonplaces,
in whatever form they circulate, function primarily to help publics see themselves and envision their interconnections with the imagined community."[137]
In this instance, Kennedy activated the multifaceted dynamics of West Berlin
as place—location, container, network—to solidify the city as a representative symbol of the "Free World" within the larger Cold War global imaginary.
This elevation of West Berlin as a democratic icon was so successful that numerous other presidents returned to the same spot with the hope they could
emulate Kennedy's performance. Years later, Martin Hillenbrand, the deputy
chief of mission in West Berlin in 1963, noted how Kennedy's visit established
a rhetorical precedent. "It was absolutely part of the required drill that the
high-level visitor go to Berlin and repeat the American commitment to the
protection of the city," he recalled. "Every subsequent president has been in
exactly the same position. The problem that we have faced—parenthetically, I
might add this—with subsequent presidents was that Kennedy's visit to both
West Germany and to Berlin was such a triumphal thing that subsequent
presidents have always felt somehow or other that they had to duplicate it
at least."[138]

Examples of these rhetorical returns abound. In 1969, Richard Nixon told
West Berliners that it was "a very moving occasion . . . to travel through this
city and to realize again what Berlin means to all the people of the world."[139]
Similarly, Jimmy Carter reinforced the city's symbolic status for the West when
he compared Berlin to a "city on a hill" during a 1978 visit. "As a city of human
freedom, human hope, and human rights, Berlin is a light to the whole world;
a city on a hill—it cannot be hidden; the eyes of all people are upon you," he
said.[140] In 1982, Ronald Reagan reaffirmed the United States' commitment to
the city, declaring that "a[s] long as Berlin exists, there can be no doubt about
the hope for democracy." To conclude, Reagan channeled Kennedy's memory
directly: "We all remember John Kennedy's stirring words when he visited
Berlin. I can only add that we in America and in the West are still Berliners, too, and always will be."[141] Five years later, in what perhaps is the most
famous reappropriation of West Berlin after Kennedy's "Ich bin ein Berliner"
declaration, Reagan spoke in front of the Brandenburg Gate and uttered this
well-known line: "Mr. Gorbachev, tear down this wall!"[142]

Even after the wall fell, however, US presidents continued their pilgrim-
ages to Berlin to reaffirm the special relationship between the United States

and Germany. In 1994, William J. Clinton recounted the United States' ongoing commitment to the city and told the German people that *"Amerika steht an ihrer Seite, jetzt und fur immer.* America is on your side, now and forever."[143] Less than a year after 9/11, George W. Bush visited Berlin and addressed a special session of the German Bundestag, telling his audience that "the history of our time is written in the life of Berlin. . . . One American president came here to proudly call himself a citizen of Berlin. Another President dared the Soviets to tear down that wall. And on a night in November, Berliners took history into their hands and made your city whole."[144] In the remainder of his address, the president argued that the United States and Germany should support each other in the war on terror, just as they did during the Cold War. For Bush, speaking in Berlin provided him the opportunity to reactivate the US–West German alliance so central to US foreign policy against the Soviet Union.

Speaking in Berlin has also come to represent a presidential rite of passage. In 2008, then–US senator and Democratic presidential candidate Barack Obama delivered a major foreign policy speech in front of the Victory Column in the Tiergarten in Berlin. Although the Obama campaign wanted the senator to speak at the Brandenburg Gate, German chancellor Angela Merkel vocalized her opposition to this plan because, in the words of her spokesman, she did not want the national landmark to be used "as a campaign backdrop."[145] In his speech, Obama told a crowd of more than two hundred thousand Berliners: "I come to Berlin as so many of my countrymen have come before. Tonight, I speak to you not as a candidate for president, but as a citizen—a proud citizen of the United States, and a fellow citizen of the world."[146] Here Obama suggested that he and the rest of his audience were joined not just by their common identification with the city of Berlin, but as members of a global community. In 2013, Obama returned to Berlin as president and spoke in front of the Brandenburg Gate. Throughout his remarks, Obama used the location of his speech—and the symbolic associations of previous US presidential rhetoric in this place—to argue that "the tests of our time demand the same fighting spirit that defined Berlin a half-century ago." Kennedy's famous words delivered in this city, Obama said, were "timeless because they call upon us to care more about things than just our own self-comfort, about our own city, about our own country. They demand that we embrace the common endeavor of all humanity." To reinforce the point, Obama (re)appropriated Kennedy's "Ich bin ein Berliner" declaration for his twenty-first-century audience when he stated, "we are not only citizens of America or Germany, we are also citizens of the world. And our fates and fortunes are linked like never before."[147] Through his rhetoric in place, Obama attempted to bolster US foreign policy abroad by arguing that the United States (and the rest of the world) should consider how to achieve Kennedy's vision in a new era of globalization.

These examples of presidential returns to Berlin demonstrate how certain places shape and condition rhetorical action. For studies of the global rhetorical presidency more broadly, however, these instances also affirm the idea that US presidents—and the American people more broadly—gravitate toward places that affirm shared values and ideals. During Kennedy's visit, Berlin stood as a symbol of US determination, a place-as-container housing memories of America's enduring commitment and moral resolve against the spread of communism. Berlin, in other words, could stand as a symbol of American resolve—qualities Kennedy and other Cold War presidents were eager to display to the watching world. In an ideological contest that was simultaneously spatial and symbolic, West Berlin became the consummate rhetorical resource. Its geographical position constituted a literal outpost of freedom in the heart of enemy territory, representing the hope that democratic forces could infiltrate the Soviet Bloc. Berlin's historical progression from the epicenter of Nazi Germany to a bright symbol of democratic resolve continually reaffirmed the importance of US leadership on the global stage. It reminded the US public of what the nation had done and what it must continue to do to protect the "Free World." These repeated histories and memories also elevated Berlin as an aspirational example to the rest of the world. This connectivity linked Berlin to the rest of the "Free World," a network of peoples and nations who, although separated by physical allegiance, were united in their shared opposition to Soviet communism.

5

Nixon and the "Opening to China"

Our planning should be to maximize the positive value of this unique, historic moment—President Nixon's visit to a country which has been the "enemy" for more than twenty-five years. The news interest in this at home and around the world must not be underestimated. If, after having billed this as a "journey for peace," we do not follow through with reasonable news planning to exploit the acclaim the President has already received, we are being shortsighted in the extreme.

JOHN SCALI TO H. R. HALDEMAN, September 11, 1971[1]

Richard Nixon had a penchant for drama. A master of the political spectacle, he was obsessed with creating moments where he could dominate the Cold War stage. Early in his political career, Nixon embraced the role of a young, committed anticommunist who could articulate the stark image of the Cold War as a battle between good and evil, democracy and communism. In 1948, he gained national prominence for his testimony against Alger Hiss, the accused Russian spy. "Red-hunting was now the state religion," writes historian Rick Perlstein, and Nixon "spotted the chance to engineer his investiture as its pope."[2] And he succeeded, positioning himself and the Republican Party as the true defenders of American democracy.[3] This unapologetic stance put him on Eisenhower's short list for vice president two years later. As one campaign advisor recalled, "Eisenhower wanted above all a vice-presidential nominee with a demonstratable record of anti-Communism"—and Nixon was the man for the job.[4] As Eisenhower's vice president, Nixon undertook several "Good Will" tours of his own, positioning the United States as the natural defender of the "Free World." He also traveled behind enemy lines. In July 1959, he flew to the Soviet Union to attend the opening of the American Exhibition in Moscow, where he and Nikita Khrushchev held their famous "kitchen debate" about the future of capitalism versus communism.[5]

But even as Nixon toured the globe, there was one place that remained elusive: the PRC. After the 1949 Chinese Revolution and Mao Tse-tung's military victory over Chinese nationalist Chiang Kai-shek, many US politicians—Nixon included—mourned the "loss" of China to the communists. An enormous blow to US prestige, the move put "Red China" firmly in the Soviet camp. After the USSR and the PRC signed the "Sino-Soviet Treaty of Friendship, Alliance and Mutual Assistance" in February 1950 and the North Korean invasion of South Korea in July 1950, Republicans blamed the Truman administration for a rapidly increasing communist presence in Asia. Indeed, the Soviet support for communist-backed military actions in Korea and Vietnam further underscored the severity of the threat.[6] But on February 21, 1972, after twenty-two years of no formal diplomatic contact between the United States and the PRC, Richard Nixon became the first US president to set foot on Chinese soil. This move had been a long time in coming, the result of many months of back-channel messages, secret negotiations, and a president determined to use the trip for his own political gain. For Nixon, the visit was about much more than a renewal of diplomatic relations between two countries. It offered him the opportunity to go where no US president had gone before—and to do so on live television for the entire world to see.

Nixon's "Opening to China" looms large in US-centric narratives of the Cold War for at least three reasons. First, it offered a positive image of American presence abroad at a time when US military action in Vietnam, Laos, and Cambodia threatened to derail the United States' image as a force for good in the world. To a US public weary of the Vietnam War and the loss of national prestige on the world stage, Nixon's widely celebrated tour offered a strikingly different account of what American involvement in Asia might entail. Second, Nixon's visit displayed in vivid detail the idea that former ideological enemies could become strategic partners and even friends. But the final reason that the "Opening to China" continues to fascinate is because this is precisely what Nixon and other White House officials intended. Where most historical accounts focus on how the renewed US-China partnership shifted the balance of Cold War geopolitics, there is more to the story.[7] Recently declassified documents from the Nixon White House and US State Department reveal the ultimate purpose behind this trip: to create a televised political spectacle that would portray the president as a skilled diplomat, global leader, and clear frontrunner in the upcoming 1972 presidential election. In fact, these historical records suggest that the goal of elevating Nixon's personal prestige surpassed any hopes for a formal rapprochement with the PRC. Attending to these backstage, behind-the-scenes maneuvers reveals how the White House designed the "Opening to China" to allow one specific actor—Nixon himself—to use this historic occasion to elevate his own image on the world stage.

In this chapter, I detail how Nixon's 1972 visit to the PRC extended and expanded the boundaries of where US presidents could go, what they could do, and how they could control the media narrative of these global movements. Although numerous accounts of the "Opening to China" focus their attention on the geopolitical, historical, and diplomatic ramifications of the trip, my purpose here is not to recount every last detail of the trip. Instead, I focus on how Nixon and other US officials designed this moment to create a political spectacle that would simultaneously capture public attention, elevate his presidential image, distract from the quagmire of Vietnam, boost his re-election chances in November 1972, and feed his obsession with controlling the media landscape. Deeply cognizant of the widespread interest in the trip from the US public and the rest of the world, US officials carefully orchestrated the words Nixon would utter and the moves he would make. Because of recent advances in communication technology and the ability of network television to transmit live footage of Nixon in China to audiences around the world, the president could see and be seen behind the mysterious "Bamboo Curtain,"[8] step into the highly controlled media spotlight, and know the entire world was watching.

China in the US Imaginary

As I have detailed in the preceding chapters, US presidents used their travels abroad to paint a picture of American global dominance during the Cold War. Their bodily movements to and through various regions accentuated the nation's ideological presence on the world stage. Even when they visited lands far removed from the general US public's imaginary, they made these places accessible and relatable to audiences at home and abroad. Nixon's visit to China is no exception. But where American audiences could reference images of the other places and regions aligned with the "West," China remained elusive, mysterious, and distant. Indeed, images of China throughout US history have bordered on the exotic, the sensual, the mysterious, the unknown. Portrayed as a land of the Oriental "other," it was often described as a place full of bounty and beauty, one ready and waiting for European conquest.[9] Despite China's rich and lengthy history, one that extends far beyond the comparably brief existence of the United States, US politicians and intellectuals followed Britain's example to frame the Chinese as Oriental "others" different and less than "Western," European ideals. The discursive creation of "the Orient" offered a "contrasting image, idea, personality, experience" to Europe and the "West."[10] As Oliver Turner contends, these "Western classifications of the global East as exotic, alluring and passive have traditionally provided the logic and rationale for imperial penetration and control."[11] For Chinese immigrants living in the United States, however, circulating discourses of Orientalism and white supremacy only reinforced their marginalized status and, as historian Ronald Takaki argues, this "status of racial inferiority assigned to the Chinese had been prefigured in the [B]lack and Indian past."[12] The 1882 passage of the Chinese Exclusion Act makes this fact plain. While on the surface lawmakers presented the legislation as designed to prevent Chinese immigrants from overwhelming the American workforce, it was a blatant act of white supremacy, an attempt to keep anyone out of the country who did not resemble what "true Americans" looked like.[13]

Even as the United States was quick to exclude the Chinese laborers under the guise of protecting American interests, the nation also embraced any opportunity to profit monetarily from a trading relationship with China. At the dawn of the twentieth century—and at the same time that Frederick Jackson Turner noted that the "Frontier Thesis" should be extended to the global stage and William McKinley began contemplating a presidential visit to Cuba— Secretary of State John Hay initiated the first "Open Door" policy toward China, a move that established opportunities for economic trade between China and other nations, including the United States, Great Britain, France, Russia, Germany, and Japan. In truth, these policies were designed to give the United States access to China's wealth and resources—and to beat their European rivals to the punch. The mythic narrative of American exceptionalism, rugged individualism, capitalism, and westward expansion continued across the Pacific Ocean. After the violent Boxer Uprising against the Qing dynasty in 1899–1901 and the formal creation of the Republic of China in 1912, the United States adopted a paternalistic, benevolent gaze toward China and its evolution from a centuries-old imperial dynasty to a democracy. Americans also began to compare this new country—one made possible because of a political revolution against a dynastic state—against the origins, customs, and ideologies of their own. The American Revolution was the model revolution, the US political structure was the gold standard, and any nation hoping to achieve political freedom would do well to follow this example. In his message formally recognizing China as a legitimate government, Woodrow Wilson welcomed "the new China" and asserted "that in perfecting a republican form of government the Chinese nation will attain to the highest degree of development and well-being."[14] In Wilson's estimation, China's intentional pursuit of a true democracy would enable them to enter the community of "civilized" nations.

But where themes of paternalism, American exceptionalism, and missionary-style diplomacy dominated US-Chinese relations during the first half of the twentieth century, the 1949 Chinese Revolution shattered the United States' self-appointed role as a benevolent benefactor to a fledgling democracy. At the time, the Truman administration faced a choice between recognizing the new communist state or supporting Chiang Kai-shek, who had retreated to Taiwan (or, as US officials often referred to it, Formosa). Faced with escalating tensions with the Soviet Union, a conservative "China bloc" calling for support for the "democratic" Republic of China, and Mc-Carthy's "Red Scare," the president was stuck. After the Korean War broke out in June 1950, US officials were faced with compelling evidence that communism was spreading through Asia, and a hard stance against "Red China" seemed to be the only option.[15]

From 1949 on, US officials described the PRC as "Red China," a country "lost" to communism. Richard Nixon played a pivotal role in creating and sustaining this narrative. A central member and instigator of the American anticommunist crusade, Nixon was "the Republican hatchet man on China" for nearly two decades.[16] In 1953, he stated that "as we look at China on the map, we can see that China is the basic cause of all our troubles in Asia. If China had not gone Communist, there would be no war in Indochina, no war in Malaya."[17] Although Nixon's reference here was to the French-Indochina War, this argument would continue long after the 1954 Geneva Conference. In fact, a primary reason for sending US troops to South Vietnam was the threat "Red China" posed to the rest of the Asian continent.[18] And yet, as Denise M. Bostdorff demonstrates in remarkable detail, Nixon's rhetoric about China slowly evolved between 1952 to 1971 because, "like all good politicians, [Nixon] hedged his claims in preparation for the possibility that he might someday need to change his position."[19] In fact, during the 1960 presidential campaign, Nixon articulated a flexible rhetoric on China, simultaneously denouncing "Red China" while also leaving open the possibility that new diplomatic relations between the US and the PRC could emerge in the right circumstances.

But it was his 1967 essay in *Foreign Affairs* that signaled a monumental shift in how Nixon conceived of the United States' relationship with the PRC. To frame his argument, Nixon first reaffirmed the United States' role of protector and defender of democracies in Asia. The US military presence in Vietnam had provided "a shield behind which the anti-communist forces [in Indonesia] found the courage and capacity to . . . rescue their country from the Chinese orbit" and "diverted Peking from such other potential targets [such] as India, Thailand and Malaysia."[20] But one of the "legacies of Viet Nam" would be a "deep reluctance on the part of the United States to become involved once again in a similar intervention on a similar basis."[21] It was in the United States' best interest, Nixon argued, to consider how the country might begin diplomatic relations with PRC so as to prevent another armed conflict. "We simply cannot afford to leave China forever outside the family of nations, there to nurture its fantasies, cherish its hates and threaten its neighbors." Instead, the US should aim to "induce change . . . to persuade China that it *must* change."[22] And yet, even as Nixon presented the case for rapprochement

as based in US interests and suggested that the nation's role as "world police-
man" would be "limited in the future," he subtly reaffirmed the United States'
position of global superiority and hegemony—and used decidedly racist ter-
minology to do so:[23]

> Dealing with Red China is something like trying to cope with the more explo-
> sive ghetto elements in our own country. In each case a potentially destruc-
> tive force has to be curbed; in each case an outlaw element has to be brought
> within the law; in each case dialogues have to be opened; in each case aggres-
> sion has to be restrained while education proceeds; and, not least, in neither
> case can we afford to let those now self-exiled from society stay exiled forever.
> We have to proceed with an urgency born of necessity and a patience born of
> realism, moving step by calculated step toward the final goal.[24]

The contest to determine which Cold War superpower would influence Asia
had already begun, Nixon said. "Without turning our backs on Europe," he
concluded, "we have now to reach out westward to the East, and to fashion
the sinews of a Pacific community."[25] In Nixon's telling, extending American
influence and ideology to "Red China" was the next logical step in the insatiable quest to conquer the western frontier—even if that meant crossing
the Pacific Ocean and negotiating with communist outlaws in dire need of
American education and civilization. These ideas, first expressed in the pages
of an elite academic journal, would begin to shape US foreign policy just two
years later.

The Opening Gambit

From the moment he took office, Nixon set the stage for what would become
a hallmark of his presidency. Although the formal "Opening to China" would
not occur until February 1972, the beginnings of this Cold War diplomatic
revolution can be traced back to Nixon's first day in office. In his inaugural
address, Nixon described his administration's foreign policy as one directed
toward "an open world—open to ideas, open to exchange of goods and people—a world in which no people, great or small, will live in angry isolation."[26]
Less than two weeks later, the president directed his national security advisor,
Henry Kissinger, to "give every encouragement to the attitude that the administration was exploring possibilities of rapprochement with the Chinese."[27]
At the time, Kissinger could hardly believe his ears, scoffing to one deputy
that Nixon had "taken leave of reality." In time, however, senior administration officials would recognize the strategic nature of the move. As General
Alexander Haig Jr. later recalled, the normalization of relations would be a

positive step "for our relations with the U.S.S.R., the rest of the world, and the political opposition in the United States."[28] For years, the United States had been concerned with the rising influence of two communist powers in Asia: the Soviet Union and the PRC. But after the Sino-Soviet split over ideological differences and Khrushchev's call for "peaceful coexistence" with the United States, US officials had to contend with two communist powers in Asia intent on the domination of the other.[29] Normalizing relations with the Chinese would shift the balance of power away from the Soviet Union and toward the United States.[30] White House officials also believed that renewed US-China relations could shift the US public's focus away from Vietnam and demonstrate that a foreign policy of détente could actually succeed. To a US public wary of another overseas conflict and American intervention abroad more broadly, the "Opening to China" could offer a strikingly different picture of what Cold War diplomacy might look like. Instead of fighting a jungle war against the communists to defend a particular "way of life," Nixon's visit would articulate a new foreign policy, one designed "to build a lasting peace in the world."[31] And instead of measuring the success of the United States' Cold War global leadership based upon a victory in Vietnam, the president could offer an alternative image: the "Leader of the Free World" leading a diplomatic revolution from the capital of "Red China."[32]

Although many of the early back-channel exchanges between the United States and the PRC happened through unofficial means, Nixon made several purposeful public statements designed to defrost the chilly relationship between Washington and Peking. At a banquet in October 1970 for Romanian president Nicolae Ceaușescu, Nixon praised the communist leader for being one of few who had "good relations with the United States, good relations with the Soviet Union, and good relations with the People's Republic of China"—the first time a US president had referred to the PRC by name.[33] Four months later, Nixon used the same title in a radio address on US foreign policy, noting that "when the Government of the People's Republic of China is ready to engage in talks, it will find us receptive to agreements that further the legitimate national interests of China and its neighbors."[34] This time, Chou En-lai, the Chinese premier and Mao's deputy, took note and sent a back-channel message to Nixon stating that he was welcome to visit the PRC and continue an exchange of ideas.

As Nixon and Kissinger debated how to best approach the potential visit, PRC officials also discussed how they might utilize it to increase their own geopolitical strength. To them, "Beijing's opening to America" would encourage a withdrawal of US troops in North Vietnam and convince Nixon that the Soviet threat was in Europe, not Asia.[35] In April 1970, PRC officials invited the US table tennis team to visit Beijing, a move that signaled a willingness to continue a gradual rapprochement. But Chinese officials were also aware that this growing potential for a renewed friendship with the United States might offset the global balance of power in Vietnam. Their concern was that "China's détente with the United States might push Hanoi further into the arms of the Soviet Union, a development that would run counter to the very objective that underlay Beijing's opening to America."[36] Despite these concerns, however, Chou En-lai told the visiting American team that their "trip to China has opened the gate for friendly visits by people of the two countries."[37] After this successful instance of "Ping-Pong" diplomacy, Kissinger sent a message to the Chinese premier through Pakistani president Yahya Khan suggesting Nixon visit the PRC. Two weeks later, the White House received a formal invitation. The "Opening to China" had begun.

Choreographing the "Opening to China"

When Nixon announced his intention to visit the PRC, he described the trip as a "major development in our efforts to build a lasting peace in the world."[38] But the trip was about much more than achieving world peace or elevating the United States' stature in the Cold War global imaginary. Instead, White House officials designed the "Opening to China" as a political spectacle of epic proportions, one that would showcase Nixon's starring role as a visionary leader, global statesman, and emissary for peace on the world stage. Ever mindful of the upcoming 1972 presidential election, the White House wanted to get "maximum mileage" out of the trip.[39]

From the very beginning, senior US officials obsessed over how to amplify the president's political image and the historical nature of the trip. By going to the PRC, Nixon could solidify his foreign policy legacy and forever be known as the first US president to set foot on Chinese soil. Indeed, as one White House reporter recalled, Nixon "always liked to stress he was the first U.S. president to visit some foreign land."[40] White House officials also sought to coordinate the visit in ways that would overcome a perceived media bias against the president. In one conversation with Chou En-lai in January 1972, Haig stressed that because "most American journalists are shallow idiots" who concocted stories "from the immediate atmospherics of the situation," it was "crucial that there be no public embarrassment to the President as a result of his visit to Peking. It is in our mutual interest that the visit reinforce President Nixon's image as a world leader."[41] Chou, however, was not impressed and replied that Nixon's image should "evolve from his actions— not theatrics."[42] And it seems Chou struck a nerve, for Haig later clarified that he spoke "strictly in [the] context of affording enemies an opportunity to place obstacles in [the] way of our policies. Imagery has never been a factor in President's calculus for decisions as his past performance confirms."[43] In short, were Nixon primarily concerned with his public image, then he likely would be more popular with both global leaders and US citizens.

Given the historic nature of the visit to China, the White House developed and implemented a massive public relations campaign both before and during the trip. Archival documents make plain how the Nixon administration worked to ensure "the instantaneous transmission of color television images of Nixon's visit all over the world."[44] To both the president and his closest advisors, television would have the strongest effect, one they were determined to use for the president's political advantage. As Kissinger later recalled, Nixon and White House chief of staff H. R. Haldeman believed that written journalistic accounts did little to alter public opinion, but "television could change perceptions in a matter of minutes."[45] Because of this fact, the White House set its sights on ensuring that all television coverage of the "Opening to China" was favorable to Nixon. This was the plan from the very beginning: allow the US public to watch the spectacle of Nixon's visit unfold live on TV, as one might experience a Broadway show—but from the comfort of one's living room.

White House officials refused to leave any element of this political spectacle to chance, obsessing over how to control press coverage of the trip. One way they worked around the media filter was to broadcast the trip live to the US public as much as possible—despite the thirteen-hour time difference between Washington and Beijing. "It is critically important that we make available the maximum amount of picture[s] of the President in China so that we can wind up controlling, to a considerable extent, what appears on the screen," wrote former journalist and White House special advisor John Scali. "The more picture[s] we make available of the spectacle of the President in China, the more we wind up dominating in a positive way what appears."[46] Without this live coverage, Scali predicted, network producers would rely on delayed sound bites and "China experts" who would no doubt be critical of the president. Instead, Scali recommended that the administration "dominate" the news coverage by providing the networks with a cleverly packaged spectacle ready to air on live television.[47] Ultimately, the goal was to use this moment to capitalize on the "sheer drama of the President's visit to Peking," Scali wrote, since "a prudent man would plan on this as the big 'plus' as the President faces re-election."[48] The president's trip to China, he predicted, would be "one of the great publicity coups of all time."[49]

To capitalize on the "sheer drama" of the president's trip, White House officials scheduled all major events—arrivals, departures, banquets, tours of cultural landmarks—to align with the morning or evening news cycle back in the United States. This would ensure that

> Richard Nixon, the man, would dominate the television screens back home like no public figure has ever done before. No network could resist carrying it live because of the sheer drama. In addition, the availability of this "live" coverage would guarantee that [it] would become the backbone of any special that was scheduled. Furthermore, the prospect that viewers back home could see the President "live" from Peking would ensure huge audiences—far, far greater than any hour-long special put together earlier in more leisurely fashion as a wrap up of his activities of the previous day.[50]

Because of the historic nature of the trip, Scali predicted that this live featuring of Nixon in China would be worth "millions and millions of extra viewers. . . . Viewers will want to be present in front of their television screens for the first 'live' broadcasts from Peking."[51] This opportunity was "a press agent's dream," one that would not come again. As such, it was worth a monetary investment. "I do not know what we will have to 'pay' the Chinese in order to get the press arrangements we want," Scali wrote to Haldeman. "But, I suggest that it is worth the cost because of the result we can help guarantee— unprecedented, positive exposure for the President in an election year."[52] The construction of this political spectacle was about Nixon, and Nixon alone.

But to make this live television coverage possible, the White House had to convince the Chinese to embrace technological change. Due to what Nixon press secretary Ron Ziegler described as "China's inadequate internal communications network," it was impossible to transmit live television feeds from Peking to the rest of the world.[53] The only solution, explained senior White House communication officials, was to build a ground satellite station in Peking. This proposed station would provide space for a network pool production center and allow news outlets to transmit live footage, still images, and written copy to US audiences and the rest of the world in an instant. But without this ground station, all content would have to be flown to Hong Kong, Seoul, or Tokyo to be processed, edited, and sent via satellite to New York. Overall, this delay in transmission would be anywhere between eighteen and twenty-four hours.[54] Even more concerning for Nixon, however, was the fact that this time delay would mean that the "first television pictures and [the] majority of [the] trip coverage [that] would be provided first [would be] by foreign news representatives either already in Peking or accredited by [the] Chinese for [the] visit."[55] It also "almost certainly would arouse [a] storm of protests from [the] American press which would charge [that the] President, because of weakness, did not insist on adequate communications to cover [this] highly important visit for [the] American people."[56] White House press secretary Ron Ziegler told Haig that the only option was to set up a ground station, since live television coverage "could have profound impact on the American people and the world, and due to the isolation of China for the past twenty-five years would take on the drama similar to live coverage of the moon walk."[57]

After lengthy negotiations between Kissinger and his Chinese counterparts, PRC officials approved visas for eighty-seven US journalists and several dozen technicians.[58] The task of assigning these coveted spots fell to the White House press secretary—with direct involvement from Nixon himself. The president saw this trip as an opportunity to reward journalists he considered "friendly" to the administration and to punish those he characterized as his political enemies. Initially, he refused to let anyone from the New York Times or the Washington Post accompany him on the trip—an ultimatum his staff finally convinced him to surrender after much coaxing.[59] Ultimately, forty-four visas were allotted to print journalists and photographers, and forty-three were given to broadcast news media. With the additional media technicians sent to China to construct the network ground station, broadcast representatives outnumbered the print press by almost three to one.[60] As Ron Ziegler told a UPI reporter at one point, the trip to China was, after all, "a picture story."[61]

There were two press contingents, however, that almost got left behind: the official White House photographer and representatives from the USIA. After the highly coveted slots had been doled out to members of the White House press corps, administration officials realized that none had been set aside for the president's own photographer or the nation's global propaganda arm. In a memorandum to Haig, White House deputy press secretary Les Janka argued that "a good case can be made, on foreign policy grounds, for including a minimum representation for USIA," whose coverage would be fast, global, and—most likely—positive. It would give the non-American, foreign-language press an alternative to possible propaganda coming from Radio Peking or the New China News Agency. Finally, the USIA would provide good materials for producing the historical archive—and, ultimately, the public's experience of the president's visit.[62] Although the network ground station would allow US audiences to witness Nixon's "Opening to China" in real time, the administration could not control how non-US press outlets would cover the trip. What they could dictate, however, was USIA coverage and how the agency distributed related materials in the weeks and months to come. Such coverage would also elevate the president's image leading up to the 1972 presidential election.

As the White House considered how to best transmit the president's visit to US audiences, officials also sought to capitalize on the international media's interest—obsession, even—with the "Opening to China." Twenty-two national networks associated with the Eurovision Broadcasting Company applied to cover the president's trip, and network executives agreed that if the Chinese did not approve the American ground station, Eurovision would ask for their own. "Europeans firmly believe Peking would not have agreed to the Nixon visit unless it had also made a decision to permit substantial television and written news coverage," wrote Vittorio Boni, the chairman of Eurovision, to Scali. There was "intense European interest in television coverage of the President's visit," Boni explained, predicting that live coverage of Nixon's tour would "attract more viewers in Europe than did the Apollo first moon walk."[63] This widespread global interest also extended beyond Western Europe. The same day Nixon touched down in the PRC, State Department officials reported that Intervision, the East European counterpart of Eurovision, would transmit live satellite coverage of the president's visit throughout the USSR, Bulgaria, Czechoslovakia, the GDR (East Germany), Hungary, Romania, and Poland. Together, these Eastern European countries made up a viewing audience of 114 million people, where the audience in Western Europe was estimated at 250 million people.[64] State Department officials also carefully monitored media preparations in Asia, focusing particularly on reporting from outlets in North Vietnam, South Vietnam, the ROK, Japan, Taiwan, the PRC, and the Philippines.[65] As with previous presidential trips abroad, US officials were determined to use the president's visit to reaffirm the United States' leadership role in the world. This time, however, they had to contend with an unpopular war in South Asia. The "Opening to China" provided the perfect opportunity to redirect the global public away from the quagmire of Vietnam and showcase the United States' commitment to deescalating tensions on the Cold War global stage.

By the time the president left for the PRC, White House officials had choreographed every detail of the trip and arranged the best press coverage possible. In fact, they suggested that Nixon and journalists covering the trip each had a role to play in this historic "Opening to China." In talking points prepared for a meeting Nixon would hold with the White House press pool just prior to landing in the PRC, officials suggested that the president should frame journalists as strategic partners. "You both have a task in opening the connections between these two countries. . . . You want the press to know that you consider their role critical to the success of this visit. The press is indeed the eyes and ears of the American people as a new world is opened to America."[66] The unstated premise here was, of course, the fact that Nixon was dependent upon this sustained media coverage. Only they could ensure that this dramatic political spectacle imagined, designed, and enacted by the president himself would be seen, heard, and experienced by audiences at home and abroad.

"The Week That Changed the World"

On February 17, 1972, President and Mrs. Nixon walked onto the South Lawn of the White House, where a crowd of eight thousand people waited to bid them farewell.[67] After shaking hands with members of Congress and other senior US officials, Nixon declared this undertaking to be a "historic mission" and "a journey for peace," one he hoped would bring about "a much safer world." If he could write a postscript for this trip, Nixon concluded, "it would be the words on the plaque which was left on the moon by our first astronauts when they landed there: 'We came in peace for all mankind.'"[68] Ten days later, in a toast to Chinese officials on his final night in China, the president declared: "This magnificent banquet marks the end of our stay in the People's Republic of China. We have been here a week. This was the week that changed the world."[69] And Nixon had reason to celebrate. Where previous US presidents relied on harsh rhetoric characterizing "Red China" as a communist foe, Nixon went behind the "Bamboo Curtain" and showed the nation and the world that the United States was willing to work with a former adversary. As the administration had hoped for during its planning of the trip, all three news networks (ABC, CBS, NBC) featured live programming of the president's movements, sightseeing tours, and formal remarks each morning and evening. This vivid visual display of the president of the United States traveling to and moving throughout the PRC made the country visible, accessible, and tangible to the American public watching at home.

In what follows, I highlight five major scenes from the president's trip that the White House designed for Nixon's political advantage. As will become clear, White House officials—and the president himself—saw the trip as a means to a particular end. Although this dramatic encounter between a pro-democracy US president and devout Chinese communists would shift the power balance in Asia, it also gave Nixon a first-term legacy that he hoped would both cement his reelection and ensure that history would remember him as the president who opened the East to the West.

THE DEPARTURE

Although the president left Washington, DC, on February 17, he did not arrive in Peking until four days later. Doctors advised against traveling without adequate rest, and no doubt Nixon's staff wanted to avoid any appearance of a haggard American president with a five o'clock shadow—an image that still haunted Nixon from his first debate with John F. Kennedy in 1960. Instead, Air Force One (which Nixon christened the *Spirit of '76* during his time in office) stopped first in Hawaii and then in Guam. This gradual progression across the Pacific Ocean intensified the dramatic appeal, the feeling that this was a historic journey to an unknown, foreign land. As he flew from Washington to Hawaii, Nixon recorded that he felt "we were embarking on a voyage of philosophical discovery as uncertain, and in some respects as perilous, as the voyages of geographical discovery of a much earlier time." To the US public watching at home, there was also some "ingredient of excitement about the boldness of the move, and [about] visiting a land that was unknown to so many Americans."[70] The press also reflected this sense of anticipation. NBC's John Chancellor described their final destination as a "mysterious domain across the sea about which we know very little. . . . This is a very old fashioned assignment for reporters to go to a place where your countrymen have not been, to tell a little how it smells and tastes and feels. . . . American reporters can't go to the moon yet, but life in China is the last great uncovered story on the planet."[71]

Archival speech drafts prepared for Nixon's departure statements reflected similar themes of exploration, discovery, and missionary-style diplomacy.[72] In remarks prepared for the departure ceremonies in Hawaii, speechwriters suggested that the president reference Theodore Roosevelt's 1905 prediction that "our history will be more determined by our position on the Pacific facing China than by our position on the Atlantic facing Europe." It would be appropriate, the draft continued, "that the last American State we visit on this journey is the westernmost American State, the one with the closest historic and cultural ties to the great peoples of Asia." The president would ask his audience for their "support" and "prayers—that our mission will be a success, so that this greatest of oceans can truly be what its name portends—a sea of peace for all peoples."[73] White House speechwriters also suggested that Nixon invoke the memory of Ferdinand Magellan, the Portuguese explorer whose voyage to the East Indies resulted in the first circumnavigation of the earth, in remarks prepared for a stop in Guam. "If, as historians believe, Magellan did stop at Guam on his voyage around the world," Nixon would begin, "this island's involvement with historic journeys and relations of East and West now dates back four and a half centuries." It was fitting, the president would continue, that "Guam should be the home soil from which we take our departure on this journey for peace—this first visit of an American President to the People's Republic of China. We are embarked, as Magellan was, on a voyage of discovery. He proved that the world was one round globe; we seek to prove that all the nations around it are one indivisible community."[74] Although Nixon underlined this specific passage on his copy of the draft remarks, he did not use the reference to Magellan. Instead, he stressed the historic nature of his own visit to China. "I would hope that all of you here today would join me in this prayer," Nixon said, "that with this trip to China a new day may begin for the whole world."[75] While the president avoided these historical allusions to European and American exploration, the numerous archival references to geographical discovery demonstrate how the White House understood Nixon's visit as a significant milestone in the relationship between West and East.

As the US public awaited Nixon's arrival in the PRC, American journalists tried to articulate just how radical this diplomatic move was. "When Mr. Nixon arrives in Peking," reported one host of the NBC *Nightly News*, "it'll mark one of the most drastic and dramatic about faces in the history of American foreign policy."[76] ABC's Al Smith declared the trip a "short step for one American, but a giant step in foreign policy for Americankind."[77] Journalist Bill Moyers explained that Nixon made a "radical" shift in his foreign policy toward the PRC and argued that his trip to China was significant due to the president's "dramatic reversal" from being a "champion" of a tough stance on "Red China" early in his political career.[78] It was for this reason, ABC's Harry Reasoner explained, that Nixon was the only one who could undertake this "dramatic journey."

> If we had recognized the fact of Mao's successful revolution in 1949, a lot of things might've been different and more peaceful in the years since. Well, that's wishful thinking, but at least Mr. Nixon has at last had the courage to reopen communication. He is, of course, the only president who could have done it. Even General Eisenhower would have been bought by the bitterness and sense of defeat that we nourished in the '50s. And Mr. Kennedy and Mr. Johnson would have been called traitors. Now, in both real and symbolic senses, we are on our way. And no matter what happens in the next eight days, I think the president deserves a salute for arranging this little excursion.[79]

Here, Reasoner articulated what would become a popular refrain: only Nixon could go to China.

THE ARRIVAL

Although the White House carefully designed all elements of the president's trip, US officials approached Nixon's arrival and first full day in the PRC with particular care. Knowing full well that the first televised images would set the tone for Nixon's entire visit, the White House went to extraordinary lengths to make sure that the optics were just right. On Monday, February 21, the president's party flew from Guam to Shanghai, where a Chinese navigator boarded the plane to accompany the *Spirit of '76* to Peking. An hour and a half later, the presidential plane touched down at 11:28 a.m. in Peking—and 10:28 p.m. EST the previous day in the United States, a slot that aligned perfectly with the 10 o'clock evening news.

Live network pool coverage showed the president's plane taxi to the Chinese airport hangar. As the *Spirit of '76* rolled to a complete stop, TV cameras focused on what one CBS journalist described as a "very small delegation" gathered to greet the president of the United States. There were "no large crowds, no banners, no groups of smiling school children waving flowers."[80] Instead, forty-two Chinese officials and around five hundred members of a Chinese military honor guard were assembled on the tarmac.[81] Nixon was adamant that he be the only US official (besides Mrs. Nixon) to greet Chou En-lai and shake his hand for the first time. This gesture was doubly symbolic, for it also would rectify a very public slight Chou still talked about, when then secretary of state John Foster Dulles refused to shake his hand at the 1954 Geneva Summit. So intent were Nixon and Haldeman that the president be the center of attention that a military aide blocked the aircraft aisle once Nixon and his wife exited the plane. No one would get through until the handshake was complete. The president walked down the stairs, extended his hand to Chou En-lai, and smiled for the television cameras. "When our hands met," Nixon later wrote, "one era ended and another began."[82] As Kissinger described the scene, the "historic Nixon-Chou handshake had been consummated in splendid solitude."[83] The rest of the US delegation deplaned while Chou introduced Nixon to several high-ranking Chinese officials assembled on the tarmac. After reviewing the military troops, the president listened to the Chinese band play "The Star-Spangled Banner." The US national anthem, Nixon later wrote, "had never sounded so stirring to me as on that windswept runway in the heart of Communist China"[84] (figures 5.1 and 5.2).

But to a president accustomed to a roaring public welcome on his previous global tours, the arrival ceremony was disappointing. Nixon and other senior officials worried about how the US media would report the sparse crowds and sorely lacking pomp and circumstance. As the president's motorcade moved from the airport to the center of the city, Kissinger recalled that "there was still some errant hope crackling over Haldeman's radio to Ziegler that perhaps the real welcoming ceremony involving photogenic Chinese multitudes might be awaiting us at Tien An Men Square. The hope was in vain."[85] One

FIGURE 5.1. President Richard Nixon and First Lady Pat Nixon disembark at the Peking Airport in the People's Republic of China, February 21, 1972. White House Photo Office. Courtesy of the Richard Nixon Library. Accession Number: WHPO-8521-06A.

FIGURE 5.2. President Richard Nixon and Chinese premier Chou En-lai shake hands upon Nixon's arrival at the Peking Airport in the People's Republic of China, February 21, 1972. White House Photo Office. Courtesy of the Richard Nixon Library. Accession Number: WHPO-8498-17.

NBC commentator summarized the president's airport arrival as a "proper but restrained welcome" from the Chinese. Reporting from the president's motorcade route in Peking, reporter John Rich told viewers that only a few people in Tiananmen Square seemed to realize "something is happening," but "nobody seemed very excited, and there was certainly no official ceremony or salute or anything else laid on for the president. Perhaps that will come later."[86]

Once the president arrived at his guest quarters, he and Haldeman discussed how to control the media narrative about the less than spectacular
arrival ceremony. Nixon insisted that Haldeman and Ziegler put out the line
that "they weren't concerned about lack of people, [or the] welcoming crowd."
In fact, they should stress "that this was exactly what we'd expected, and point
out the significance of other things, such as Chou En-lai being at the airport,
their playing 'The Star Spangled Banner,' and that sort of thing."[87] This media
strategy session was interrupted by Chou's sudden announcement that Mao
Tse-tung wanted to meet with Nixon—an invitation the president craved.
The meeting was closed to US journalists, but Chinese photographers captured the meeting in vivid detail and shared the images with US officials. "We
should get some great coverage as a result of that," Haldeman recorded in
his diary—and he was correct.[88] Reporting live from Peking for NBC's *Today
Show*, Herbert Kaplow described the Nixon-Mao meeting as the "high point
of the day" and suggested that "the fact that Chairman Mao saw fit to see the
American President as practically the first function of the President's week
here . . . seemed to have given the whole visit sort of a blessing, and get it off
to a good start."[89]

Back in the United States, one of Kissinger's deputies described the media scene as one of "sudden euphoria." Despite their initial anxiety about the
"coolness" of the airport reception, he explained, these narratives had been
"replaced by surge of euphoric reaction" to the events of Nixon's first day in
the PRC. In fact, the "U.S. media, television and press is now totally dominated by coverage of [the] visit. I anticipate this will level off sharply since it
has built so drastically in past twenty four hours."[90] Overall, he reported, "We
are all greatly impressed with [the] performance of [the] President and [the]
U.S. team thus far. It is evident that painstaking planning on all details has
paid off handsomely."[91]

THE RECIPROCAL BANQUETS

The vivid imagery and political spectacle of Nixon's arrival extended to the
pomp and circumstance of the diplomatic banquets scheduled throughout
the week. If the images of Nixon in China displayed the almost unbelievable
reality of the president of the United States being welcomed to the PRC by devout communists, the reciprocal toasts between Nixon and Chinese officials
gave voice to a new chapter in US-China diplomatic relations. The president
delivered five official toasts at five banquets over the course of the week: the
February 21 Welcoming Banquet hosted by Chou En-lai at the Great Hall
of the People; the February 24 American and Chinese Delegations' Private

Dinner; the February 25 Reciprocal Banquet hosted by President Nixon at the Great Hall of the People; the February 26 Welcoming Banquet for Nixon hosted by the Provincial Revolutionary Committee of the Province in Hangchow; and the February 27 Banquet for Nixon hosted by the Shanghai Municipal Revolutionary Committee. The White House sought to capitalize on both the visual and verbal elements of these banquets for, as Kissinger explained, these dramatic events were "televised live on the morning shows in America [and] performed a deadly serious purpose. They communicated rapidly and dramatically to the peoples of both countries that a new relationship was being forged."[92]

A central feature of these banquets was the exchange of toasts between the president and various Chinese officials. The White House prepared numerous possible drafts of these short speeches prior to the trip, but nothing was finalized until the president arrived in China. Nixon played an active role in writing and editing, and the archival record contains dozens of pages of Nixon's handwritten notes outlining the themes he wished to stress. As Michelle Murray Yang argues, the president's toasts during his week in the PRC showcased his ability to address "multiple audiences with often conflicting agendas" and allowed him to "traverse a rhetorical tightrope, balancing the needs of each audience with the objectives of his mission."[93] The president had to indicate a willingness to partner with his Chinese hosts, reassure conservative US audiences that he was not "selling out" Taiwan, and convince the American public that this "Opening to China" marked the beginning of a new, productive friendship. Nevertheless, while Nixon's rhetorical challenge was to address several audiences, none was more important to his reelection chances than the US public. As with the president's arrival in Peking, the White House scheduled these banquets—minus the private dinner on February 24—to coincide with American news programming. The dinners and corresponding toasts happened at the same hour as the morning shows, such as the *Today Show* on NBC. Unlike the ongoing war in Vietnam, the live footage of Nixon's "Opening to China"—and the diplomatic rhetoric that made this opening possible—suggested that perhaps this "journey for peace" might succeed.

To US audiences tuning in at home, the February 21 Welcoming Banquet in Peking offered the first real look into the president's public activities in the PRC. After watching Nixon's arrival on the late Sunday evening news, US audiences awoke Monday morning to live footage of President and Mrs. Nixon walking up a grand staircase to be greeted by the Chinese premier and his accompanying delegation. Filming mere inches from US and Chinese dignitaries, network camera crews enabled the American public to feel as if they

FIGURE 5.3. President Richard Nixon and Chinese premier Chou En-lai speak at a banquet in Peking, February 21, 1972. Photograph by Oliver F. Atkins, White House Photo Office. Courtesy of the Richard Nixon Library. Accession Number: NLRN-WHPO-C8488-02A.

were *there*, in Peking, attending the banquet vicariously with and through the president of the United States. CBS network news correspondents Dan Rather and Bernard Kalb offered detailed commentary on what US audiences saw on their television screens. Although it would be quite a while until the public knew the full extent of the diplomatic negotiations, they explained, the initial "appearance of the China visit was off to a very good start." Moreover, Kalb continued, the "fact that Chairman Mao for his part and Nixon for his part committed their prestige to the Sino-American rendezvous so early in the visit" suggested that substantive changes in US-Chinese diplomatic relations might come out of the visit (figure 5.3).[94]

Halfway through an elegant dinner of spongy bamboo shoots, shark's fin, prawns, steamed chicken with coconut, almond junket, and fruit, Chinese premier Chou En-lai rose to deliver the first toast.[95] Although Chou delivered the toast in Mandarin, his remarks were translated for the US delegation attending the dinner—and news networks also relayed this translation to American audiences. The Chinese premier began by welcoming President and Mrs. Nixon and extended "cordial greetings to the American people on the other side of the great ocean" on behalf of the Chinese citizenry. Chou no doubt knew that these proceedings were being broadcast live in the United States and took this moment to address the US public directly. While the "social systems of China and the United States are fundamentally different," Chou continued, he hoped that United States and the PRC could "find common ground" and make a "new start . . . in the relations between our two countries."[96]

Nixon, who had seen a copy of Chou's toast prior to the banquet, was able to make edits to his own. In one early draft for the February 21 toast, speechwriters suggested that the president note that "when Columbus discovered America, he did so because he had set out in search of China." But if the diplomatic negotiations of this week succeeded, Nixon would continue, "it may be said that even as Columbus set out for China and discovered America, that we set out from America for China, and that together we opened the way to a new world in which future generations, whatever their differences, at long last can live at peace with one another."[97] This passage, which Nixon first underlined for emphasis but later crossed out, did not appear in the final version of the toast. However, like his other prepared statements prior to arriving in China, this draft reflected the White House's view of this trip as a historic mission to an unknown world, one they hoped would bring about peace, friendship, and harmony between the United States and the PRC.

In the final version of his February 21 banquet toast, Nixon began by thanking the prime minister for his "incomparable hospitality" and "gracious and eloquent remarks." It was a marvel of modern telecommunications, the president continued, that at this moment "more people are seeing and hearing what we say than on any other occasion in the whole history of the world." Despite the hyperbolic nature of this statement, Nixon had a point. Due to the massive public relations efforts of the White House and international news outlets, no previous presidential trip had received such sustained global media coverage. And yet, Nixon stated, "what we say here will not be long remembered. What we do here can change the world." A clear invocation of Lincoln's "Gettysburg Address" ("The world will little note nor long remember what we say here, but it can never forget what they did here"), the president intimated that any future relationship between the United States and the PRC would be shaped by tangible actions, not only words. The goal, Nixon continued, was to "find common ground to work together" to achieve world peace. Here, the president did not call for ideological conformity, but instead acknowledged clear differences between the two countries. He proposed that he and the Chinese premier "start a long march together, not in lockstep, but on different roads leading to the same goal, the goal of building a world structure of peace and justice in which all may stand together with equal dignity and in which each nation, large or small, has a right to determine its own form of government, free of outside interference or domination." It was up to them, Nixon concluded, "to rise to the heights of greatness which can build a new and a better world."[98]

In their live network coverage from Peking, US journalists stressed the friendly nature of these reciprocal toasts and suggested that Nixon's visit was off to an excellent start. After the cool airport reception dampened expectations for the president's first day, the unexpected meeting with Mao Tse-tung and the warm hospitality of the Chinese premier set a new tone for the trip. NBC's Frank McGee described the banquet as "historic" and "absorbing," and fellow anchor Donald Klein noted that the "extraordinary frankness" of both toasts suggested that "we may be in high gear in Peking already."[99] After reporting live from Peking for the *Today Show*, NBC reporter Herbert Kaplow asked the host what the response was like back in the United States. Anchor Frank McGee noted the "enormous public interest" in the trip. "Everybody's being inundated with visual impressions and deluged with words, and trying to keep their eye on the significant aspects of the journey, which have not yet surfaced, and which may not for several days to come. This is the nature of television, we take it as it comes along, and do with it what we can at the time."[100] White House officials seemed to draw a similar conclusion. As Haldeman wrote in his diary that evening after the banquet, "The network coverage of four hours, live, of the banquet period was apparently very impressive and they got all the facts the P[resident] wanted, such as his use of chopsticks, his toast, Chou's toast, the P[resident]'s glass-clinking, etc. So that came off very well."[101] After an eventful first day in the PRC, Nixon reveled in the positive news coverage coming out of Peking, convinced that the trip was off to an excellent start.

The president delivered four more formal toasts during his weeklong stay in the PRC, each of which stressed similar themes of peaceful coexistence, goodwill, and a desire to begin the relationship between the United States and the PRC anew. A powerful form of diplomatic rhetoric, these reciprocal exchanges between the US president and senior Chinese officials offered clues as to what was being said behind closed doors. Indeed, many US journalists interpreted these toasts as markers of the top-secret negotiations between the two sides over the course of the week. But it was not just what Nixon said that mattered. Perhaps even more significant to US audiences was the sight of the president of the United States delivering a toast—an epideictic address, a speech of praise—to the developing friendship between the two countries. In a toast to Chou En-lai at a private dinner on February 24, Nixon noted that both the United States and the PRC were working toward a world where "no walls will divide people and divide nations, and in which they exist only for our protection and never for our division."[102] The next evening, at a banquet

FIGURE 5.4. President Richard Nixon and Chinese premier Chou En-lai at a banquet, February 26, 1972. White House Photo Office. Courtesy of the Richard Nixon Library. Accession Number: WHPO-C8616-29.

honoring the Chinese premier, the president stated that although "for almost a generation there has been a wall between the People's Republic of China and the United States of America," both leaders had "begun the long process of removing that wall between us." Great differences existed, Nixon acknowledged, but "we are determined that those differences do not prevent us from living together in peace."[103] In contrast to his strong anticommunist rhetoric against "Red China" and the Soviet Union as US senator and vice president, these statements struck some US conservatives as too deferential, too willing to embrace nuance and complexity instead of maintaining a hard line against totalitarian rule. But it was precisely *because* Nixon had been one of the most vocal opponents of the communist state that he could now embark on this diplomatic revolution in Peking (figure 5.4).

THE SPECTACLE OF CHINA

If the "Opening to China" would allow Nixon to display his foreign policy skill and position as global statesman to the US public, the president's visit also enabled PRC officials to showcase their history and culture to the rest of the world. In Kissinger's estimation, the Chinese "wanted to use the majesty of their civilization and the elegance of their manners to leave an impression that nothing was more natural than an increasingly intimate relationship between the world's most avowedly revolutionary Marxist state and the embodiment of capitalism." And, because the White House wanted to create a compelling political spectacle for US audiences, these two purposes "intersected to produce a spectacular show."[104]

Some of the president's sightseeing tours took place at famous national landmarks of Chinese history and culture. Vivid images of Nixon touring the Great Wall, exploring the Ming tombs, and visiting the Forbidden City dominated television news coverage. The American press contingent tried to get the best photos, camera angles, and interviews possible. At the Great Wall, the president peered over the structure to imagine what Chinese soldiers would have seen while defending the country from northern invaders. As he walked up the steep incline, Nixon shook hands with various spectators and talked with his Chinese tour guides. "The president was the perfect tourist and campaigner, handshaking when appropriate," Harry Reasoner reported. When ABC's Tom Jarriel asked what he thought of the scenery, Nixon used his immediate location to allude to his larger foreign policy objectives. "What is most important is if we have an open world, as we look at this wall, we do not want walls of any kind between peoples," he said, and that he hoped that as a result of this trip, "the walls that are erected, whether they are physical walls like this or whether they are other walls, ideology or philosophy will not divide peoples in the world."[105] Fully aware that these remarks would be circulated to American audiences and a wider global public, Nixon used this moment to tie the visit to his larger Cold War strategy that included a new rhetoric of rapprochement. Stressing themes of peace, friendship, and mutual respect, these remarks offered a distinctly different characterization of how the United States could— and would—interact with nations with whom they did not agree (figure 5.5).

But the White House had another goal for these tourist stops. The president had planned for "a television extravaganza," *Washington Post* correspondent Stanley Karnow recalled—and he got it.[106] Watching from home, US audiences were transported to a distant, foreign land as tourists along for the ride, one made possible by the president of the United States. After years of hostility between the United States and communist countries, Nixon opened another world through his physical travel to and through the PRC. This was precisely Nixon's intent, as Kissinger aide Winston Lord recalled, since the president wanted "above all" for his trip "to be covered as widely as possible by the American media, not to mention the world media."[107] Those responsible for covering the president's every move recalled feeling as if they were pawns in a larger campaign operation, one designed to portray a positive presidential image to audiences at home and abroad. *New York Times* bureau chief Max Frankel explained that "it's an election year. The fact that all of this

FIGURE 5.5. President Richard Nixon and First Lady Pat Nixon tour the Great Wall of China, February 24, 1972. White House Photo Office. Courtesy of the Richard Nixon Library. Accession Number: WHPO-C8548-26A.

was happening at the beginning of 1972 was hardly lost on us. And so, to that extent, we're part of a partisan propaganda effort." Dan Rather concurred, noting that "this had all the trappings and all the inner core of a campaign trip. No doubt that we were on a re-elect President Nixon campaign trip."[108]

Chinese officials planned various cultural events for President and Mrs. Nixon to attend in the evening, including a performance by the Chinese Revolutionary Opera and a sports exhibition. News networks featured these events on live television, always coinciding with the morning news in the United States. On their second night in China, President and Mrs. Nixon returned to the Great Hall of the People to attend the opera with Chou En-lai. A pet project of Chiang Ch'ing, Mao Tse-tung's wife, the opera was, according to the White House official description, an event "designed at the same time to entertain and indoctrinate."[109] True to form, "The Red Detachment of Women" celebrated the triumph of the Red Army over Chinese nationalist Chiang Kai-shek. The next evening, the President and Mrs. Nixon attended a sports exhibition featuring badminton, table tennis, and gymnastics. Held in a colorful hall that some journalists compared to Madison Square Garden, the event was attended by eighteen thousand men, women, and children who "applauded vigorously" as the president entered the building—the kind of reception Nixon had hoped for when he first landed in Peking (figures 5.6 and 5.7).[110]

FIGURE 5.6. Chinese gymnasts and table tennis athletes at the Peking Capitol Gymnasium during the athletic show honoring President and Mrs. Nixon, February 23, 1972. White House Photo Office. Courtesy of the Richard Nixon Library. Accession Number: NLRN-WHPO-8540-34A.

FIGURE 5.7. Scene from the ballet attended by President and Mrs. Nixon at the Great Hall of the People, February 22, 1972. Photograph by Byron E. Schumaker, White House Photo Office. Courtesy of the Richard Nixon Library. Accession Number: NLRN-WHPO-C8520-05A.

Collectively, Nixon's participation in these sightseeing tours and cultural events translated Chinese history and culture for American audiences watching at home and provided a human, on-the-ground counterpart to the diplomatic negotiations happening behind closed doors. US television journalists used this opportunity to display China to the nation and the world—and to portray Nixon as the one who had opened the door. These presidential "sight-seeing trips went off as magnificent spectacles," Kissinger later wrote, in which "hordes of famous television commentators and senior journalists converged on each set piece" to capture "the profound thoughts of the leading actors" and display a long-forbidden land to the US public. In fact, he concluded, "the fact that the excursions were geared to television only reinforced that here, if ever, the medium was the message. In the mind of the American public, television established the reality of the People's Republic and the grandeur of China as no series of diplomatic notes possibly could have."[111]

THE RETURN HOME

After a full week in the PRC, with stops in Peking, Hangchow, and Shanghai, the president attended one final banquet on February 27, the night before his departure. It was here that Nixon triumphantly declared this as the "week that changed the world." If both countries could continue "working together where we can find common ground. . . . on which we can both stand," the president said, "generations in the years ahead will look back and thank us for this meeting that we have held in this past week."[112] Although US journalists did note Nixon's enthusiastic summary of the visit, the major news of the day was the long-awaited release of the Shanghai Communiqué, a carefully worded diplomatic agreement between the United States and the PRC. Although the document outlined the "respective positions and attitudes" of both sides on "important changes and great upheavals" within "the international situation," the bombshell revelation was the United States' affirmation that "there is but one China and that Taiwan is a part of China." The US also agreed to "progressively reduce its forces and military installations on Taiwan" so that the relationship between mainland China and Taiwan could be solved "by the Chinese themselves."[113] While there had been some indication that the United States was moving in this direction prior to Nixon's trip, this announcement represented a dramatic step back from earlier US policies in support of Taiwan. As Dan Rather explained to viewers, this communiqué "soften[ed] considerably the American position of support for the Chinese Nationalists on Taiwan," established the "diplomatic machinery" to increase personal contacts between the United States and China, and established the foundation for economic trade between the two countries.[114]

The next day, as the presidential party flew from Shanghai to Anchorage, Alaska, US politicians began expressing their reactions to the communiqué and the overall success of Nixon's trip. Reporting from Washington, DC, ABC's Bob Clark explained that "there were both hurrahs and jeers here in Congress today for the President's China trip and its controversial communique," and "most of the applause came from moderates and liberals, even from some Democratic presidential candidates."[115] South Dakota US senator George McGovern, who would become the Democratic presidential candidate later that summer, stated that although he would have been more direct about when and how the United States would withdraw from Taiwan, he gave Nixon "high marks for going as far as he can, or for as far as he has, on trying to settle this Taiwan question."[116] But in the view of former vice president Hubert Humphrey, also a candidate for the Democratic presidential nomination, "the rug has been pulled out from under the Taiwanese."[117] US representative John Ashbrook, a Republican from Ohio who challenged Nixon for the 1972 Republican nomination, was more direct: "The communists call on us to abandon our ally, and our response is to announce a phased unilateral withdrawal of all our forces from Taiwan."[118] Other prominent conservatives, such as Senator Strom Thurmond (R-SC) and Senator John Tower (R-TX), also expressed their dismay about the communiqué's position on Taiwan.[119]

To a president who saw the "Opening to China" as a central element of his 1972 reelection campaign and overall presidential legacy, these early reactions from US conservatives were a legitimate cause for concern. On the flight home, Nixon obsessed over US public reception of the communiqué, particularly in relation to Taiwan, and worried that the opinion of prominent Republicans could play a decisive factor in the 1972 presidential race.[120] Back in Washington, Kissinger deputy Alexander Haig reported that, in his estimation, it was too early to "slip into a self-conscious posture which tends to be defensive on the Taiwan issue." In fact, because of "all the factors which only a few of the players can fully appreciate," Haig explained, the efforts of the past week and the preceding months can be described as nothing short of brilliant."[121] But Nixon continued to stew.

To reinforce the historic nature of the president's trip (and to counteract the criticism of the Shanghai Communiqué), the White House planned a jubilant welcome ceremony for Nixon's arrival at Andrews Air Force Base. After a nine-hour layover in Anchorage, the *Spirit of '76* touched down at 9:15 p.m. EST on February 28, 1972. As the president descended the airplane stairs, he was greeted by a crowd of fifteen thousand people and the US Army

Band's rendition of "Hail to the Chief."[122] It was a hero's welcome. Vice President Spiro T. Agnew introduced the president, reminding the audience that through the "miracle of satellite television," the US public had experienced "the sights and sounds of a society that has been closed to Americans for over two decades." Through this carefully produced media spectacle, the US public felt as if they were able to travel along with Nixon into this new world. Now, Agnew told the president, he and the rest of the country were "glad to have you back" and felt "easier tonight because of the trip that you took."[123]

In his arrival statement, Nixon highlighted the diplomatic achievements of his trip while also reaffirming his belief in American exceptionalism, democratic principles, and the "greatness" of the United States. Nixon began by reminding the audience of the trip's explicit goal: to undertake a "journey for peace." Despite the "gulf of almost 12,000 miles and 22 years of noncommunication and hostility" dividing the United States and the PRC, Nixon explained, this trip had started the "long process of building a bridge across that gulf"—a process that was far from over. But even as the president celebrated the new beginnings of diplomatic contact between the two countries, he also declared that his visit offered another important lesson that extended beyond US-China relations. It "demonstrated that nations with very deep and fundamental differences can learn to discuss those differences calmly, rationally, and frankly, without compromising their principles," he explained. In fact, it was possible for two countries to "talk about differences rather than fight about them." To a public long accustomed to ideological conflict with nations who embraced communism, this was a massive shift. The president explained that he did not—and would not—pretend that major differences did not exist between the two countries. They did. Nixon recalled the "total belief" and "total dedication" Chinese leaders had to "their system of government." It was their right to pledge such allegiance, the president argued, "just as it is the right of any country to choose the kind of government it wants." The implicit argument was, of course, that if the freedom of political choice was a core principle of American democracy, the United States could not reject those countries who did not align with US political ideology. But after this week in the PRC, Nixon explained that he returned "with an even stronger faith in our system of government" and the principles that made the nation an example to the world.

As I flew across America today, all the way from Alaska, over the Rockies, the Plains, and then on to Washington, I thought of the greatness of our country and, most of all, I thought of the freedom, the opportunity, the progress that 200 million Americans are privileged to enjoy. I realized again this is a beautiful country. And tonight my prayer and my hope is that as a result of this trip, our children will have a better chance to grow up in a peaceful world.[124]

Here, Nixon drew on themes of American exceptionalism to reaffirm the "greatness" of the United States and celebrate the core values that set it apart from the rest of the world: "freedom," "opportunity," and "progress." It was this reverence for these national ideals, he argued, that made the "Opening to China" a hopeful symbol for future generations.

Public Response

The White House carefully monitored US and global public opinion before, during, and after the president's trip, commissioning various polls to ascertain how the "Opening to China" would impact public perceptions of the president and his reelection chances that November. In the hours and days that followed Nixon's return to the United States, senior administration officials turned their attention to tracking how much audiences at home and abroad had heard about the trip—and what they thought about it.

At home, domestic polling data revealed that the administration's massive public relations campaign to increase awareness of the trip had been wildly successful. A Gallup poll taken just days after Nixon's return revealed that 98 percent of those surveyed had heard or read about the president's trip—the highest awareness score of any event registered in the history of the organization.[125] In their post-trip analysis, NBC's research department estimated that one hundred million viewers saw some portion of the three networks' coverage of the "Opening to China."[126] In an Opinion Research Corporation (ORC) survey conducted mere days after Nixon's return, a whopping 81 percent of respondents said they watched either a "great deal" or a "fair amount" of the president's visit. As part of the survey, respondents listened to a series of statements that had "been made by those who disapprove and those who approve of President Nixon's China visit" and then were asked whether they agreed or disagreed. Statements included queries about whether Nixon's trip "resulted in a sellout of the non-Communist Chinese on Taiwan" (25 percent agreed, 57 percent disagreed), if the president's trip "eased tensions and made world peace more likely" (69 percent agreed, 23 percent disagreed), and whether the visit to China was "mainly a publicity stunt to get more votes in the 1972 Presidential election" (34 percent agreed, 61 percent disagreed).[127] These questions, which Haldeman and other senior White House officials developed immediately after Nixon's return, reveal an administration desperate to gauge how the "Opening to China" would shape the president's image as global statesman and influence US voters in the 1972 presidential campaign.

According to a final poll analysis provided by the ORC, "the trip to Peking was a great plus for President Nixon in terms of favorable public relations, enhancing his already strong image in foreign affairs." Public awareness of the trip was "extensive—only three percent say they heard or read nothing at all about the trip and only 4 percent say they saw nothing on T.V." Perhaps even more significant, this widespread media coverage of the trip meant that both Republicans and Democrats were exposed to the trip—and with very favorable results for the president. Eighty-one percent of those surveyed "applauded President Nixon's conduct in China as an American representative," and when compared against other world leaders, he stood "head and shoulders above all others in capability of conducting negotiations with Communist China."[128] Ultimately, the president's trip to the PRC "may well prove to be the deciding event of the 1972 political campaign," the report concluded. "The President has moved the public's attention to the largest issue of all—world peace" and "has held out hope that a major break through [sic] in the tensions of the last 30 years may be at an end. At the same time, he has firmly established for himself in the public's mind, a unique role as the initiator and moving factor in this changing picture."[129]

Abroad, USIA officials commissioned several surveys to capture global opinion regarding the "Opening to China" around the world before and after Nixon's trip.[130] In the final report issued in May 1972, USIA officials detailed the results of post-trip surveys in nine countries (Great Britain, West Germany, France, Italy, Sweden, Canada, Japan, Australia, and Israel) and "major city samplings" from six others (Manila, Kuala Lumpur, Mexico City, Caracas, Beirut, and Nairobi).[131] These findings were significant for several reasons. First, the USIA found that the president's visit to the PRC achieved "one of the highest levels of awareness ever recorded in international public opinion surveys." In fact, in comparison to other USIA surveys taken since the early 1950s, "only the Soviet's first space satellite and America's manned moon landing registered higher levels of awareness." Abroad, "the average (median) awareness [of the trip] . . . was 82 percent for the general public and 94 percent for the 'educated elite.'"[132] Second, the data revealed that an average (median) of 70 percent of the general public read about the trip in newspapers and 67 percent watched it on television.[133] These two facts supported a third major finding: this widespread public awareness of Nixon's "Opening to China" increased positive judgments about the trip's success in easing world tensions.[134]

In many ways, the administration's massive efforts to capture domestic and international public opinion reflect Nixon's obsession with using the "Opening to China" to elevate his own image and guarantee an easy reelection campaign. In the days and weeks following his return to Washington, the president was consumed by public perception of the trip, arguing that senior officials were not doing enough to emphasize his diplomatic skill and presidential image. As Haldeman recalled, Nixon believed the "main thing for us in China is the P[resident]'s position as a big-league operator. . . . The unusual world statesman capability, the personal qualities of the man. He wants to refer to this as a classic battle between a couple of heavyweights, each with his own style."[135] The irony here, of course, was even as Nixon publicly called for open dialogue and mutual understanding, behind the scenes he longed to be seen as the victor in a diplomatic battle on the world stage.

Conclusion

On the evening of February 28, as the presidential party flew across the continent toward the nation's capital and Nixon brooded over how his Republican base would respond to the Shanghai Communiqué, *ABC Evening News* cohost Howard K. Smith suggested that the president's trip was motivated by three main goals: win the 1972 presidential election, end the war in Vietnam without surrendering to the communists, and cease US military interventions abroad while maintaining—and even increasing—American influence on the global stage. "In China," Smith argued, "he achieved forward movement on all three."[136] To a US public tired of a never-ending American military presence in Asia, the president's visit suggested that ideological opponents could disagree but still seek common ground. To a nation accustomed to a Cold War foreign policy grounded in narratives of American exceptionalism, the "Opening to China" offered a vivid display of how a daring act of international diplomacy could reshape the geopolitical landscape. And to an electorate wondering whether Nixon deserved four more years, his journey to the heart of "Red China" offered a memorable—and, for some, compelling—image of a global statesman willing to move beyond two decades of isolation to bridge an ideological gulf between the United States and the PRC.

Ultimately, however, the "Opening to China" looms large in the global imaginary because that was Nixon's intention from the very beginning. It was a trip designed to capture the US public's attention and dominate the global media landscape. As I have shown in the preceding pages, the president and senior White House officials envisioned a live television spectacle broadcast from the capital of "Red China," and they believed that this near-constant news coverage would so mesmerize the US public that they would not be able to look away. This televised drama between two former enemies would cement Nixon's legacy in world affairs and propel him to reelection in November 1972. These explicit political goals were not some accessory or casual aside. They motivated, animated, and dictated every detail of the trip.

There was one final element of Nixon's presidential image the White House hoped—albeit discreetly—to portray. Not only would he be the first one to visit the PRC, but his travel through the "Bamboo Curtain" would allow the US president to reach and ultimately liberate a Chinese people held captive by communism. At first glance, this claim seems to depart from the rest of Nixon's public statements praising a spirit of US-PRC cooperation despite ideological differences. But behind the scenes, senior administration officials revealed their ultimate hope: that "Chinese communism can be made to erode, and finally fall."[137] In a top-secret report prepared for the president's briefing book (and one that Nixon heavily notated), an unnamed US official (most likely NSC or CIA) reported that Mao Tse-tung's "anti-American feeling" was a clear "manifestation of the hatreds felt by an inferior for one superior; by a slave for his master; by one who is poor for a rich man; by one who is crude for those who are genteel; and by the conquered for the conqueror."[138] In Mao's mind, Americans were "outer barbarians. . . . to be controlled or pacified when we are strong, or conquered and driven away when he is strong."[139] The best analogy for Nixon's visit, the report argued, was the historical example of the Manchus, a barbarian tribe the Chinese emperor invited into Peking during the seventeenth century to defend the city from enemy attack. In the end, however, the Manchus refused to leave and instead set up their own dynasty in China.

The Americans, US officials argued, should learn from the Manchus. "We must emulate the Manchus of 1644 A.D.," the report concluded, "and although we may help drive away the brigands Emperor Mao Tse-tung fears [the Soviets], let us hope we can remain in Peking in the ways described above [the exchange of news, students, scientists, doctors, businessmen, and trade] and thereby bring about the fall of the emperor."[140] This erosion of communism and the fall of Mao Tse-tung would allow the Chinese to "resume their own basic characteristics, those of warmth, friendliness and individuality." Finally unshackled from an oppressive political regime, they would be able to return to their rightful, normal selves. These blatantly racist descriptions of the Chinese reflect earlier discourses of US-China diplomacy—such as US imperialism, paternalism, missionary-style diplomacy—even as they positioned Nixon and the United States as uniquely qualified to "save" the Chinese people from totalitarian rule. Although such discourses would not appear in

Nixon's public statements (and if they had, they would directly contradict the White House's highly scripted narratives of the trip), they reveal the long and enduring history of racist tropes animating US foreign policy toward China. And they suggest that while the president may have celebrated this new diplomatic partnership, he also saw the "Opening to China" as just that—the United States' first reconnaissance mission into a communist state they hoped to dismantle brick by brick.

6

Reagan at Normandy

The ceremonies in Normandy will celebrate the victory and mourn the dead. They will also mourn, almost subliminally, a certain moral clarity that has been lost, a sense of common purpose that has all but evaporated. Never again, perhaps, would the Allies so handsomely collaborate. The invasion of Normandy was a thunderously heroic blow dealt to the evil empire. Never again, it may be, would war seem so unimpeachably right, so necessary and just. Never again, perhaps, would American power and morality so perfectly coincide.

LANCE MORROW, *Time*, May 28, 1984[1]

If the Cold War was a drama enacted in various places and moments on the world stage, Ronald Reagan played a starring role. His was the marquee name, the actor who appeared on set at pivotal junctures in this geopolitical contest. In fact, for many US Americans, the fortieth president of the United States spoke as the ultimate Cold Warrior—a persona that Reagan deliberately cultivated, embodied, and embraced.

A central theme woven throughout Reagan's Cold War rhetorical performances was his active, avid stance against the Soviet Union. In fact, his political career was made possible because of his strident anticommunism. Reagan appeared on the national political scene in October 1947, just as the United States was beginning to extend economic aid to Greece, Turkey, and other European countries under the Truman Doctrine and the Marshall Plan. Reagan testified before the House Un-American Activities Committee (HUAC) in his role as president of the Hollywood Screen Actors Guild.[2] Although he was a "New Deal Liberal," Reagan's HUAC file explained, "he has no fear of any one, is a nice talker, well informed on the subject, and will make a splendid witness."[3] Seventeen years later, in October 1964, the newly minted Republican took center stage once again to speak on behalf of another strident anticommunist: the GOP nominee for president of the United States, Arizona US senator Barry Goldwater. Known as the "Time for Choosing" speech, Reagan used the occasion to articulate a conservative response to President Lyndon Johnson's "Great Society" programs and a foreign policy of Soviet accommodation or détente. "Those who would trade our freedom for the soup kitchen of the welfare state have told us they have a utopian solution of peace without victory [in Vietnam]," he said. Reagan described the moment in stark moral terms, a choice between individual liberty and communist oppression.

"The martyrs of history were not fools, and our honored dead who gave their lives to stop the advance of the Nazis didn't die in vain," he said. The "road to peace," Reagan declared, could be achieved only through courage, moral resolve, duty, and sacrifice. "You and I have a rendezvous with destiny," he concluded. "We'll preserve for our children this, the last best hope of man on earth, or we'll sentence them to take the last step into a thousand years of darkness."[4] In this vivid depiction, Reagan presented the United States of America as tall, proud, strong—an example to the rest of the world.

More than any other Cold War figure, Reagan also modernized and popularized the mythic narrative of America as a "shining city on a hill." It was the story he used to announce his presidential campaign in November 1979 and the image he portrayed in his "Farewell Address" to the nation in January 1989. The enduring appeal of this "shining city on a hill" depiction was due in no small part to its historical reflexivity, its ability to connect past events to the present moment and to inspire future action. As Reagan put it in 1979: "We who are privileged to be Americans have had a rendezvous with destiny since the moment in 1630 when John Winthrop, standing on the deck of the tiny *Arbella* [*Arabella*] off the coast of Massachusetts, told the little band of Pilgrims [Puritans], 'We shall be a city upon a hill.'" This image, however, was particularly effective because Reagan used it as a moral justification for his vision for the United States' reassertion of global leadership. "A troubled and afflicted mankind looks to us," he explained, "pleading with us to keep our rendezvous with destiny; that we will uphold the principles of self-reliance, self-discipline, morality, and—above all—responsible liberty for every individual [so] that we will become that shining city on a hill."[5] In this telling, the nation could remain true to its mythic founding narrative by remembering and returning to those principles that made America truly great. As Reagan explained in his final address to the nation, this city was now "more prosperous, more secure, and happier than it was 8 years ago. . . . And she's still a beacon, still a magnet for all who must have freedom, for all the pilgrims from all the lost places who are hurtling through the darkness, toward home."[6]

Reagan's rhetorical skill lay in his ability to spark vivid imagery in the minds of his audience and to invite listeners to see themselves as principal actors in the national narrative he retold.[7] He constituted the US public as witnesses to this story, individuals who could draw inspiration from the heroic actions of their forebears to embody yet again the values and ideals that made America a shining example to the rest of the world. It was this narrative that gave active support to Reagan's Cold War foreign policy frame. But where this mythic ideal was often described in metaphorical terms, Reagan used the fortieth anniversary of D-day to make this vision come, quite literally, to life.

If the global rhetorical presidency describes how chief executives forward a particular image of the nation, Reagan made his vision accessible, tangible, and materially real in his speech at Pointe du Hoc. Deploying themes of sight, vision, image, light, and rhetorical display, Reagan transported the US public to the scene of his address through compelling historical narratives, striking imagery, and the physical display of D-day veterans he honored from the very ground they fought and died to free. Although Reagan's speech was itself eloquent and moving, the real emotional punch came from the scene of address. Television crews beamed images and live footage of the jagged cliffs of Pointe du Hoc, expansive beaches on the Normandy coastline, and rows of marble crosses and Stars of David to viewers in the United States and around the world. Millions of Americans were transported to the place where D-day happened from their kitchens and living rooms as they finished their morning coffee. As White House speechwriter Peggy Noonan recalled, the goal was for "American teenagers to stop chewing their Rice Krispies for a minute and hear about the greatness of those tough kids who are now their grandfathers. . . . Pause, sink in, bring it back to now, history is real."[8]

Where Truman, Eisenhower, and Kennedy addressed a US public who could remember the lessons of the Second World War in personal, intimate terms, Reagan spoke to many who came of age in the 1960s and 1970s, decades during which the earlier vision of American greatness was called into question. For many, the widely circulated images of the 1968 My Lai massacre, the hasty evacuation of the US embassy in Saigon in 1975, and the 1979 Iran Hostage Crisis were a stark and painful reminder of what American intervention overseas might actually entail. But at Normandy, the moral clarity and purpose enacted by the "Greatest Generation" on D-day became a clear and compelling justification for the United States' postwar leadership on the global stage. In Reagan's retelling, threats to political freedom in other areas of the world—such as in Central America—required present and future American intervention. The mythic quest to protect freedom and defeat totalitarianism at home and abroad was as noble in 1984 as it had been forty years earlier.

In this chapter, I detail how Reagan used his visit to Normandy and the ceremonial act of commemoration to paint a vivid, emotional argument for US global leadership on the Cold War world stage. Where traditional examples of foreign policy rhetoric ask audiences to assess past actions or make decisions about future initiatives, ceremonial addresses constitute the audience as witnesses who have seen and must act differently because of these experiences. These moments invite—even require—the public to remember and reflect together. Acts of commemoration, what Edward Casey defines as "*intensified remembering*" of the past, usher individuals into shared rituals and common texts, practices and discourses tethered to and extending beyond space and time. It is through these communal experiences that people "overcome the effects of anonymity and spatio-temporal distance and pay homage to people and events [they] have never known and will never know face-to-face."[9] Commemoration constitutes communities, and commemorative rhetorics sketch an overarching narrative depicting who communities have been, are, and will become. At Normandy, Reagan invited his audience to enter into the scene of battle and remember, intensely, together. Vivid images of sheer cliffs on the Normandy coastline and the bodies of military veterans withered with age made the past viscerally present. As the president pointed the audience to these compelling visuals and iconic heroes situated in the place of address, he offered a potent, irrefutable argument for his Cold War campaign. Within this mythic commemorative narrative, the only possible response was to honor the extraordinary sacrifices displayed at Normandy with a renewed commitment to defending democracy around the world.[10]

Normandy as a Place of Return

Few other places and moments occupy the same mythic status as Normandy does in American public memory. This is due in large part to how narratives of D-day have evolved to encapsulate larger national commitments. What we remember, cherish, or even abhor about the past is always already shaped by our communal identification and association with others. "It is in society that people normally acquire their memories," Maurice Halbwachs famously wrote, and in community "that they recall, recognize, and localize their memories."[11] These memories also construct a shared sense of the world, inviting multiple groups to participate in imagined communities that transcend time and space.[12] The past, in other words, "is not preserved but is reconstructed on the basis of the present."[13] Within the Cold War mythic framework, Normandy offered a powerful set of rhetorical resources. As both a physical place and metaphorical model, Normandy embodied and displayed ideals of American moral commitment, duty, and sacrifice—qualities that, for many US presidents, justified the United States' leadership of the Cold War struggle against Soviet communism.

From the very beginning, Normandy was rhetorically constructed as a moral struggle between good and evil, an episode of heroic sacrifice, and the expression of duty to a cause greater than oneself.[14] In his June 6, 1944, "Order of the Day," General Dwight D. Eisenhower described D-day as a "Great Crusade" to liberate "the oppressed peoples of Europe" and attain "security for ourselves in a free world."[15] When Franklin D. Roosevelt spoke for the first time about the invasion to the US public over radio, he described the Allied landing at Normandy as "a mighty endeavor, a struggle to preserve our Republic, our religion, and our civilization, and to set free a suffering humanity."[16] In the days and weeks after the invasion, the US public encountered photographs, newsreel footage, and speeches by public officials that portrayed American soldiers and their counterparts as allies united in a righteous battle to free Europe from Nazi oppression. In this context, Normandy became a living, breathing warrant for US global leadership of the "Free World." After the Allied victory in World War II, US presidents frequently invoked Normandy's mythic status to support America's expanding intervention in the Cold War world. This occurred most often during ceremonies commemorating the anniversary of D-day.[17] But as the United States increased its military presence in Vietnam, presidential invocations of Normandy were used as an implicit justification for US military action in South Asia.[18] Just as the United States did not abandon its moral responsibility to defend liberty during World War II, Lyndon Johnson pledged in 1964, so too would the United States honor its duty in other places "where we have commitments to the cause of freedom."[19] Implied here was the presence of twenty thousand US military advisors in South Vietnam, a country whose "freedom" from North Vietnamese communist influence the United States took seriously.[20]

These early invocations of Normandy as a mythic Cold War commonplace occurred through words alone, but in 1964 Eisenhower elevated the physical scene of battle in the American public consciousness by going there himself. To commemorate the twentieth anniversary of D-day in 1964, CBS News aired a special broadcast entitled "D-Day + 20." In this ninety-minute special, news anchor Walter Cronkite and the former supreme commander of the Allied Expeditionary Force and former president led the nation on a tour of the battlefield's key sites. CBS's announcement of the broadcast described the program as one in which Eisenhower would give "his personal recollections of D-Day and the liberation of France, as well as his reflections on the meaning of the wartime events for today's world." According to the executive producer Fred W. Friendly, "There will be no other generals or politicians or statesmen on the program. It will be one soldier's personal way of saying it was all worthwhile."[21] The program aired on Friday night, June 5, from 8:30 p.m. to 10:00 p.m. around the country, and the *New York Times* reported that "West Germany and 18 other countries . . . purchased [access to] the show."[22] There was much press anticipation of the broadcast, and the news media focused on the eyewitness account Eisenhower would provide of June 6, 1944. The *Los Angeles Times* wrote that the general and former president would offer "personal recollections of D-Day decisions and experiences as well as place the day and the invasion in historical perspective."[23]

This special broadcast transported the nation—and world—to the scene of battle, with the D-day commanding general as the narrator of the story. The audience saw images of Pointe du Hoc, Omaha Beach, and the bunkers where German soldiers tried to stop the Allied advance. The program also offered sweeping views of the French coastline and moving images of the thousands of white crosses at the Normandy American Cemetery. Although the US public would have seen print images of Normandy and perhaps even newsreel footage of D-day just weeks after the invasion, these televised images would offer a new personal connection to the events of twenty years earlier. Eisenhower offered his own recollections of D-day as they moved from place to place, and these reflections were interspersed from camera footage CBS obtained of the D-day landings. In the final segment of the broadcast, with Eisenhower and Cronkite sitting on a stone wall with white crosses in the background, the former president explained that on June 6, 1944, "these men came here, British, and our other Allies, and Americans, to storm these beaches for one purpose only, not to gain anything for ourselves, not to fulfill any ambitions that America had for conquest, but just to preserve freedom, systems of self-government in the world."[24] New York Times writer Jack Gould described the program as "90 minutes of quietly moving television." He noted that "little was added to history's record of the turning point in World War II," but he emphasized the power of listening to Eisenhower's memory in place. "Sharing first-hand the Allied commander's illustrated remembrance of D-Day was an effective and novel commemoration of the occasion," he wrote. "For both General Eisenhower and the individual viewer it was an experience in nostalgia and a reminder of D-Day's cost."[25] These visual images of Pointe du Hoc, Omaha Beach, the German bunkers, and the US military cemetery, coupled with the general's firsthand account, made the events of the past come alive to those watching in the present moment, even if they were far removed from the scene of battle. Normandy had become a physical, material, tangible, visible place of return that provided new meaning and symbolism for a Cold War context. Reagan would appropriate a similar approach twenty years later.

By the 1970s, the mythic narrative of Normandy no longer provided the same image of American moral clarity and purpose.[26] Other places in the Cold War global imaginary—Vietnam, Laos, Cambodia—took center stage. As I detailed in chapter 5, Nixon sought to redirect public focus from Vietnam to the PRC through his 1972 visit, a trip that was designed to showcase US economic leadership in global affairs and a triumphant American presence in Asia. Although this new narrative may have been successful in the short term, it receded in the shadow of Watergate. With national morale at an all-time low after the withdrawal of US forces from Vietnam, economic inflation, energy shortages, and the Iran Hostage Crisis, the lessons of D-day—and the idea of American leadership abroad—seemed like a relic of the past. Michael R. Dolski argues that the "striking descent of D-Day's prominence from 1964 to 1974 indicates the rapid withdrawal from Second World War–related cele-brationism in American society. D-Day had shown America at its greatest, as the stories went; dulled by the pain and defeat abroad and dissent at home, that tale seemed less relevant."[27] The moral certainty and democratic convic-tions characterizing the "Good War" to defeat Hitler did not apply as cleanly and clearly to Vietnam.[28] Likewise, as *Time* essayist Lance Morrow observed, "If there has sometimes been a messianic note in American foreign policy in postwar years, it derives in part from the Normandy configuration. . . . But when the U.S. has sought to redeem other lands—South Viet Nam, notably—from encroaching evil, the drama has proved more complex."[29] This was the economic, cultural, and geopolitical climate that set the stage for the 1980 presidential contest between President Jimmy Carter and former California governor Ronald Reagan.

"Make America Great Again"

Throughout the 1980 presidential campaign, Reagan's optimistic faith in the American experiment and his campaign pledge to "make America great again" signaled a return to the past, a history that revolved around mythic narratives of individualism, self-reliance, and a divine mission to defend de-mocracy around the world. Indeed, a hallmark of Reagan's rhetorical style was this narrative retrospection. In his speech accepting the Republican nomination for president, Reagan argued it was "once again time to renew our compact of freedom" and "make this a new beginning" where the nation would once again stand as an "island of freedom" and "a refuge for all those people in the world who yearn to breath[e] freely."[30] When Reagan defeated Carter by more than eight million votes, many interpreted the upset as a di-rect rejection of the incumbent's foreign policy of détente and a sharp decline in the United States' image as the "Leader of the Free World."[31] In his first in-augural address, Reagan promised to address this decline in American pres-tige, arguing that as the nation took steps to "renew ourselves here in our own land, we will be seen as having greater strength throughout the world. We will again be the exemplar of freedom and a beacon of hope for those who do not now have freedom."[32] During his first term, Reagan's foreign policy rhetoric displayed what White House speechwriter Tony Dolan described as the "evolution of a counter-strategy to the Soviets" that rejected two things: "the notion that you cannot be morally candid and confront the Soviet Union" and the idea of "containment." This strategy, Dolan explained, "said the Soviet Union is about to collapse and we're gonna push it. That's all it's ever really needed."[33] After a long history of Soviet appeasement, Reagan took a bold—and, to many, idealistic—approach. Yet Reagan's strength, argues John Lewis Gaddis, "lay in his ability to see beyond complexity to simplicity. And what he saw was simply this: that because détente perpetuated—and had been meant to perpetuate—the Cold War, only killing détente could end the Cold War."[34]

Given his rhetorical ability to repurpose mythic themes of American patriotism, idealism, and exceptionalism for a Cold War world, it is not surprising that Reagan invoked the lessons of the Second World War as inspiration for his approach to US foreign policy.[35] Two speeches in particular set the tone for Reagan's "peace through strength" approach to US foreign policy during his first term.[36] In an address to members of the British Parliament on June 8, 1982, Reagan predicted that "the march of freedom and democracy . . . will leave Marxism-Leninism on the ash-heap of history." The United States and Great Britain had a responsibility to learn from the Second World War and act as "free people, worthy of freedom and determined not only to remain so but to help others gain their freedom as well."[37] Less than a year later, on March 8, 1983, Reagan spoke at the annual meeting of the National Association of Evangelicals in Orlando, Florida. The president called on his audience to resist the temptation "to ignore the facts of history and the aggressive impulses of an evil empire, to simply call the arms race a giant misunderstanding and thereby remove yourself from the struggle between right and wrong and good and evil." Reagan also maintained that the struggle between democracy and communism was not ultimately a matter of military might, but a spiritual crisis, "a test of moral will and faith."[38] Instead of simply presenting US democracy and Soviet communism as two competing views of the world, Reagan pronounced one good and the other evil. The explicit argument was that the United States was on the side of what was right and just.[39]

Like many of his Cold War predecessors, Reagan believed that the Soviet threat to political freedom could be found in the nation's own backyard. During his first term, Reagan took several steps to counteract Moscow's influence in Latin America. Some of these actions were overt. In October 1983, Reagan sent US troops to Grenada, an island nation just north of Venezuela. Earlier that year, the president had warned of the "Soviet-Cuban militarization of Grenada [that], in short, can only be seen as a power projection into the region."[40] After government officials ousted and executed Grenada's president, Maurice Bishop, the leaders of several Caribbean nations called for American military assistance. White House officials were also concerned about the safety of American medical students attending Saint George's University Medical School on the island. They could not afford another hostage situation. But Reagan also saw the situation in Grenada as an opportunity to counteract painful memories of Vietnam, and to make American influence and military power visible in the region. As H. W. Brands writes, "Reagan recognized that Grenada wasn't quite a dagger at America's heart, yet it *was* a place he could make a statement that would keep other daggers away."[41] In a speech to the nation after the invasion, the president recounted how brave US military forces came to this "Soviet-Cuban colony being readied as a major military bastion to export terror and undermine democracy." The lesson of Grenada, Reagan explained, was that "our national security can be threatened in faraway places. It's up to all of us to be aware of the strategic importance of such places and be able to identify them." To ensure that the next generation of Americans could enjoy political freedom, the president concluded, "we have to keep working for it and sacrificing for it just as long as we live."[42]

Other actions in Central America, however, took place in secret—or at least they started that way. Soon after Reagan took office, officials in the White House, the State Department, the NSC, and the CIA raised alarm over Soviet-sponsored arms and supplies being sent to Nicaragua and El Salvador by way of Cuba. In November 1981, Reagan authorized the CIA to engage in "political and paramilitary operations against the Cuban presence and the Cuban-Sandinista support infrastructure in Nicaragua."[43] Although Congress was informed of the administration's decision to provide support to pro-democratic forces in Nicaragua, the actual details of the plan were obscured. By early 1982, however, members of Congress sought additional information about the administration's actions in Central America and, under the Boland amendments, limited congressional financial support for the program. But in January 1984, CIA-backed local operatives began planting bombs in various harbors throughout Nicaragua to counteract a growing Cuban influence—an action Reagan had approved. On April 6, the *Wall Street Journal* reported the CIA's involvement in and the president's support for the covert operation. Members of Congress—both Democrats and Republicans—were incensed. Senator Barry Goldwater, now the chairman of the Senate Intelligence Committee and a strong supporter of the president, was unbridled in his criticism. In a letter he made public to the press, the Senate Republican told William Casey, Reagan's director of the CIA, that mining the harbors of Nicaragua was "an act violating international law. It is an act of war."[44] Although Reagan would later defend these covert operations as the natural progression of the

Monroe Doctrine and his commitment to the nation's "special responsibility to help others achieve and preserve the democratic freedoms we enjoy," the president struggled to articulate this message to the US public.[45]

It was in this context that the Reagan-Bush '84 campaign raised alarm over US public perceptions regarding Reagan's "handling of the situation in Central America and Nicaragua."[46] By May 1984, new internal polling suggested that the president was particularly vulnerable on several key issues: his perceived image as a world leader, US foreign policy overall, and the country's relations with Central America.[47] The nation was sharply divided over support for Reagan's foreign policy: 49 percent of US voters approved; 48 percent disapproved.[48] The most concerning issue to these Republican pollsters, however, were the "*serious* challenges" Reagan faced "over administration policies in Central America."[49] Only 37 percent of respondents indicated support for the president's foreign policy in Central America, where 51 percent disapproved, and 12 percent had no opinion. An even higher number—53 percent—disapproved of Reagan's "handling of the situation in Nicaragua." These results, cautioned Republican pollster Dick Wirthlin, suggested that "Central America remains a potentially explosive and divisive issue." Moreover, Wirthlin predicted, "Democratic demagoguery is certain to center on our involvement there, attempting to illustrate parallels, however remote, to Vietnam."[50] As history would reveal, however, these parallels were far from remote.

Reagan sought to allay such fears in an Oval Office address to the nation on May 9, 1984. Located "at our doorstep," he explained, Central America had also "become the stage for a bold attempt by the Soviet Union, Cuba, and Nicaragua to install communism by force throughout the hemisphere." The president referenced John F. Kennedy's warning against "the threat of Communist penetration in our hemisphere" and argued that that supporting prodemocratic forces in Central America was akin to the United States' military and economic aid for Greece under the Truman Doctrine in 1947. Quoting Truman's address to a Joint Session of Congress directly, Reagan stated: "The free peoples of the world look to us for support in maintaining their freedoms. If we falter . . . we may endanger the peace of the world, and we shall surely endanger the welfare of the nation." The world, the president added, was "shrinking," and the nation "could not pretend otherwise if we wish to protect our freedom, our economic vitality, and our precious way of life." In this narrative, US support for anticommunist forces in Central America was the natural extension of the Truman Doctrine and, importantly, a rejection of the isolationist ignorance that had blinded the US public in the early days of the Second World War. If the United States stood idly by as communists tried to gain geographical and ideological ground in this hemisphere, the country would be abandoning its moral imperative to "defend freedom in the world."[51]

Reagan would make a similar argument in his Pointe du Hoc address just four weeks later. America's past leadership set the precedent for the current moment. Present actions to protect individual freedom around the world were the natural progression of the nation's heritage. Although the White House characterized the president's visit to Normandy as a ceremonial event, in fact it was carefully timed, cleverly staged, and deliberately designed to address three underlying political exigencies. First, the visit underscored what Reagan and other US officials saw as the moral imperative of American global leadership. Because the domestic and foreign policy crises of the 1970s had severely damaged public confidence at home and American prestige abroad, the US public—and, by extension, the rest of the world—needed to be reminded of earlier American triumphs in the contest between good and evil. Second, the president's presence in Normandy reaffirmed his image as a confident, capable "Leader of the Free World" going into the 1984 presidential contest. Together, these two arguments were designed to convince US citizens of a third: that through Reagan's leadership, America's standing on the world stage had been restored. Unlike the failures of previous administrations, noted one briefing memo from the president's trip itinerary, Reagan's "strong leadership and clarity of purpose in the conduct of U.S. foreign policy" had replaced a previously "doubtful prognosis for the nation's future." Most significantly, Reagan had "restored the belief of the American people in themselves" and "re-asserted the pre-eminence of the United States in world affairs."[52] It was this strong global leadership that made the president deserving of a second term.

Setting the Stage for Normandy

Where earlier US presidents used their own body to symbolize America's expanding role in the world, Reagan chose to feature the bodies who fought to make this vision possible: the surviving military veterans of D-day. These were the men who risked their lives to preserve a democratic "way of life" from totalitarian aggression. The best way to honor their courage and sacrifice, the president suggested, was to ensure that political freedom was never again threatened, in Europe or elsewhere. By displaying these bodies in place, the president offered his audience a common text, a visible icon of D-day heroism. These vivid, living, breathing images created a space for remembrance, that intensified remembering communities do together.

The president's trip to Normandy in June 1984 was part of a ten-day European tour designed to strengthen US ties with its Western allies, particularly Great Britain, France, and Ireland. "Our objective by the time this trip is completed," wrote National Security Advisor Robert C. McFarlane to Deputy Chief of Staff Michael K. Deaver, "will be to reassert U.S. interest in a stronger and viable Europe within a larger policy context embracing both the Atlantic and Pacific communities, while stressing shared democratic values."[53] The White House chose specific geographic locations that would highlight these themes. In an April 1984 memo, William Flynn Martin, the director of international economic affairs for the NSC, noted that certain places would play a significant role in the president's trip. He wrote that Reagan's visits to Ireland, Normandy, and London would "provide the President with an ideal backdrop for his themes of peace and prosperity and the importance of Allied support and cooperation in the achievement of both." At Normandy, wrote Martin, Reagan should

> focus on Normandy as a landmark in the transatlantic relationship. Pay tribute to the Americans and other Allies who gave their lives in the fight for liberation and link the events at Normandy forty years ago with the reconciliation of former adversaries and the establishment of the current period of unprecedented peace and prosperity of Europe, based on the continued and continuing US commitment to the security of Europe.[54]

As both an "ideal backdrop" for the president's foreign policy goals and "a landmark in the transatlantic relationship," the physical scene and symbolic significance of Normandy in US public memory offered powerful visual imagery. In addition, as Martin noted, this place would provide a tangible link between past and present; what happened at Pointe du Hoc forty years earlier offered an inspiration for future Allied cooperation in Europe.

Although Reagan would deliver two addresses on the fortieth anniversary of D-day, it was his speech at Pointe du Hoc that the White House and other US officials considered particularly significant.[55] "It was here on June 6, 1944 that the US Army Rangers scaled the cliffs under heavy fire and secured the area to protect the landings at Omaha and Utah Beaches," explained Secretary of State George P. Shultz in a memorandum for the president. "Here you will make your principal statement of the day—a 15 minute speech stressing the bravery of the fallen and the survivors of this battle and emphasizing that Normandy marked the beginning of a continuous U.S. commitment to the security of Europe."[56] Secretary Shultz stressed the foreign policy goals of Reagan's address at Pointe du Hoc: memorialize the dead, honor the living, and show how the events of D-day worked to strengthen US-European ties in the future. A handwritten note on the top of a May 21, 1984, speech draft summarized this theme: "Pointe du Hoc a symbol of our selfless effort—against impossible odds men willing to do great deeds."[57] This notation hinted at the connection Reagan would draw between the US Army Rangers' heroic action in 1944 and the United States' ongoing commitment to defending democracy against Soviet expansion. In fact, a miscellaneous note in the speechwriting files suggested that the president should tie the US Army Rangers' action in 1944 to the 1983 US invasion of Grenada: "Tie Rangers of WWII to Modern Rangers; Point Salinas in Grenada."[58]

But it was not simply what happened at Pointe du Hoc that made this place significant; the power of the visuals associated with this place was of great importance. A speech draft from the NSC focused specifically on what one saw from the site: "The Cliffs which fall away to this often rough sea witnessed extraordinary heroism. Forty years ago—as part of a great Allied effort—brave American Rangers scaled these heights under fire. This ceremony and this place honors them."[59] A month later, in an article for the *New York Post* just a few days before the commemorative ceremonies, journalist Jack Schnedler noted that Pointe du Hoc offered the best "real" view of D-day. "It is hard to visualize that a great and fearsome battle raged only 40 years ago" at many of the historical sites at Normandy, he wrote. "Time and reconstruction have erased the evidence. But Pointe du Hoc, eight miles northwest of the U.S. cemetery, is an exception. Atop this 100-foot cliff, which the Germans were thought to have fortified with massive 155-mm. guns, the terrain is still a moonscape of craters and shattered bunkers from the Allied bombardment of June 6, 1944."[60] Not only did this place symbolize extraordinary heroism and sacrifice; it offered a glimpse into the past and the ideal backdrop for Reagan's retelling of D-day.

Reagan administration officials recognized, however, that most potent symbol of Pointe du Hoc was not the place itself. Instead, it was the bodies of the US Army Rangers who scaled the cliffs of France forty years earlier who offered the most powerful link between past and present. The White House invited the surviving US Army Rangers to attend the president's speech and made arrangements for these men to sit on the stage directly in front of the president. A miscellaneous note scratched on the back of a White House notepad described the set up: "RR stands in front of memorial dagger w/ Rangers, Mrs. Rudder & Mrs. Reagan seated in front on same level—In horseshoe—vets dependents[,] other veterans[,] VIP—military brass[,] official. RR won't even be announced. No one else speaks."[61] The president and the US Army Rangers would be featured together on the elevated stage, with the larger audience assembled around the stage in a "horseshoe" formation.

In this arrangement, Reagan could speak directly to an intimate group of sixty-two US Army Rangers while live cable television carried images of the president flanked by military veterans to audiences around the world. This staging also influenced the construction of the speech. "The Rangers were going to be sitting all together in the front rows, sitting right there five feet from the president," Peggy Noonan recalled. "Well then he should refer directly to them. He should talk to them. He should describe what they did and then say . . . 'These are the boys of Pointe du Hoc.'"[62] For the broader audience assembled around the stage—and the millions watching over live television—it would be impossible to look at Reagan without seeing the now gray-haired soldiers sitting on either side of him.

Miscellaneous notes by an unidentified author found in the archives of the White House Office of Speechwriting reveal a mixture of enthusiasm about the rhetorical potency of these images and a concern as to whether this arrangement might appear to be pure political spectacle. One notation suggested that reporters might see the speech as "a media show rather than an address directed toward the Rangers (who are sitting right there)."[63] Another read: "We're playing to the cameras rather than recognizing the heroes in front of him."[64] A third note mused that perhaps the focus on the US Army Rangers was "too anecdotal—doesn't seize the moment; bland treatment of heavy emotions, need to feel and communicate emotional rather than the factual." Further down on the yellow legal pad, however, other ruminations appeared: "Here the West Stood." "The Free World." Finally, this gem: "visual and his words make whole movie."[65] These notes, which seem to document key points of a meeting of Reagan's speechwriting team, reveal internal tensions over what the president's rhetorical display of these bodies would communicate to the watching world. Would these images seem opportunistic, calculated, and a political stunt? Or, would the combination of Reagan's historical narrative and the bodies of the men who enacted this daring feat reinforce the overarching themes the White House hoped to express—namely, that "Here the West Stood" to protect and defend "The Free World"?

A final clue to these internal deliberations comes from an obscure reference to an ancient text of political oratory. The same unidentified author scratched out the following passage from Thucydides's famed account of Pericles's funeral oration: "For her[oes] have the E[arth] for their tomb; and in lands far from their own, where the column w/ its epitaph declares it, there is enshrined in every breast a record unwritten w/ no tablet to preserve it, except that of the heart."[66] Below this paragraph, the author wrote: "Remind people this was written in [the] 400 b.c. Funeral oration of Pericles."[67] Although the date of Pericles's oration was incorrect, the author of these notes undoubtedly recognized that Reagan's speech at Pointe du Hoc followed the ancient Athenian tradition of memorializing the dead through public speech. This specific quotation suggests the commemorative function Reagan's speech would fulfill. Although he would not confront the immediate shock of death in 1984, he would use this occasion to honor the heroes of D-day who epitomized the values driving the Allied forces in 1944: freedom from tyranny, love of country, and moral resolve. Just as the citizens of Athens would listen to a revered orator deliver a eulogy over the dead, Reagan's audience would hear the president retell the story of Pointe du Hoc to the very men who enacted the daring feat forty years earlier. Overall, the White House designed Reagan's speeches in Normandy to "be forward-looking and positive, stressing a future mission for the broadened post-war alliance which can find inspiration in the sacrifices of Normandy."[68] The president would commemorate the fortieth anniversary of D-day by displaying bodies in place.

Broadcasting Reagan's Commemorative Campaign

Reagan's appearance at Pointe du Hoc was a made-for-TV event. It was an opportunity to reaffirm the centrality of US global leadership to the "Free World" global imaginary—a community that encompassed past events, present realities, and future possibilities. This vibrant image also would underscore the importance of reelecting Reagan to lead this Cold War campaign. "The public relations highlight of your trip to Europe will undoubtedly be the celebrations in Normandy," Shultz wrote to the president. "The intense media interest provides an opportunity for you personally, and allied leaders as a group, to reach an unprecedented audience on both sides of the Atlantic."[69]

The White House capitalized on this widespread media coverage, even granting Walter Cronkite (the same broadcaster who interviewed General Eisenhower in Normandy twenty years earlier) an exclusive interview with Reagan just after the president's speech at Pointe du Hoc. Five days before the event, Michael Dobbs of the *Washington Post* offered this synopsis of the White House's adaptation for prime time:

> With its gaze firmly fixed on the presidential elections in November, the White House has been anxious to see that photogenic ceremonies coincide with breakfast-time television back home. A speech by Reagan at the Pointe du Hoc, scene of a heroic assault by 225 U.S. Rangers to seize a gun emplacement at the top of a 100-foot cliff, will be beamed back live by all major U.S. networks Wednesday morning. Pool arrangements between U.S., French and British television stations will provide live coverage by over 30 camera crews of ceremonies at the American cemetery above Omaha Beach and at

Utah Beach. . . . Each network is planning to deploy its big guns, from Walter
Cronkite broadcasting live from Pointe du Hoc for CBS to Ted Koppel hosting
a one-hour reconstruction of the D-Day events on ABC's Nightline. The biggest effort is being mounted by NBC, which has hired its own satellite ground
station and is fielding 12 camera crews.[70]

Indeed, by the time Reagan arrived in Normandy on June 6, 1984, the US
public had been reminded of the significance of this commemorative occasion for several weeks. In May, NBC and CBS aired evening specials on the
Allied preparations for and rehearsals of D-day.[71] The week before the anniversary, *NBC Nightly News* featured a five-part special offering a play-by-play
of June 6, 1944.[72] Newspapers around the country editorialized the meaning
and significance of D-day, with op-ed columnists often drawing comparisons
between 1944 and the current moment. These television specials, images, and
newspaper accounts provided important historical context to an audience
who may have forgotten what this moment and this place symbolized. Reagan's Cold War stage had been set.

Reagan at Pointe du Hoc

In 2004, *Washington Post* reporter Lou Cannon described Reagan's speech
at Pointe du Hoc as "elegiac," a term that captures the cadence or repeated
rhythms adopted by Greek poets to recite national history and memorialize
the dead.[73] Where most mythic depictions ask the audience to imagine the
story in their minds, Reagan physically displayed the heroes of his narrative
in the very place where they enacted their daring feats forty years earlier. The
president's repeated references to the bodies of the US Army Rangers and
Pointe du Hoc as place provided a tangible link between past and present, an
enthymematic rhetorical resource that visually and physically displayed the
lessons of Normandy—courage, sacrifice, moral resolve—to the nation and
the world.

The White House timed the president's address so it would be broadcast
live on US networks over the morning news.[74] President and Mrs. Reagan arrived at Pointe du Hoc via Marine One at 8:02 a.m. EDT (2:02 p.m. local time)
and departed for Omaha Beach exactly one hour and one minute later.[75] This
hour slot perfectly coincided with television news network morning broadcasts, ensuring that Reagan's speech would receive full coverage. Network
news correspondents on the ground editorialized the president's hour-long
stop at Pointe du Hoc, offering poignant insights into how this place moved
them personally. ABC correspondent Pierre Salinger described the effect:

"You relive the day of D-Day, you see these enormous German bunkers . . . it still has the look of war around it."[76] As the camera crew panned to the hundred-foot cliffs, Peter Jennings asked his viewers to look carefully and consider what it must have been like to scale the heights under enemy fire. "Look at how high above the water [Reagan] is, forty years ago today, imagine people trying to climb up there."[77] CNN anchor Bernard Shaw narrated the scene for those watching at home. "You can see how rocky the terrain is," he said, explaining that Pointe du Hoc offered the most realistic picture of what D-day actually looked like forty years earlier. And when the president listened to two of the rangers recount their climb on D-day, reporter Richard Blystone encapsulated what everyone else had attempted to articulate: "These are men to stand in awe of when you stand at the place where they did what they did"[78] (figures 6.1 and 6.2).

President Reagan spoke with his back to the English Channel with the "boys of Pointe du Hoc" seated in a horseshoe formation around him. During the president's address, the network cameras focused their attention on Reagan and the sixty-two US Army Rangers assembled on the platform, with images of the jagged cliffs and rocky coastline sprinkled throughout. To those watching at home, this striking visual images became one with the text of Reagan's speech. The president began by noting the significance of the histori-

FIGURE 6.1. President Ronald Reagan speaks with two US Army Rangers who scaled the cliffs of Pointe du Hoc on D-day while members of the media look on, June 6, 1984. White House Photographic Office Collection. Courtesy of the Ronald Reagan Library. Accession Number: C22404-18.

FIGURE 6.2. President Ronald Reagan speaks with two US Army Rangers who scaled the cliffs of Pointe du Hoc on D-day, June 6, 1984. White House Photographic Office Collection. Courtesy of the Ronald Reagan Library. Accession Number: C22424-9.

cal occasion: "We're here to mark that day in history when the Allied armies joined in battle to reclaim this continent to liberty."[79] In his very first sentence, the president situated his audience in time and place. "We"—he and the rest of the audience, both those assembled at Normandy and the millions watching via television—were gathered "here" atop the cliffs of Pointe du Hoc to "mark" or commemorate an event in the past. Reagan then invited the audience to imagine the historical context of June 6, 1944: "For 4 long years, much of Europe had been under a terrible shadow. Free nations had fallen, Jews cried out in the camps, millions cried out for liberation. Europe was enslaved, and the world prayed for its rescue." After situating his audience in the present moment while pointing them toward the past, Reagan rooted his audience in place: "Here in Normandy the rescue began. Here the Allies stood and fought against tyranny in a giant undertaking unparalleled in human history." The successive use of "here" reminded the audience that this place was a marker not only on the timeline of "human history," but also the physical location where the Allied rescue of Europe began.

"We stand on a lonely, windswept point on the northern shore of France," Reagan continued. In this sentence, the president defined the physical scene and setting even as he located his audience geographically on the cliffs of Normandy. Although the air was now "soft," Reagan reminded his audience that "40 years ago at this moment, the air was dense with smoke and the cries of men, and the air was filled with the crack of rifle fire and the roar of cannon." Again, the president transported his audience back in time to what had happened in this place. These powerful metaphors of sight, sound, and smell made the realities of war viscerally present. Booming verbs such as "crack" and "roar" anchored the sentence, causing it to flow rhythmically and heavily, almost like the sharp popping of artillery. When Reagan recounted the scene of battle, network news coverage played historical footage taken of the Allied invasion. These black-and-white images depicted crowded boats motoring toward shore, dead bodies floating in the water, and smoke billowing in the distance. These images offered a physical display of the courage, honor, and sacrifice of those who fought on D-day.

Reagan moved from a general description of the events at Normandy to a vivid description of what happened at this exact spot—Pointe du Hoc:

> At dawn, on the morning of the 6th of June, 1944, 225 Rangers jumped off the British landing craft and ran to the bottom of these cliffs. Their mission was one of the most difficult and daring of the invasion: to climb these sheer and desolate cliffs and take out the enemy guns. The Allies had been told that some of the mightiest of these guns were here and they would be trained on the beaches to stop the Allied advance. The Rangers looked up and saw the enemy soldiers—[at] the edge of the cliffs shooting down at them with machine-guns and throwing grenades. And the American Rangers began to climb. They shot rope ladders over the face of these cliffs and began to pull themselves up. When one Ranger fell, another would take his place. When one rope was cut, a Ranger would grab another and begin his climb again. They climbed, shot back, and held their footing. Soon, one by one, the Rangers pulled themselves over the top, and in seizing the firm land at the top of these cliffs, they began to seize back the continent of Europe. Two hundred and twenty-five came here. After 2 days of fighting, only 90 could still bear arms.

In this passage, Reagan relied on what was visually evident and physically present: "these sheer and desolate cliffs," the beachhead at "the bottom of these cliffs," the hazardous climb to "the top of these cliffs." These repeated references to the jagged boulders lining the shore of France fused Reagan's spoken texts with its material context. "These cliffs" offered a powerful material testament to the courage, bravery, and sacrifice of the 225 US Army Rangers who persevered under heavy German artillery fire to make it to the top of the embankment. Through his vivid verbal imagery, Reagan transported the audience back to the sights, sounds, and smells of the past, inviting them to respond kinesthetically with the rangers who jumped and ran to the bottom of the cliffs upon which they were seated (figure 6.3).

FIGURE 6.3. President Ronald Reagan speaks at Pointe du Hoc, June 6, 1984. White House Photographic Office Collection. Courtesy of the Ronald Reagan Library. Accession Number: C22418-10.

Reagan then made the past immediately present by introducing the human actors of his narrative:

> Behind me is a memorial that symbolizes the Ranger daggers that were thrust into the top of these cliffs. And before me are the men who put them there. These are the boys of Pointe du Hoc. These are the men who took the cliffs. These are the champions who helped free a continent. These are the heroes who helped end a war.

To Reagan's immediate audience and the millions watching via television, it would have been impossible to look at the president and not see the sixty-two US Army Rangers seated on either side of him. With the physical presence of these former soldiers immediately before the eyes of all who were watching, Reagan amplified these visual images by pointing to these heroes with his words: "These are the boys of Pointe du Hoc." The president used the same word, "these," to describe the physical scene and heroes of the historical narrative. This word choice allowed Reagan to draw the audience's attention to the jagged rocks directly behind him and the middle-aged men in front of him. This physical display of the US Army Rangers' bodies offered a tangible instantiation of the sacrifices of D-day. History was alive, living and breathing, by the very men who enacted it (figure 6.4).

With the former soldiers now front and center for his immediate and extended audience, Reagan linked these brave men to other Allied troops, using vignettes vivid in their specificity to describe other soldiers and nations who had fought beside the US Army Rangers. Reagan enumerated "a rollcall of honor": the Royal Winnipeg Rifles, Poland's Twenty-Fourth Lancers, the Royal Scots Fusiliers, the Screaming Eagles, the Yeomen of England's armored divisions, the forces of Free France, and the Coast Guard's "Matchbox Fleet." By specifically naming these groups, the president made their sacrifices present to the assembled audience and emphasized that the US Army Rangers had not won the battle alone. This listing also underscored the need for Allied cooperation in the present-day struggle against Soviet communism. After recognizing the other nations who fought to free Europe in this historical narrative, Reagan returned to the present moment and spoke directly to the heroes of his story. "Forty summers have passed since the battle that you fought here," he said.

> You were young the day you took these cliffs; some of you were hardly more than boys, with the deepest joys of life before you. Yet, you risked everything here. Why? Why did you do it? What impelled you to put aside the instinct for self-preservation and risk your lives to take these cliffs? What inspired all the men of the armies that met here? We look at you, and somehow we know the answer. It was faith and belief. It was loyalty and love.

FIGURE 6.4. President Ronald Reagan addresses sixty-two US Army Rangers and other guests on the fortieth anniversary of D-day, June 6, 1984. White House Photographic Office Collection. Courtesy of the Ronald Reagan Library. Accession Number: C2420-13.

As Reagan translated the heroic actions of the men sitting before him, their physical bodies displayed the lessons of Normandy that so many US presidents had referenced earlier. The enthymematic argument Reagan started developing was this: if these men had been willing to risk their lives and give up the "deepest joys of life" to free other nations and defend their own country from Nazi tyranny, the United States had a moral obligation to follow their example forty years later.

The president continued his interpretation of the soldiers' bravery, extending the US Army Rangers' action at Pointe du Hoc to the broader Allied alliance in 1944—and 1984.

> The men of Normandy had faith that what they were doing was right, faith that they fought for all humanity, faith that a just God would grant them mercy on this beachhead or on the next. It was the deep knowledge—and pray God we have not lost it—that there is a profound, moral difference between the use of force for liberation and the use of force for conquest.

Again, the president's verbal pointing to the US Army Rangers—and, by extension, all those who fought on D-day—made their faith, courage, and sacrifice physically present. Reagan emphasized that the "men of Normandy" fought a battle "for all humanity" and explained that it was this enduring belief in the justice of their cause that motivated the Allied forces forty years earlier. This reflection on the past quickly shifted to the immediate present when the president expressed his hope that the Allies had not forgotten the "profound, moral difference" between liberation and conquest.

The president then interpreted the US Army Rangers' action in light of this moral lesson: "You were here to liberate, not to conquer, and so you and those others did not doubt your cause. And you were right not to doubt." Although Reagan did not mention US military action after the Second World War explicitly, his language implied that any involvement by the United States overseas designed to "liberate, not to conquer" should receive similar support from the citizenry and government officials—such as more recent actions in Vietnam, Grenada, El Salvador, and Nicaragua. "You all knew that some things are worth dying for," Reagan continued. "One's country is worth dying for, and democracy is worth dying for, because it's the most deeply honorable form of government ever devised by man. All of you loved liberty. All of you were willing to fight tyranny, and you knew the people of your countries were behind you." This bold claim positioned democratic freedom above all other governmental structures, in particular the "tyranny" the men of Normandy came to fight.

After focusing the first half of his speech on the events of June 6, 1944, the president continued the historical narrative up to the present moment—all while still relying on bodies in place to intensify his commemoration and the arguments that flowed from it. "When the war was over, there were lives to be rebuilt and governments to be returned to the people. There were nations to be reborn. Above all, there was a new peace to be assured. These were huge and daunting tasks. But the Allies summoned strength from the faith, belief, loyalty, and love of those who fell here." Despite the difficulties of the post-war years in Europe and the rest of the world, Reagan argued that the Allies found inspiration because of the courage and sacrifice of those who died at Normandy. Again, the bodily presence of the sixty-two US Army Rangers seated on stage offered a vivid reminder of the thousands who fought to free France. Here men fell and died while holding true to their faith, belief, loyalty, and love; thus, it was here, at Normandy, that strength and resolve could be found for the future.

From this inspiration, Reagan explained, the Allies "rebuilt a new Europe together." The United States "did its part, creating the Marshall plan to help rebuild our allies and our former enemies. The Marshall plan led to the Atlantic alliance—a great alliance that serves to this day as our shield for freedom, for prosperity, and for peace." What had been decimated by war, famine, and poverty was rebuilt through reconciliation and joint resolve. Those who were once enemies—most notably, the German people—were now friends and allies, and this friendship provided "our shield" for freedom, and against the spread of communism. There was, however, a sober part of the story. Despite these shared efforts, "not all that followed the end of the war was happy or planned. Some liberated countries were lost. The great sadness of this loss echoes down to our own time in the streets of Warsaw, Prague, and East Berlin." The "loss" of nations to Soviet communism was a bitter blow still evident in specific foreign locations. Warsaw, Prague, and East Berlin offered tangible examples of the Soviet march across Europe:

> Soviet troops that came to the center of this continent did not leave when peace came. They're still there, uninvited, unwanted, unyielding, almost 40 years after the war. Because of this, allied forces still stand on this continent. Today, as 40 years ago, our armies are here for only one purpose—to protect and defend democracy. The only territories we hold are memorials like this one and graveyards where our heroes rest.

Unlike the Allied troops who came to Normandy "to liberate, and not to conquer," Russian troops came and never left. It was because of their continued presence in places like Poland, Czechoslovakia, and East Germany that the United States (and other Western nations) remained. Their one purpose, argued Reagan, was "to protect and defend democracy"—a mission that,

according to his earlier historical narrative, was morally right. In this interpretation, the present-day Soviet presence in Europe was a continuation of
the Second World War.

In the final minutes of the speech, Reagan offered the moral to this story,
what was to be learned from these events:

> We in America have learned bitter lessons from two World Wars: It is better
> to be here ready to protect the peace, than to take blind shelter across the sea,
> rushing to respond only after freedom is lost. We've learned that isolationism
> never was and never will be an acceptable response to tyrannical governments
> with an expansionist intent.

It was more important to be "here"—here in Normandy, here in Europe,
and the metaphorical here of other places threatened by "tyrannical governments"—than living in willful ignorance. This was the lesson of the nation's
isolationist impulse prior to US entry into World War II. The underlying
implication was that earlier US action against Nazi Germany would have
saved thousands of lives—including those who died here at Pointe du Hoc.
Yet learning was not enough; specific actions were necessary. "We try always
to be prepared for peace; prepared to deter aggression; prepared to negotiate the reduction of arms; and yes, prepared to reach out again in the spirit
of reconciliation." The rhythm underscored the importance of preparation
to respond to possibilities and risks. Reagan stated that the United States
welcomed reconciliation with the Soviet Union so that both countries could
"lessen the risks of war, now and forever." The shift was subtle and somewhat
unexpected, the language reflecting a desire to reunite in an effort that echoed
their past alliance.

This spirit of reconciliation was underscored by Reagan's public recognition of Russian casualties during the Second World War. "It's fitting to
remember here the great losses also suffered by the Russian people during
World War II: 20 million perished, a terrible price that testifies to all the
world the necessity of ending war." This reference was a last-minute addition
by the NSC and State Department. Officials pushed the speechwriting staff
to include this line, noting that "an addition of a short paragraph alluding to
Soviet losses . . . will assist us in maintaining the moral high ground we have
secured in our public diplomacy struggle with the Soviets."[80] This mention
also served as an indirect refutation to Soviet press reports charging that the
president was attempting to "falsify the historic events of 40 years ago" and
discount the Soviet Union's role in defeating Hitler.[81] This acknowledgment of
the millions of Russian citizens who perished during World War II human-
ized the Russians. They, too, had lost men, women, and children—including

the more than four million that died during the siege of Leningrad.[82] Reagan's statement also worked as a metaphorical olive branch to the Russians. "I tell you from my heart that we in the United States do not want war. We want to wipe from the face of the Earth the terrible weapons that man now has in his hands." However, Reagan placed responsibility on the Soviet Union, stating that the Russians needed to demonstrate a willingness to work together with the United States and other Western allies. "We look for some sign from the Soviet Union that they are willing to move forward, that they share our desire and love for peace, and that they will give up the ways of conquest. There must be a changing there that will allow us to turn our hope into action."

After describing his vision for a post–Cold War world, Reagan shifted his audience back to the present moment, the immediate scene, and the bodies of the US Army Rangers on stage. "But for now, particularly today," Reagan said, "it is good and fitting to renew our commitment to each other, to our freedom, and to the alliance that protects it." The president's temporal references to "now" and "today" reminded his audience of their present obligation as witnesses to what happened at Normandy forty years earlier. Today, on this commemorative occasion, how should they respond? The president offered this answer: "We are bound today by what bound us 40 years ago, the same loyalties, traditions, and beliefs. We're bound by reality. The strength of America's allies is vital to the United States, and the American security guarantee is essential to the continued freedom of Europe's democracies." Reagan's use of "bound" implied a covenanting; here, in this place where Allied troops fought and died together for freedom, he was renewing the United States' commitment to defending liberty against Soviet communism. Moreover, the temporal shift between "today" and "40 years ago" reaffirmed the enduring covenant that neither time nor distance could sever. The president continued:

> We were with you then; we are with you now. Your hopes are our hopes, and your destiny is our destiny. Here, in this place where the West held together, let us make a vow to our dead. Let us show them by our actions that we understand what they died for. Let our actions say to them the words for which Matthew Ridgway listened: "I will not fail thee nor forsake thee." Strengthened by their courage and heartened by their value [valor], and borne by their memory, let us continue to stand for the ideals for which they lived and died.

In these final lines, Reagan described the United States' commitment to its Allied partners in the present moment as motivated by those who fought at Normandy forty years earlier. It was "here, in this place where the West held together," that the president called on the United States and other Western democracies to make a solemn vow—a vow not just to each other, but "to our dead." The bodily presence of the sixty-two US Army Rangers who climbed the cliffs at Pointe du Hoc offered a physical, tangible display of those men who had lived and died to liberate Europe. How could all freedom-loving nations not vow to honor their sacrifice and the thousands who perished on these very beaches forty years earlier? Just as the Allies had found strength in the "faith, belief, loyalty, and love" of the Allied soldiers during the postwar reconstruction of Europe, Reagan argued that the United States and the rest of the world had a moral responsibility to continue that mission in the present and future.

Public Reception and the 1984 Presidential Campaign

To the millions watching in the United States and throughout Western Europe, the live network news coverage offered a unique front row seat to Reagan's commemoration in place. Sweeping panorama shots of Pointe du Hoc transported viewers to the beaches of Normandy, and camera crews followed the President and Mrs. Reagan as they inspected the concrete German bunkers and walked along the edge of the cliffs. Viewers heard the waves crashing against the rocky shore below and saw gusts of wind blow Reagan's hair out of place. A lone seagull flew out over the English Channel as Reagan spoke. Although it was impossible to fully appreciate the multisensory dimensions of Pointe du Hoc without being there in person, the dramatic visuals and live media coverage of Reagan's presidential presence in place further amplified the president's moving narrative (figures 6.5 and 6.6).[83]

During the live coverage of the president's thirteen-minute address, the network cameras focused their attention on Reagan and the sixty-two US Army Rangers assembled on the platform, with images of the jagged cliffs and rocky coastline sprinkled throughout. When Reagan reminded his audience of Bill Millin, ABC showed a picture of the British soldier playing the bagpipes. Several minutes later, as Reagan recounted the scene of battle, the network played historical footage taken of the Allied invasion. These black-and-white images depicted crowded boats motoring toward shore, dead bodies floating in the water, and smoke billowing in the distance. After this brief return to the past, ABC returned to the immediate scene and zoomed in on the US Army Rangers as Reagan asked what motivated these men to sacrifice so much for their country. These images—both past and present—offered a physical display of the courage, honor, and sacrifice of those who fought on D-day. "You really do hope that a lot of the very young are watching," Peter Jennings remarked just after the president's speech, "because . . . there's been this sense of urgency and almost sense of wistfulness" that the current generation "don't have a real sense of what men and women went through to regain their freedom."[84]

FIGURE 6.5. President Ronald Reagan and First Lady Nancy Reagan tour a German bunker above the English Channel at Pointe du Hoc, June 6, 1984. White House Photographic Office Collection. Courtesy of the Ronald Reagan Library. Accession Number: C22411-11.

FIGURE 6.6. President Ronald Reagan greets several US Army Rangers after his speech at Pointe du Hoc, June 6, 1984. White House Photographic Office Collection. Courtesy of the Ronald Reagan Library. Accession Number: C22392-25A.

Stationed in Pointe du Hoc and along the Normandy coastline, US journalists played a critical role in narrating the significance of this moment for audiences watching at home. Throughout this live network commentary, reporters repeatedly noted the symbolism of Reagan's location, the US Army Rangers' bodies sitting atop the cliffs they climbed forty years earlier, and the narrative thread connecting past, present, and future. As NBC's Chris Wallace put it, "For Ronald Reagan, this was a day to honor the past, and use it to shape the future."[85] ABC reporter Sam Donaldson noted that the president relied on the sixty-two veterans "to set the tone for the American remembrance."[86] On the *CBS Evening News*, commentators highlighted how these men offered a living link between past and present:

> The president of the United States came to the beaches of Normandy to touch history. The wind and waves were almost calm, unlike 1944, and the sun, not seen then, sparkled today over the legions of the dead. At Pointe du Hoc, a sheer granite knife-edge 100 feet above the sea, Mr. Reagan heard from men of the second ranger battalion how they scaled the cliff under a hail of machine gun fire, losing more than half their number before they took the summit, only to be trapped there for several days.[87]

As one CBS reporter explained, "This solemn occasion was the kind of opportunity that comes only to a president to demonstrate statesmanship to the world at large, as well as to those back home."[88]

But the press also emphasized Reagan's larger goals for his commemoration at Normandy on June 6, 1984. "The White House saw Mr. Reagan's participation today as the perfect moment to reassure Europe that the alliance is strong and to argue dramatically that he wants no war," explained a CBS commentator.[89] Tom Brokaw noted that the president "used this occasion to reach out to the Soviet Union, an American ally forty years ago."[90] But perhaps it was NBC reporter Chris Wallace's assessment that so perfectly described the symbolic significance of this occasion and the White House's goals for the president's presence at Pointe du Hoc:

> For Ronald Reagan, this was a day to honor the past, and use it to shape the future. He began at Pointe du Hoc, a one-hundred-foot-high spike of rock that U.S. Rangers scaled with heavy casualties against a German barrage. Thirty [*sic*] of the 225 Rangers who fought here returned today. Mr. Reagan said they saved democracy. As he would all day, [he] compared the alliance against the Nazis then, to the alliance against the Soviets now. . . . The White House saw this as a big event for the President, and used it. He spoke here before meeting French President Mitterrand to get on U.S. morning television. Every move had been carefully choreographed. White House advance men rushed children in to wave goodbye to the Reagans and then tried to rush their teacher

out of the picture. . . . The president drew parallels between D-Day and now. But the real pull of that June day may be that it seems so far off. The U.S. was fighting for right, and it won. After Vietnam and Lebanon, the world no longer seems so uncomplicated.[91]

For the millions of US citizens watching at home, Reagan's rhetoric at Pointe du Hoc—and the bodies he displayed as evidence—presented a moral narrative of the past that also supported his present Cold War foreign policy.

Although the Reagan White House was particularly focused on how live network news would cover the president's speech, print journalists also played an important role. In a special report for the *New York Times*, military correspondent Drew Middleton noted that Reagan's speeches on the fortieth anniversary of D-day "touched common themes, including the bravery of the German enemy and sacrifices made by the Soviet Union during World War II."[92] The *Los Angeles Times* described how Reagan "issued a call to 'wipe from the face of the earth the terrible weapons man now has in his hands,'" and made special mention of the president's emphasis on "the 20 million Soviet citizens who lost their lives in the war."[93] According to Benjamin Taylor, a writer for the *Boston Globe*, "the now peaceful beaches of Normandy served as a dramatic backdrop yesterday for a ceremony commemorating the 40th anniversary of D-Day. . . . In remarks laced with emotion and patriotism, Reagan castigated the Soviet Union for its military domination of Eastern Europe even as he continued to extend the olive branch of reconciliation if 'they will give up their ways of conquest.'"[94] These reports further emphasized the clear dual message of Reagan's speeches at Normandy: commemorate the past Allied triumph over Nazi tyranny and rededicate the Western alliance to defending—and spreading—democracy during the Cold War.

These visually potent images of Reagan at Normandy continued to circulate during the summer and fall of 1984. This was always part of the plan. In a February 1984 memorandum, the Reagan-Bush '84 campaign stressed the importance of using "the pre-convention period to positively reinforce the President's image as President and leader."[95] Between March and June, campaign officials sought to create what they called "'ideal image' events" that would "weave together and advance our themes and issues and blanket the target groups and areas. In effect, we are creating commercials for the President's campaign."[96] But even though the White House and the Reagan-Bush '84 campaign anticipated featuring the president's visit to Normandy in their campaign materials, internal documents suggest that Reagan's performance at Pointe du Hoc was more successful than anyone could have anticipated. In a strategy memo dated June 19, 1984, the producers of the convention docu-

mentary detailed their plan for the film, noting that there would be no inter-
viewer or narrator—only the voice of the president. "He is our guide, in effect,
through the film. . . . As the President speaks, we begin to dissolve through
and *see* those actual events of which he's speaking. The verbal images become
visual images. We see—and hear—those moments the President is talking
about. And we begin to re-live those events and experiences on film." To emphasize the point, the producers highlighted one possible scenario for the film:

> For example, he might say something like: "On our trip to Normandy June 6th
> for the Anniversary of D-Day, I'll never forget that feeling of walking down
> that line of Rangers who climbed those cliffs 40 years ago. I felt like I was
> touching hands with history . . ."
>
> Now, at this point, we begin to actually *see* that moment on film. And as
> he shakes their hands, the President's voice continues over and he says, "as
> I looked into those faces, with the scars of war still around us, I thought to
> myself . . . 'Never again.'"

Through this production strategy, the producers concluded, the president's
"verbal images would become visual."[97] Reagan's rhetoric in place—and the
images of him at this sacred site—would enable the audience to imagine the
events he recounted in his speech at Pointe du Hoc.

On the final evening of the 1984 Republican National Convention in Dal-
las, the US public encountered these striking images in an eighteen-minute
campaign film. Entitled "A New Beginning," the video montage featured
snippets of Reagan's speeches at Pointe du Hoc and Omaha Beach, including
sweeping panoramic shots of the cliffs at Pointe du Hoc, endless rows of white
crosses and Stars of David in the Normandy American Cemetery, and the
large audience assembled for the joint ceremony at Omaha Beach. The most
poignant aspect of this section was how the campaign interspersed Reagan's
speeches at Pointe du Hoc and Omaha Beach with actual footage of men
storming the beaches on June 6, 1944. In addition, the video also contained
close shots of the sixty-two "boys of Pointe du Hoc." As the audience listened to Reagan's narrative of the Allied landings at Normandy, they watched
black-and-white footage of soldiers swimming to shore. When Reagan recounted the courageous climb of the US Army Rangers forty years earlier, the
camera zoomed in on the faces of the D-day veterans. This juxtaposition of
text and image provided a striking tribute not just to the men who fought at
Normandy, but it also reinforced Reagan's image as a focused, patriotic head
of state dedicated to protecting US democracy at home and preventing the
spread of communism abroad.

Four years after his promise to "make America great again," Reagan-Bush

'84 campaign officials sought to portray Reagan as the one who could honor America's past, lead the country through the challenges of the present moment, and paint a vision for the nation's future. In their view, the president's bold and innovative leadership had returned the United States to its rightful place in the world after the domestic and geopolitical tumult of the 1960s and 1970s. Reagan had shepherded the country out of a decade of decline into a prosperous "New Beginning." In this narrative, the nation should once again put its faith in Reagan's optimism that America's greatest days were still ahead. A vote for Reagan would be a vote for patriotism, duty, love of country, and US global leadership—the ideals that motivated the heroes of D-day and the values that gave meaning to the present moment. A vote for Reagan, then, was a vote for a bright and hopeful future, a new "Morning in America," and the continuation of America's elevated role as the "Leader of the Free World." And on November 6, 1984, the US public embraced this vision, reelecting Reagan in a landslide.[98]

Conclusion

Ronald Reagan's speech on the fortieth anniversary of D-day at Pointe du Hoc stands as an exemplar of presidential commemoration. Indeed, Reagan is to Normandy as Kennedy is to Berlin. All future presidential addresses at Normandy would be compared to Reagan's commemorative campaign.[99]

Part of this is due to Reagan's rhetorical ability to crystallize the meaning and symbolism of D-day into a vivid, compelling narrative that his immediate and extended audience could see, hear, and imagine. Commemoration is, after all, a form of epideictic address, speech designed to display or extol individuals and actions worthy of communal celebration.[100] It looks backward and forward even as it remains in the immediate situation, the temporal present.[101] As a sacred act of remembrance, commemoration "points both backward to the vanished event or person and forward . . . to preserve the memory of the event or person, or even to act on it."[102] And when commemoration happens at or in relation to a specific site, this space provides "the ground and resource, the location and scene of the remembering we do in common."[103] But commemoration in place does more than designate a site as sacred. It constitutes the audience as witnesses (*theōros*), individuals who have seen and heard and must now respond in kind. As *theōros*, notes Megan Foley, the audience engages in "a seeing-seen, a seen-seeing, a double vision in double time. The vision of the *theōros* is doubled in its temporality, simultaneously progressive and perfect: 'One is seeing and one has seen at the same time.'"[104] Commemoration in place, then, is both rooted in space and time while also extending beyond the present moment. With their location fully fixed, individuals can look backward to what happened here many years ago and apply the lessons of these events to present and future circumstances. This is what Reagan accomplished at Pointe du Hoc.

Although on the surface Reagan's address was a commemorative act, the president used this occasion to advance his broader Cold War foreign policy, a vision of the United States—and, by extension, the US president—as the rightful "Leader of the Free World." In a 2013 interview, Peggy Noonan noted that what "Reagan was really saying to all the gathered leaders of the West who were there that day" was that "if we hold together as they did, we are going to defeat together the tyranny of our time—and that is Soviet communism." In fact, Noonan added, "by lauding the World War II generation, Reagan was also trying to inspire those who now still had to hold together . . . to push that wall [the Berlin Wall] over. So, he very consciously . . . used that speech to say, 'Look what we did last time. We can still do it!'"[105] As Noonan's reflections make clear, Reagan appropriated the moral clarity and purpose of D-day for the present moment. The only possible response to their extraordinary sacrifice was a renewed commitment to protecting and defending democracy around the world. Anything less would betray the heroes and story of D-day. Reagan's commemoration at Normandy engendered much more than ceremonial oratory. It was a deliberate reassertion of American leadership on the Cold War world stage.

After Reagan's commemoration in place in 1984, four additional presidents—William J. Clinton, George W. Bush, Barack Obama, and Donald J. Trump—have traveled to Normandy to commemorate the anniversary of D-day. In 1994, Clinton promised the D-day veterans assembled at Normandy, "We commit ourselves, as you did, to keep [freedom's] lamp burning for those who will follow. You completed your mission here. But the mission of freedom goes on; the battle continues."[106] Ten years later, on the sixtieth anniversary of D-day, George W. Bush told the surviving veterans, "You will be honored ever and always by the country you served and by the nations you freed."[107] In 2009, President Barack Obama commented on the historical significance of June 6, 1944, noting, "D-Day was a time and a place where the bravery and selflessness of a few was able to change the course of an entire century."[108] Five years later, on the seventieth anniversary of the Normandy invasion, Obama drew a parallel between the "Greatest Generation" and present-day military heroes fighting in Iraq and Afghanistan. As Reagan had done before him, Obama used the story of D-day to inspire patriotic sentiment and humble appreciation for these "generations of men and women who proved once again that the United States of America is and will remain the greatest force for freedom the world has ever known."[109]

But in 2019, on the seventy-fifth anniversary of D-day, Donald J. Trump offered a strikingly nationalistic interpretation of D-day, a tale of what Normandy meant for the American "way of life." Like Reagan, Trump detailed a historical narrative featuring individual actors who participated in the Allied landings—and their children and grandchildren. These were men who "enlisted their lives in a Great Crusade," who undertook a mission Trump described as "the story of an epic battle and the ferocious, eternal struggle between good and evil." He declared that the "warriors of D-Day" won "a future for our nation" and the "survival of our civilization." In fact, Trump described these heroes as motivated by "the confidence that America can do anything because we are a noble nation, with a virtuous people, praying to a righteous God." The use of present tense here was key.

Where earlier US presidents used the moment to underscore a historic partnership between the United States and other Western democracies, Trump spoke about American superiority. Where his predecessors used their speeches at Normandy to set forth a clear example of US global leadership, Trump emphasized that the heroes of D-day "did not just win a battle" or even "just win a war." Instead, "those who fought here won a future for our nation. They won the survival of our civilization. And they showed us the way to love, cherish, and defend our way of life for many centuries to come." And where past chief executives emphasized a national commitment to protecting and defending democracy around the world, Trump's statements were focused on "America First." His concern was over winning "a future for our nation," ensuring the "survival of our civilization," and defending "our way of life."[110] This is not surprising, given Trump's "America First" foreign policy and repeated public dismissals of several historically important geopolitical organizations, including the United Nations, the North Atlantic Treaty Organization, and the G7. And yet, in a speech explicitly described by the White House as one of commemoration, Trump shifted the narrative. Where US presidents from Reagan to Obama explicitly elevated ideals or virtues such as moral clarity, unity of purpose, and a commitment to defending democratic freedom as the motivating factor behind the American sacrifice at Normandy, Trump focused on something else: a nationalistic zeal for "our way of life" that proclaimed, above all, a distinction and division between "our nation" and the rest of the world.

Conclusion

On June 9, 2021, Joseph R. Biden, the forty-sixth president of the United States, departed for an eight-day visit to Europe. In an op-ed published in the *Washington Post* five days before he flew to the United Kingdom, Biden described his first presidential trip abroad as an opportunity to reclaim the United States' position of leadership on the world stage. "In this moment of global uncertainty, as the world still grapples with a once-in-a-century pandemic," he wrote, "this trip is about realizing America's renewed commitment to our allies and partners, and demonstrating the capacity of democracies to both meet the challenges and deter the threats of this new age." Citing the ongoing threats of the COVID-19 pandemic, climate change, and "the harmful activities of the governments of China and Russia," Biden asserted his view that the United States "must lead the world from a position of strength."[1]

Biden's explicit commitment to reinstating the nation's position of global leadership was a common refrain throughout the trip, one that mirrored comments he made during the 2020 US presidential campaign. During a town hall event in October 2020, Biden stated that because the United States had failed to lead by the "power of our example," the country had become "more isolated in the world than we've ever been. . . . [because] America first has made America alone."[2] In many ways, the Biden administration saw the president's first international trip as a direct rejection of Trump's "America First" foreign policy approach. *New York Times* journalists David E. Sanger and Steven Erlanger went so far as to describe the visit as Biden's "comeback tour," noting that "at every stop he opened with the same three words: 'America is back.'"[3] In a press briefing one day after Biden returned from Europe, White House National Security Advisor Jake Sullivan described what he saw as the "foundational outcome for the trip": "The bottom line is that Joe Biden confidently and skillfully donned the mantle of leader of the free world on this trip. The previous president had ceded that mantle, and this president has now emphatically reclaimed it."[4] Although this desire to reinstate the president's global leadership role was a direct response to the previous administration, it also invoked a long-standing tradition of US foreign policy dating back to the earliest days of the Cold War, if not before: asserting, maintaining, and rhetorically displaying a strong, confident image of the United States as the "Leader of the Free World."

In fact, it is difficult to imagine rhetorical articulations of US foreign policy apart from the act of going global. The precedent set by Theodore Roosevelt in 1906 has evolved to become a central feature of US presidential rhetoric and foreign policy in the post–Cold War world. As I detailed in the introduction, it is no accident that US presidents began to travel overseas and speak directly to foreign leaders and international audiences just as the nation began to expand its power and influence abroad. Tracing the rise, evolution, and extension of the global rhetorical presidency also tells the story of the United States' determination to conquer a new global frontier throughout the twentieth century. As chief executives sought to elevate US prestige in the minds of an international audience, they also attempted to remind the US public that the nation was, at its core, a force for good in the world—that "city on a hill" Winthrop described so many years ago.

A defining aspect of these tours is how US presidents used their travels to and physical presence within international locales to display American power and influence abroad. Although scholarly considerations of US foreign policy rhetoric often focus on the language of formal communiqués or joint statements, this book demonstrates how the visual, spatial, embodied, and emplaced elements of presidential performance have contributed to the United States' position on the world stage. Attending to these tactics of rhetorical display also underscores the central role epideictic oratory plays in US foreign policy discourse. In Aristotle's original formulation, epideictic speech invited the audience to bear witness to a shared national past, present, and future, to celebrate moments of communal pride or achievement, and to recommit themselves to the cause at hand. Within the context of US foreign policy, chief executives and other political officials utilized the global rhetorical presidency to create scenes or image events that invited—required, even—their audience to see, envision, or imagine what American global leadership might accomplish for the rest of the world. Theodore Roosevelt saw his visit to the Panama Canal Zone as a unique opportunity to make American ingenuity and grit visible, accessible, and translatable to the US public. If the nation's best and brightest technological minds could forge a path across the

Panamanian isthmus, what other unimagined feats might they accomplish? Woodrow Wilson traveled to Europe convinced that the United States should play a central role in global affairs. But he also went to be seen, not just by an international public but by American citizens watching at home. In his estimation, if the nation was to make the world "safe for democracy," the president needed to play a visible role.[5] And despite his physical limitations and very real security concerns, Franklin D. Roosevelt made the explicit decision to cross oceans and international boundaries so that he could be seen performing his duties as commander in chief and as the leader of the "Big Three" alliance during the Second World War.

The presidential impulse to go global only increased during the Cold War. Through their carefully orchestrated tours abroad, chief executives rhetorically constructed and physically displayed a robust, active image of the United States on the metaphorical and literal world stage. This was not just a war of words alone. It was a contest between two "ways of life" and the images, borders, bodies, and places that symbolized, structured, and sustained that ideological divide. When Truman toured the wreckage of a decimated Nazi Germany, he declared that the United States would continue to defend a free "way of life" even after the Second World War ended. To a public well aware of the dangers posed to democracies by totalitarian expansion, this diplomatic move seemed to be a natural extension of US foreign policy—even if this meant sending military and economic aid to European countries fighting to defend themselves from Soviet encroachment. Fourteen years later, with the Cold War fully underway, Eisenhower developed his "Good Will" tours to sketch the boundaries of US global influence, demarcate critical points on the Cold War ideological battlefield, and rally international public opinion behind the United States in the ongoing contest of global prestige. For Kennedy, the decision to go to West Berlin was as much about elevating his own presidential image as it was reaffirming the United States' commitment to an enduring symbol of "Free World" determination. His place of address—and all it contained—became a powerful presidential platform, one numerous chief executives have deployed ever since. Amid the escalating crisis in South Vietnam, Nixon redirected the narrative by extending a diplomatic hand of friendship to the PRC. He broke through the "Bamboo Curtain" through his travel to the PRC and, through the novel affordances of live network news, took the nation and the world along for the ride. And at Normandy, Reagan deployed themes of sight, vision, image, light, and rhetorical display to recenter the global stage around the mythic ideal of American exceptionalism and those quintessential American heroes who fought and died to make this vision possible.

But these presidential tours were never neutral or apolitical. Chief executives of both parties used the act of going global to forward their own political agenda. Rather than limiting their political ambitions to the confines of the United States, they saw the global rhetorical presidency as a mechanism to extend their presidential influence, expand their role in foreign affairs, cement their historical legacy in American public memory, and marshal public support for their presidential campaigns. As the nation's chief diplomat and emissary for US foreign policy, the president's travel in, between, and through select spaces and regions marked them as meaningful and significant for US interests. For each of the episodes recounted in this book, there are dozens of stories of telegrams, letters, and phone calls from various political leaders clamoring for a presidential visit. Heads of state around the world knew it meant something for the "Leader of the Free World" to commit time, attention, and material resources to a specific country. For many, securing a spot on the president's traveling roadshow symbolized belonging and membership in this "Free World." And yet, as I have shown in the preceding chapters, the White House always had competing motives for the trips they planned, granted, and choreographed.

Indeed, the president's embodied movements spun a geopolitical web of inclusion and exclusion, privilege and dismissal, attention and deflection. The political nature of these tours extended beyond where the president chose to go. A common refrain throughout these episodes is how various administrations designed these tours as a strategy of redirection or obfuscation. As I noted in chapter 3, "Operation Amigo" allowed Eisenhower to see and be seen in Latin America at the same moment that senior US officials outlined several containment strategies for Castro's Cuba, including the beginnings of a plan that would culminate in the Bay of Pigs fiasco in April 1961. Although he would never mention the island nation by name in his public remarks, Eisenhower's presence in Latin America redirected attention away from a growing communist influence ninety miles from Florida and toward an image of US power and influence in the region. Strategies of deflection also extended to the domestic front. Where chief executives struggled to articulate clear support for civil rights and racial equity at home, they embraced any opportunity to showcase the superiority of American democracy on the world stage. As chapter 4 shows, when faced with the choice to visit Birmingham or Berlin, Kennedy decided to go abroad. To the president and senior White House officials, it was more important to reaffirm Kennedy's status as the "Leader of the Free World" overseas than to demonstrate support for civil rights at home. Nothing could replace the sight of the US president being cheered by over a million West Berliners.

To American audiences watching from home, seeing the image of the president touring the globe reinforced the idea of US leadership of and pre-eminence in world affairs. In the aftermath of Roosevelt's sudden death and Truman's ascendence to the presidency, the nation watched to see how the former junior senator from Missouri would fare next to Stalin and Churchill at the third and final conference of the "Big Three." As chapter 2 demonstrates, Truman used his public appearances at Potsdam to articulate the United States' commitment to winning the Second World War and the peace that followed. For some US presidents, going global offered a sure and steady way to reaffirm their image of global statesman. Such was the case with Nixon's 1972 "Opening to China" and Reagan's visit to Normandy in 1984. As I detailed in chapters 5 and 6, these visits occurred just months before their respective re-election campaigns—and that was the point. Images of Nixon shaking hands with Mao Tse-tung and Chou En-lai displayed a new vision for US foreign policy, one defined not by military action but a desire to bridge the long-established ideological gulf between the United States and the PRC. For Reagan, the fortieth anniversary of D-day allowed him to repurpose themes of duty, courage, and sacrifice for the present moment, arguing that the United States and its Western allies had the same moral duty to stand against communism in 1984 as they did Nazi aggression in 1944. In both cases, these presidential tours deflected attention from unpopular US interventions abroad (Vietnam and Central America) and refocused the narrative to portray the president as a strong, confident "Leader of the Free World."

The evolution of the global rhetorical presidency also reflects the rapidly changing media environment and telecommunications technology during the twentieth century. Where Theodore Roosevelt could rely on the novelty of publishing images in the *Congressional Record* and journalists eager to cover his every move, Wilson had to contend with a press and a public who were less than thrilled about the idea of an American president spending several months in Europe—and, in their minds, absent from the job they elected him to do. But in the postwar years, US officials devoted considerable time and energy to developing a coordinated media platform from which to market the superiority of American democracy to the rest of the world. Images of Truman surveying the wreckage in Berlin and meeting with the "Big Three" at Potsdam reaffirmed his presidential role in the aftermath of FDR's sudden death and portrayed US leadership of the postwar world as necessary and justified. Both Eisenhower and Kennedy relied on photographic images, newsreels, and feature films to extend the reach of their global tours to audiences around the world. For Nixon and Reagan, the advent of cable news and live satellite feeds allowed US officials to choreograph and produce carefully curated political spectacles in the PRC and Pointe du Hoc, image events that displayed American power and influence on the world stage.

Although the preceding case studies provide key representative examples of how the global rhetorical presidency evolved to meet the needs of the historical moment and to respond to various political exigencies, there are many more that deserve careful study and analysis. This project offers an entry point for analyzing how other presidential acts of going global have reflected and directed US foreign priorities and commitments. By attending to the rhetorical dynamics of body, place, image, audience, and circulation, this approach underscores the fact that foreign policy discourse is not limited to words delivered from a platform or written on a page. Instead, it is a dynamic, multifaceted encounter between the US president and a multitude of audiences. It is simultaneously verbal and visual, situated and emplaced, a symbolic act that reflects and redefines complicated geopolitical histories while mediating, transmitting, and circulating the presence of the president to the international arena. The act of going global also represents a form of direct presidential address, a way for the chief executive to speak to the nation and the world. Of course, this is not the only way US presidents address international audiences, but it does matter where they speak and why they choose to speak there.

Within a twenty-first-century context, the global rhetorical presidency has evolved to reflect the differing foreign policy priorities of various administrations and the post–Cold War international landscape. Some of these moves were made to justify US military intervention overseas and affirm the United States' self-appointed role as a protector and defender of political freedom. In June 2003, George W. Bush traveled to the Middle East after his infamous "Mission Accomplished" declaration on the deck of the aircraft carrier USS Abraham Lincoln one month earlier. During a speech to US military personnel at Camp As Sayliyah, Qatar, the president reminded his audience that they had been sent "on a mission to remove a grave threat and to liberate an oppressed people, and that mission has been accomplished." It was from "right here"—this military base—that the "very first strike in the liberation of Iraq started," he said. "Missions of mercy are directed from here." For Bush, like Kennedy before him, place was everything. As he praised the bravery of American men and women in uniform, Bush articulated his rationale for why the United States was in Iraq and Afghanistan. The nation, he explained, did not "seek the expansion of territory. We're not interested in more territory. Our goal is to enlarge the realm of liberty. . . . We believe people have the right to think and speak and worship in freedom. That's what we believe in America, and that's what you showed the world."[6] This narrative, which bore a striking resemblance to Truman's argument for keeping US troops in Europe after the Second World War, reaffirmed the idea that US intervention overseas is warranted and justified when the aim is to liberate the oppressed. And like Reagan did at Pointe du Hoc, Bush laid out this rationale in front of an audience who had risked their lives to make this liberation possible. The implication, of course, was that any disagreement with the president's characterization of the present military mission would dishonor those who served.

Other instances reveal how US presidents have gone global to articulate a new vision for American foreign policy. Where Bush traveled to a US military base in the Middle East to declare US victory over an oppressive Islamic regime, Obama went to Cairo to propose "a new beginning" between the United States and Muslim nations around the world.[7] In a speech co-hosted by Cairo University, Egypt's premier public university, and Al-Azhar University, one of the oldest and most prestigious Islamic universities in the world, Obama emphasized the significance of his presidential presence in place. "I have come to Cairo to seek a new beginning between the United States and Muslims around the world," he said, "one based on mutual interest and mutual respect, and one based upon the truth that America and Islam are not exclusive and need not be in competition." The president acknowledged the long and complex history between the United States and Muslim nations, one complicated by 9/11 and the US invasion of Iraq and Afghanistan. But Obama told his audience that to "move forward," both parties needed to engage in "a sustained effort to listen to each other; to learn from each other; to respect one another; and to seek common ground." Throughout the speech, the president took the unusual but important step of acknowledging that the United States could not—and should not—dictate the affairs of other countries. "America does not presume to know what is best for everyone," he said, "but I do have an unyielding belief that all people yearn for certain things"—such as freedom of speech, democratic representation, governmental transparency, and equal treatment under the law. These ideals did not belong to the United States, Obama insisted, but were instead "human rights. And that is why we will support them everywhere." By framing these principles as universal rights that should be available to all, Obama departed from a narrative that posited these ideals to be uniquely American. Instead, he argued for a pluralistic understanding of the world, one in which the United States acted instead as an equal partner and friend. In Obama's view, it was this commitment to mutual collaboration that would allow the "people of the world [to] live together in peace."[8]

And yet, as I have detailed throughout this book, the articulation and enactment of US foreign policy narratives is largely dependent on the person who occupies the Oval Office. Where Obama argued for an open, inclusive global society, Donald J. Trump used his presence abroad to present the United States as set apart—and isolated—from the rest the world. A hallmark of Trump's foreign policy approach was his repeated declaration of "America First." Where Cold War US presidents actively cultivated a strong international coalition with other nations through US-backed organizations such as the United Nations, NATO, and various iterations of the current G7, Trump took steps to undermine these relationships throughout his time in office. As I noted at the end of chapter 6, Trump's rhetoric at Normandy on the seventy-fifth anniversary of D-day represents a stark departure from previous anniversary ceremonies. Although US presidents routinely emphasize American global leadership—preeminence, even—Trump offered a strikingly US-centered nationalistic narrative. In his telling, D-day was a battle for the American "way of life," but a life in which the "shining city" Reagan depicted three decades ago was defined not by who it welcomed, but who it ignored, excluded, and erased.[9]

Despite Trump's repeated rejections of the global democratic alliance forged during the Cold War, he embraced one specific element of the global rhetorical presidency: the penchant for historical firsts. On June 30, 2019, Donald J. Trump became the first sitting US president to set foot in North Korea—a step that sent diplomatic shock waves around the world. During his 2016 presidential campaign, Trump suggested that he, and he alone, had the gumption and political skill to negotiate with North Korea. Then, in June 2018, Trump met with Kim Jong-un in Singapore, a moment that marked the first time in history that a US president had interacted with the leader of North Korea. One year later, and less than eighteen months before the 2020 US presidential election, Trump decided to stage another presidential first. Although he was scheduled to visit the demilitarized zone (DMZ) on the border of North and South Korea, his step onto North Korean soil was a hastily arranged political spectacle, one Trump first suggested on Twitter. He would soon be in South Korea, the president tweeted, and "if Chairman Kim of North Korea sees this, I would meet him at the Border/DMZ just to shake his hand and say Hello(?)!"[10] According to several administration officials, it was only after Trump issued this tweet that the White House began planning for such a meeting between the two leaders.[11] This historic step into North Korea was a highly publicized political spectacle made possible because of a 230-character tweet and a US president who rejected traditional channels of US diplomacy and the recommendations of his own advisors so he could claim a presidential first. But perhaps this was his point. Where earlier diplomatic overtures were carefully planned, staged, and orchestrated, Trump took this symbolic and physical step because he tweeted that he could. Whatever else the global rhetorical presidency may be, it is a mechanism directed by and dependent upon the president's rhetorical leadership—or lack thereof.

And the global rhetorical presidency lives on. As these contemporary anecdotes and the preceding chapters make plain, the decision to go global is itself a form of symbolic action, an acknowledgment and articulation of the complex foreign policy choices all chief executives encounter while in office. It is a geopolitical act and a hegemonic move, one designed to elevate the nation's position and the US president's role in matters of state. In the end, this rhetorical strategy allows chief executives to use their travel to and bodily presence in place to expand US political and psychological dominance beyond the nation's shores and, in so doing, extend the "empire for liberty" to the global frontier.

Acknowledgments

Every book tells a story that extends beyond the words contained within. The people, places, and moments that made this work possible are a tangible evidence of grace and good fortune in my life.

Some of my earliest teachers encouraged a love of reading, history, and language. My parents, Ben and Rochelle Platter, ensured that I received the best possible education and funded some of my earliest "research" endeavors. Tammy Feigal taught me how to write (and braved many poor attempts), and Kirstin Kiledal introduced me to the study of rhetoric.

At the University of Minnesota, I benefited from generous faculty mentors and a robust intellectual community of fellow graduate students. John Archer, Karlyn Kohrs Campbell, Richard Graff, Ronald Walter Greene, Elaine Tyler May, Lary May, Edward Schiappa, Mary Vavrus, and Arthur Walzer engaged my work with care and constructive criticism. Classes and conversations with Sky LaRell Anderson, Shelby Bell, Matt Bost, Heather Ashley Hayes, Al Hiland, Emma Bedor Hiland, Daniel Horvath, Rebecca Kuehl, Margaret Kunde, Kaitlyn Patia, Dana Schowalter, Shannon Stevens, Svilen Trifonov, David Tucker, and Sarah Wolter helped me test out new ideas and provided a welcome respite from the rigors of graduate school. Generous financial support from the Department of Communication Studies and the Graduate School's Doctoral Dissertation Fellowship allowed me to devote my final year of graduate school to research and writing.

I was fortunate to begin faculty life in the Department of Communication Studies at Colorado State University surrounded by colleagues who became good friends. I thank Karrin Vasby Anderson, Eric Aoki, Carl Burghardt, Tom Dunn, Evan Elkins, Meara Faw, Katie Gibson, Kit Hughes, Katie Knobloch, Ziyu Long, Nick Marx, Elizabeth Parks, and Elizabeth Williams for their encouragement of this project at various stages. As department chair, Greg

Dickinson provided crucial support for my research and teaching endeavors. Gloria Blumanhorst, Eliza Kenyon-Wagner, and Dawn McConkey did the behind the scenes work that made my archival trips possible. Jordin Clark, Kristina Lee, Hailey Nicole Otis, and E. Brooke Phipps accomplished crucial research tasks, kept impeccable notes, and willingly went down many a scholarly rabbit hole on my behalf. Lori Lessing, Vince Lopez, Bella Martinez, Taylor Mockridge, Megan Palizzi, Rory Plunkett, and Josh Wolberg compiled hundreds of archival news stories and did so without complaint. Kristina Quynn, the director of CSU Writes, created the time, space, and community where many of these chapters first took form. I am grateful for generous funding both from the department and the College of Liberal Arts at Colorado State University that allowed me to conduct archival research and fieldwork for this book.

My colleagues at the University of Wisconsin–Madison deserve special recognition for their support and advocacy. Kelley Conway, Stephen Lucas, and Susan Zaeske offered a warm welcome to campus and the Department of Communication Arts. Vickie Groth, Linda Lucey, Lynn Malone, James Runde, Clara Schanck, and Peter Sengstock helped me transition this project from one university to another. Robert Asen, Robert Glenn Howard, Jenell Johnson, and Sara McKinnon have been remarkable senior colleagues, mentors, and friends. I am grateful to Russ Castronovo and Megan Massino at the University of Wisconsin–Madison's Center for the Humanities for supporting a First Book Program workshop discussion on an earlier iteration of this manuscript and to Robert Asen, Roderick P. Hart, Kenneth Mayer, Christa Olson, Mary Stuckey, and Jessica Weeks for taking the time to participate in the conversation (particularly the day before the 2020 US presidential election). Monthly get-togethers with fellow assistant professors Jason Kido Lopez, Darshana Mini, and Lillie Williamson buoyed my spirits through the ups and downs of pandemic writing and teaching. Kelly Jensen conducted crucial last-minute research tasks. Support for this research was provided by the University of Wisconsin–Madison Office of the Vice Chancellor for Research and Graduate Education with funding from the Wisconsin Alumni Research Foundation.

I am indebted to a generous community of scholars who have read and engaged my work across time zones, conference locations, and varying degrees of development. In particular, I thank Karrin Vasby Anderson, Bill Balthrop, Tim Barney, Vanessa Beasley, Carole Blair, Denise Bostdorff, Bonnie Dow, George Edwards III, Cara Finnegan, Ronald Walter Greene, Atilla Hallsby, Kelly Happe, Debra Hawhee, Theon Hill, J. Michael Hogan, Kathleen Hall Jamieson, Michele Kennerly, Zornitsa Keremidchieva, Martin J. Medhurst, John Murphy, Charles E. Morris III, Ned O'Gorman, Julia Scatliff O'Grady, Christa Olson, Shawn Parry-Giles, Angela Ray, Robin Rowland,

Alyssa Samek, Brad Serber, Belinda Stillion Southard, Mary Stuckey, Dave Tell, Brad Vivian, Arthur Walzer, Isaac West, Kirt Wilson, Emily Winderman, Carly Woods, and David Zarefsky for the conversations that shaped my thinking and sharpened my arguments.

Although academic life is not for the faint of heart, I have been surrounded by remarkable friends at every stage. Zoë Hess Carney, Megan Fitzmaurice, Elizabeth Gardner, and Esther Liu remain the greatest gifts of my graduate school days. Virtual weekly writing dates with Emily Winderman motivated me to keep going, especially during the challenges of finishing a book manuscript during COVID-19. Stephanie A. "Sam" Martin believed in this project when I almost gave up. Her loyal friendship, guts, and grit challenge and inspire me daily. The support of our little village in Madison during the pandemic—particularly Peter Bakken and Martha Nack, Curt and Michelle Hanke, Grace McCluskey, and Phil and Terri Pellitteri—helped us weather the viral storm. Special thanks go to the splendid pups Arthur Wallace Nack Bakken and Harry O. Prasch for their loyal companionship, licks, and romps.

My academic journey would not have been possible without several remarkable mentors. In the fall of 2009, Karlyn Kohrs Campbell took a chance on a naive, overeager, non–degree seeking student desperate to enter the graduate program in the Department of Communication Studies at the University of Minnesota. She taught me how to read, write, and think as a rhetorical critic, and her presence pervades every page of this book. Arthur Walzer championed my work from the very beginning. His integrity, kindness, and thoughtful criticism sustained me at crucial moments, and I hope to be the kind of mentor he has been for me. Carole Blair welcomed me to the discipline with warmth and enthusiasm. Our conference coffee chats inspired the early beginnings of this project and motivated me to take scholarly risks. Angela Ray took me under her wing when I needed it most. Her wit and wisdom are unmatched, and I will always be grateful to be academic siblings. Mary Stuckey is one of the most generous scholars I know. She volunteered to read iterations of this project (and many others) at various points, and her impeccable work remains a model for my own. In addition to her brilliance and keen editorial eye, Karrin Vasby Anderson is a woman of valor, through and through. Her example and influence changed the course of my life and career. Sara McKinnon has been an incredible colleague, confidante, and friend. She read every page of this manuscript more times than I care to admit and cheered me on toward the finish line.

For their assistance over the past eight years, I am indebted to the archivists and staff at the National Records and Archives Administration in College Park, Maryland; the Franklin D. Roosevelt Presidential Library in Hyde Park,

New York; the Harry S. Truman Presidential Library in Independence, Missouri; the Dwight D. Eisenhower Presidential Library in Abilene, Kansas; the John F. Kennedy Presidential Library in Boston, Massachusetts; the Richard Nixon Presidential Library in Yorba Linda, California; and the Ronald Reagan Presidential Library in Simi Valley, California. Some of the material in the introduction, chapter 1, and chapter 3 first appeared in "The Rise of the Global Rhetorical Presidency," *Presidential Studies Quarterly* 50, no. 2 (2021): 327–56, and "Reading the Presidency In Situ: Obama in Cuba and the Significance of Place in U.S. Presidential Public Address," in *Reading the Presidency: Advances in Presidential Rhetoric*, ed. Stephen J. Heidt and Mary E. Stuckey (New York: Peter Lang, 2019), 44–64. Some of the material in chapter 6 first appeared in "Reagan at Pointe du Hoc: Deictic Epideictic and the Persuasive Power of 'Bringing before the Eyes,'" *Rhetoric & Public Affairs* 18, no. 2 (2015): 247–76.

My editor at the University of Chicago Press, Kyle Wagner, provided tireless support for this project over many months and unexpected turns. Kristin Rawlings helped me navigate image permissions, author checklists, and final tasks with good humor and grace. Mark Reschke provided a meticulous review of every sentence and citation. Nathan Petrie helped me launch this book into the world with his marketing and promotion expertise. The talented designers at Faceout Studios took my fragmented ideas for a book cover and produced a work of art. Amy Murphy did the painstaking work of indexing. Weston Platter and Bethany Schrock contributed their time, talents, and eye for detail in the last stages of the project. Finally, I am grateful to three anonymous reviewers whose careful reading of and engagement with this manuscript made it an infinitely better book. Any errors that remain are mine and mine alone.

My two children are precious bookends to this project. Oliver has been with me from the very beginning. His contagious joy, energy, and curiosity sustained me over the past eight years. Since he frequently tells people that I have been writing this book his entire life (a true statement), his hope of becoming an author brings tears to my eyes and has taught me that these two worlds can, in fact, coexist. Lucy joined our family circus days after I turned in the final manuscript. Her impending arrival gave me a hard deadline, but more importantly, her growing presence was a constant reminder of what really matters.

This book would not exist without the love, encouragement, and partnership of my husband, Jason. For the past twenty years, he has supported me in ways big and small, seen and unseen. Words cannot adequately express how grateful I am to him for believing in me and daring me to build a life that exceeds our wildest dreams. He is, and will always be, my best.

Notes

Introduction

1. David Pietrusza, Harry S. Truman's Speech at the 1948 Democratic National Convention—Harry S. Truman (July 15, 1948), National Recording Preservation Plan, Library of Congress, https://www.loc.gov/static/programs/national-recording-preservation-board/documents/Truman.pdf.

2. For additional context, see David Pietrusza, *1948: Harry Truman's Improbable Victory and the Year That Transformed America* (New York: Union Square Press, 2011), and W. H. Lawrence, "Victory Sweeping: President Wins, 947½ to 263, over Russell on the First Ballot," *New York Times*, July 15, 1948, 1.

3. Lawrence, "Victory Sweeping."

4. Harry S. Truman, "Address in Philadelphia upon Accepting the Nomination of the Democratic National Convention," July 15, 1948, online by Gerhard Peters and John T. Woolley, *The American Presidency Project*, https://www.presidency.ucsb.edu/node/232683.

5. "Vandenberg Backs Nonpartisanship: Republicans Will Halt Politics at the Water's Edge, He Tells Party in Michigan," *New York Times*, September 26, 1948, 50.

6. Arthur Vandenberg, "Lincoln Day Dinner Speech," February 10, 1949, as quoted in *The Private Papers of Senator Vandenberg*, ed. Arthur H. Vandenburg and Joe Alex Morris (Boston: Houghton Mifflin, 1952), 472–73.

7. My use of "going global" draws deliberately on Samuel Kernell's influential argument about "going public," a concept to which I return later in the chapter. Samuel Kernell, *Going Public: New Strategies of Presidential Leadership* (Washington, DC: CQ Press, 1986).

8. Interested parties should consult "Travels Abroad of the President," US Department of State Office of the Historian, https://history.state.gov/departmenthistory/travels/president.

9. Vanessa B. Beasley, *You, the People: American National Identity in Presidential Rhetoric* (College Station: Texas A&M University Press, 2004), 22.

10. Mary E. Stuckey, *The President as Interpreter-in-Chief* (Chatham, NJ: Chatham House Publishers, 1991), 1.

11. Richard Slotkin, *Gunfighter Nation: The Myth of the Frontier in Twentieth-Century America* (New York: Atheneum, 1992), 5.

12. For more on this point, see Allison M. Prasch and Mary E. Stuckey, "'An Empire for Liberty': Reassessing US Presidential Foreign Policy Rhetoric," *Quarterly Journal of Speech* 108, no. 4 (2022): forthcoming.

13. Although Article II of the US Constitution assigns executive power and oversight to the president of the United States, it says much less about the president's role in the doing and making of US foreign policy. The only clear foreign policy powers articulated include a president's position as commander in chief of the US military, the power to make treaties with foreign governments (by and with the "advice and consent of the Senate"), the authority to appoint US ambassadors, and the ability to receive other foreign ambassadors and heads of state. There is nothing in the US Constitution that outlines the president's rhetorical role in communicating US foreign interests to the nation and the world. Of course, the powers of the presidency have grown and extended to account for political needs, historical changes, and the growing demands of the Executive Office of the President.

14. John Winthrop, "A Modell of Christian Charity," 1630, Collections of the Massachusetts Historical Society (Boston, 1838), 3rd ser., 7:31-48, Hanover Historical Texts Collection, https://history.hanover.edu/texts/winthmod.html.

15. This phrase comes from a sermon delivered by Samuel Danforth, a Puritan pastor in Massachusetts, in 1670. For more on the rhetorical construction of this idea, see Stephen H. Browne, "Samuel Danforth's 'Errand into the Wilderness' and the Discourse of Arrival in Early American Culture," *Communication Quarterly* 40, no. 2 (1992): 91-101.

16. For more on the implications of this perspective, see Carroll Smith-Rosenberg, *This Violent Empire: The Birth of an American National Identity* (Chapel Hill: Omohundro Institute and the University of North Carolina Press, 2012); Jason Edward Black, *American Indians and the Rhetoric of Removal and Allotment* (Jackson: University Press of Mississippi, 2015); Claudio Saunt, *Unworthy Republic: The Dispossession of Native Americans and the Road to Indian Territory* (New York: W. W. Norton, 2020).

17. Thomas Jefferson to James Madison, April 27, 1809; Library of Congress Manuscript Division, Thomas Jefferson, https://www.loc.gov/exhibits/jefferson/149.html.

18. George Washington, "Farewell Address," September 17, 1796, online by Gerhard Peters and John T. Wooley, *The American Presidency Project*, https://www.presidency.ucsb.edu/node/200675. Historian Walter A. MacDougall persuasively argues that Washington's caution was as much about preserving American liberty at home as it was preventing the United States from getting involved in foreign policy squabbles overseas. See Walter A. MacDougall, *Promised Land, Crusader State: The American Encounter with the World since 1776* (Boston: Houghton Mifflin, 1997), 44-49.

19. Jon Meacham, *Thomas Jefferson: The Art of Power* (New York: Random House, 2012), 269.

20. Thomas Jefferson, "Inaugural Address," March 4, 1801, online by Gerhard Peters and John T. Woolley, *The American Presidency Project*, https://www.presidency.ucsb.edu/node/201948.

21. For more on this idea, see Gordon S. Wood, *Empire of Liberty: A History of the Early Republic, 1789-1815* (New York: Oxford University Press, 2009).

22. James Monroe, "Seventh Annual Message," December 2, 1823, online by Gerhard Peters and John T. Wooley, *The American Presidency Project*, https://www.presidency.ucsb.edu/node/205755.

23. MacDougall, *Promised Land, Crusader State: The American Encounter with the World since 1776*, 73. See also Mark T. Gilderhus, "The Monroe Doctrine: Meanings and Implications," *Presidential Studies Quarterly* 36, no. 1 (2006): 5-16; Jay Sexton, *The Monroe Doctrine: Empire and Nation in Nineteenth-Century America* (New York: Hill and Wang, 2011); Christa J. Olson,

"'But in Regard to These (the American) Continents': U.S. National Rhetorics and the Figure of Latin America," *Rhetoric Society Quarterly* 45, no. 3 (2015): 264–77.

24. John O'Sullivan, "The Great Nation of Futurity," *United States Democratic Review*, November 1839, 427 (emphasis in original).

25. John O'Sullivan, "Annexation," *United States Magazine and Democratic Review* 17, no. 1 (July–August 1845): 5.

26. I put this in quotes not only because it is Turner's phrase, but because it connotes how the "American frontier" was defined and conquered by the United States even as it ignored the existence of Indigenous peoples whose lands they claimed as their own.

27. Frederick Jackson Turner, "The Significance of the Frontier in American History," paper delivered at the meeting of the American Historical Society in Chicago, July 12, 1893, reprinted in Frederick Jackson Turner, *Frontier in American History* (New York: Henry Holt, 1920), 1. See also Ronald H. Carpenter, "Frederick Jackson Turner and the Rhetorical Impact of the Frontier Thesis," *Quarterly Journal of Speech* 63, no. 2 (1977): 117–29; Mary E. Stuckey and John M. Murphy, "By Any Other Name: Rhetorical Colonialism in North America," *American Indian Culture and Research Journal* 25, no. 4 (2001): 73–98.

28. Turner, "The Significance of the Frontier in American History," 4.

29. Turner, 37. For more on the rhetorical appropriations of the frontier myth, see Richard Slotkin, *Regeneration through Violence: The Mythology of the American Frontier, 1600–1860* (Middleton, CT: Wesleyan University Press, 1973); Richard Slotkin, *The Fatal Environment: The Myth of the Frontier in the Age of Industrialization, 1800–1890* (New York: Atheneum, 1985); Slotkin, *Gunfighter Nation*; Leroy G. Dorsey, "The Frontier Myth in Presidential Rhetoric: Theodore Roosevelt's Campaign for Conservation," *Western Journal of Communication* 59, no. 1 (1995): 1–19; Tiffany Lewis, "Winning Woman Suffrage in the Masculine West: Abigail Scott Duniway's Frontier Myth," *Western Journal of Communication* 75, no. 2 (2011): 127–47; Leroy G. Dorsey, "Managing Women's Equality: Theodore Roosevelt, the Frontier Myth, and the Modern Woman," *Rhetoric & Public Affairs* 16, no. 3 (2013): 423–56; Greg Grandin, *The End of the Myth: From the Frontier to the Border Wall in the Mind of America* (New York: Metropolitan Books, 2019); E Cram, *Violent Inheritance: Sexuality, Land, and Energy in Making the North American West* (Oakland: University of California Press, 2022).

30. Frederick Jackson Turner, "Contributions to American Democracy," *Atlantic Monthly*, January 1903, reprinted in Turner, *Frontier in American History*, 246.

31. McKinley, as quoted in Richard Ellis, *Presidential Travel: The Journey from George Washington to George W. Bush* (Lawrence: University Press of Kansas, 2008), 169.

32. McKinley, as quoted in Louis L. Gould, *The Modern American Presidency* (Lawrence: University Press of Kansas, 2003), 8.

33. Theodore Roosevelt, "Second Annual Message," December 2, 1902, online by Gerhard Peters and John T. Wooley, *The American Presidency Project*, https://www.presidency.ucsb.edu/node/206194.

34. See David McCullough, *The Path between the Seas: The Creation of the Panama Canal, 1870–1914* (New York: Simon and Schuster, 1977), and Edmund Morris, *Theodore Rex* (New York: Random House, 2001).

35. According to Joseph Bucklin Bishop, the secretary of the Panama Canal Commission, precautions were taken to ensure that although the president would venture outside US borders during his trip, he would land on US soil in Panama. "This visit was notable as being the first instance in which an American President had passed out of United States territory while holding

the office," wrote Bishop. "A special station was erected on the Panama Railroad near the Canal Zone boundary at Panama in order that he might land on United States territory, and this was used by him and his party during the visit." Joseph Bucklin Bishop, *The Panama Gateway* (New York: Charles Scribner's Sons, 1913), 169.

36. "President to Visit Panama Canal Zone," *New York Times*, June 24, 1906, 1.

37. Bishop, *The Panama Gateway*, 172–73; "Mr. Roosevelt on the Panama Canal," *New York Times*, December 18, 1906, PRTM1.

38. Bishop, *The Panama Gateway*, 174.

39. For a more extensive discussion of how Roosevelt's trip visit contributed to the rise of the global rhetorical presidency, see Allison M. Prasch, "The Rise of the Global Rhetorical Presidency," *Presidential Studies Quarterly* 50, no. 2 (2021): 336–38.

40. After Roosevelt's visit to the Panama Canal Zone, William Howard Taft made similar visits to Mexico and Cuba. Taft also visited the Panama Canal Zone in 1909 as president-elect and as president in 1910 and 1912. "William Howard Taft—Travels of the President, U.S. Department of State Office of the Historian," https://history.state.gov/departmenthistory/travels/president/taft-william-howard. Curiously, this State Department record omits Taft's visits in 1910 and 1912 and does not mention his stop in Cuba on the 1910 trip. For details on these two trips, see "Taft Home Again from Panama Trip," *New York Times*, November 24, 1910, 8, and "President Sails for Colon," *New York Times*, December 22, 1912, 4 (among other reports).

41. Woodrow Wilson, "Address Delivered at the First Annual Assemblage of the League to Enforce Peace: 'American Principles,'" May 27, 1916, online by Gerhard Peters and John T. Wooley, *The American Presidency Project*, https://www.presidency.ucsb.edu/node/206570.

42. Woodrow Wilson, "Address to a Joint Session of Congress Requesting a Declaration of War against Germany," April 2, 1917, online by Gerhard Peters and John T. Wooley, *The American Presidency Project*, https://www.presidency.ucsb.edu/node/207620.

43. Woodrow Wilson, "Sixth Annual Message," December 2, 1918, online by Gerhard Peters and John T. Woolley, *The American Presidency Project*, https://www.presidency.ucsb.edu/node/207603. For more on Wilson's visit, see H. W. Brands, *Woodrow Wilson* (New York: Henry Holt, 2003), 99–130; Arthur Walworth, *America's Moment: 1918* (New York: W. W. Norton, 1977), 110–20; August Heckscher, *Woodrow Wilson* (New York: Charles Scribner's Sons, 1991), 438–536; John Milton Cooper, *Woodrow Wilson: A Biography* (New York: Alfred A. Knopf, 2009), 454–505.

44. Heckscher, *Woodrow Wilson*, 495.

45. Lansing as quoted in Walworth, *America's Moment: 1918*, 138.

46. For more on these attempts, see J. Michael Hogan, *Woodrow Wilson's Western Tour: Rhetoric, Public Opinion, and the League of Nations* (College Station: Texas A&M University Press, 2006); Cooper, *Woodrow Wilson: A Biography*, 506–34, 40–60.

47. For a more extensive discussion of how Wilson's visit contributed to the rise of the global rhetorical presidency, see Prasch, "The Rise of the Global Rhetorical Presidency," 338–43.

48. Susan Schulten, *The Geographical Imagination in America, 1880–1950* (Chicago: University of Chicago Press, 2001).

49. Ellis, *Presidential Travel: The Journey from George Washington to George W. Bush*, 131.

50. Max Paul Friedman, "The Good Neighbor Policy," in *Oxford Research Encyclopedia, Latin American History* (New York: Oxford University Press, 2020), https://oxfordre.com/latinamericanhistory/view/10.1093/acrefore/9780199366439.001.0001/acrefore-9780199366439-e-222?print=pdf.

51. See, for example, Greg Grandin, *Empire's Workshop: Latin America, the United States, and*

the Rise of New Imperialism (New York: Metropolitan Books, 2006); Greg Grandin, *The End of the Myth* (New York: Henry Holt, 2019); Daniel Immerwahr, *How to Hide an Empire: A History of the Greater United States* (New York: Farrar, Straus and Giroux, 2019).

52. David M. Kennedy, *Freedom from Fear: The American People in Depression and War, 1929–1945* (New York: Oxford University Press, 1999), 386.

53. Given Roosevelt's physical disabilities, his international trips were particularly noteworthy. See Davis W. Houck, "Reading the Body in the Text: FDR's 1932 Speech to the Democratic National Convention," *Southern Communication Journal* 63, no. 1 (1997): 20–36, and Amos Kiewe and Davis W. Houck, *FDR's Body Politics: The Rhetoric of Disability* (College Station: Texas A&M University Press, 2003).

54. Franklin D. Roosevelt, "Inaugural Address," March 4, 1933, online by Gerhard Peters and John T. Woolley, *The American Presidency Project*, https://www.presidency.ucsb.edu/node/208712.

55. Franklin Delano Roosevelt, "Address before a Joint Session of the National Congress and the Supreme Court of Brazil at Rio de Janeiro," November 27, 1936, online by Gerhard Peters and John T. Woolley, *The American Presidency Project*, https://www.presidency.ucsb.edu/node/208499.

56. Mary E. Stuckey, *The Good Neighbor: Franklin D. Roosevelt and the Rhetoric of American Power* (East Lansing: Michigan State University Press, 2013), 21.

57. Stuckey, 23.

58. Manfred B. Steger, *The Rise of the Global Imaginary: Political Ideologies from the French Revolution to the Global War on Terror* (Oxford: Oxford University Press, 2008), 10–11, 131.

59. Franklin D. Roosevelt, "Annual Message to Congress on the State of the Union," January 6, 1941, online by Gerhard Peters and John T. Woolley, *The American Presidency Project*, https://www.presidency.ucsb.edu/documents/annual-message-congress-the-state-the-union.

60. Franklin D. Roosevelt, "Fireside Chat," May 26, 1940, online by Gerhard Peters and John T. Woolley, *The American Presidency Project*, https://www.presidency.ucsb.edu/documents/fireside-chat-10.

61. Franklin Delano Roosevelt, "On the Declaration of War with Japan," December 9, 1941, http://docs.fdrlibrary.marist.edu/120941.html.

62. The Cold War has been the subject of extensive scholarly consideration and analysis. For several indispensable accounts of the rhetorical construction of this conflict, see Timothy Barney, *Mapping the Cold War: Cartography and the Framing of America's International Power* (Chapel Hill: University of North Carolina Press, 2015); Wayne Brockriede and Robert L. Scott, *Moments in the Rhetoric of the Cold War* (New York: Random House, 1970); John F. Cragan, "The Origins and Nature of the Cold War Rhetorical Vision, 1946–1972," in *Applied Communication Research: A Dramatistic Approach*, ed. John F. Cragan and Donald C. Shields (Prospect Heights, IL: Waveland Press, 1981), 47–66; Lynn Boyd Hinds and Theodore Otto Windt, *The Cold War as Rhetoric: The Beginnings, 1945–1950* (New York: Praeger, 1991); Robert J. McMahon, *The Cold War in the Third World* (New York: Oxford University Press, 2013); Martin J. Medhurst, Robert L. Ivie, Philip Wander, and Robert L. Scott, *Cold War Rhetoric: Strategy, Metaphor, and Ideology* (East Lansing: Michigan State University Press, 1990); Martin J. Medhurst and H. W. Brands, eds., *Critical Reflections on the Cold War: Linking Rhetoric and History* (College Station: Texas A&M University Press, 2000); Ned O'Gorman, *Spirits of the Cold War: Contesting Worldviews in the Classical Age of American Security Strategy* (East Lansing: Michigan State University Press, 2012); Kenneth Osgood, *Total Cold War: Eisenhower's Secret Propaganda*

Battle at Home and Abroad (Lawrence: University Press of Kansas, 2006); Shawn J. Parry-Giles, *The Rhetorical Presidency, Propaganda, and the Cold War, 1945–1955* (Westport, CT: Praeger, 2002); Mary E. Stuckey, "Competing Foreign Policy Visions: Rhetorical Hybrids after the Cold War," *Western Journal of Communication* 59, no. 3 (1995): 214–27; Odd Arne Westad, *The Global Cold War: Third World Interventions and the Making of Our Times* (Cambridge: University of Cambridge, 2007).

63. Ernest G. Bormann, John F. Cragan, and Donald C. Shields, "An Expansion of the Rhetorical Vision Component of the Symbolic Convergence Theory: The Cold War Paradigm Case," *Communication Monographs* 63, no. 1 (1996): 9.

64. George Orwell, "You and the Atom Bomb," *Tribune*, October 19, 1945, 8. Odd Arne Westad provides additional insight: "Although a critical term at first, the term 'Cold War' in the 1950s came to signal an American concept of warfare against the Soviet Union: aggressive containment without a state of war. The Soviets, on their side, never used the term officially before the Gorbachev era, since they clung to the fiction that their country was 'peaceful' and only 'imperialism' was aggressive, in a way similar to how US (and Western European) leaders used the 'Cold War' to imply a Soviet threat." Westad, *The Global Cold War: Third World Interventions and the Making of Our Times*, 2.

65. Walter Lippmann, *The Cold War: A Study in American Foreign Policy* (New York: Harper and Brothers, 1947).

66. Hinds and Windt, *The Cold War as Rhetoric: The Beginnings, 1945–1950*, 220.

67. Winston Churchill to Harry S. Truman, May 12, 1945; Meetings of Heads of State, 2 of 2; Box 6; Naval Aide to the President; Papers of Harry S. Truman; Harry S. Truman Presidential Library, Independence, Missouri (hereafter HSTL).

68. Winston Churchill, "The Sinews of Peace ('Iron Curtain Speech')," March 5, 1946, Westminster College, Fulton, Missouri, https://winstonchurchill.org/resources/speeches/ 1946–1963-elder-statesman/the-sinews-of-peace/.

69. Upon his death, the *New York Times* described Franklin D. Roosevelt as the "chief author of the democratic coalition. Certainly in the eyes of the people of the free world beyond our shores no more towering figure has come upon the American scene in the times of men now living." "The Road Leads Forward," *New York Times*, April 15, 1945, E8.

70. Harry S. Truman, "Special Message to the Congress on Greece and Turkey: The Truman Doctrine," March 12, 1947, online by Gerhard Peters and John T. Woolley, *The American Presidency Project*, https://www.presidency.ucsb.edu/node/232818.

71. Barbara Ward, "'The Marshall Plan Is Not Enough': To Meet the Challenge of the Communists the Non-Communist World Needs a Real Union," *New York Times Magazine*, November 14, 1948, 71.

72. "1952 Democratic Party Platform," July 21, 1952, online by Gerhard Peters and John T. Woolley, *The American Presidency Project*, https://www.presidency.ucsb.edu/node/273228.

73. Kenneth Burke, "Ways of Placement," in *Kenneth Burke: On Symbols and Society*, ed. Joseph R. Gusfield (Chicago: University of Chicago Press, 1989), 146, 150.

Chapter One

1. For more on these approaches to history, see Carlo Ginzburg, John Tedeschi, and Anne C. Tedeschi, "Microhistory: Two or Three Things That I Know about It," *Critical Inquiry* 20, no. 1 (1993): 10–35; Debra Hawhee and Christa J. Olson, "Pan-Historiography: The Challenges of

Writing History across Time and Space," in *Theorizing Histories of Rhetoric*, ed. Michelle Ballif (Carbondale: Southern Illinois University Press, 2013), 90–105.

2. Here I draw on David Zarefsky's description of viewing rhetoric as a "force in history" and call to approach the study of history "as a series of rhetorical problems." See David Zarefsky, "Four Senses of Rhetorical History," in *Doing Rhetorical History*, ed. Kathleen J. Turner (Tuscaloosa: University of Alabama Press, 1998), 29, 30.

3. Michael Leff, "Textual Criticism: The Legacy of G. P. Mohrmann," *Quarterly Journal of Speech* 72, no. 4 (1986): 382.

4. Kernell, *Going Public: New Strategies of Presidential Leadership*; Richard Ellis, ed., *Speaking to the People: The Rhetorical Presidency in Historical Perspective* (Amherst: University of Massachusetts Press, 1998).

5. For an initial explication of this theory, see Prasch, "The Rise of the Global Rhetorical Presidency."

6. James W. Ceaser et al., "The Rise of the Rhetorical Presidency," *Presidential Studies Quarterly* 11, no. 2 (1981): 159; Jeffrey K. Tulis, *The Rhetorical Presidency* (Princeton, NJ: Princeton University Press, 1987), 18.

7. Mary E. Stuckey and Fred J. Antczak, "The Rhetorical Presidency: Deepening Vision, Widening Exchange," *Communication Yearbook* 21 (1998): 405–42; Chad Murphy, "The Evolution of the Modern Rhetorical Presidency: A Critical Response," *Presidential Studies Quarterly* 38, no. 2 (2008): 300–307; Terri Bimes, "Understanding the Rhetorical Presidency," in *The Oxford Handbook of the American Presidency*, ed. George C. Edwards and William G. Howell (Oxford: Oxford University Press, 2009), 208–31; David A. Crockett, "'The Rhetorical Presidency': Still Standing Tall," *Presidential Studies Quarterly* 39, no. 4 (2009): 932–40; Mel Laracey, "'The Rhetorical Presidency' Today: How Does It Stand Up?," *Presidential Studies Quarterly* 39, no. 4 (2009): 908–31; Mary E. Stuckey, "Rethinking the Rhetorical Presidency and Presidential Rhetoric," *Review of Communication* 10, no. 1 (2010): 38–52; Joshua M. Scacco and Kevin Coe, "The Ubiquitous Presidency: Toward a New Paradigm for Studying Presidential Communication," *International Journal of Communication* 10 (2016): 2014–37.

8. Martin J. Medhurst, ed., *Before the Rhetorical Presidency* (College Station: Texas A&M University Press, 2008).

9. Martin J. Medhurst, "A Tale of Two Constructs: The Rhetorical Presidency versus Presidential Rhetoric," in *Beyond the Rhetorical Presidency*, ed. Martin J. Medhurst (College Station: Texas A&M University Press, 1996), xi–xxv; John M. Murphy, *John F. Kennedy and the Liberal Persuasion* (East Lansing: Michigan State University Press, 2019), 13–28.

10. Some of this recent work includes George C. Edwards, "The Bully in the Pulpit," *Presidential Studies Quarterly* 50, no. 2 (2020): 286–324; Roderick P. Hart, "Donald Trump and the Return of the Paranoid Style," *Presidential Studies Quarterly* 50, no. 2 (2020): 348–65; Roderick P. Hart, *Trump and Us: What He Says and Why People Listen* (New York: Cambridge University Press, 2020); Jennifer R. Mercieca, *Demagogue for President: The Rhetorical Genius of Donald Trump* (College Station: Texas A&M University Press, 2020); Mary Stuckey, "'The Power of the Presidency to Hurt': The Indecorous Rhetoric of Donald J. Trump and the Rhetorical Norms of Democracy," *Presidential Studies Quarterly* 50, no. 2 (2020): 366–91.

11. Kernell, *Going Public: New Strategies of Presidential Leadership*; Ellis, *Speaking to the People*.

12. Raka Shome and Radha Hegde, "Culture, Communication, and the Challenge of Globalization," *Critical Studies in Media Communication* 19, no. 2 (2002): 174.

13. Steger, *The Rise of the Global Imaginary: Political Ideologies from the French Revolution to the Global War on Terror.*

14. Shome and Hegde, "Culture, Communication, and the Challenge of Globalization," 176.

15. Scacco and Coe, "The Ubiquitous Presidency: Toward a New Paradigm for Studying Presidential Communication"; Joshua M. Scacco and Kevin Coe, *The Ubiquitous Presidency: Presidential Communication and Digital Democracy in Tumultuous Times* (New York: Oxford University Press, 2021).

16. Roderick P. Hart, *The Sound of Leadership: Presidential Communication in the Modern Age* (Chicago: University of Chicago Press, 1987), 58; Kernell, *Going Public: New Strategies of Presidential Leadership*, 125; Richard Rose, *The Postmodern President: The White House Meets the World* (Chatham, NJ: Chatham House Publishers, 1988), 31.

17. Benjamin E. Goldsmith and Yusaku Horiuchi, "Spinning the Globe? U.S. Public Diplomacy and Foreign Public Opinion," *Journal of Politics* 71, no. 3 (2009): 863–75; Kevin Coe and Rico Neumann, "International Identity in Theory and Practice: The Case of the Modern American Presidency," *Communication Monographs* 78, no. 2, (2011): 139–61; Benjamin E. Goldsmith and Yusaku Horiuchi, "In Search of Soft Power: Does Foreign Public Opinion Matter for US Foreign Policy?," *World Politics* 64, no. 3 (2012): 555–85; Jason Gilmore, "Translating American Exceptionalism: Comparing Presidential Discourse about the United States at Home and Abroad," *International Journal of Communication* 8 (2014): 2416–37; Jeffrey E. Cohen, "Presidential Attention Focusing in the Global Arena: The Impact of International Travel on Foreign Publics," *Presidential Studies Quarterly* 46, no. 1 (2016): 30–47; Jason Gilmore and Charles M. Rowling, "Lighting the Beacon: Presidential Discourse, American Exceptionalism, and Public Diplomacy in Global Contexts," *Presidential Studies Quarterly* 48, no. 2 (2018): 271–91.

18. Karlyn Kohrs Campbell and Kathleen Hall Jamieson, *Presidents Creating the Presidency: Deeds Done in Words* (Chicago: University of Chicago Press, 2008).

19. For more on the relationship between the presidency as an institution versus as an individual, see Allison M. Prasch, "A Tale of Two Presidencies: Trump and Biden on the National Mall," *Quarterly Journal of Speech* 107, no. 4 (2021): 472–79.

20. Kenneth Burke, "Four Master Tropes," *Kenyon Review* 3, no. 4 (1941): 427.

21. Ralph Citrón, "Democracy and Its Limitations," in *The Public Work of Rhetoric: Citizen-Scholars and Civic Engagement*, ed. John M. Ackerman and David J. Coogan (Columbia: University of South Carolina Press, 2010), 100.

22. Christa J. Olson, "Performing Embodiable Topoi: Strategic Indegeneity and the Incorporation of Ecuadorian National Identity," *Quarterly Journal of Speech* 96, no. 3 (2010): 303.

23. Kiewe and Houck, *FDR's Body Politics: The Rhetoric of Disability.*

24. James Darsey, "Barack Obama and America's Journey," *Southern Communication Journal* 74, no. 1 (2009): 88–103; Robert C. Rowland and John M. Jones, "One Dream: Barack Obama, Race, and the American Dream," *Rhetoric & Public Affairs* 14, no. 1 (2011): 125–54; Susanna Dilliplane, "Race, Rhetoric, and Running for President: Unpacking the Significance of Barack Obama's 'A More Perfect Union' Speech," *Rhetoric & Public Affairs* 15, no. 1 (2012): 127–52; Robert E. Terrill, *Double-Consciousness and the Rhetoric of Barack Obama* (Columbia: University of South Carolina Press, 2015).

25. Kristina Horn Sheeler and Karrin Vasby Anderson, *Woman President: Confronting Postfeminist Political Culture* (College Station: Texas A&M University Press, 2013), 3.

26. Yi-Fu Tuan, *Space and Place: The Perspective of Experience* (Minneapolis: University of Minnesota Press, 1977), 6.

27. Raka Shome, "Space Matters: The Power and Practice of Space," *Communication Theory* 13, no. 1 (2003): 39, 40.

28. Benedict Anderson described these shared social relations as imagined communities, noting that even if "the members of even the smallest nation will never know most of their fellow-members, meet them, or even hear of them, yet in the minds of each lives the image of their communion." Building on Anderson's work, sociologist Charles Taylor offered the related concept of the "social imaginary," a term that describes "the ways people imagine their social existence, how they fit together with others, how things go on between them and their fellows, the expectations that are normally met, and the deeper normative notions and images that underlie these expectations." Taylor is explicit about using the term "imaginary" because he is focused "on the ordinary way people 'imagine' their social surroundings . . . [and how this] is carried in images, stories, and legends." This image, he writes, is often "shared by large groups of people" and is a "common understanding that makes possible common practices and a widely shared sense of legitimacy." The use of language—rhetoric—plays a critical role in creating and sustaining this shared social imaginary, for it is through language that individuals articulate a shared understanding of one's position in the world and in relation to others. Rhetoric, then, is the glue that cements these communities or imaginaries together. Benedict Anderson, *Imagined Communities: Reflections on the Origin and Spread of Nationalism*, 2nd ed. (London: Verso, 2006), 6, 188; Charles Taylor, *Modern Social Imaginaries* (Durham, NC: Duke University Press, 2004), 23.

29. Edward S. Casey, *Getting Back into Place: Toward a Renewed Understanding of the Place-World* (Bloomington: Indiana University Press, 1991), 71.

30. For more on this perspective see, for example, David Lowenthal, "Past Time, Present Place: Landscape and Memory," *Geographical Review* 65, no. 1 (1975): 1–36; Henri Lefebvre, *The Production of Space*, trans. Donald Nicholson-Smith (Malden, MA: Blackwell Publishing, 1991); John Bodnar, *Remaking America: Public Memory, Commemoration, and Patriotism in the Twentieth Century* (Princeton, NJ: Princeton University Press, 1992); Pierre Nora, *Realms of Memory: Rethinking the French Past* (New York: Columbia University Press, 1996); Carole Blair, "Reflections on Criticism and Bodies: Parables from Public Places," *Western Journal of Communication* 65, no. 3 (2001): 271–94; Carole Blair, Greg Dickinson, and Brian L. Ott, "Introduction: Rhetoric/Memory/Place," in *Places of Public Memory: The Rhetoric of Museums and Memorials*, ed. Greg Dickinson, Carole Blair, and Brian L. Ott (Tuscaloosa: University of Alabama Press, 2010), 1–54; Danielle Endres and Samantha Senda-Cook, "Location Matters: The Rhetoric of Place in Protest," *Quarterly Journal of Speech* 97, no. 3 (2011): 257–82.

31. Doreen Massey, *Space, Place, and Gender* (Minneapolis: University of Minnesota Press, 1994), 5.

32. For more on how discourse constituted the space of the Cold War global imaginary, see Gearóid Ó Tuathail and John Agnew, "Geopolitics and Discourse: Practical Geopolitical Reasoning in American Foreign Policy," *Political Geography* 11, no. 2 (1992): 190–204; Barney, *Mapping the Cold War*.

33. For more on the relationship between Cold War public diplomacy and visual rhetoric see, for example, Nathan S. Atkinson, "Newsreels as Domestic Propaganda: Visual Rhetoric at the Dawn of the Cold War," *Rhetoric & Public Affairs* 14, no. 1 (2011): 69–100; Timothy Barney, "Power Lines: The Rhetoric of Maps as Social Change in the Post–Cold War Landscape," *Quarterly Journal of Speech* 95, no. 4 (2009): 412–34; Timothy Barney, "'Gulag'-Slavery, Inc.: The Power of Place and the Rhetorical Life of a Cold War Map," *Rhetoric & Public Affairs* 16, no. 2 (2013): 317–53; Kevin Hamilton and Thomas E. O'Gorman, *Lookout America! The Secret*

Hollywood Studio at the Heart of the Cold War (Lebanon, NH: University Press of New England, 2018).

34. Davi Johnson, "Martin Luther King Jr.'s 1963 Birmingham Campaign as Image Event," *Rhetoric & Public Affairs* 10, no. 1 (2007): 2. See also Kevin Michael DeLuca and Jennifer Peeples, "From Public Sphere to Public Screen: Democracy, Activisim, and the 'Violence' of Seattle," *Critical Studies in Mass Communication* 19, no. 2 (2002): 125–51; Kevin Michael DeLuca, *Image Politics: The New Rhetoric of Environmental Activism* (New York: Routledge, 2005).

35. Cara A. Finnegan and Jennifer L. Jones Barbour, "Visualizing Public Address," *Rhetoric & Public Affairs* 9, no. 3 (2006): 504.

36. Kenneth Burke, "Identification," in *Kenneth Burke on Symbols and Society*, ed. Joseph R. Gusfield (Chicago: University of Chicago Press, 1989), 191.

37. Michael Warner, *Publics and Counterpublics* (Cambridge: Zone Books, 2002). A number of important works in rhetoric and communication studies also inform this line of scholarly inquiry. See, for example, the special forum in *Rhetoric & Public Affairs* 15, no. 4 (2012): 609–94; Benjamin Lee and Edward LiPuma, "Cultures of Circulation: The Imaginations of Modernity," *Public Culture* 14, no. 1 (2002): 191–213; Ronald Walter Greene, "Rhetorical Pedagogy as a Postal System: Circulating Subjects through Michael Warner's 'Publics and Counterpublics,'" *Quarterly Journal of Speech* 88, no. 4 (2002): 434–43; Cara A. Finnegan and Jiyeon Kang, "'Sighting' the Public: Iconoclasm and Public Sphere Theory," *Quarterly Journal of Speech* 90, no. 4 (2004): 377–402; Jenny Edbauer, "Unframing Models of Public Distribution: From Rhetorical Situation to Rhetorical Ecologies," *Rhetoric Society Quarterly* 35, no. 4 (2005): 5–24; Lester C. Olson, "Pictorial Representations of British America Resisting Rape: Rhetorical Re-Circulation of a Print Series Portraying the Boston Port Bill of 1774," *Rhetoric & Public Affairs* 12, no. 1 (2009): 1–45; Catherine Chaput, "Rhetorical Circulation in Late Capitalism: Neoliberalism and the Over-determination of Affective Energy," *Philosophy & Rhetoric* 43, no. 1 (2010): 1–25.

38. Chaput, "Rhetorical Circulation in Late Capitalism: Neoliberalism and the Overdetermination of Affective Energy," 13.

39. Finnegan and Kang, "'Sighting' the Public: Iconoclasm and Public Sphere Theory," 396.

40. Murray Edelman, *The Symbolic Uses of Politics* (Urbana and Chicago: University of Illinois Press, 1964); Hart, *The Sound of Leadership: Presidential Communication in the Modern Age*; Kathleen Hall Jamieson, *Eloquence in an Electronic Age: The Transformation of Political Speechmaking* (New York: Oxford University Press, 1988); Murray Edelman, *Constructing the Political Spectacle* (Chicago: University of Chicago Press, 1988); Bruce E. Gronbeck, "The Presidency in the Age of Secondary Orality," in *Beyond the Rhetorical Presidency*, ed. Martin J. Medhurst (College Station: Texas A&M University Press, 1996), 30–49; Keith V. Erickson, "Presidential Rhetoric's Visual Turn: Performance Fragments and the Politics of Illusionism," *Communication Monographs* 67, no. 2 (2000): 138–57; Karen S. Hoffman, "Visual Persuasion in George W. Bush's Presidency: Cowboy Imagery in Public Discourse," *Congress & the Presidency* 38, no. 3 (2011): 322–43; Megan D. McFarlane, "Visualizing the Rhetorical Presidency: Barack Obama in the Situation Room," *Visual Communication Quarterly* 23, no. 1 (2016): 3–13.

41. In a fascinating study published in 1967, political scientist Bernard Rubin explained how television influenced political life in the United States. "First and perhaps foremost," he wrote, "the medium can transmit sounds and sights from the locales where news events are unfolding. Consequently . . . interest in on-the-spot news reporting has grown tremendously. Before World War II, it was difficult for the average person to picture news events in real-life settings. Today, most Americans can visualize a civil rights demonstration, a political party convention, a Presi-

dential address, or a rocket launching through television presentations." For Rubin, the "where" (or the place) of a particular rhetorical act or news event was particularly important, and the visual images that act provided became a powerful form of public education and persuasion. Bernard Rubin, *Political Television* (Belmont, CA: Wadsworth Publishing, 1967), 1–2. For more on the relationship between television and politics, see, for example, Edelman, *The Symbolic Uses of Politics*; Erik Barnouw, *Tube of Plenty: The Evolution of American Television* (Oxford: Oxford University Press, 1975); William C. Spragens, *The Presidency and the Mass Media in the Age of Television* (Lanham, MD: University Press of America, 1979); Edelman, *Constructing the Political Spectacle*; David E. Fisher and Marshall Jon Fisher, *Tube: The Invention of Television* (Washington, DC: Counterpoint, 1996); Stephen Cushion and Justin Lewis, eds., *The Rise of the 24-Hour News Television: Global Perspectives* (New York: Peter Lang, 2010).

42. The claim that certain places, sites, or backdrops of political acts can have a persuasive impact is not new, however. Political scientist Murray Edelman criticized politicians who exploited political scene or setting for their own ideological ends, writing that political actors take "great pains . . . to call attention to settings and to present them conspicuously, as if the scene were expected either to call forth a response of its own or to heighten the response to the act it frames." Edelman, *The Symbolic Uses of Politics*, 95.

Chapter Two

1. Robert G. Nixon, "President Truman Gains Popularity and Prestige Overseas," *Washington Post*, July 22, 1945, B1.

2. Truman's parents "gave him the middle initial S to honor and please his grandfathers, Shipp Truman and Solomon Young." "Harry S. Truman Biography," Harry S. Truman White House, https://www.trumanlittlewhitehouse.com/key-west/president-truman-biography.

3. When Franklin D. Roosevelt died of a massive stroke, the former US senator from Missouri had virtually no foreign policy experience. In fact, Roosevelt and Truman had met just twice in private since their inauguration and at neither meeting did they discuss anything significant. David McCullough, *Truman* (New York: Simon and Schuster Paperbacks, 1992), 339.

4. Tony Judt, *Postwar: A History of Europe since 1945* (New York: Penguin Books, 2005), 106. A number of US officials were concerned about Truman's preparedness, including US secretary of war Henry Stimson, who wrote in his diary that he was "very sorry for the President because he is new on his job and he has been brought into a situation which ought not to have been allowed to come his way." Stimson diary entry as quoted in Michael S. Neiberg, *Potsdam: The End of World War II and the Remaking of Europe* (New York: Basic Books, 2015), 24.

5. Charles E. Bohlen, *Witness to History, 1929–1969* (New York: Norton, 1973), 212.

6. Harry S. Truman Diary Entry, April 12, 1945, as printed in Harry S. Truman, *Off the Record: The Private Papers of Harry S. Truman*, ed. Robert H. Ferrell (New York: Harper & Row, 1980), 16.

7. Masao Tomonaga, "The Atomic Bombings of Hiroshima and Nagasaki: A Summary of the Human Consequences, 1945–2018, and Lessons for *Homo sapiens* to End the Nuclear Weapon Age," *Journal for Peace and Nuclear Disarmament* 2, no. 2 (2019): 493.

8. In the immediate aftermath of the "Big Three" meeting and the early years of the Cold War, US officials attributed little significance to the Potsdam Conference. Charles Bohlen, for example, wrote that "while Potsdam reached a number of decisions, some of which lasted, many of which did not, it cannot be regarded as a vital conference. Most of the policy lines on both

sides had been laid down before the meeting. After Potsdam, there was little that could be done to induce the Soviet Union to become a reasonable and cooperative member of the world community." Bohlen, *Witness to History, 1929–1969*, 240. More recent historical work has challenged this assessment. See, for example, Michael Dobbs, *Six Months in 1945: FDR, Stalin, Churchill, and Truman—from World War to Cold War* (New York: Vintage Books, 2012); Wilson D. Miscamble, *From Roosevelt to Truman: Potsdam, Hiroshima, and the Cold War* (New York: Cambridge University Press, 2007); Michael S. Neiberg, *Potsdam: The End of World War II and the Remaking of Europe* (New York: Basic Books, 2015); Chris Tudda, *Cold War Summits: A History from Potsdam to Malta* (London: Bloomsbury Academic, 2015).

9. For more on the use of strategic ambiguity in a rhetorical context, see Leah Ceccarelli, "Polysemy: Multiple Meanings in Rhetorical Criticism," *Quarterly Journal of Speech* 84, no. 4 (1998): 395–415; David Zarefsky, *Lyndon Johnson, Vietnam, and the Presidency: The Speech of March 31, 1968* (College Station: Texas A&M University Press, 2021).

10. Daniel F. Harrington, *Berlin on the Brink: The Blockade, the Airlift, and the Early Cold War* (Lexington: University Press of Kentucky, 2012).

11. Focusing on the symbolic resonances of Truman's performance at Potsdam is unconventional for studies of the Potsdam Conference. Analyses of the three-week summit often focus on the parallels to—or departures from—previous "Big Three" summits at Tehran and Yalta and speculate on the ultimate implications of the meeting for the Cold War years to come. Such histories also have included discussions of the conference in relation to Truman's decision to drop the atomic bomb and the chronicling of the behind-the-scenes work of newly appointed Secretary of State James Byrnes at the conference. See, for example, Tudda, *Cold War Summits: A History from Potsdam to Malta*, 7–36; Charles L. Mee, *Meeting at Potsdam* (New York: M. Evans, 1975); Neiberg, *Potsdam: The End of World War II and the Remaking of Europe*; John Lewis Gaddis, *The United States and the Origins of the Cold War, 1941–1947* (New York: Columbia University Press, 1972); Gar Alperovitz, *Atomic Diplomacy: Hiroshima and Potsdam* (London: Pluto Press, 1994); Miscamble, *From Roosevelt to Truman: Potsdam, Hiroshima, and the Cold War*.

12. Bohlen, *Witness to History, 1929–1969*, 227.

13. Harry S. Truman, "Radio Report to the American People on the Potsdam Conference," August 9, 1945, online by Gerhard Peters and John T. Woolley, *The American Presidency Project*, https://www.presidency.ucsb.edu/node/230985.

14. "First Hundred Days," *Life*, August 6, 1945, 18.

15. William E. Leuchtenburg, *In the Shadow of FDR: From Harry Truman to Barack Obama*, 4th ed. (Ithaca, NY: Cornell University Press, 2009).

16. Harry S. Truman Diary Entry, July 9, 1945, as printed in Truman, *Off the Record: The Private Papers of Harry S. Truman*, 49.

17. Bohlen, *Witness to History, 1929–1969*, 228.

18. Anne O'Hare McCormick, "Two Mighty Tests for the Big Three," *New York Times*, July 15, 1945, 47.

19. "The Potsdam Palace Conference," *Los Angeles Times*, July 17, 1945, A4.

20. "Mr. Truman to Berlin," *Chicago Daily Tribune*, July 9, 1945, 10.

21. Judt, *Postwar: A History of Europe since 1945*, 109.

22. "The Quarter's Polls," *Public Opinion Quarterly* 9, no. 3 (Autumn 1945): 389.

23. Winston Churchill to Harry S. Truman, May 12, 1945; Meetings of Heads of State (2 of 2), Box 6, Staff Member Office Files (hereafter SMOF): Naval Aide to the President Files, Harry S. Truman Papers, HSTL.

24. The 1943 Tehran Conference took place on the grounds of the Soviet embassy. The 1945 Yalta Conference took place on the Crimean Peninsula along the coast of the Black Sea.

25. Winston Churchill to Harry S. Truman, May 11, 1945; Meetings of Heads of State (2 of 2), Box 6, SMOF: Naval Aide to the President Files, Harry S. Truman Papers, HSTL.

26. On May 28, Truman relayed the following note to Churchill: "Stalin has informed me through Mr. Hopkins that he would like to have our three party meeting in the Berlin area and I will reply that I have no objection to the Berlin area." Harry S. Truman to Winston Churchill, May 28, 1945; Meetings of Heads of State (2 of 2), Box 6, SMOF: Naval Aide to the President Files, Harry S. Truman Papers, HSTL.

27. Tania Long, "Ruins of Berlin a Spur to Peace," *New York Times*, July 22, 1945, 63.

28. William L. Shirer, *The Rise and Fall of the Third Reich: A History of Nazi Germany* (New York: Simon & Schuster, 1960), 196–97.

29. Mee, *Meeting at Potsdam*, 71.

30. Harry S. Truman to Winston Churchill, May 12, 1945.

31. "The Presidency: On His Way," *Time*, July 16, 1945, 13–14.

32. "Again the Big Three," *New York Times*, June 14, 1945, 18.

33. "The First 100 Days," *New York Herald Tribune*, July 22, 1945, A8.

34. "The Potsdam Palace Conference" *Los Angeles Times*, July 17, 1945, A4.

35. Anne O'Hare McCormick, "Man from Missouri Meets Man from Georgia," *New York Times*, July 18, 1945, 26.

36. McCormick, "Two Mighty Tests for the Big Three."

37. Barnet Nover, "The Big Three Meet: The Basic Issue at Potsdam," *Washington Post*, July 17, 1945, 6.

38. "Mr. Truman's Role at Potsdam," *Chicago Daily Tribune*, July 19, 1945, 14.

39. McCormick, "Two Mighty Tests for the Big Three."

40. McCormick.

41. James Reston, "Three Big Uncertainties at Big Three Meeting," *New York Times*, July 22, 1945, 61.

42. Truman to Churchill, May 12, 1945.

43. "The Presidency: Missourian Abroad," *Time*, July 23, 1945, 21.

44. "Stalin Absent as Churchill, Truman Meet," *Chicago Daily Tribune*, July 17, 1945, 1.

45. McCullough, *Truman*, 406–7.

46. "Big Three Open Parley near Berlin," 200 Universal Newsreel 18-418, National Archives and Records Administration, College Park, Maryland (hereafter NARA II).

47. Raymond Daniell, "Parley Curbs Irk Berlin Newsmen," *New York Times*, July 15, 1945, 11.

48. In late June, Churchill wrote to Truman: "I suggest that following the precedent of the Crimea Conference the press should not be allowed at TERMINAL [Churchill's codename for the conference], but that photographers should be permitted." The president approved of this plan. William D. Leahy to Harry S. Truman, June 23, 1945; Meetings of Heads of State (1 of 2), Box 6, SMOF: Naval Aide to the President Files, Harry S. Truman Papers, HSTL.

49. An exasperated *New York Times* reporter wrote: "Most of the American and British newspaper correspondents now in Berlin came here when they did chiefly to report the Big Three conference. But that is the one thing they cannot write about, not even to the extent of speculating on the time and place of the meeting." The *Washington Post* was more direct in its criticism. "It has become the habit of these statesmen of the freedom-loving nations to discuss and decide questions involving the future of the world as though they were matters of no legiti-

mate interest to the hundreds of thousands of human beings whose destines are concerned," the editorial page read. "It was precisely thus that Hitler and Mussolini once discussed, at the Brenner Pass, the destinies of Europe." Raymond Daniell, "Parley Curbs Irk Berlin Newsmen," *New York Times*, July 15, 1945, 11; "Lid on Potsdam," *Washington Post*, July 19, 1945, 6.

50. The press body present at Potsdam contained more than 100 representatives of the American, British, French, Belgian, Brazilian, and Chinese press and radio, according to a report from the *New York Herald Tribune*. Russell Hill, "News Blackout on Conference Now Complete," *New York Herald Tribune*, July 18, 1945, 5.

51. Truman, *Off the Record: The Private Papers of Harry S. Truman*, 52.

52. "Half an hour after Churchill's departure [from meeting with Truman], Fred Canfil, a Federal marshal from Kansas and a former sergeant in the President's World War I regiment, turned up at the temporary White House from a sightseeing tour of Berlin. He was excited about it, and wanted the President to go out and see the devastation for himself." Truman had been scheduled to go on Wednesday, but decided to move the trip up to Monday. Russell Hill, "Stalin Late; Big 3 Parley Start Delayed," *New York Herald Tribune*, July 19, 1945, 2.

53. "Silence on Stalin," *New York Times*, July 17, 1945, 5.

54. Neiberg, *Potsdam: The End of World War II and the Remaking of Europe*, 119.

55. "Stalin's Absence Delays Parley," *Los Angeles Times*, July 17, 1945, 5.

56. "Silence on Stalin," *New York Times*, July 17, 1945.

57. "Stalin's Absence Delays Parley," *Los Angeles Times*, July 17, 1945.

58. Truman, *Off the Record: The Private Papers of Harry S. Truman*, 52.

59. "Silence on Stalin," *New York Times*, July 17, 1945.

60. "Stalin's Absence Delays Parley," *Los Angeles Times*, July 17, 1945, 5.

61. Churchill "stood aside defiantly near the spot where Hitler's body was supposedly burned and asked Russian escorts how the Nazis had died there," reported the *New York Times*. "He inspected Hitler's office, visited older parts of the Chancellery and descended through the stench into the underground shelter where Hitler and his sweetheart, Eva Braun, were said to have spent the last days of the siege of Berlin." There also were some reports that Stalin and Molotov conducted their own driving tour of Berlin in secrecy at some point during the conference. "Silence on Stalin," *New York Times*, July 17, 1945; "Stalin Guarded by Living Wall of Soviet Police," *New York Herald Tribune*, August 3, 1945, 7A.

62. Truman, *Off the Record: The Private Papers of Harry S. Truman*, 52.

63. *Time*, July 16, 1945, 29–30.

64. "Berlin," *Life*, July 23, 1945, 21.

65. "Berlin," *Life*, July 23, 1945, 19.

66. Paramount Newsreel, "Film Log of Harry S. Truman's Historical Trip to Berlin, July 1945 (MP72-36)," HSTL.

67. Pathé News, "Harry S. Truman's Movie Memory Album, July 7, 1945–August 7, 1945 (MP-72-5)," HSTL.

68. Kiewe and Houck, *FDR's Body Politics: The Rhetoric of Disability*, 10.

69. "First Hundred Days," *Life*, August 6, 1945, 18.

70. Harry S. Truman, "Remarks at the Raising of the Flag over the U.S. Group Control Council Headquarters in Berlin," July 20, 1945, online by Gerhard Peters and John T. Woolley, *The American Presidency Project*, https://www.presidency.ucsb.edu/node/231266.

71. "The Presidency," *Time*, July 30, 1945, 21.

72. "The Presidency," *Time*, July 30, 1945.

73. Tania Long, "Ruins of Berlin a Spur to Peace," *New York Times*, July 22, 1945, 63.

74. Truman, "Remarks at the Raising of the Flag." A press release version of this speech also can be found in White House Press Releases, July 1945, Box 55, President's Secretary's Files, HSTL.

75. Truman, "Remarks at the Raising of the Flag."

76. William A. Fowlkes, "Seeing and Saying: Home, Mr. Truman," *Atlanta Daily World*, August 5, 1945, 4.

77. "Paradox at Potsdam," *Chicago Defender*, August 18, 1945, 12.

78. Truman, "Remarks at the Raising of the Flag."

79. Long, "Ruins of Berlin."

80. W. E. B. DuBois, "The Winds of Time," *Chicago Defender*, August 11, 1945, 13.

81. Long, "Ruins of Berlin."

82. "The American Goal," *New York Herald Tribune*, July 21, 1945, 10.

83. See, for example, Edwin Black, "The Second Persona," *Quarterly Journal of Speech* 56, no. 2 (1970): 109–19.

84. "The American Goal," *New York Herald Tribune*, July 21, 1945.

85. "Truman Sees Flag Go Up in Berlin," *Chicago Daily Tribune*, July 22, 1945, 11; "The Presidency," *Time*, July 30, 1945, 21.

86. "Big Three Open Parley near Berlin," July 23, 1945, Universal Newsreel, 200 Universal 18-418, NARA II, https://web.archive.org/web/20070411224306/http://history.sandiego.edu/gen/newsreels/57.html.

87. Paramount Newsreel, "Film Log."

88. "Photographers Observe Truman Keeps No. 1 Seat," *Los Angeles Times*, August 1, 1945, 4.

89. Kiewe and Houck, *FDR's Body Politics: The Rhetoric of Disability*; Houck, "Reading the Body in the Text."

90. "A Show of Unity" exhibit, Schloss Cecilienhof, Potsdam, Germany, fieldwork conducted in August 2017.

91. "Photographers Observe Truman Keeps No. 1 Seat," *Los Angeles Times*, August 1, 1945.

92. See *Atlanta Daily World*, July 20, 1945, 5; "Minuet in Potsdam," *Time*, July 30, 1945, 31; "At Potsdam Attlee and Truman Look with Pleased Expression at the Sole Remaining Member of the First Big Three, Stalin, Who Looks Pleased Himself," *Life*, August 13, 1945, 28; "The Nations," *Time*, August 6, 1945, 32.

93. Universal Newsreel, "Big Three Conference Has Ended," 200-UN-18-421, August 1945, NARA II.

94. Of course, photos of the leaders together began circulating as soon as the conference began. For example, the *New York Times* published pictures of Truman and Churchill meeting for the first time and an image of the large meeting room at the Cecilienhof Palace. After Churchill's defeat, *Life* featured an image of Truman and Stalin above a headline that read: "The Berlin Conference: Without Churchill, Truman Meets Stalin to Discuss Peace in Europe and War in the Pacific." The next two pages provided an aerial view of the round table in the main conference room of the first formal meeting of the "Big Three" (when Churchill was still prime minister). But of particular significance in thinking about Truman's presidential ethos were those images taken of the "Big Three" together. See "Silence on Stalin," *New York Times*, July 17, 1945, 1; "At Potsdam Truman Talks to Stalin through Russian Interpreter Pavlov While Byrnes Links His Arm through Molotov's," *Life*, August 6, 1945, 15; "First Formal Meeting," *Life*, August 6, 1945, 16–17.

95. Due to copyright restrictions, the image displayed here (figure 2.7) was taken from a slightly different angle than the one printed in color in US periodicals, but the setting, image composition, and placement of the "Big Three" leaders remains the same.

96. "First Color Photo Radioed across the Atlantic," *Philadelphia Inquirer*, August 19, 1945, 3. Clipping found in the Papers of Arthur Grant Anderson, Box 1, World War II Collection, HSTL.

97. Urlich Calvosa, "The First Telechrome," *Collier's*, September 8, 1945, 19. Clipping found in the Papers of Arthur Grant Anderson, Box 1, World War II Collection, HSTL.

98. Truman, "Radio Report to the American People on the Potsdam Conference," August 9, 1945; "Expect Truman to Tell Big 3 Facts on Radio," *Chicago Daily Tribune*, July 26, 1945, 5.

99. Wilson, "Address to a Joint Session of Congress," April 2, 1917.

100. Franklin D. Roosevelt, "Annual Message to Congress on the State of the Union," January 6, 1941, online by Gerhard Peters and John T. Woolley, *The American Presidency Project*, https://www.presidency.ucsb.edu/documents/annual-message-congress-the-state-the-union; Franklin D. Roosevelt, "Radio Address before the Pan American Governing Board," April 15, 1940, online by Gerhard Peters and John T. Woolley, *The American Presidency Project*, https://www.presidency.ucsb.edu/documents/radio-address-before-the-pan-american-governing-board.

101. Truman, "Radio Report to the American People on the Potsdam Conference," August 9, 1945.

102. "The President Reports," *New York Herald Tribune*, August 10, 1945, 18.

103. Roscoe Drummond, "Free WORLD's Headliner: Truman," *Free World* 30 (1945): 30, 31, 33. A copy of this article is found in Potsdam Conference, White House Official File 190, Harry S. Truman Papers, HSTL.

104. Wat Arnold to Harry S. Truman, August 4, 1945; Potsdam Conference, White House Official File 190, Harry S. Truman Papers, HSTL.

105. Herbert Baynard Swope to Harry S. Truman, August 6, 1945; Potsdam Conference, White House Official File 190, Harry S. Truman Papers, HSTL.

106. J. C. Nichols to Harry S. Truman, August 6, 1945; Potsdam Conference, White House Official File 190, Harry S. Truman Papers, HSTL.

107. George H. Hodges and Frank Hodges to Harry S. Truman, August 8, 1945; Potsdam Conference, White House Official File 190, Harry S. Truman Papers, HSTL

108. C. Conner Makin to Harry S. Truman, August 8, 1945; Potsdam Conference, White House Official File 190, Harry S. Truman Papers, HSTL.

109. C. H. Bryson to Harry S. Truman, August 8, 1945; Potsdam Conference, White House Official File 190, Harry S. Truman Papers, HSTL.

110. "Paradox at Potsdam," *Chicago Defender*, August 18, 1945, 12.

111. "Dr. Goebbels Rides Again," *Pittsburgh Courier*, July 7, 1945, 6.

112. See Bohlen, *Witness to History, 1929–1969*, 240; George F. Kennan, *Memoirs, 1925–1950* (Boston: Little, Brown, 1967), 258.

113. Joseph Stalin, "Speech Delivered by Stalin at a Meeting of Voters of the Stalin Electoral District, Moscow," February 9, 1946, History and Public Policy Program Digital Archive, Gospolitizdat, Moscow, 1946, http://digitalarchive.wilsoncenter.org/document/116179. For more on the internal White House reaction to this speech, see Denise M. Bostdorff, *Proclaiming the Truman Doctrine: The Cold War Call to Arms* (College Station: Texas A&M University Press, 2008), 18–19.

114. George F. Kennan to the Secretary of State, "Long Telegram," Moscow, 861.00/2-2246:

Telegram, February 22, 1946, National Security Archive, Washington, DC, https://nsarchive2
.gwu.edu//coldwar/documents/episode-1/kennan.htm.

115. Bostdorff, *Proclaiming the Truman Doctrine: The Cold War Call to Arms*, 23. See also Denise M. Bostdorff, "Dean Acheson's May 1947 Delta Council Speech: Rhetorical Evolution from
the Truman Doctrine to the Marshall Plan," in *World War II and the Cold War: The Rhetoric of
Hearts and Minds*, ed. Martin J. Medhurst, A Rhetorical History of the United States, vol. 8 (East
Lansing: Michigan State University Press, 2018), 167–214.

116. Harry S. Truman, "Special Message to the Congress on Greece and Turkey: The Truman Doctrine," March 12, 1947, online by Gerhard Peters and John T. Woolley, *The American
Presidency Project*, https://www.presidency.ucsb.edu/documents/special-message-the-congress
-greece-and-turkey-the-truman-doctrine.

117. Truman, "Remarks at the Raising of the Flag Over the U.S. Group Control Council
Headquarters in Berlin."

Chapter Three

1. "Information Aspects of Non-Information Activities of Government," 7-8; Image—Public
Opinion, 1, Box 15, Papers of the US President's Committee on Information Activities Abroad
(Sprague Committee), Dwight D. Eisenhower Presidential Library (hereafter DDEL).

2. William I. Hitchcock, *The Age of Eisenhower: America and the World in the 1950s* (New
York: Simon & Schuster, 2018), 28.

3. Hitchcock, 27.

4. Harry S. Truman, "Statement by the President on the Situation in Korea," June 27, 1950,
online by Gerhard Peters and John T. Wooley, *The American Presidency Project*, https://www
.presidency.ucsb.edu/node/230845.

5. Dwight D. Eisenhower, "Text of the Address by Dwight D. Eisenhower, Republican Nominee for President, Delivered at Detroit, Michigan, October 24, 1952," https://www
.eisenhowerlibrary.gov/sites/default/files/research/online-documents/korean-war/i-shall-go-to
-korea-1952-10-24.pdf. For a detailed analysis of this speech, see Martin J. Medhurst, "Text and
Context in the 1952 Presidential Campaign: Eisenhower's 'I Shall Go to Korea' Speech," *Presidential Studies Quarterly* 30, no. 3 (2000): 464–84.

6. For more on these propaganda campaigns during the Cold War, see Leo Bogart, *Premises
for Propaganda: The United States Information Agency's Operating Assumptions in the Cold War*
(New York: Free Press, 1976); Nicholas J. Cull, *The Cold War and the United States Information Agency: American Propaganda and Public Diplomacy, 1945–1989* (New York: Cambridge
University Press, 2008); Michael Curtin, *Redeeming the Wasteland: Television Documentary and
Cold War Politics* (New Brunswick, NJ: Rutgers University Press, 1995); Walter L. Hixon, *Parting
the Curtain: Propaganda, Culture, and the Cold War, 1945–1961* (New York: St. Martin's Press,
1997); David F. Krugler, *The Voice of America and the Domestic Propaganda Battles, 1945–1953*
(Columbia: University of Missouri Press, 2000); James Schwoch, *Global TV: New Media and
the Cold War, 1946–69* (Urbana: University of Illinois Press, 2009); Holly Cowan Shulman, *The
Voice of America: Propaganda and Democracy, 1941–1945* (Madison: University of Wisconsin
Press, 1990).

7. Eisenhower's shrewd management of US and global public opinion has been the subject
of many a scholarly study and much recent historical scholarship. The thirty-fourth president
governed with a "hidden hand," Fred I. Greenstein argued in 1994, making choices behind the

scenes that demonstrate his innate—and, at times, ruthless—political calculus. For more on
Eisenhower's rhetorical leadership, see Robert A. Divine, *Eisenhower and the Cold War* (New
York: Oxford University Press, 1981); Fred I. Greenstein, *The Hidden-Hand Presidency: Eisen-
hower as Leader* (Baltimore: Johns Hopkins University Press, 1982); R. Gordon Hoxie, "Eisen-
hower and Presidential Leadership," *Presidential Studies Quarterly* 13, no. 4 (1983): 589–612;
H. W. Brands, *Cold Warriors: Eisenhower's Generation and American Foreign Policy* (New York:
Columbia University Press, 1988); J. Michael Hogan, "Eisenhower and Open Skies: A Case Study
in Psychological Warfare," in *Eisenhower's War of Words: Rhetoric and Leadership*, ed. Martin J.
Medhurst (East Lansing: Michigan State University Press, 1994), 137–56; Shawn J. Parry-Giles,
"The Eisenhower Administration's Conceptualization of the USIA: The Development of Overt
and Covert Propaganda Strategies," *Presidential Studies Quarterly* 24, no. 2 (1994): 263–76;
Shawn J. Parry-Giles, "'Camouflaged' Propaganda: The Truman and Eisenhower Administra-
tions' Covert Manipulation of News," *Western Journal of Communication* 60, no. 2 (1996): 146–
67; Martin J. Medhurst, "Eisenhower and the Crusade for Freedom: The Rhetorical Origins of a
Cold War Campaign," *Presidential Studies Quarterly* 27, no. 4 (1997): 646–61; Ira Chernus, *Eisen-
hower's Atoms for Peace* (East Lansing: Michigan State University Press, 2002); Ned O'Gorman,
"Eisenhower and the American Sublime," *Quarterly Journal of Speech* 94, no. 1 (2008): 44–72;
Ned O'Gorman, *Spirits of the Cold War: Contesting Worldviews in the Classical Age of American
Security Strategy* (East Lansing: Michigan State University Press, 2012); Richard M. Filipink,
Dwight Eisenhower and American Foreign Policy during the 1960s: An American Lion in Winter
(Lanham, MD: Lexington Books, 2015); Hitchcock, *The Age of Eisenhower: America and the
World in the 1950s.*

8. Dwight D. Eisenhower, "Radio and Television Address to the American People before
Leaving on Good Will Trip to Europe, Asia, and Africa," December 3, 1959, online by Gerhard
Peters and John T. Woolley, *The American Presidency Project*, https://www.presidency.ucsb
.edu/node/234625.

9. "The President's Committee on International Information Activities: Report to the President," June 30, 1953, 58; US President's Committee on International Information Activities (Jackson Committee): Records, 1950–53, Box 14, DDEL.

10. "Notes on 'The Image of America,' a Presentation by Mr. George V. Allen, Director of
USIA, at the Planning Board, September 30, 1958," 44; USIA, 1, 1954–60, Box 18, NSC Series,
Briefing Notes Subseries, White House Office of the Special Assistant for National Security, Re-
cords, DDEL.

11. "Summary Conclusions and Recommendations of the President's Committee on Information Activities Abroad," n.d., 4; Summary Conclusions and Recommendations, Box 26,
Sprague Committee, DDEL.

12. "The Communication Dimension in American Foreign Policy," n.d., 1; US Resources for
Communications and Political Warfare, Box 19, Sprague Committee, DDEL.

13. "A Strategy for Peace," July 20, 1959, 3; Coordination of Informational and Public Opinion, Box 1, Operation Coordinating Board Series, Subject Subseries, White House Office of the
Special Assistant for National Security Affairs, Records, DDEL.

14. James C. Hagerty to Dwight D. Eisenhower, December 9, 1958, 6; Political Committee
1959 (1), Box 26, Dwight D. Eisenhower Papers as President, 1953–61, Name Series, DDEL.

15. Hagerty to Eisenhower, December 9, 1958, 7–8.

16. Dwight D. Eisenhower, *Waging Peace, 1956–1961: The White House Years* (Garden City,
NY: Doubleday, 1965), 485.

17. Eisenhower, 485–86.

18. Eisenhower, 487.

19. Allen W. Dulles to Dwight D. Eisenhower, December 2, 1959; OF 116-XX, President's Trip to Asia, Europe, and Africa, December 1959, Box 508, White House Central Files, Official File, DDEL.

20. Eisenhower, "Radio and Television Address to the American People," December 3, 1959.

21. Murphy to Secretary of State, Washington, DC, December 10, 1959; The President's' Goodwill Trip—December 1959—Matters for Specific Follow Up (8), Box 4, International Meetings Series, Papers of Dwight D. Eisenhower as President (Ann Whitman File), DDEL.

22. "Spain, Morocco and Home," New York Times, December 23, 1959, 26.

23. Dwight D. Eisenhower, "Radio and Television Address to the American People on the Eve of South American Trip," February 21, 1960, online by Gerhard Peters and John T. Woolley, The American Presidency Project, https://www.presidency.ucsb.edu/documents/radio-and -television-address-the-american-people-the-eve-south-american-trip.

24. Eisenhower, "Radio and Television Address to the American People on the Eve of South American Trip."

25. "Memorandum of Conversation, Subject: Possible Presidential Trip to Brazil," November 27, 1959; Brazil (1), May 1958–January 1960, Box 2, International Series, White House Office of the Special Assistant for National Security, Records, DDEL.

26. This is not to suggest that there was not imperialist, hegemonic intent in these two other tours. Comparatively, however, Eisenhower's visit to South America was markedly different than the other two.

27. "A Strategy for Peace," July 20, 1959, 13; Coordination of Informational and Public Opinion, Box 1, Operation Coordinating Board Series, Subject Subseries, White House Office of the Special Assistant for National Security Affairs, Records, DDEL.

28. For more on US imperialist intervention in Central and South America under Eisenhower and other US presidents, see Stephen G. Rabe, Eisenhower and Latin America: The Foreign Policy of Anticommunism (Chapel Hill and London: University of North Carolina Press, 1988); Stephen G. Rabe, "The Caribbean Triangle: Betancourt, Castro, and Trujillo and U.S. Foreign Policy, 1958–1963," Diplomatic History 20, no. 1 (1996): 55–78; Grandin, Empire's Workshop: Latin America, the United States, and the Rise of New Imperialism; Greg Grandin, The Last Colonial Massacre: Latin America in the Cold War (Chicago: University of Chicago Press, 2004); Luis L. Schenoni and Scott Mainwaring, "US Hegemony and Regime Change in Latin America," Democratization 26, no. 2 (2019): 269–87.

29. Karl G. Harr, "Memorandum for the President," August 4, 1959, 1; Miscellaneous (9), November 1959–February 1960, Box 4, Operation Coordinating Board Series, Subject Subseries, White House Office of the Special Assistant for National Security Affairs, Records, DDEL.

30. "TV, Radio Carrying Khrushchev Today," New York Times, September 27, 1959, 41. The full text of the speech was printed as "Text of Khrushchev's News Conference on this Talks with the President," New York Times, September 28, 1959, 18–19. Text also available in Nikita Sergeyevich Khrushchev, Khrushchev in America (New York: Crosscurrents Press, 1960), 198–207. This work was the American version of Nikita Sergeyevich Khrushchev, Let Us Live in Peace and Friendship: Full Texts of the Speeches Made by N. S. Khrushchev on His Tour of the United States, September 15–27, 1959 (Moscow: Foreign Languages Publishing House, 1959).

31. N. S. Khrushchev, "Speech at Andrews Field," September 15, 1959, as published in Khrushchev, Khrushchev in America, 14.

32. CIA, "Survey of Recent Communist Policies and Activities," October 23, 1959, 3; Communist Policies and Activities, Report re: 1959, Box 5, NSC Series, Briefing Notes Subseries, White House Office of the Special Assistant for National Security, Records, DDEL.

33. CIA, "Survey of Recent Communist Policies and Activities," November 1959, 18; Communist Policies and Activities, Report re: 1959, Box 5, NSC Series, Briefing Notes Subseries, White House Office of the Special Assistant for National Security, Records, DDEL.

34. "Jet Age Diplomacy," *New York Times*, February 14, 1960, E8.

35. "The News of the Week in Review: Two on Tour," *New York Times*, February 28, 1960, E1.

36. Daniel Schorr, "Traveling Salesmen for Two Ways of Life," *New York Times*, March 13, 1960, SM22.

37. Vincent P. Wilbert to the Department of State, Washington, DC, March 9, 1960; 711.11 EI/3-960a, Box 1440, Record Group 59—State Department Central Files (hereafter RG 59), NARA II.

38. Robert B. Hill to the State Department, Washington, DC, March 8, 1960; 711.11 EI/3-160, Box 1440, RG 59, NARA II.

39. Robert G. Barnes to the State Department, Washington, DC, March 14, 1960; 711.11 EI/3-960b, Box 1440, RG 59, NARA II.

40. "Travels of the Big-Two Leaders," *New York Times*, February 28, 1960, E3.

41. "Southern Swing," *Time*, March 7, 1960, 12.

42. "President's Trip to Latin America, February—March, 1960, Policy Information Statement ARA-305," 3; Advance South American Trip—General, President, Box 27, Papers of James C. Hagerty, DDEL.

43. "President's Trip to Latin America, February—March, 1960, Policy Information Statement ARA-305," 5.

44. "President's Trip to Latin America, February—March, 1960, Policy Information Statement ARA-305," 3-4.

45. Victor Rosenberg, *Soviet-American Relations, 1953–1960: Diplomacy and Cultural Exchange during the Eisenhower Presidency* (Jefferson, NC: McFarland, 2005), 106.

46. Christian Herter as captured in Memorandum of Telephone Conversation with the President, February 11, 1960; Presidential Telephone Calls 1–6 1960 (2), Box 10, Papers of Christian A. Herter, DDEL.

47. For more on this history, see Amy Kaplan, *The Anarchy of Empire in the Making of U.S. Culture* (Cambridge, MA: Harvard University Press, 2005); Charles R. Venator-Santiago, *Puerto Rico and the Origins of US Global Empires: The Disembodied Shade* (New York: Routledge, 2015); Sam Erman, *Almost Citizens: Puerto Rico, the U.S. Constitution, and Empires* (Cambridge: Cambridge University Press, 2019).

48. Arturo Morales Carrion to Roy Rubottom, January 15, 1960; 711.11 EI/1-1560, Box 1438, RG 59, NARA II.

49. "Memorandum to the President (Draft)," January 27, 1960, attached to Roy Rubottom to Christian A. Herter, January 22, 1960; 711.11 EI/1-2060, Box 1438, RG 59, NARA II.

50. Dwight D. Eisenhower, "Remarks upon Arrival at International Airport, San Juan, Puerto Rico," February 22, 1960, online by Gerhard Peters and John T. Woolley, *The American Presidency Project*, https://www.presidency.ucsb.edu/node/234944.

51. "The Start in Puerto Rico," *New York Times*, February 23, 1960, 30.

52. "Current Basic United States Policy towards Cuba (November 1959)," 1; Cuban Situation,

2 (1959–60), Box 6, NSC Series, Briefing Notes Subseries, White House Office of the Special Assistant for National Security, Records, DDEL.

53. Walter Lippmann, "Eisenhower's Policy on Cuba Is Correct," *Los Angeles Times*, January 31, 1960, C4.

54. Robert G. Barnes to the State Department.

55. US Embassy Moscow to Christian A. Herter, March 5, 1960; 711.11 EI/3-160, Box 1440, RG 59, NARA II.

56. Beam to Christian A. Herter, March 5, 1960; 711.11 EI/3-160, Box 1440, RG 59, NARA II.

57. Braddock to Christian A. Herter, March 3, 1960; 711.11 EI/3-160, Box 1440, RG 59, NARA II.

58. Braddock to Christian A. Herter, March 10, 1960; 711.11 EI/3-960a, Box 1440, RG 59, NARA II.

59. Samuel E. Belk, "Memorandum for Mr. Gray, Subject: Background for the Cuba and Dominican Republic Items on the Council's Agenda for January 14, 1960," January 13, 1960, 1; Cuban Situation, 2 (1959–60), Box 6, NSC Series, Briefing Notes Subseries, White House Office of the Special Assistant for National Security, Records, DDEL.

60. Belk, 2.

61. On February 26, Admiral Arleigh Burke, the chief of naval operations, Department of the Navy, penned a note to Livingston Merchant, the undersecretary of political affairs at the Department of State, outlining his concerns about the growing communist influence in Cuba. This letter exchange is significant, for it was then sent along to Gordon Gray, special assistant to the president for national security affairs to be used at the NSC meeting just after Eisenhower's return from "Operation Amigo." In his note to Merchant, Burke expressed his concern over Cuba's "strategic location with respect to the sea approaches to the southern United States and the Panama Canal, and because of the location there of the Guantanamo Naval Base." Moreover, he noted that "a communist controlled state in Cuba would serve as a base of operations for the further spread of communistic influence in the Western Hemisphere having as its aim the isolation of the United States of America." Here, metaphors of disease and isolation suggested that a growing communist presence in the region would infect and strangle the country—two outcomes the "Leader of the Free World" could never allow. "The U.S. has never renounced the Monroe Doctrine," Burke noted in an attached memorandum, and the "worst extreme" would be the "possibility of direct support for Cuba by the Soviet Bloc." In his response to Burke on March 10, Merchant expressed his agreement that the "*maximum objective* of International Communism—in the immediate future—is the consolidation of a radical, anti-American Revolution friendly to the USSR in Cuba and the utilization of Cuba as a base to promote similar revolutionary movements in the Caribbean." The "primary objective of U.S. policy," therefore, "should be the creation of an affective, patriotic movement friendly to the United States within Cuba and among Cuban exiles to counter Cuba's current trend." The undersecretary continued to acknowledge in no uncertain terms that the administration was engaged in efforts to "encourage such elements to organize more effectively and to expect our support and collaboration in their efforts." Indeed, such "covert activities [were] underway towards this end." However, Livingston cautioned that the administration must "exercise the greatest care that we do not necessarily transform the developing dissatisfaction of the Cuban people with Castro into a fight between the United States and Cuba, for no self-respecting Cuban could then afford to support us against his own country." Arleigh Burke to Livingston T. Merchant, February 26, 1960; Cuba,

May 1959–September 1960 (2), Box 4, NSC Series, Subject Subseries, White House Office of the Special Assistant for National Security, Records, DDEL; "Recommendations for U.S. Action in Cuba," February 26, 1960, 1, 3; Cuba, May 1959–September 1960 (2), Box 4, NSC Series, Subject Subseries, White House Office of the Special Assistant for National Security, Records, DDEL; Livingston T. Merchant to Arleigh Burke, March 10, 1960, 1, 2, 3; Cuba, May 1959–September 1960 (2), Box 4, NSC Series, Subject Subseries, White House Office of the Special Assistant for National Security, Records, DDEL.

62. "Memorandum for the National Security Council, Subject: U.S. Policy Toward Cuba," March 15, 1960; Cuba, May 1959–September 1960 (2), Box 4, NSC Series, Subject Subseries, White House Office of the Special Assistant for National Security, Records, DDEL.

63. Christian A. Herter to Dwight D. Eisenhower, "Memorandum for the President," March 17, 1960; Herter, Christian, March 1960 (2), Box 12, Dulles-Herter Series, DDEL.

64. Craig Allen, *Eisenhower and the Mass Media: Peace, Prosperity, and Prime-Time TV* (Chapel Hill: University of North Carolina Press, 1993), 167, 68.

65. James C. Hagerty to American Embassy Santiago, Buenos Aires, Rio de Janeiro, and Montevideo, January 8, 1960, 2, 3; Advance South American Trip—General, Press, Box 27, Papers of James C. Hagerty, DDEL .

66. "Memorandum: The President's Trip to Latin America, January 11, 1960," 1; Advance South American Trip—General, Press, Box 27, Papers of James C. Hagerty, DDEL.

67. "Memorandum: The President's Trip to Latin America, January 11, 1960," 3.

68. "President's Trip to Latin America, February–March, 1960, Policy Information Statement ARA-305," 3.

69. "President's Trip to Latin America, February–March, 1960, Policy Information Statement ARA-305," 3-4.

70. USIA Office of Research and Analysis, "Brazil Preoccupation Profile," January 15, 1960, 2; South American Trip—Confidential Data on Each Country, Box 27, Papers of James C. Hagerty, DDEL.

71. Dwight D. Eisenhower, "Address before a Joint Session of the Congress of Brazil," February 24, 1960, online by Gerhard Peters and John T. Woolley, *The American Presidency Project*, https://www.presidency.ucsb.edu/node/235007.

72. William P. Cochran Jr. to Christian A. Herter, March 18, 1960, 2; 711.11 EI/3-1760, Box 1440, RG 59, NARA II; "Rio Gives Eisenhower Heart-Warming Welcome" (ARF 25); Brazil—General Information, Plane Crash, Press Kits, etc., Box 28, Papers of James C. Hagerty, DDEL.

73. "The News of the Week in Review: Two on Tour," *New York Times*, February 28, 1960, E1.

74. "The President in Rio," *New York Times*, February 25, 1960, 28.

75. Robert B. Hill to the State Department, Washington, DC, March 8, 1960, 3; 711.11 EI/3-160, Box 1440, RG 59, NARA II.

76. Robert G. Barnes to the State Department, Washington, DC, March 14, 1960, 2; 711.11 EI/3-960b, Box 1440, RG 59, NARA II.

77. Hill to Christian A. Herter, March 11, 1960, 1; 711.11 EI/3-960b, Box 1440, RG59, NARA II.

78. Houghton to Christian A. Herter, February 27, 1960; 711.11 EI/2-2060, Box 1439, RG59, NARA II.

79. "Stocktaking after President Eisenhower's Tour," *London Times*, March 11, 1960, 9.

80. "Aide-Mémoire: Political Aspects of Operation Pan-American," 1; DDE to South Amer-

ica, Chronology, Brazil, February 23–26, 1960 (1), Box 10, International Trips and Meetings Series, White House Office of the Staff Secretary, DDEL.

81. Christian A. Herter to Dwight D. Eisenhower, Subject: Latin American Press Comment on Your Tour, March 12, 1960; 711.11 EI/3-960, Box 1440, RG 59, NARA II.

82. Detailed media reports from various countries throughout Latin America and Europe can be found in Box 1439 and Box 1440, RG 59, NARA II.

83. Sparks to Christian A. Herter, March 8, 1960; 711.11 EI/3-160, Box 1440, RG 59, NARA II.

84. Farland to Christian A. Herter, March 9, 1960; 711.11 EI/3-960, Box 1440, RG 59, NARA II.

85. Neal to Christian A. Herter, March 7, 1960; 711.11 EI/3-160, Box 1440, RG 59, NARA II.

86. Tad Szulc, "Eisenhower's Tour: The Promises and the Expectations," *New York Times*, March 6, 1960, E6.

87. "The Presidency: Benvindo Eekee!," *Time*, March 7, 1960, 12.

88. "Good Will's Fine, but What's in It for Us?," *Chicago Daily Tribune*, March 7, 1960, 18.

89. Szulc, "Eisenhower's Tour."

90. Robert Hartmann, "Eisenhower Lauds Ties with Latins," *Los Angeles Times*, March 9, 1960, 1.

91. "And Castro's Still There," *Los Angeles Times*, March 10, 1960, B4.

92. Polyzoides, "Frondizi Setback Shows Need of Urgent Action," *Los Angeles Times*, March 30, 1960, 25.

93. "Fights Flare in the South," *Chicago Defender*, February 29, 1960, 1.

94. "Faltering Leadership," *Chicago Defender*, May 22, 1960, A10.

95. Negro Physician, "Dignity of the Individual," *Los Angeles Times*, February 8, 1960, B4.

96. C. L. Sulzberger, "Heads of State Now Traveling Salesmen," *Los Angeles Times*, March 16, 1960, 2.

97. "The Presidency: On with the Trip," *Time*, June 27, 1960, 9.

98. Eisenhower, *Waging Peace*, 563.

99. William J. Jorden, "Chagrin Is Voiced," *New York Times*, June 17, 1960, 1.

100. Fulbright, Khuchel, and Johnson as quoted in Carroll Kilpatrick, "Congress Is Shocked by U.S. 'Defeat' as Japan Cancels Eisenhower's Visit," *Washington Post*, June 17, 1960, A1.

101. C. L. Sulzberger, "What May Be Learned from Disaster," *New York Times*, June 18, 1960, 22.

102. These detailed media reports can be found in 711.11 EI/6-1260, Box 1443 and 711.11 EI/6-1860, Box 1444, RG 59, NARA II.

103. Christian A. Herter to J. Graham Parsons, June 21, 1960; 711.11 EI/5-1360, Box 1442, RG 59, NARA II.

104. Herter to Parsons, June 21, 1960.

105. Hugh S. Cunning Jr. to Christian A. Herter, June 27, 1960; 711.11-EI-6-60, Box 1443, RG 59, NARA II.

106. Herter to Parsons, June 21, 1960.

107. "We Must Find Ways to Win Friends and Influence People," *Atlanta Daily World*, June 18, 1960, 4.

108. "Another Fiasco," *Chicago Defender*, June 20, 1960, A10.

109. "First Things First," *Los Angeles Sentinel*, June 30, 1960, A6.

110. President's Committee on Information Activities Abroad, "The Problem of U.S. Public Understanding of International Affairs," August 8, 1960, 6; President's Committee on Information Activities Abroad 21 (1), Box 22, Sprague Committee, DDEL.

111. "Draft: U.S. Resources for Foreign Communication and Political Warfare," June 21, 1960; US Resources for Foreign Communications and Political Warfare (1), Box 19, Sprague Committee, DDEL.

112. "Conclusions and Recommendations of the President's Committee on Information Activities Abroad," December 1960, 3; Printed Committee Report, Box 26, Sprague Committee, DDEL.

113. "Conclusions and Recommendations of the President's Committee on Information Activities Abroad," December 1960, 4; Printed Committee Report, Box 26, Sprague Committee, DDEL.

114. "Conclusions and Recommendations of the President's Committee on Information Activities Abroad," December 1960, 45; Printed Committee Report, Box 26, Sprague Committee, DDEL.

Chapter Four

1. US Department of State, Bureau of Public Affairs, Office of Public Services, "Background: Berlin—1961" (Washington, DC: US Government Printing Office, August 1961), 28–29.

2. John F. Kennedy, "Statement of Senator John F. Kennedy," January 2, 1960; Speeches and the Press, Speech Files, 1953–60, Papers of John F. Kennedy, Pre-Presidential Papers, Senate Files, John F. Kennedy Presidential Library, Boston, Massachusetts (hereafter JFKL).

3. Truman, "Remarks at the Raising of the Flag Over the U.S. Group Control Council Headquarters in Berlin."

4. John F. Kennedy, "Remarks in the Rudolph Wilde Platz, Berlin," June 26, 1963, online by Gerhard Peters and John T. Woolley, The American Presidency Project, https://www.presidency.ucsb.edu/node/236863.

5. Andreas W. Daum, Kennedy in Berlin, trans. Dona Geyer (New York: Cambridge University Press, 2008), xviii.

6. Robert Dallek, An Unfinished Life: John F. Kennedy, 1917–1963 (Boston: Little, Brown, 2003), 623.

7. Ted Sorenson, Kennedy (New York: Harper & Row, Publishers, 1965), 600.

8. Murphy, John F. Kennedy and the Liberal Persuasion, 196.

9. Isabel Fay and Jim A. Kuypers, "Transcending Mysticism and Building Identification through Empowerment of the Rhetorical Agent: John F. Kennedy's Berlin Speeches on June 26, 1963," Southern Communication Journal 77, no. 3 (2012): 199.

10. Kennedy, "Remarks in the Rudolph Wilde Platz, Berlin."

11. John F. Kennedy, "Our Stake in Berlin," March 24, 1960, 2; Speeches, Statements, and Sections, 1958–60, Speeches and the Press, Papers of John F. Kennedy, Pre-Presidential Papers, Presidential Campaign Files, 1960, JFKL.

12. Massey, Space, Place, and Gender, 5.

13. Edward T. Lilly, "Political Objectives in Berlin," n.d.; Berlin, Box 44, Papers of Edward Lilly, DDEL.

14. Royce E. Eckwright, United States Air Access to Berlin, 1945–1965: Part I, the Political-Military Background (Historical Division, Office of Information, US Air Forces in Europe, 1966), 1.

15. The city's "special status stems from the fact that it was the capital not only of Hitler's Third Reich but of the German nation formed in the latter half of the 19th century," explained

one State Department publication. "In essence, the four major allies agreed to hold Berlin, as the traditional capital, in trust for a democratic and united Germany." US State Department, "Background: Berlin—1961," 1.

16. Eckwright, *United States Air Access to Berlin*, 5-6.

17. Eckwright, xi. For more details on the Berlin Airlift, see Robert P. Grathwol and Donita M. Moorhus, *Berlin and the American Military: A Cold War Chronicle* (New York: New York University Press, 1999); Daniel F. Harrington, *Berlin on the Brink: The Blockade, the Airlift, and the Early Cold War* (Lexington: University Press of Kentucky, 2012); Michael D. Haydock, *City under Siege: The Berlin Blockade and Airlift, 1948-1949* (Washington, DC: Brassey's, 1999); Roger G. Miller, *To Save a City: The Berlin Airlift, 1948-1949* (College Station: Texas A&M University Press, 2000); Thomas Parrish, *Berlin in the Balance, 1945-1949: The Blockade, the Airlift, and the First Major Battle of the Cold War* (Reading, MA: Addison-Wesley, 1998).

18. John G. Norris, "Firmness Can Win 'Cold' War, U.S. Chiefs in Berlin Agree," *Washington Post*, July 14, 1948, 7.

19. Lilly, "Political Objectives in Berlin."

20. I draw here on Hitchcock, *The Age of Eisenhower: America and the World in the 1950s*, 410-17.

21. Kennedy, "Our Stake in Berlin."

22. John F. Kennedy, "Radio and Television Report to the American People on the Berlin Crisis," July 25, 1961, online by Gerhard Peters and John T. Woolley, *The American Presidency Project*, https://www.presidency.ucsb.edu/node/235247.

23. This was not their first meeting. The two men met during Khrushchev's tour of the United States in 1959, when Kennedy was a junior senator from Massachusetts.

24. Sorenson, *Kennedy*, 583.

25. As historian Michael Beschloss explains, Kennedy's insistence "came just six weeks after he himself had tried to change [the power balance] at the Bay of Pigs. . . . Now, in Khrushchev's view, he was arrogantly brandishing the superior might of the United States. Despite his earlier rhetoric about parity, Kennedy seemed to be saying that since America was more powerful, it could afford to ignore Soviet concerns about Berlin." Michael R. Beschloss, *The Crisis Years: Kennedy and Khrushchev, 1960-1963* (New York: Edward Berlingame Books, 1991), 217. For a detailed account of the conversations between Kennedy and Khrushchev in Vienna, see Beschloss, 191-236.

26. John F. Kennedy, as quoted in Frederick Kempe, *Berlin 1961: Kennedy, Khrushchev, and the Most Dangerous Place on Earth* (New York: Berkley Books, 2011), 252.

27. Nikita Khrushchev, as quoted in Kempe, 252.

28. John F. Kennedy, as quoted in Beschloss, *The Crisis Years: Kennedy and Khrushchev, 1960-1963*, 223.

29. Nikita Khrushchev, as quoted in Beschloss, 223-24.

30. The "Berlin Crisis" of 1961 has been the subject of ample scholarship. See, for example, Sorenson, *Kennedy*, 583-601; Beschloss, *The Crisis Years: Kennedy and Khrushchev, 1960-1963*; Kempe, *Berlin 1961: Kennedy, Khrushchev, and the Most Dangerous Place on Earth*; Grathwol and Moorhus, *Berlin and the American Military: A Cold War Chronicle*, 79-106; Dallek, *An Unfinished Life: John F. Kennedy, 1917-1963*, 418-35.

31. Vito N. Silvestri, *Becoming JFK: A Profile in Communication* (Greenwood, CT: Praeger, 2000), 184.

32. John F. Kennedy, "Radio and Television Report to the American People on Returning

from Europe," June 6, 1961, online by Gerhard Peters and John T. Woolley, *The American Presidency Project*, https://www.presidency.ucsb.edu/node/234830.

33. John F. Kennedy, "The President's News Conference," June 28, 1961, online by Gerhard Peters and John T. Woolley, *The American Presidency Project*, https://www.presidency.ucsb.edu/node/234940.

34. Theodore C. Sorenson to John F. Kennedy, "Memorandum to the President: The Decision on Berlin," July 17, 1961, 3; Germany: General, July 1961, Box 116b, Papers of John F. Kennedy, Presidential Papers, President's Office Files, JFKL.

35. Kempe, *Berlin 1961: Kennedy, Khrushchev, and the Most Dangerous Place on Earth*, 312.

36. Kennedy, "Radio and Television Report to the American People on the Berlin Crisis."

37. Kennedy, "Radio and Television Report to the American People on the Berlin Crisis."

38. Kempe, *Berlin 1961: Kennedy, Khrushchev, and the Most Dangerous Place on Earth*, 323–62.

39. Beschloss, *The Crisis Years: Kennedy and Khrushchev, 1960–1963*, 277.

40. Robert Schlesinger, *White House Ghosts: Presidents and Their Speechwriters* (New York: Simon and Schuster, 2008), 138–39; Beschloss, *The Crisis Years: Kennedy and Khrushchev, 1960–1963*, 275.

41. Kempe, *Berlin 1961: Kennedy, Khrushchev, and the Most Dangerous Place on Earth*, 375.

42. Daum, *Kennedy in Berlin*, 52.

43. Lyndon B. Johnson, as quoted in Sydney Gruson, "300,000 Applaud: Vice President Tells Them Washington Will Not Forget," *New York Times*, August 20, 1961, 1.

44. Gruson.

45. Gerald S. Strober and Deborah H. Strober, *"Let Us Begin Anew": An Oral History of the Kennedy Presidency* (New York: HarperCollins Publishers, 1993), 367–68. When Johnson returned to the United States, he reported his observations to the president in a memo marked "SECRET": "I returned from Germany with new pride in America's leadership but with an unprecedented awareness of the responsibility which rests upon this country. The world expects so much from us, and we must measure up to the need, even while we seek more help from our allies. For if we fail or falter or default, all is lost, and freedom may never have a second chance." Kempe, *Berlin 1961: Kennedy, Khrushchev, and the Most Dangerous Place on Earth*, 389–90.

46. "Berlin Salutes Robert Kennedy: He Vows Support," *New York Times*, February 23, 1962, 1.

47. Robert F. Kennedy as quoted in "Berlin Salutes Robert Kennedy: He Vows Support," *New York Times*, February 23, 1962.

48. "Berlin Salutes Robert Kennedy: He Vows Support," *New York Times*, February 23, 1962.

49. "Background Briefing (European Trip) at the White House with Pierre Salinger," June 19, 1963, 7; Trips: Germany, June 1963: 22–26, Box 108, President's Office Files, Papers of John F. Kennedy, Presidential Papers, JFKL.

50. E. Allan Lightner to Dean Rusk, February 5, 1963; President's Trip: Europe, June–July 1963, Germany, January 17–June 10, 1963 (1 of 2 folders), Box 241, National Security Files, Trips and Conferences, JFKL.

51. Robert Magill to Department of State, March 8, 1963; President's Trip: Europe, June–July 1963, Germany, January 17–June 10, 1963 (1 of 2 folders), Box 241, National Security Files, Trips and Conferences, JFKL.

52. "Review of West German Press, Radio and Television Comment 14 March 1963," attached to Memorandum, L. J. Legere to Carl Kaysen, March 15, 1963; President's Trip: Europe, June–July

1963, Germany, January 17–June 10, 1963 (1 of 2 folders), Box 241, National Security Files, Trips and Conferences, JFKL.

53. Memorandum, William H. Brubeck to McGeorge Bundy, March 14, 1963, 1; President's Trip: Europe, June–July 1963, Germany, January 17–June 10, 1963 (1 of 2 folders), Box 241, National Security Files, Trips and Conferences, JFKL (emphasis in original).

54. Memorandum, "Reasons Why President Should Visit Berlin," no author, n.d., attached to Memorandum, L. J. Legere to Carl Kaysen, March 20, 1963; President's Trip: Europe, June–July 1963, Germany, January 17–June 10, 1963 (1 of 2 folders), Box 241, National Security Files, Trips and Conferences, JFKL.

55. Memorandum, Edward R. Morrow to McGeorge Bundy, February 13, 1963; President's Trip: Europe, June–July 1963, Germany, January 17–June 10, 1963 (1 of 2 folders), Box 241, National Security Files, Trips and Conferences, JFKL.

56. Thomas C. Sorenson to McGeorge Bundy, "Memorandum on Reasons for the President's Trip to Europe," June 14, 1963, 1; President's Trip: Europe, June–July 1963, General (2 of 4 folders), Box 239, National Security Files, Trips and Conferences, JFKL.

57. Memorandum, George R. Ball to John F. Kennedy, June 20, 1963, 12, 13; President's Trip: Europe, June–July 1963, General (3 of 4 folders), Box 239, National Security Files, Trips and Conferences, JFKL.

58. Telegram, US Berlin Mission to Dean Rusk, May 1, 1963; President's Trip: Europe, June–July 1963, Germany, January 17–June 10, 1963 (1 of 2 folders), Box 241, National Security Files, Trips and Conferences, JFKL.

59. Memorandum, John A. Calhoun to McGeorge Bundy, April 30, 1963; President's Trip: Europe, June–July 1963, Germany, January 17–June 10, 1963 (1 of 2 folders), Box 241, National Security Files, Trips and Conferences, JFKL.

60. Telegram, US Berlin Mission to Dean Rusk, May 1, 1963; President's Trip: Europe, June–July 1963, Germany, January 17–June 10, 1963 (1 of 2 folders), Box 241, National Security Files, Trips and Conferences, JFKL.

61. US Berlin Mission to Rusk, May 1, 1963.

62. US Berlin Mission to Rusk, May 1, 1963.

63. Telegram, Charles E. Hulick to Dean Rusk, May 10, 1963; President's Trip: Europe, June–July 1963, Germany, January 17–June 10, 1963 (1 of 2 folders), Box 241, National Security Files, Trips and Conferences, JFKL.

64. For more on the Birmingham Campaign and international responses to the civil rights movement during Kennedy's administration, see Mary L. Dudziak, *Cold War Civil Rights: Race and the Image of American Democracy* (Princeton, NJ: Princeton University Press, 2000), 152–202; Johnson, "Martin Luther King Jr.'s 1963 Birmingham Campaign as Image Event," 1–26.

65. Johnson, "Martin Luther King Jr.'s 1963 Birmingham Campaign as Image Event," 2–3.

66. "Segregation: Is the Dam Breaking in Dixie, North?," *Chicago Defender*, June 8, 1963, 9.

67. *Berliner Zeitung* and *Novidades* as quoted in "Austrians Call Negro Rights Fight Revolution," *Chicago Defender*, June 8, 1963, 19.

68. "U.S. Race Problems Evoke Brandt's 'Sorrow,'" *Chicago Defender*, June 13, 1963, 4.

69. "2 Senators Rap Kennedy Trip Abroad: Has Problems in U.S., They Say," *Chicago Tribune*, June 17, 1963, 3.

70. Walter Lippmann, "Today and Tomorrow: On Seeing It Through," *Washington Post*, June 4, 1963, A15.

71. "Civil Rights Program," *New York Times*, June 5, 1963, 14; "Cancel That Trip," *New York Times*, June 5, 1963, 14.

72. John F. Kennedy, "Radio and Television Report to the American People on Civil Rights," June 11, 1963, online by Gerhard Peters and John T. Woolley, *The American Presidency Project*, https://www.presidency.ucsb.edu/node/236675.

73. Memorandum, Frederick D. Vreeland to John F. Kennedy, June 12, 1963, 1, 2; President's Trip: Europe, June–July 1963, Germany, June 11–July 12, 1963 (1 of 4 folders), Box 241, National Security Files, Trips and Conferences, JFKL.

74. Theodore C. Sorenson, recorded interview by Carl Kaysen, May 3, 1964, 132, John F. Kennedy Library Oral History Program.

75. Caroll Kilpatrick, "Kennedy Differs with His Critics on Necessity of European Trip," *Washington Post*, June 16, 1963, A2.

76. US Berlin Mission to Department of State, "Program for Presidential Visit, Berlin June 26, 1963," June 1, 1963, 12; POL 7 6-1-63—US-Kennedy, Box 4090, RG 59, NARA II.

77. Val Adams, "22 TV Shows Set on Kennedy Trip," *New York Times*, June 17, 1963, 39.

78. "Kennedy Off to Spur European Good Will," *Los Angeles Times*, June 23, 1963, E1.

79. "German TV to Follow Kennedy," *Los Angeles Times*, May 15, 1963, 5.

80. Telegram, US Embassy Berlin to Department of State, "Presidential Visit Berlin Press Aspects," June 1, 1963; President's Trip: Europe, June–July 1963, Germany, January 17–June 10, 1963 (2 of 2 folders), Box 241, National Security Files, Trips and Conferences, JFKL.

81. Telegram, Unnamed CIA Source to State Department, May 31, 1963; President's Trip: Europe, June–July 1963, Germany, January 17–June 10, 1963 (2 of 2 folders), Box 241, National Security Files, Trips and Conferences, JFKL.

82. "Background Briefing (European Trip) at the White House with Pierre Salinger," June 19, 1963, 7; Trips: Germany, June 1963: 22–26, Box 108, Papers of John F. Kennedy, Presidential Papers, President's Office Files, JFKL.

83. Final European Itinerary, June 21, 1963, 6; President's Trip: Europe, June–July 1963, General (3 of 4 folders), Box 239, National Security Files, Trips and Conferences, JFKL.

84. Laurence Burd and Larry Rue, "Berlin, Irish Hail Kennedy," *Chicago Tribune*, June 27, 1963, 1.

85. Burd and Rue.

86. Burd and Rue.

87. "Berlin Acclaims President's Words: Spontaneous Welcome," *Christian Science Monitor*, June 27, 1963, 1.

88. Michael Goldsmith, "Thousands in East Berlin Defy Reds to Hear Kennedy Welcome," *Chicago Tribune*, June 27, 1963, 3.

89. Kenneth P. O'Donnell, David F. Powers, and Joe McCarthy, *"Johnny, We Hardly Knew Ye": Memories of John Fitzgerald Kennedy* (Boston: Little, Brown, 1970), 360–61.

90. Burd and Rue, "Berlin, Irish Hail Kennedy."

91. O'Donnell, Powers, and McCarthy, *"Johnny, We Hardly Knew Ye,"* 360–61.

92. O'Donnell, Powers, and McCarthy, 360.

93. Arthur M. Schlesinger, *A Thousand Days: John F. Kennedy in the White House* (Boston: Houghton Mifflin, 1965), 884.

94. "Background Briefing (European Trip)," 13.

95. Lawrence Townsend, "Kennedy Stirs Tears in Berlin Address," *Chicago Tribune*, June 27, 1963, 2.

96. Robert H. Estabrook, "JFK Realism Impresses Berlin," *Washington Post*, June 27, 1963, A10.

97. Memorandum, Morrill Cody to Mr. Tyler, May 3, 1963; President's Trip: Europe, June–July 1963, Germany, January 17–June 10, 1963 (1 of 2 folders), Box 241, National Security Files, Trips and Conferences, JFKL.

98. Telegram, Arthur R. Ray to Department of State, May 28, 1963; President's Trip: Europe, June–July 1963, Germany, January 17–June 10, 1963 (2 of 2 folders), Box 241, National Security Files, Trips and Conferences, JFKL. Kennedy asked Arthur M. Schlesinger Jr., a special assistant to the president, to review speech drafts for the European tour prepared by the State Department. His assessment, Schlesinger later wrote, was "of their predominant banality and vapidity. These speeches could have been given just as easily by President Eisenhower—or President Nixon. They fail to convey any sense of a fresh American voice or distinctive Kennedy approach." The problem was that the State Department was "constitutionally opposed to exploiting abroad the benefits of the change in administration in Washington. . . . This attitude denies one of the most powerful weapons we have in winning the confidence and the enthusiasm of other peoples." Memorandum, Arthur M. Schlesinger to John F. Kennedy, June 8, 1963; President's Trip: Europe, June–July 1963, General (2 of 4 folders), Box 239, National Security Files, Trips and Conferences, JFKL. See also Schlesinger, *A Thousand Days: John F. Kennedy in the White House*, 883–84.

99. Speech Cards, "Remarks at the Berlin Rathaus, June 26"; Remarks on Signing the Golden Book, Rudolph Wilde Platz, Berlin, 26 June 1963, Papers of John F. Kennedy, President's Office Files, Speech Files, JFKL.

100. Meeting recorded in the president's daily schedule for June 18, 1963; President's Appointments, June 1963, Evelyn Lincoln Personal Papers, Schedules and Diaries, 1953–63, JFKL. See also Daum, *Kennedy in Berlin*, 149–51.

101. For a complete account of Plischke's meetings with Kennedy, see Margarete Plischke, "Teaching the Berliner," *American Heritage* 48, no. 4 (1997): 26–27. According to Daum, Plischke kept the original document with Kennedy's handwritten notation and put it up for sale in January 1978. The West Berlin Senate bought it for $8,000, and it remains at the city archives in Berlin, Germany. See Daum, *Kennedy in Berlin*, 151 and notes 60 and 62.

102. "Berlin," no author, n.d., found in President's Trip: Europe, June–July 1963, Germany, June 11–July 12, 1963 (2 of 4 folders), Box 241, National Security Files, Trips and Conferences and Germany: JFK visit, June 1963, Box 117a, Papers of John F. Kennedy, President's Office Files, JFKL.

103. During the afternoon and evening of June 25, Bundy (who was traveling with the president) and Kaysen (who was on call in Washington, DC) exchanged "emergency" telegrams making last-minute changes to the president's Rudolph Wilde Platz speech. These sentences do not appear anywhere in these final drafts.

104. O'Donnell, Powers, and McCarthy, *"Johnny, We Hardly Knew Ye": Memories of John Fitzgerald Kennedy*, 361.

105. Strober and Strober, *"Let Us Begin Anew": An Oral History of the Kennedy Presidency*, 371.

106. Cody to Tyler, May 3, 1963.

107. Daum, *Kennedy in Berlin*, 148.

108. Daum, 148.

109. Kenneth Burke, *A Rhetoric of Motives* (Berkeley: University of California Press, 1969), 20–23.

110. John Donne, "No Man Is an Island," lines 1–4. Ernest Hemmingway used the quotation (in Donne's original spelling) as the epigraph for his classic work *For Whom the Bell Tolls*.

111. Schlesinger, *A Thousand Days: John F. Kennedy in the White House*, 885.

112. Ted Sorenson, *Counselor: A Life at the Edge of History* (New York: HarperCollins Publishers, 2008), 323–24.

113. O'Donnell, Powers, and McCarthy, *"Johnny, We Hardly Knew Ye": Memories of John Fitzgerald Kennedy*, 360.

114. Sorenson, *Counselor: A Life at the Edge of History*, 325.

115. Arthur J. Olsen, "Bonn-Washington Ties Are Seen Stronger," *New York Times*, June 30, 1963, 110.

116. Sorenson, *Kennedy*, 601. According to West Berlin mayor Willy Brandt's autobiography, Jackie Kennedy later told him that the president watched the documentary of his visit to Berlin several times after the trip. Willy Brandt, *People and Politics: The Years, 1960–1975*, trans. J. Maxwell Brownjohn (Boston: Little, Brown, 1976), 73.

117. Willy Brandt to John F. Kennedy, July 3, 1963; Germany: General, 1963: July–August, Box 117, Papers of John F. Kennedy, Presidential Papers, President's Office Files, JFKL.

118. Brandt, *People and Politics: The Years 1960–1975*, 72.

119. Telegram, George McGhee to Dean Rusk, June 27, 1963; President's Trip: Europe, June–July 1963, Germany, June 11–July 12, 1963 (3 of 4 folders), Box 241, National Security Files, Trips and Conferences, JFKL.

120. Telegram, George McGhee to Dean Rusk, June 28, 1963; President's Trip: Europe, June–July 1963, Germany, June 11–July 12, 1963 (3 of 4 folders), Box 241, National Security Files, Trips and Conferences, JFKL.

121. Burd and Rue, "Berlin, Irish Hail Kennedy."

122. McGhee to Rusk, June 27, 1963.

123. "Opinion of the Week: Kennedy and Europe," *New York Times*, June 30, 1963, 115.

124. Walter K. Scott to Secretary of State, July 1, 1963; POL-7-7-5-63-US Kennedy, Box 4091, RG 59, NARA II.

125. Robert H. Estabrook, "JFK Tour Valve: Renewed Idealsim," *Washington Post*, June 30, 1963, E6.

126. Kramer to Secretary of State, July 5, 1963; POL-7-6-22-63-US Kennedy, Box 4090, RG 59, NARA II.

127. Hare to Secretary of State, July 5, 1963; POL-7-7-5-63-US Kennedy, Box 4091, RG 59, NARA II.

128. Elbrick to Secretary of State, July 2, 1963; POL-7-7-7-63-US Kennedy, Box 4091, RG 59, NARA II.

129. Larry Rue, "E. Berliners Await Visit by Nikita Today," *Chicago Tribune*, June 28, 1963, 5.

130. Murrey Mardner, "2 K's in Berlin. . . . The Aim's the Same," *Washington Post*, June 28, 1963, A19.

131. Larry Rue, "Sparse Crowd Greets Nikita in East Berlin," *Chicago Tribune*, June 29, 1963, N4.

132. Katharine Clark, "K Berlin Visit Fails to Offset JFK Trip," *Washington Post*, June 29, 1963, A1.

133. Kennedy, "Remarks in the Rudolph Wilde Platz."

134. "Western European Reaction to President Kennedy's Trip, R-125-63," July 8, 1963, i; Box 15, Office of Research, P142, Record Group 306—USIA/USIS (hereafter RG 306), NARA II.

135. "West German Opinion on President Kennedy," August 13, 1963, 1; Box 3, Office of Research and Media Reaction, P64, RG 306, NARA II.

136. Christa J. Olson, *Constitutive Visions: Indigeneity and Commonplaces of National Identity in Republican Ecuador* (University Park: Pennsylvania State University Press, 2014), 6.

137. Olson, 9.

138. Strober and Strober, *"Let Us Begin Anew": An Oral History of the Kennedy Presidency*, 369-70.

139. Richard Nixon, "Remarks at the Signing of the Golden Book at the Charlottenburg Palace, West Berlin," February 27, 1969, online by Gerhard Peters and John T. Woolley, *The American Presidency Project*, https://www.presidency.ucsb.edu/node/240698.

140. Jimmy Carter, "Berlin, Federal Republic of Germany Remarks at a Wreathlaying Ceremony at the Airlift Memorial," July 15, 1978, online by Gerhard Peters and John T. Woolley, *The American Presidency Project*, https://www.presidency.ucsb.edu/node/247915.

141. Ronald Reagan, "Remarks to the People of Berlin," June 11, 1982, online by Gerhard Peters and John T. Woolley, *The American Presidency Project*, https://www.presidency.ucsb.edu/node/245269.

142. Ronald Reagan, "Remarks on East-West Relations at the Brandenburg Gate in West Berlin," June 12, 1987, online by Gerhard Peters and John T. Woolley, *The American Presidency Project*, https://www.presidency.ucsb.edu/node/252499. For a detailed analysis of Reagan's address, see Robert C. Rowland and John M. Jones, "Reagan at the Brandenburg Gate: Moral Clarity Tempered by Pragmatism," *Rhetoric & Public Affairs* 9, no. 1 (2006): 21-50.

143. William J. Clinton, "Remarks to the Citizens of Berlin," July 12, 1994, online by Gerhard Peters and John T. Woolley, *The American Presidency Project*, https://www.presidency.ucsb.edu/node/220270. Clinton also spoke to the German people in West Berlin in 1998. See William J. Clinton, "Remarks to the People of Germany in Berlin," May 13, 1998, online by Gerhard Peters and John T. Woolley, *The American Presidency Project*, https://www.presidency.ucsb.edu/node/225396.

144. George W. Bush, "Remarks to a Special Session of the German Bundestag," May 23, 2002, online by Gerhard Peters and John T. Woolley, *The American Presidency Project*, https://www.presidency.ucsb.edu/node/212942.

145. Nicholas Kulish and Jeff Zeleny, "Prospect of Obama at Brandenburg Gate Divides German Politicians," *New York Times*, July 10, 2008, https://www.nytimes.com/2008/07/10/us/10germany.html.

146. "Obama Live Ticker: 'America Has No Better Partner than Europe,'" Spiegel Online International, July 24, 2008, http://www.spiegel.de/international/germany/obama-live-ticker-america-has-no-better-partner-than-europe-a-567821.html.

147. Barack Obama, "Remarks at the Brandenburg Gate in Berlin, Germany," June 19, 2013, online by Gerhard Peters and John T. Woolley, *The American Presidency Project*, https://www.presidency.ucsb.edu/node/304616.

Chapter Five

1. John Scali to H. R. Haldeman, "China Trip News Coverage," September 11, 1971, 3-4; China Trip, Box 192, Papers of H. R. Haldeman, Richard Nixon Presidential Library, Yorba Linda, California (hereafter RNL).

2. Rick Perlstein, *Nixonland: The Rise of a President and the Fracturing of America* (New York: Scribner, 2008), 31.

3. In a speech on the House floor on January 26, 1950, Nixon called for a renewed national

effort to weed out communists in all levels of government. Richard M. Nixon, "The Hiss Case—a Lesson for the American People," January 26, 1950, as printed in "Proceedings January 26, 1950," Annals of Congress, House of Representatives, 81st Congress, 2nd Session, Vol. 96, Part 1, 999–1007, https://www.congress.gov/81/crecb/1950/01/26/GPO-CRECB-1950-pt1-18.pdf.

4. Hitchcock, *The Age of Eisenhower: America and the World in the 1950s,* 72.

5. As the *New York Times* reported at the end of Nixon's trip, movers and shakers in Washington felt that the vice president's performance "succeeded in building up his claim to standing not only as a politician but also as something of a statesman and a leader in the struggle for world peace." "Now the Summit?," *New York Times,* August 2, 1959, E1.

6. As Dean Acheson, Truman's secretary of state, wrote to the British foreign minister, "There can be little doubt, but that Communism, with Chi[na] as one spear-head, was now embarked upon an assault against Asia with immediate objectives in Korea, Indo-China, Burma, the Philippines and Malaya and with medium-range objectives in Hong Kong, Indonesia, Siam, India and Japan." In 1954, Eisenhower would explain that the "loss" of any country in Asia would be disastrous to "free world" interests. "You have a row of dominoes set up," he said, and when "you knock over the first one . . . what will happen to the last one is the certainty that it will go over very quickly." Acheson as cited in Margaret MacMillan, *Nixon and Mao: The Week That Changed the World* (New York: Random House, 2007), 102–3; Dwight D. Eisenhower, "The President's News Conference," April 7, 1954, online by Gerhard Peters and John T. Woolley, *The American Presidency Project,* https://www.presidency.ucsb.edu/node/233655.

7. For some of the best accounts of this move, see Evelyn Goh, *Constructing the U.S. Rapprochement with China, 1961–1974* (Cambridge: Cambridge University Press, 2005); MacMillan, *Nixon and Mao: The Week That Changed the World;* Michelle Murray Yang, "President Nixon's Speeches and Toasts during His 1972 Trip to China: A Study in Diplomatic Rhetoric," *Rhetoric & Public Affairs* 14, no. 1 (2011): 1–44; Chris Tudda, *A Cold War Turning Point: Nixon and China, 1969–1972* (Baton Rouge: Lousiana State University Press, 2012). Henry Kissinger offers a helpful, albeit one-sided, perspective in Henry Kissinger, *White House Years* (Boston: Little, Brown, 1979), and Henry Kissinger, *On China* (New York: Penguin Press, 2011).

8. The idea of the "Bamboo Curtain" emerged after the Chinese revolution as way to describe peoples "lost" to communism. The phrase clearly played off the idea of the "Iron Curtain" popularized by Winston Churchill. In a *New York Times* article entitled "Behind the Bamboo Curtain," the paper wrote: "the Peiping Government raised another question, and that question deserves consideration. To what extent can that Government speak for the whole people of China? Some recent reports from behind what might be called the Bamboo Curtain cause speculation. These reports, including official pronouncements, leave little doubt that the Communist regime, despite its continued show of strength, is still far from either stability or complete control of the country, and that it is working under difficulties which render its future at the very least uncertain." This is one of the first uses of the term I can find in journalist accounts, but it grew more common in the years to come and was a frequent descriptor deployed by US journalists covering Nixon's trip to the PRC in 1972. "Behind the Bamboo Curtain," *New York Times,* August 26, 1950.

9. See, for example, Harold R. Isaacs, *Scratches on Our Minds: American Images of China and India* (New York: John Day, 1958); Edward W. Said, *Orientalism* (New York: Pantheon Books, 1978); Oliver Turner, *American Images of China: Identity, Power, Policy* (London: Routledge, 2014).

10. Said, *Orientalism,* 2.

11. Turner, *American Images of China: Identity, Power, Policy*, 68.

12. Ronald Takaki, *A Different Mirror: A History of Multicultural America*, rev. ed. (New York: Back Bay Books, 2008), 188.

13. See, for example, Erika Lee, *At America's Gates: Chinese Immigration During the Exclusion Era, 1882–1943* (Chapel Hill: University of North Carolina Press, 2004); Beth Lew-Williams, *The Chinese Must Go: Violence, Exclusion, and the Making of the Alien in America* (Cambridge, MA: Harvard University Press, 2018).

14. Wilson as quoted in Cooper, *Woodrow Wilson: A Biography*, 211. For more here on the religious underpinnings of Wilson's views on China, see Eugene P. Trani, "Woodrow Wilson, China, and the Missionaries, 1913–1921," *Journal of Presbyterian History* 49, no. 4 (1971): 328–51.

15. For a remarkable analysis of the "China myths" of this period, see Robert P. Newman, "Lethal Rhetoric: The Selling of the China Myths," *Quarterly Journal of Speech* 61, no. 2 (1975): 113–28.

16. Denise M. Bostdorff, "The Evolution of a Diplomatic Surprise: Richard M. Nixon's Rhetoric on China, 1952–July 15, 1972," *Rhetoric & Public Affairs* 5, no. 1 (2002): 33.

17. Nixon as cited in Bostdorff, 33.

18. See, for example, Goh, *Constructing the U.S. Rapprochement with China, 1961–1974*, 38–42.

19. Bostdorff, "The Evolution of a Diplomatic Surprise: Richard M. Nixon's Rhetoric on China, 1952–July 15, 1972," 37.

20. Richard Nixon, "Asia after Viet Nam," *Foreign Affairs* 46, no. 1 (1967): 111.

21. Nixon, 113.

22. Nixon, 121.

23. Nixon, 114.

24. Nixon, 123.

25. Nixon, 124.

26. Richard Nixon, "Inaugural Address," January 20, 1969, online by Gerhard Peters and John T. Woolley, *The American Presidency Project*, https://www.presidency.ucsb.edu/node/239549. In his post-presidential memoirs, Nixon noted that this reference was an intentional—albeit indirect—one to the PRC. Richard Nixon, *RN: The Memoirs of Richard Nixon, Volume 2* (New York: Warner Books, 1979), 8.

27. Nixon, *RN: The Memoirs of Richard Nixon, Volume 2*, 8.

28. Alexander Haig Jr. and Charles McCarry, *Inner Circles: How America Changed the World* (New York: Warner Books, 1992), 257.

29. Goh, *Constructing the U.S. Rapprochement with China, 1961–1974*, 34.

30. According to one report from the CIA, the Soviet Union and China had "come to regard the other as its principal antagonist. Their rivalry is now so pervasive that, when any major new international issue arises, they instinctively tend to range themselves on opposing sides." "The Soviet Union: Chinese Perception of the Problem," n.d., p. 2; Book V, The President's Briefing Papers for the China Trip, 1972, NSC Files, For the President's File—China Trip, Box 847, RNL.

31. Richard Nixon, "Remarks to the Nation Announcing Acceptance of an Invitation to Visit the People's Republic of China," July 15, 1971, online by Gerhard Peters and John T. Wooley, *The American Presidency Project*, https://www.presidency.ucsb.edu/node/240410.

32. "If Richard Nixon could quote Mao Tse-tung to support American foreign policy on Washington's birthday," wrote Kissinger, "a diplomatic revolution had clearly taken place." Kissinger, *White House Years*, 1070.

33. Richard Nixon, Toasts of the President and President Ceaușescu of Romania, October 26, 1970, online by Gerhard Peters and John T. Woolley, *The American Presidency Project*, https://www.presidency.ucsb.edu/node/240102. As Kissinger explained, it was the "first time they had been referred to by this name in a public statement by the President"—and Ceaușescu knew it. "Off the Record Conversation with Dr. Henry Kissinger, Assistant to the President for National Security Affairs," July 19, 1971, 6; China Trip—July 19, 1971 [3 of 3], Box 2, Papers of John Scali, RNL. A search of the Public Papers of the President (housed online at *The American Presidency Project*) supports this claim.

34. Richard Nixon, "Radio Address about Second Annual Foreign Policy Report to the Congress," February 25, 1971, online by Gerhard Peters and John T. Woolley, *The American Presidency Project*, https://www.presidency.ucsb.edu/node/240718.

35. Qiang Zhai, *China and the Vietnam Wars, 1950–1975* (Chapel Hill: University of North Carolina Press, 2000), 195, 96–97.

36. Zhai, 195.

37. Chou En-lai as quoted in Zhai, 195.

38. Richard Nixon, "Remarks to the Nation Announcing Acceptance of an Invitation to Visit the People's Republic of China," July 15, 1971, online by Gerhard Peters and John T. Woolley, *The American Presidency Project*, https://www.presidency.ucsb.edu/node/240410.

39. H. R. Haldeman to Chuck Colson, "ORC Release," July 23, 1971; Distribution of China Trip. Announcement Poll ORC [July] 20–21, 1971, Box 354, Papers of H. R. Haldeman, RNL.

40. Helen Thomas, *Dateline: White House* (New York: Macmillan Publishing, 1975), 132; Helen Thomas, *Front Row at the White House: My Life and Times* (New York: Simon and Schuster, 1999), 185.

41. Memorandum of Conversation, January 3, 1972, 7; Haig China Trip [Haig Advance Party] December 29, 1971–January 10, 1972 [1 of 2], Box 1015, NSC Files, Alexander M. Haig Special File, RNL.

42. Al Haig to Henry Kissinger, January 8, 1972, 3; Haig China Trip [Haig Advance Party] December 29, 1971–January 10, 1972 [1 of 2], Box 1015, NSC Files, Alexander M. Haig Special File, RNL.

43. Al Haig to Henry Kissinger, January 8, 1972, 5.

44. Haig and McCarry, *Inner Circles: How America Changed the World*, 262.

45. Kissinger, *White House Years*, 1049–50.

46. John Scali to H. R. Haldeman, "China Trip News Coverage," September 11, 1971, 1; China Trip, Box 192, Papers of H. R. Haldeman, RNL.

47. John Scali to H. R. Haldeman, "China Trip News Coverage," September 11, 1971, 3.

48. John Scali to H. R. Haldeman, "China Trip News Coverage," September 11, 1971, 4.

49. John Scali to H. R. Haldeman, September 13, 1971, 1; China Trip, Box 192, Papers of H. R. Haldeman, RNL.

50. John Scali to H. R. Haldeman, September 13, 1971, 1.

51. John Scali to H. R. Haldeman, September 13, 1971, 3.

52. John Scali to H. R. Haldeman, September 13, 1971, 4.

53. Ron Ziegler, John Scali, and Tim Elborn to Dr. Henry A. Kissinger, "Press Plans for China Coverage," October 9, 1971, 2; HAK China Trip October 1971 [1 of 3], NSC HAK Office Files, Country Files—Near East, Box 87, RNL.

54. Ron Ziegler, John Scali, and Tim Elborn to Dr. Henry A. Kissinger, "Press Plans for China Coverage," October 9, 1971, 3.

55. Ron Ziegler, John Scali, and Tim Elborn to Dr. Henry A. Kissinger, "Press Plans for China Coverage," October 9, 1971, 3.

56. Ron Ziegler, John Scali, and Tim Elborn to Dr. Henry A. Kissinger, "Press Plans for China Coverage," October 9, 1971, 3.

57. Ron Ziegler to Al Haig, "Press Arrangements for the China Trip," September 9, 1971, 2; China Trip, Box 192, Papers of H. R. Haldeman, RNL.

58. "Assignment: China—the Week That Changed the World," University of Southern California US-China Institute, https://www.youtube.com/watch?v=uyCZDvec5sY.

59. "Assignment: China."

60. Joseph C. Spear, Presidents and the Press: The Nixon Legacy (Cambridge, MA: MIT Press, 1984), 98.

61. Spear, 98.

62. Les Janka to Al Haig, "Official Media on China Trip," December 23, 1971, 1–2; China—President's Trip, December 1971–February 17, 1972 [2 of 4], NSC HAK Office Files, Country Files—Near East, Box 88, RNL.

63. John Scali to Dwight Chapin, "Chinese Government Attitude toward TV News Coverage," October 8, 1971, 2, 3; HAK China Trip October 1971 [3 of 3], NSC HAK Office Files, Country Files—Near East, Box 87, RNL.

64. US Mission Geneva to USIA Washington, DC, February 21, 1972; POL 7—US Nixon—2-21-72, Box 2698 (Nixon), RG 59, NARA II.

65. There is little mention of media monitoring in Latin America and Africa in these files. However, later USIA reports do mention surveying public opinion and awareness in Mexico City, Caracas, and Nairobi. However, this omission does reveal an administration focused primarily on how the president's trip would affect public opinion in countries they considered strategic partners and friends. For detailed records of these exchanges, see telegrams and memoranda held in Boxes 2696–99 (Nixon), RG 59, NARA II.

66. Ron Ziegler to Henry Kissinger, "President's Talking Points for Hawaii," February 16, 1972, 1, 2; China—President's Trip, February 15–29, 1972 [3 of 3], NSC HAK Office Files, Country Files—Near East, Box 88, RNL.

67. Richard Nixon, "Toasts of the President and Chairman Chang Ch'un-ch'iao at a Banquet in Shanghai," February 27, 1972, online by Gerhard Peters and John T. Woolley, The American Presidency Project, https://www.presidency.ucsb.edu/node/255132.

68. Richard Nixon, "Remarks on Departure from the White House for a State Visit to the People's Republic of China," February 17, 1972, online by Gerhard Peters and John T. Woolley, The American Presidency Project, https://www.presidency.ucsb.edu/node/255095.

69. Nixon, "Toasts of the President and Chairman Chang Ch'un-ch'iao at a Banquet in Shanghai."

70. Nixon, RN: The Memoirs of Richard Nixon, Volume 2, 26.

71. China Trip Summary Tape I, 14:58; White House Communication Agency Videotape Collection (WHCA-5146), RNL.

72. For an analysis of the spatial metaphors present in Nixon's discourse about the "Opening to China," see Zoë Hess Carney and Allison M. Prasch, "'A Journey for Peace': Spatial Metaphors in Nixon's 1972 'Opening to China,'" Presidential Studies Quarterly 47, no. 4 (2017): 646–64.

73. "Draft Departure Remarks—Hawaii," February 16, 1972; Nell Yates [China Trip Daily Schedules], Box 27, Papers of Dwight L. Chapin, SMOF, White House Special Files, RNL.

74. "Remarks for Guam Departure," February 15, 1972; February 20–21, 1972, Arrival-Departure—Guam, President's Speech File, Box 72, President's Personal File, RNL.

75. Nixon remarks as reported in "Nixon, on Guam, Asks Prayer for 'New Day,'" *New York Times*, February 21, 1972, 12. The formal text of the president's remarks in Hawaii and Guam do not appear in the Public Papers of the President or on *The American Presidency Project* website. Here, I rely on news accounts from journalists traveling with the president.

76. China Trip Summary Tape I, 34:28; White House Communication Agency Videotape Collection (WHCA-5146), RNL.

77. Lyndon "Mort" Allin to Warren Higby aboard *Spirit of '76*, 3; China News Coverage [I] (1 of 3), Box 131, H. R. Haldeman Alpha Subject Files, SMOF, White House Special Files, RNL.

78. "China News Summary No. 6: Friday Wires and Sat. Post," February 18, 1972, 2; China News Coverage [I] (2 of 3), Box 131, H. R. Haldeman Alpha Subject Files, SMOF, White House Special Files, RNL.

79. China Trip Summary Tape I, 10:10; White House Communication Agency Videotape Collection (WHCA-5146), RNL.

80. "Nixon Arrival in Peking (2/20/1972)," CBS News; White House Communication Agency Videotape Collection (WHCA-5085), RNL.

81. Yang, "President Nixon's Speeches and Toasts during His 1972 Trip to China: A Study in Diplomatic Rhetoric," 10.

82. Nixon, *RN: The Memoirs of Richard Nixon, Volume 2*, 26.

83. Kissinger, *White House Years*, 1054–55.

84. Nixon, *RN: The Memoirs of Richard Nixon, Volume 2*, 26–27.

85. Kissinger, *White House Years*, 1055.

86. "Today Show" (February 21, 1972): Summary of President Nixon's first day in China (People's Republic of China), February 21, 1972; White House Communication Agency Videotape Collection (WHCA-5098), RNL.

87. H. R. Haldeman, *The Haldeman Diaries: Inside the Nixon White House* (New York: G. P. Putnam's Sons, 1994), 413.

88. Haldeman, 416.

89. "Today Show" (February 21, 1972): Summary of President Nixon's First Day in China (People's Republic of China), February 21, 1972; White House Communication Agency Videotape Collection (WHCA-5098), RNL.

90. Al Haig to Henry A. Kissinger, February 27, 1972; China—President's Trip, February 15–29 [3 of 3], NSC HAK Office Files, Country Files—Near East, Box 88, RNL.

91. Al Haig to Henry A. Kissinger, February 27, 1972; China—President's Trip, February 15–29 [3 of 3], NSC HAK Office Files, Country Files—Near East, Box 88, RNL.

92. Kissinger, *White House Years*, 1069.

93. Yang, "President Nixon's Speeches and Toasts during His 1972 Trip to China: A Study in Diplomatic Rhetoric," 2.

94. "NBC Live from China," February 21, 1972; White House Communications Agency Videotape Collection (WHCA-5088), RNL.

95. "Menu," February 21, 1972; February 1972, China—Place Cards, Invitations, etc., Box 73, President's Speech File, President's Personal File, RNL.

96. Translation of Premier Chou En-lai's Toast at the Banquet in Honor of President Nixon, February 21, 1972; February 21, 1972, Peking, China, Box 72, President's Speech File, President's Personal File, RNL.

97. "Suggested Toast," 3; February 21, 1972, Peking China, Box 72, President's Speech File, President's Personal File, RNL.

98. Richard Nixon, "Toasts of the President and Premier Chou En-lai of the People's Republic of China at a Banquet Honoring the President in Peking," February 21, 1972, online by Gerhard Peters and John T. Woolley, *The American Presidency Project*, https://www.presidency.ucsb.edu/node/255103.

99. "Today Show" (February 21, 1972): Summary of President Nixon's first day in China (People's Republic of China); White House Communication Agency Videotape Collection (WHCA-5098), RNL.

100. "Today Show" (February 21, 1972), Summary of President Nixon's first day in China (People's Republic of China); White House Communication Agency Videotape Collection (WHCA-5098), RNL.

101. Haldeman, *The Haldeman Diaries: Inside the Nixon White House*, 416.

102. Richard Nixon, "Private Dinner Toast, Peking," February 24, 1972, as printed in Yang, "President Nixon's Speeches and Toasts during His 1972 Trip to China: A Study in Diplomatic Rhetoric," 18–19.

103. Richard Nixon, "Toasts of the President and Premier Chou En-lai of China at a Banquet Honoring the Premier in Peking," February 25, 1972, online by Gerhard Peters and John T. Woolley, *The American Presidency Project*, https://www.presidency.ucsb.edu/node/255121.

104. Kissinger, *White House Years*, 1066.

105. Nixon as quoted in China Trip Summary Tape II, 1:19:57; White House Communication Agency Videotape Collection (WHCA-5146), RNL.

106. Stanley Karnow interview in "Assignment: China—the Week That Changed the World."

107. Winston Lord interview in "Assignment: China—the Week That Changed the World."

108. Max Frankel and Dan Rather interviews in "Assignment China—the Week That Changed the World."

109. "Revolutionized Chinese Opera," as contained in "Folders and Their Contents for President's Trip to People's Republic of China," February 17–29, 1972; Nell Yates [China Trip Daily Schedules], Box 27, Papers of Dwight L. Chapin, SMOF, White House Special Files, RNL.

110. China Trip Summary Tape II, 1:15:300; White House Communication Agency Videotape Collection (WHCA-5146), RNL.

111. Kissinger, *White House Years*, 1067.

112. Nixon, "Toasts of the President and Chairman Chang Ch'un-ch'iao at a Banquet in Shanghai," February 27, 1972.

113. "Joint Statement Following Discussions with Leaders of the People's Republic of China," Shanghai, February 27, 1972; *Foreign Relations of the United States, 1969–1976*, vol. 27, *China, 1969–1972*, https://history.state.gov/historicaldocuments/frus1969–76v17/d203.

114. China Trip Summary Tape III, 1:18:57; White House Communication Agency Videotape Collection (WHCA-5148), RNL.

115. China Trip Summary Tape IV, 03:16; White House Communication Agency Videotape Collection (WHCA-5149), RNL.

116. George McGovern as quoted in China Trip Summary Tape IV, 03:39; White House Communication Agency Videotape Collection (WHCA-5149), RNL.

117. Hubert Humphrey as quoted in China Trip Summary Tape IV, 20:50; White House Communication Agency Videotape Collection (WHCA-5149), RNL.

118. John Ashbrook as quoted in China Trip Summary Tape IV, 15:05; White House Communication Agency Videotape Collection (WHCA-5149), RNL.

119. China Trip Summary Tape IV, 4:49; White House Communication Agency Videotape Collection (WHCA-5149), RNL.

120. Haldeman, *The Haldeman Diaries: Inside the Nixon White House*, 422–24.

121. General Haig to Henry Kissinger, February 27, 1972, 1–2; China—President's Trip, February 15–29, 1972 [3 of 3], NSC HAK Office Files, Country Files—Near East, Box 88, RNL.

122. MacMillan, *Nixon and Mao: The Week That Changed the World*, 319. See also "President Home after China Trip; Reassures Allies," *New York Times*, February 29, 1972, 1.

123. Spiro T. Agnew, as quoted in Richard Nixon, "Remarks at Andrews Air Force Base on Returning from the People's Republic of China," February 28, 1972, online by Gerard Peters and John T. Woolley, *The American Presidency Project*, https://www.presidency.ucsb.edu/node/255133.

124. Nixon, "Remarks at Andrews Air Force Base on Returning from the People's Republic of China."

125. "American Image of China," March 12, 1972, Interviewing Date: March 3–5, 1972, Survey #846-K, as printed in *The Gallup Poll: Public Opinion, 1972–1977*, vol. 1 (Wilmington, DE: Scholarly Resources, 1978), 20.

126. Alvin Snyder to Larry Higby, "China Visit—Network Coverage," March 7, 1972; China Follow Up, Box 2, Papers of John Scali, RNL.

127. "Post China Poll," 7–8; Post-China Poll O—March 4–5, 1972, Box 361, Papers of H. R. Haldeman, RNL.

128. "Comments on the March 3–4, 1972 Telephone Survey, Post China Poll," 3, found in Distribution of China Trip Announcement Poll ORC [July] 20–21, 1971, Box 354, Papers of H. R. Haldeman, RNL.

129. Thomas W. Benham, "Comments on the March 3–5, 1972 Telephone Survey," March 6, 1972, 3, 4, 5; Post-China Poll O—March 4–5, 1972, Box 361, Papers of H. R. Haldeman, RNL.

130. The pre-trip surveys allowed the USIA to chart any changes in public opinion because of Nixon's visit to the PRC—and this was their explicit intent. "Besides describing foreign public opinion about the U.S. at this important time," explained the introduction to one such survey, "these measures will provide a set of benchmarks against which to evaluate the impact of the China visit. After the visit U.S. standing on the same indices will again be measured in the same countries plus some others." "Public Opinion in Western Europe and Asia on the President's Visits to China and the USSR," February 15, 1972, ii; Box 39, Office of Research, P142, RG 306, NARA II.

131. "The Impact of the President's Visit to China on Foreign Public Opinion," May 16, 1972; Box 39, Office of Research, P142, RG 306, NARA II.

132. "The Impact of the President's Visit to China on Foreign Public Opinion," May 16, 1972, 1; Box 39, Office of Research, P142, RG 306, NARA II.

133. "The Impact of the President's Visit to China on Foreign Public Opinion," May 16, 1972, 2; Box 39, Office of Research, P142, RG 306, NARA II.

134. "The Impact of the President's Visit to China on Foreign Public Opinion," May 16, 1972, 24; Box 39, Office of Research, P142, RG 306, NARA II.

135. Haldeman, *The Haldeman Diaries: Inside the Nixon White House*, 424.

136. China Trip Summary Tape IV, 08:34; White House Communication Agency Videotape Collection (WHCA-5149), RNL.

137. "Evaluations of Mao Tse-tung and Chou En-lai by an American Lawyer," 2; Book IV, The President's Readings on Mao Tse-tung and Chou En-lai, NSC Files, For the President's File—China Trip, Box 847, RNL.

138. Nixon underlined this sentence of his briefing book and placed a checkmark next to this passage in the margins.

139. "Evaluations of Mao Tse-tung and Chou En-lai by an American Lawyer," 1–2.

140. "Evaluations of Mao Tse-tung and Chou En-lai by an American Lawyer," 3.

Chapter Six

1. Lance Morrow, "June 6, 1944," *Time*, May 28, 1984, 18.

2. Reagan also served as an FBI informant in the 1940s and, along with his first wife, Jane Wyman, passed along names of possible pro-communist actors and influences in Hollywood. Scott Herhold, "Reagan Played Informant Role for FBI in '40s," *Chicago Tribune*, August 26, 1985, https://www.chicagotribune.com/news/ct-xpm-1985-08-26-8502250710-story.html.

3. "Ronald Reagan," Witness Memo, House of Representatives, Committee on Un-American Activities, Washington, DC, from Smith Report of September 2, 1947; "From the Archives: Reagan, Hollywood, and the Red Scare," Reagan Foundation, Simi Valley, California, https://www.reaganfoundation.org/media/51313/red-scare.pdf.

4. Ronald Reagan, "A Time for Choosing," October 27, 1964, Ronald Reagan Presidential Library and Museum, Simi Valley, California (hereafter RRL), https://www.reaganlibrary.gov/reagans/ronald-reagan/time-choosing-speech-october-27-1964.

5. Ronald Reagan, "Remarks Announcing Candidacy for the Republican Presidential Nomination," November 13, 1979, online by Gerhard Peters and John T. Woolley, *The American Presidency Project*, https://www.presidency.ucsb.edu/node/255827.

6. Ronald Reagan, "Farewell Address to the Nation," January 11, 1989, online by Gerhard Peters and John T. Woolley, *The American Presidency Project*, https://www.presidency.ucsb.edu/node/251303.

7. For more on Reagan's use of narrative form, see Ernest G. Bormann, "A Fantasy Theme Analysis of the Television Coverage of the Hostage Release and the Reagan Inaugural," *Quarterly Journal of Speech* 68, no. 2 (1982): 133–45; Walter R. Fisher, "Romantic Democracy, Ronald Reagan, and Presidential Heroes," *Western Journal of Speech Communication* 46, no. 3 (1982): 299–310; William F. Lewis, "Telling America's Story: Narrative Form and the Reagan Presidency," *Quarterly Journal of Speech* 73, no. 3 (1987): 280–302; Mary E. Stuckey, *Playing the Game: The Presidential Rhetoric of Ronald Reagan* (New York: Praeger, 1990); Mary E. Stuckey, *Slipping the Surly Bonds: Reagan's* Challenger *Address* (College Station: Texas A&M University Press, 2006); Rowland and Jones, "Reagan at the Brandenburg Gate: Moral Clarity Tempered by Pragmatism," 21–50; Robert C. Rowland and John M. Jones, *Reagan at Westminster: Foreshadowing the End of the Cold War* (College Station: Texas A&M University Press, 2010).

8. Peggy Noonan, *What I Saw at the Revolution: A Political Life in the Reagan Era* (New York: Random House, 1990), 86.

9. Edward S. Casey, *Remembering: A Phenomenological Study*, 2nd ed. (Bloomington: Indiana University Press, 2000), 217, 18.

10. For more on the relationship between epideictic speech, visual imagery, and place in Reagan's commemoration of the fortieth anniversary of D-day, see Allison M. Prasch, "Reagan at Pointe du Hoc: Deictic Epideictic and the Persuasive Power of 'Bringing before the Eyes,'" *Rheto-*

ric & Public Affairs 18, no. 2 (2015): 247–76. For other examples of how Reagan and other US presidents have displayed physical bodies as evidence for their larger argument, see Craig Allen Smith, "Mistereagan's Neighborhood: Rhetoric and National Unity," *Southern Speech Communication Journal* 52, no. 3 (1987): 219–39; Denise M. Bostdorff, "Epideictic Rhetoric in the Service of War: George W. Bush on Iraq and the 60th Anniversary of the Victory over Japan," *Communication Monographs* 78, no. 3 (2011): 296–323; Allison M. Prasch, "Toward a Rhetorical Theory of Deixis," *Quarterly Journal of Speech* 102, no. 2 (2016): 166–93; Allison M. Prasch and Julia Scatliff O'Grady, "Saluting the 'Skutnik': Special Guests, the First Lady's Box, and the Generic Evolution of the State of the Union Address," *Rhetoric & Public Affairs* 20, no. 4 (2017): 571–604; Allison M. Prasch, "Obama in Selma: Deixis, Rhetorical Vision, and the 'True Meaning of America,'" *Quarterly Journal of Speech* 105, no. 1 (2019): 42–67.

11. Maurice Halbwachs, *On Collective Memory*, ed. Lewis A. Coser (Chicago: University of Chicago Press, 1992), 38.

12. Benedict Anderson writes about this when he notes how particular groups conceive of themselves as living parallel lives to those who existed hundreds of years earlier. Even if they never meet, they are "certainly proceeding along the same trajectory." Anderson, *Imagined Communities: Reflections on the Origin and Spread of Nationalism*, 188.

13. Halbwachs, *On Collective Memory*, 40.

14. For additional accounts of D-day in these early years, see Michael R. Dolski, "'Portal of Liberation': D-Day Myth as American Self-Affirmation," in *D-Day in History and Memory*, ed. Michael Dolski, Sam Edwards, and John Buckley (Denton: University of North Texas Press, 2014), 45–54; Michael R. Dolski, *D-Day Remembered: The Normandy Landings in American Collective Memory* (Knoxville: University of Tennessee Press, 2016), 17–58.

15. Dwight D. Eisenhower, "Order of the Day," June 6, 1944, http://www.americanrhetoric .com/speeches/dwighteisenhowerorderofdday.htm.

16. Franklin D. Roosevelt, "Prayer on D-Day," June 6, 1944, online by Gerhard Peters and John T. Woolley, *The American Presidency Project*, https://www.presidency.ucsb.edu/node/ 210815.

17. On the tenth anniversary of D-day, Eisenhower intimated that the United States' current offensive against Soviet communism found its inspiration on the beaches of Normandy. In 1954, then president Dwight D. Eisenhower told the US public that what happened in Normandy "set in motion a chain of events which affected the history of the entire world" and suggested that the same "courage, devotion and faith which brought us through the perils of war will inevitably bring us success in our unremitting search for peace, security and freedom." Dwight D. Eisenhower, "Statement by the President on the 10th Anniversary of the Landing in Normandy," June 6, 1954, online by Gerhard Peters and John T. Woolley, *The American Presidency Project*, https://www.presidency.ucsb.edu/node/232111.

18. In 1964, on the twentieth anniversary of D-day, Lyndon B. Johnson recalled the remarkable resolve "born on that D-Day," calling Americans to find similar resolve and "stand together" so that "light of freedom [would not] be extinguished on any continent again." Lyndon B. Johnson, "Remarks to Members of the Delegation to the D-Day Ceremonies," June 3, 1964, online by Gerhard Peters and John T. Woolley, *The American Presidency Project*, https://www.presidency .ucsb.edu/node/239517.

19. Johnson, "Remarks to Members of the Delegation to the D-Day Ceremonies."

20. Karlyn Kohrs Campbell, *The Great Silent Majority: Nixon's 1969 Speech on Vietnamization* (College Station: Texas A&M University Press, 2014), 29. Nine months later, on March 8,

1964, US Marines landed at Da Nang as a "defensive" force in South Vietnam. Just three months later, on the twenty-first anniversary of D-day, Johnson argued that Normandy offered the prime example of the "moral duty" behind the "wellsprings of American purpose." He explicitly linked the decision "to intervene in the destiny of the continent of Europe where our culture was cradled" with the country's current motivation "to stand her sons by the sons of Europe and Asia and Latin America in keeping a vigil of peace and freedom for all mankind. What America has done—and what America is doing around the world—draws from deep and flowing springs of moral duty, and let none underestimate the depth of flow of those wellsprings of American purpose." Again, Johnson suggested that the moral conviction guiding the Allies in 1944 similarly justified US action in South Vietnam. Lyndon B. Johnson, "Commencement Address at Catholic University," June 6, 1965, online by Gerhard Peters and John T. Woolley, *The American Presidency Project*, https://www.presidency.ucsb.edu/node/241308.

21. Val Adams, "Eisenhower Going to Normandy to Film D-Day Program for TV," *New York Times*, July 15, 1963, 43.

22. Paul Gardner, "D-Day Remembered: Sites of Normandy Invasion Visited by Old Soldier Who Was There," *New York Times*, May 31, 1964, X11.

23. "Eisenhower to Return to Normandy for TV," *Los Angeles Times*, July 15, 1963, 6.

24. Dwight D. Eisenhower and Walter Cronkite, "D-Day Plus 20 Years: Eisenhower Returns to Normandy: CBS Reports," *CBS Evening News*, June 5, 1964, https://www.youtube.com/watch?v=qNsi4Z8Q12M.

25. Jack Gould, "TV: Omaha Beach, As It Was and Is," *New York Times*, June 6, 1964, 53.

26. For a detailed discussion on D-day commemoration during the 1970s, see Dolski, *D-Day Remembered: The Normandy Landings in American Collective Memory*, 91–112.

27. Dolski, 111.

28. Studs Terkel, *"The Good War": An Oral History of World War II* (New York: New Press, 2011).

29. Morrow, "June 6, 1944." Clipping of this article included in Current News: Special Edition, D-Day + 40 Years, July 23, 1984, 41–42; President's Trip to Normandy (5), Box 161, White House Office of Speechwriting, Research Office, 1981–89, RRL.

30. Ronald Reagan, "Address Accepting the Presidential Nomination at the Republican National Convention in Detroit," July 17, 1980, online by Gerhard Peters and John T. Woolley, *The American Presidency Project*, https://www.presidency.ucsb.edu/node/251302.

31. H. W. Brands, *Reagan: The Life* (New York: Doubleday, 2015), 237. According to one *New York Times*/CBS News Poll, voters ousted Carter because of two main issues: the precarious US economy and the nation's foreign policy toward the Soviet Union. The *New York Times* reported that two-thirds of voters "cited economic problems such as unemployment, taxes and inflation as a key reason for their vote." Moreover, those polled said they wanted the United States "to be more forceful in dealing with the Soviet Union 'even if it increased the risk of war'" by a margin of almost two to one. Adam Clymer, "The Collapse of a Coalition," *New York Times*, November 5, 1980, 1.

32. Ronald Reagan, "Inaugural Address," January 20, 1981, online by Gerhard Peters and John T. Woolley, *The American Presidency Project*, https://www.presidency.ucsb.edu/node/246336.

33. Martin J. Medhurst, "Writing Speeches for Ronald Reagan: An Interview with Tony Dolan," *Rhetoric & Public Affairs* 1, no. 2 (1998): 247.

34. John Lewis Gaddis, *The Cold War: A New History* (New York: Penguin Press, 2005), 217.

35. Reagan delivered a radio address to the US public on the thirty-eighth anniversary of

D-day. Speaking from London, he told his audience: "One lesson of D-Day is as clear now as it was 38 years ago: Only strength can deter tyranny and aggression," he said. D-day "was a mighty endeavor, an endeavor of liberty, sacrifice, and valor. As we honor these men, I pledge to do my utmost to carry out what must have been their wish—that no other generation of young men would ever have to repeat their sacrifice in order to preserve freedom." Ronald Reagan, "Radio Address to the Nation on the Trip to Europe," June 5, 1982, online by Gerhard Peters and John T. Woolley, *The American Presidency Project*, https://www.presidency.ucsb.edu/node/245200.

36. Reagan attorney general and confidante Edwin Meese later wrote that these two speeches were significant because they "set forth [Reagan's] view of communism, the Soviet system, and the required free world response in comprehensive fashion." Edwin Meese, *With Reagan: The Inside Story* (Washington, DC: Regnery Gateway, 1992), 164.

37. Ronald Reagan, "Address to Members of the British Parliament," June 8, 1982, online by Gerhard Peters and John T. Woolley, *The American Presidency Project*, https://www.presidency.ucsb.edu/node/245236. Reflecting on the address after his presidency, Reagan called it "one of the most important speeches I gave as president." He noted that although many considered 1982 a watershed year for his domestic and economic policy initiatives, "the real story of 1982 is that we began applying conservatism to foreign affairs." Ronald Reagan, *Speaking My Mind* (New York: Simon and Schuster, 1989), 107. In their study of Reagan's Westminster address, Robert C. Rowland and John M. Jones explain that although this speech is hailed by neoconservatives "as the moment when Reagan and Britain's Prime Minister Margaret Thatcher put 'freedom on the offensive where it belonged [Thatcher's assessment],'" Reagan's address "was not recognized as particularly important or effective at the time." Instead, Rowland and Jones argue that the speech offered a vision for a post–Cold War world that was difficult to imagine in 1982: "At the time, few shared Reagan's optimism about the cold war, and almost no one thought that the survival of the Soviet Union was in doubt. . . . A quarter-century later, Reagan's claim that the cold war was at a 'turning point' seems clearly correct, but few agreed with him in 1982." Rowland and Jones, *Reagan at Westminster: Foreshadowing the End of the Cold War*, 13–15.

38. Ronald Reagan, "Remarks at the Annual Conference of the National Association of Evangelicals," March 8, 1983, online by Gerhard Peters and John T. Woolley, *The American Presidency Project*, https://www.presidency.ucsb.edu/node/262885.

39. For an analysis of this particular speech, see Paul Fessler, "Ronald Reagan, Address to the National Association of Evangelicals ('Evil Empire Speech') (8 March 1983)," *Voices of Democracy* 2 (2007): 26–49.

40. Ronald Reagan, "Address to the Nation on National Security," March 23, 1983, https://millercenter.org/the-presidency/presidential-speeches/march-23-1983-address-nation-national-security.

41. Brands, *Reagan: The Life*, 400.

42. Ronald Reagan, "Address to the Nation on Events in Lebanon and Grenada," October 27, 1983, https://www.reaganlibrary.gov/archives/speech/address-nation-events-lebanon-and-grenada. Importantly, Reagan also used this address to respond to a terrorist attack in Lebanon that killed more than two hundred US Marines while they slept. Denise M. Bostdorff notes that this attack "placed great demands on the president's credibility, demands that were too large for even the popular Reagan to meet" and argues that the president "exploited the rhetorical possibilities of Grenada in a way that drew attention from Beirut and helped to resolve the anxieties citizens felt about his foreign policy there." Denise Bostdorff, *The Presidency and the Rhetoric of Foreign Crisis* (Columbia: University of South Carolina Press, 1994), 182, 183. See also David S. Birdsell,

"Ronald Reagan on Lebanon and Grenada: Flexibility and Interpretation in the Application of Kenneth Burke's Pentad," *Quarterly Journal of Speech* 73, no. 3 (1987): 267–79.

43. Here I am aided greatly by Malcolm Byrne's painstaking research that draws heavily on thousands of declassified documents from the Iran-Contra congressional investigations. For the specific quote outlining National Security Decision Directive 17 and North's characterization of the 1984 bombings, see Malcolm Byrne, *Iran-Contra: Reagan's Scandal and the Unchecked Abuse of Presidential Power* (Lawrence: University Press of Kansas, 2014), 14, 26.

44. Goldwater as quoted in Brands, *Reagan: The Life*, 437.

45. Ronald Reagan, *An American Life* (New York: Simon and Schuster, 1990), 471.

46. Decision/Making/Information, "A National Benchmark Survey of Public Attitudes, Prepared for the Republican National Committee, May 1984," 7; RNC National Benchmark, May 1984, Box 3, Papers of David Chew, RRL.

47. The campaign had hoped that a carefully orchestrated presidential visit to People's Republic of China in April would boost these numbers. Although polling data suggested that the trip was an "immense success," it did little to change the public's perception of Reagan's handling of US foreign policy overall. Decision/Making/Information, "A National Benchmark Survey of Public Attitudes, Prepared for the Republican National Committee, May 1984," 1.

48. Decision/Making/Information, "A National Benchmark Survey of Public Attitudes, Prepared for the Republican National Committee, May 1984," 5.

49. Decision/Making/Information, "A National Benchmark Survey of Public Attitudes, Prepared for the Republican National Committee, May 1984," 1 (emphasis in original).

50. Decision/Making/Information, "A National Benchmark Survey of Public Attitudes, Prepared for the Republican National Committee, May 1984," 7.

51. Ronald Reagan, "Address to the Nation on United States Policy in Central America," May 9, 1984, https://www.reaganlibrary.gov/research/speeches/50984h.

52. "U.S. Foreign Policy: A Look Ahead," May 18, 1984, 1, 2; Foreign Policy Background for President's Trip to Europe—Notebook (1 of 2), RAC Box 8, Executive Secretariat, NSC Trip File, RRL.

53. "Preserving Peace and Prosperity: The President's Trip to Europe, June 1984 (Public Diplomacy Action Plan)," 2; June 1984 European Trip (1), Box 3, Richard G. Darman Files, RRL.

54. Memorandum, William F. Martin to Robert C. McFarlane, April 10, 1984, 2; President's Trip to Normandy (2), Box 161, White House Office of Speechwriting: Research Office, 1981–89, RRL.

55. Historian Douglas Brinkley writes that of the two speeches—one at Pointe du Hoc and the other at Omaha Beach—the second was considered the major foreign policy speech. "Some in the White House simply referred to Omaha Beach as 'the Speech' and Pointe du Hoc as 'Brief Remarks.'" White House principal speechwriter Tony Dolan was assigned the Omaha Beach speech, and "Pointe du Hoc was considered a sideshow on June 6, a feel-good, non-policy-based moment. Therefore, Peggy Noonan was tasked with penning the 'impressionistic' oration, while Dolan's 'realist' policy speech would be headlined by prominent U.S. newspapers on June 7." Brinkley's account was published in 2005, when multiple documents related to the "Pointe du Hoc" speech had not been declassified. During my visits to the Reagan Library in June 2013 and March 2019, I accessed a number of documents (all of which were declassified after 2005) that show that the Reagan White House planned for "Pointe du Hoc" to be the centerpiece of Reagan's visit to Normandy. See the NSC's official briefing book, "The President's Trip to Europe: Ireland, UK and Normandy, June 1–10, 1984," RAC Box 4, Executive Secretariat, NSC: Trip File,

RRL, and Douglas Brinkley, *The Boys of Pointe du Hoc: Ronald Reagan, D-Day, and the U.S. Army 2nd Ranger Battalion* (New York: HarperCollins, 2005), 163.

56. Memo, George P. Shultz to Ronald Reagan, May 14, 1984; The President's Trip to Europe: Ireland, UK, and Normandy, June 1–10, 1984—The President (3 of 5), RAC Box 4, Executive Secretariat, NSC: Trip File, RRL.

57. Speech Draft, "Presidential Address: Pointe du Hoc, Wednesday, June 6, 1984, (Noonan/ BE), May 21, 1984, 3:30 p.m."; President's Trip to Normandy (8), Box 162, White House Office of Speechwriting: Research Office, 1981–89, RRL.

58. Miscellaneous notation, n.d.; President's Trip to Normandy (8), Box 162, White House Office of Speechwriting: Research Office, 1981–89, RRL.

59. Speech Draft, "Draft No. 4, the President's Normandy Speech June 6, 1984," April 30, 1984; Pointe du Hoc Address, Normandy (4), Box 161, White House Office of Speechwriting: Speech Drafts, 1981–89, RRL. Draft also found in June 1984 European Trip (3), Box 3, Richard G. Darman Files, RRL.

60. Jack Schnedler, "France Ready for Another Invasion," *New York Post*, May 29, 1984. Clipping included in Current News: Special Edition, D-Day + 40 Years, July 23, 1984, 76; President's Trip to Normandy (5), Box 161, White House Office of Speechwriting, Research Office, 1981–89, RRL.

61. Miscellaneous Note, n.d.; President's Trip to Normandy (4), Box 161, White House Office of Speechwriting: Research Office, 1981–89, RRL.

62. Noonan explained that this line came easily because she had just read Roger Kahn's memoir of the Brooklyn Dodgers, *The Boys of Summer*. See Noonan, *What I Saw at the Revolution*, 87.

63. Miscellaneous notation, n.d., 2; President's Trip to Normandy (2), Box 161, White House Office of Speechwriting—Research, RRL.

64. Miscellaneous notation, n.d.; President's Trip to Normandy (7), Box 161, White House Office of Speechwriting—Research, RRL.

65. Miscellaneous notation, n.d.; President's Trip to Normandy (7), Box 161, White House Office of Speechwriting—Research, RRL.

66. This passage is almost identical to Thucydides's actual account. The only differences are that "her" is actually "heroes" and "E" stands in for "earth."

67. Miscellaneous Note, n.d.; President's Trip to Normandy (4), Box 161, White House Office of Speechwriting: Research Office, 1981–89, RRL.

68. "Memorandum for Mr. Robert C. McFarlane, the White House, Subject: The President's June Trip," March 5, 1984, 3; Europe Memos (1 of 5), CFOA 621, William Henkel Files, RRL.

69. Shultz to Reagan, May 14, 1984, RRL.

70. Michael Dobbs, "Normandy Braces Itself for Another Invasion," *Washington Post*, June 1, 1984. Clipping included in Current News: Special Edition, D-Day + 40 Years, July 24, 1984, 1–2; President's Trip to Normandy (5), Box 161, White House Office of Speechwriting, Research Office, 1981–89, RRL.

71. "NBC Saturday Night News, NBC TV, 6:30 PM, May 19, D-Day Rehearsal Tragedy" and "CBS Saturday Evening News, CBS TV, 6:30 PM, May 26, D-Day Anniversary." Transcripts of broadcasts included in Current News: Special Edition, D-Day + 40 Years, July 23, 1984, 83, 84–85; President's Trip to Normandy (5), Box 161, White House Office of Speechwriting, Research Office, 1981–89, RRL.

72. For the transcripts of this *NBC Nightly News* five-part special, see Current News: Special

Edition, D-Day + 40 Years, July 23, 1984, 86–91; President's Trip to Normandy (5), Box 161, White House Office of Speechwriting, Research Office, 1981–89, RRL.

73. Lou Cannon, "At 40th D-Day Tribute, Reagan Took the Occasion by Storm," *Washington Post*, June 7, 2004, A6.

74. The "Draft Notional Schedule—Trip of the President to Europe" dated May 7, 1984, specified that Reagan would arrive at the Pointe du Hoc landing zone at 8:20 a.m. EDT (2:20 p.m. local time), tour the Ranger Memorial for ten minutes with two survivors of the Pointe du Hoc landing, and begin his "Remarks to assembled Veterans and unveiling of plaque commemorating Point [*sic*] du Hoc" at 8:40 a.m. EDT (2:40 pm local time). See "Draft Notional Schedule, Trip of the President to Europe," May 7, 1984; President's Trip to Normandy (2), Box 161, White House Office of Speechwriting: Research Office, 1981–89, RRL.

75. Brinkley, *The Boys of Pointe du Hoc: Ronald Reagan, D-Day, and the U.S. Army 2nd Ranger Battalion*, 258.

76. "D-Day + 40," ABC News, June 6, 1984. Footage obtained from the White House Communication Agency videotape collection, "R2004A/B 06/06/1984 President Reagan at Pointe du Hoc, Normandy, France with speech (ABC, 60:00)," RRL.

77. "D-Day + 40," ABC News, June 6, 1984. Footage obtained from the White House Communication Agency videotape collection, "R2004A/B 06/06/1984 President Reagan at Pointe du Hoc, Normandy, France with speech (ABC, 60:00)," RRL.

78. "D-Day + 40," CNN, June 6, 1984. Footage obtained from the White House Communication Agency videotape collection, "R2005 06/06/1984 President Reagan visit to Pointe du Hoc, Normandy, France with speech (CNN, 60:00)," RRL.

79. Ronald Reagan, "Remarks at a Ceremony Commemorating the 40th Anniversary of the Normandy Invasion, D-Day," June 6, 1984, online by Gerhard Peters and John T. Woolley, *The American Presidency Project*, https://www.presidency.ucsb.edu/node/261649. All successive quotations from here unless otherwise noted.

80. Memorandum, Robert M. Kimmitt to Richard G. Darman, June 1, 1984; President's Trip to Normandy (11), Box 162, White House Office of Speechwriting: Research Office, 1981–89, RRL.

81. Two Soviet television programs that ran the week before Reagan's speech in Prague and Moscow blasted the president for the upcoming "propaganda hullabaloo" in Normandy. "Normandy Ceremony to Be Propaganda Show," aired on Moscow Television Service in Russian on May 30, 1984. See also "West Said to Minimize USSR's World War II Role," aired on Prague Television Service in Czech and Slovak on May 27, 1984. Transcripts of broadcasts included in Current News: Special Edition, D-Day + 40 Years, July 23, 1984, 77–78; President's Trip to Normandy (5), Box 161, White House Office of Speechwriting, Research Office, 1981–89, RRL.

82. Historian Michael Walzer writes that "more civilians died in the siege of Leningrad than in the modernist infernos of Hamburg, Dresden, Tokyo, Hiroshima, and Nagasaki, taken together." Michael Walzer, *Just and Unjust Wars: A Moral Argument with Historical Illustrations* (New York: Basic Books, 2006), 160. For more specific details, see David Glantz, *The Siege of Leningrad, 1941–44: 900 Days of Terror* (Osceola, WI: Zenith Press, 2001).

83. As Kathleen Hall Jamieson has observed, "television enabled Reagan to transport the national audience to the stage he had set in Normandy. . . . The dramatization was compelling, the staging unsurpassable, the visual argument politically potent." Jamieson, *Eloquence in an Electronic Age: The Transformation of Political Speechmaking*, 162–63.

84. "D-Day + 40," ABC News, June 6, 1984. Footage obtained from the White House Com-

munication Agency videotape collection, "R2004A/B 06/06/1984 President Reagan at Pointe du Hoc, Normandy, France with speech (ABC, 60:00)," RRL.

85. "D-Day Anniversary," *Nightly News*, NBC News (New York: June 6, 1984), Vanderbilt Television News Archive (hereafter VTNA).

86. "D-Day Anniversary," *World News Tonight*, ABC News (New York: June 6, 1984), VTNA.

87. "D-Day Anniversary," *Evening News*, CBS News (New York: June 6, 1984), VTNA.

88. "D-Day Anniversary," *Evening News*, CBS News (New York: June 6, 1984), VTNA.

89. "D-Day Anniversary," *Evening News*, CBS News (New York: June 6, 1984), VTNA.

90. "D-Day Anniversary," *Nightly News*, NBC News (New York: June 6, 1984), VTNA.

91. "D-Day Anniversary," *Nightly News*, NBC News (New York: June 6, 1984), VTNA.

92. Drew Middleton, "Reagan Honors D-Day; Calls for Spirit of Peace," *New York Times*, June 7, 1984, A1.

93. "D-Day Remembered: Allied Leaders Honor Heroes of Normandy," *Los Angeles Times*, June 6, 1984, A1.

94. Benjamin Taylor, "Reagan Lauds Men Who Died on D-Day," *Boston Globe*, June 7, 1984, 1.

95. "Election Year Scheduling," February 27, 1984, 3; "Election Year Scheduling (Binder)—2/27/1984," Series IV: Subject Files, Michael Deaver Files, RRL.

96. "Election Year Scheduling," 1.

97. Memorandum, Sig Rogich to Michael K. Deaver, June 19, 1984, 1–2; Convention Documentary (2), Box 6, Richard G. Darman Files, RRL. For a full record of how the campaign video worked within the sequence of events that final day of the campaign, see "August 23, 1984, Republican National Convention, Day 4," C-SPAN, http://www.c-span.org/video/?124909-1/republican-national-convention-day-4. For an analysis of the film itself, see Joanne Morreale, *A New Beginning: A Textual Frame Analysis of the Political Campaign Film* (Albany: State University of New York Press, 1991).

98. Howell Raines, "Reagan Wins By a Landslide, Sweeping at Least 48 States; GOP Gains Strength in House," November 7, 1984, *New York Times*, https://www.nytimes.com/1984/11/07/politics/reagan-wins-by-a-landslide-sweeping-at-least-48-states-gop-gains.html.

99. See R. W. Apple, "Clinton in Normandy: Hands across a Generation," *New York Times*, June 8, 1994; Mary L. Kahl and Michael Leff, "The Rhetoric of War and Remembrance: An Analysis of President Bill Clinton's 1994 D-Day Discourses," *Qualitative Research Reports in Communication* 7 (2006): 15–21; Jill Abramson, "Bush Speaks of Heroism and Sacrifice at Cemetery at Normandy," *New York Times*, May 28, 2002, https://www.nytimes.com/2002/05/28/international/europe/bush-speaks-of-heroism-and-sacrifice-at-cemetery-in.html; Richard W. Stevenson, "In D-Day Rite, Bush Praises Veterans of Normandy," *New York Times*, June 7, 2004, https://www.nytimes.com/2004/06/07/world/in-d-day-rite-bush-praises-veterans-of-normandy.html; John McCormick, "Family Tapestry Part of Obama's Europe Trip," *Chicago Tribune*, June 4, 2009, https://www.chicagotribune.com/news/ct-xpm-2009-06-04-0906031228-story.html; Associated Press, "Reagan Set the Tone for D-Day Observances," *Daily Herald*, June 6, 2014, https://www.dailyherald.com/article/20140605/news/140609040/; Mark Landler and Maggie Haberman, "Trump Honors D-Day Sacrifices, with Some Legacies Unspoken," *New York Times*, June 6, 2019, https://www.nytimes.com/2019/06/06/world/europe/trump-d-day-speech.html.

100. Although there is a tendency to discount the political potential of the epideictic, Jeffrey Walker argues that it is this form of rhetorical exchange that provides the underlying grounds for civic deliberation and the morals of a community, writing, "'epideictic' appears as that which

shapes and cultivates the basic codes of value and belief by which a society or culture lives; it shapes the ideologies and imageries with which, and by which, the individual members of a community identify themselves; and, perhaps most significantly, it shapes the fundamental grounds, the 'deep' commitments and presuppositions, that will underlie and ultimately determine decision and debate in particular pragmatic forums." In affirming the morals or values the nation prizes, epideictic speech cements these ideals as that which should be emulated in public life. Similarly, Mary E. Stuckey argues that "in offering praise or blame, in fact, epideictic works to affirm a community's values. . . . Epideictic, then, may well serve as a way not just to create adherence to a thesis but also to intensify allegiance to one." See Jeffrey Walker, *Rhetoric and Poetics in Antiquity* (Oxford: Oxford University Press, 2000), 9–10; Stuckey, *Slipping the Surly Bonds: Reagan's Challenger Address*, 17.

101. Classical examples of epideictic included speeches of praise (*enkomion*), speeches delivered at festivals (*panegyrikos logos*), and the funeral oration (*epitaphios logos*), categories that, as Edward Schiappa argues, collapsed into Aristotle's refiguring of the epideictic. As these various types or uses indicate, epideictic speech adapted itself for various ends, all with the purpose of displaying (*epideixis*) the skill of the orator and the evidence at hand. See Edward E. Schiappa, *The Beginnings of Rhetorical Theory in Classical Greece* (New Haven, CT: Yale University Press, 1999).

102. Edward S. Casey, "Public Memory in Place and Time," in *Framing Public Memory*, ed. Kendall R. Phillips (Tuscaloosa: University of Alabama Press, 2004), 35.

103. Casey, 36.

104. Megan Foley, "Time for Epideictic," *Quarterly Journal of Speech* 101, no. 1 (2015): 211.

105. Peggy Noonan, "Peggy Noonan on Reagan's D-Day Speech," *The Kelly File*, December 4, 2013, http://video.foxnews.com/v/2893720031001/peggy-noonan-on-reagans-d-day-speech.

106. William J. Clinton, "Remarks on the 50th Anniversary of D-Day at Pointe du Hoc in Normandy, France," June 6, 1994, online by Gerhard Peters and John T. Woolley, *The American Presidency Project*, https://www.presidency.ucsb.edu/node/219259.

107. George W. Bush, "Remarks on the 60th Anniversary of D-Day in Colleville-sur-Mer, France," June 6, 2004, online by Gerhard Peters and John T. Woolley, *The American Presidency Project*, https://www.presidency.ucsb.edu/node/214991.

108. Barack Obama, "Remarks on the 65th Anniversary of D-Day in Normandy, France," June 6, 2009, online by Gerhard Peters and John T. Woolley, *The American Presidency Project*, https://www.presidency.ucsb.edu/node/286709.

109. Barack Obama, "Remarks on the 70th Anniversary of D-Day in Normandy, France," June 6, 2014, online by Gerhard Peters and John T. Woolley, *The American Presidency Project*, https://www.presidency.ucsb.edu/node/305667.

110. Donald J. Trump, "Remarks by President Trump on the 75th Commemoration of D-Day," June 6, 2019, https://www.whitehouse.gov/briefings-statements/remarks-president-trump-75th-commemoration-d-day/.

Conclusion

1. Joseph R. Biden, "Joe Biden: My Trip to Europe Is about America Rallying the World's Democracies," *Washington Post*, June 5, 2021, https://www.washingtonpost.com/opinions/2021/06/05/joe-biden-europe-trip-agenda/.

2. Joseph R. Biden, "Remarks in a Town Hall Meeting with George Stephanopoulos of ABC

News at the National Constitution Center in Philadelphia, Pennsylvania," October 15, 2020, online by Gerhard Peters and John T. Woolley, *The American Presidency Project*, https://www.presidency.ucsb.edu/node/343839.

3. David E. Sanger and Steven Erlanger, "For Biden, Europe Trip Achieved 2 Major Goals. And Then There Is Russia," *New York Times*, June 17, 2021, https://www.nytimes.com/2021/06/17/world/europe/joe-biden-vladimir-putin-usa-russia.html.

4. "On the Record Press Call by National Security Advisor Jake Sullivan on the President's Trip to Europe," June 17, 2021, https://www.whitehouse.gov/briefing-room/press-briefings/2021/06/17/on-the-record-press-call-by-national-security-advisor-jake-sullivan-on-the-presidents-trip-to-europe/.

5. Wilson, "Address to a Joint Session of Congress Requesting a Declaration of War against Germany."

6. George W. Bush, "Remarks to the Troops at Camp As Sayliyah, Qatar," June 5, 2003, online by Gerhard Peters and John T. Woolley, *The American Presidency Project*, https://www.presidency.ucsb.edu/node/214770.

7. I draw here on how the Obama administration characterized the president's speech on the White House website. See "The President's Speech in Cairo: A New Beginning," June 4, 2009, Obama White House Archive, https://obamawhitehouse.archives.gov/issues/foreign-policy/presidents-speech-cairo-a-new-beginning.

8. Barack Obama, "Remarks in Cairo," June 4, 2009, online by Gerard Peters and John T. Woolley, *The American Presidency Project*, https://www.presidency.ucsb.edu/node/286614.

9. Trump, "Remarks by President Trump on the 75th Commemoration of D-Day."

10. @realdonaldtrump, June 28, 2019, 6:51:41 p.m. EST, accessed via https://www.thetrumparchive.com.

11. Rebecca Ballhaus and Andrew Jeong, "Trump's Twitter Invitation to Kim Set Off a 24-Hour Scramble," *Wall Street Journal*, June 30, 2019, https://www.wsj.com/articles/trumps-twitter-invitation-to-kim-set-off-24-hour-scramble-11561943026; Scott Horsley, "Trump Tweets an Invitation to North Korea's Kim—Meet in the DMZ?," NPR, June 28, 2019, https://www.npr.org/2019/06/28/737209058/trump-tweets-an-invitation-to-north-koreas-kim-meet-in-the-dmz.

Bibliography

Manuscript Collections

Dwight D. Eisenhower Presidential Library, Abilene, Kansas
    Papers as President, Ann Whitman File
    Papers of Abbott Washburn
    Papers of C. D. Jackson
    Papers of Christian A. Herter
    Papers of Edward T. Lilly
    Papers of James C. Hagerty
    Papers of Kevin McCann
    Papers of the US President's Committee on Information Activities Abroad
        (Sprague Committee)
    Papers of the US President's Committee on International Information Activities
        (Jackson Committee)
    Papers of Thomas E. Stephens
    Papers of William G. Draper
    Records of the White House Office of the Special Assistant for National Security
    White House Central Files
    White House Office of the Staff Secretary, International Trips and Meetings
        Series
Harry S. Truman Presidential Library, Independence, Missouri
    Papers of Edwin W. Pauley
    Papers of George M. Elsey
    Papers of James H. Foskett
    Papers of James W. Riddleberger
    Papers of Richard Beckman
    Papers of Samuel I. Rosenman
    Papers of the Naval Aide to the President
    President's Secretary's File

US Army Signal Corps
White House Official File
John F. Kennedy Presidential Library, Boston, Massachusetts
Evelyn Lincoln Personal Papers
McGeorge Bundy Personal Papers
Oral History Collection
Papers of Chester V. Clifton
Papers of John F. Kennedy
Pre-Presidential Papers
Presidential Campaign Files, 1960
Presidential Papers
National Security Files
President's Office Files
White House Central Files
Papers of Theodore C. Sorenson
White House Photographic Office
National Archives and Records Administration, College Park, Maryland
Foreign Service Posts (Record Group 84)
Papers of the US Information Agency and US Information Service (Record Group 306)
Paramount Newsreel Collection
State Department Central Files (Record Group 59)
Universal Newsreel Collection
National Archives, Kew, Richmond, United Kingdom
National Security Archive, George Washington University, Washington, DC, https://nsarchive.gwu.edu
Public Papers of the President, *The American Presidency Project*, University of California, Santa Barbara, https://www.presidency.ucsb.edu
Richard Nixon Presidential Library, Yorba Linda, California
Papers of David C. Hoopes
Papers of Dwight L. Chapin
Papers of H. R. Haldeman
Papers of Raymond K. Price, Speech File
Papers of Ronald Ziegler
Papers of the National Security Council, Alexander M. Haig Special File
Papers of the National Security Council, Henry A. Kissinger Office Files
Papers of the National Security Council, President's Trip Files
Papers of the National Security Council, Subject Files
President's Personal File
White House Central Files
White House Communication Agency
White House Special Files

Ronald Reagan Presidential Library, Simi Valley, California
    Papers of Anthony "Tony" R. Dolan
    Papers of David Chew
    Papers of James Rentschler
    Papers of Michael Deaver
    Papers of Richard G. Darman
    Papers of the National Security Council, Executive Secretariat: Trip File
    Papers of the White House News Summary Office
    Papers of the White House Office of Media Relations
    Papers of the White House Office of Presidential Advance
    Papers of the White House Office of Speechwriting, Research
    Papers of the White House Office of Speechwriting, Speech Drafts
    Papers of Walter Raymond
    Papers of William F. Martin
    Papers of William Henkel
    White House Communication Agency
US Department of State, Office of the Historian, Washington, DC, https://history
    .state.gov
Vanderbilt Television Archive, Nashville, Tennessee

Newspapers and Magazines

Atlanta Daily World
Boston Globe
Chicago Daily Tribune
Chicago Defender
Chicago Tribune
Christian Science Monitor
Life
Los Angeles Times
New York Herald Tribune
New York Times
Pittsburgh Courier
The Times (London)
Time
Wall Street Journal
Washington Post
Washington Times

Books, Book Chapters, and Articles

Allen, Craig. *Eisenhower and the Mass Media: Peace, Prosperity, and Prime-Time TV.* Chapel Hill
    and London: University of North Carolina Press, 1993.
Alperovitz, Gar. *Atomic Diplomacy: Hiroshima and Potsdam.* London: Pluto Press, 1994.

Anderson, Benedict. *Imagined Communities: Reflections on the Origin and Spread of Nationalism*. 2nd ed. London: Verso, 2006.

Atkinson, Nathan S. "Newsreels as Domestic Propaganda: Visual Rhetoric at the Dawn of the Cold War." *Rhetoric & Public Affairs* 14, no. 1 (2011): 69–100.

Barney, Timothy. "'Gulag'-Slavery, Inc.: The Power of Place and the Rhetorical Life of a Cold War Map." *Rhetoric & Public Affairs* 16, no. 2 (2013): 317–53.

Barney, Timothy. *Mapping the Cold War: Cartography and the Framing of America's International Power*. Chapel Hill: University of North Carolina Press, 2015.

Barney, Timothy. "Power Lines: The Rhetoric of Maps as Social Change in the Post–Cold War Landscape." *Quarterly Journal of Speech* 95, no. 4 (2009): 412–34.

Barnouw, Erik. *Tube of Plenty: The Evolution of American Television*. Oxford: Oxford University Press, 1975.

Beasley, Vanessa B. *You, the People: American National Identity in Presidential Rhetoric*. College Station: Texas A&M University Press, 2004.

Beschloss, Michael R. *The Crisis Years: Kennedy and Khrushchev, 1960–1963*. New York: Edward Berlingame Books, 1991.

Bimes, Terri. "Understanding the Rhetorical Presidency." In *The Oxford Handbook of the American Presidency*, edited by George C. Edwards and William G. Howell. Oxford: Oxford University Press, 2009.

Birdsell, David S. "Ronald Reagan on Lebanon and Grenada: Flexibility and Interpretation in the Application of Kenneth Burke's Pentad." *Quarterly Journal of Speech* 73, no. 3 (1987): 267–79.

Bishop, Joseph Bucklin. *The Panama Gateway*. New York: Charles Scribner's Sons, 1913.

Black, Edwin. "The Second Persona." *Quarterly Journal of Speech* 56, no. 2 (1970): 109–19.

Black, Jason Edward. *American Indians and the Rhetoric of Removal and Allotment*. Jackson: University Press of Mississippi, 2015.

Blair, Carole. "Reflections on Criticism and Bodies: Parables from Public Places." *Western Journal of Communication* 65, no. 3 (2001): 271–94.

Blair, Carole, Greg Dickinson, and Brian L. Ott. "Introduction: Rhetoric/Memory/Place." In *Places of Public Memory: The Rhetoric of Museums and Memorials*, edited by Greg Dickinson, Carole Blair, and Brian L. Ott, 1–54. Tuscaloosa: University of Alabama Press, 2010.

Bodnar, John. *Remaking America: Public Memory, Commemoration, and Patriotism in the Twentieth Century*. Princeton, NJ: Princeton University Press, 1992.

Bogart, Leo. *Premises for Propaganda: The United States Information Agency's Operating Assumptions in the Cold War*. New York: Free Press, 1976.

Bohlen, Charles E. *Witness to History, 1929–1969*. New York: Norton, 1973.

Bormann, Ernest G. "A Fantasy Theme Analysis of the Television Coverage of the Hostage Release and the Reagan Inaugural." *Quarterly Journal of Speech* 68, no. 2 (1982): 133–45.

Bormann, Ernest G., John F. Cragan, and Donald C. Shields. "An Expansion of the Rhetorical Vision Component of the Symbolic Convergence Theory: The Cold War Paradigm Case." *Communication Monographs* 63, no. 1 (1996): 1–28.

Bostdorff, Denise M. "Dean Acheson's May 1947 Delta Council Speech: Rhetorical Evolution from the Truman Doctrine to the Marshall Plan." In *World War II and the Cold War: The Rhetoric of Hearts and Minds*, edited by Martin J. Medhurst, 167–214. Rhetorical History of the United States, vol. 8. East Lansing: Michigan State University Press, 2018.

Bostdorff, Denise M. "Epideictic Rhetoric in the Service of War: George W. Bush on Iraq and the

60th Anniversary of the Victory over Japan." *Communication Monographs* 78, no. 3 (2011): 296–323.

Bostdorff, Denise M. "The Evolution of a Diplomatic Surprise: Richard M. Nixon's Rhetoric on China, 1952–July 15, 1972." *Rhetoric & Public Affairs* 5, no. 1 (2002): 31–56.

Bostdorff, Denise M. *The Presidency and the Rhetoric of Foreign Crisis.* Columbia: University of South Carolina Press, 1994.

Bostdorff, Denise M. *Proclaiming the Truman Doctrine: The Cold War Call to Arms.* College Station: Texas A&M University Press, 2008.

Brands, H. W. *Cold Warriors: Eisenhower's Generation and American Foreign Policy.* New York: Columbia University Press, 1988.

Brands, H. W. *Reagan: The Life.* New York: Doubleday, 2015.

Brands, H. W. *Woodrow Wilson.* New York: Henry Holt, 2003.

Brandt, Willy. *People and Politics: The Years, 1960–1975.* Translated by J. Maxwell Brownjohn. Boston: Little, Brown, 1976.

Brinkley, Douglas. *The Boys of Pointe Du Hoc: Ronald Reagan, D-Day, and the U.S. Army 2nd Ranger Battalion.* New York: HarperCollins, 2005.

Brockriede, Wayne, and Robert L. Scott. *Moments in the Rhetoric of the Cold War.* New York: Random House, 1970.

Browne, Stephen H. "Samuel Danforth's 'Errand into the Wilderness' and the Discourse of Arrival in Early American Culture." *Communication Quarterly* 40, no. 2 (1992): 91–101.

Burke, Kenneth. "Four Master Tropes." *Kenyon Review* 3, no. 4 (1941): 421–38.

Burke, Kenneth. "Identification." In *Kenneth Burke on Symbols and Society*, edited by Joseph R. Gusfield, 179–91. Chicago: University of Chicago Press, 1989.

Burke, Kenneth. *A Rhetoric of Motives.* Berkeley: University of California Press, 1969.

Byrne, Malcolm. *Iran-Contra: Reagan's Scandal and the Unchecked Abuse of Presidential Power.* Lawrence: University Press of Kansas, 2014.

Campbell, Karlyn Kohrs. *The Great Silent Majority: Nixon's 1969 Speech on Vietnamization.* College Station: Texas A&M University Press, 2014.

Campbell, Karlyn Kohrs, and Kathleen Hall Jamieson. *Presidents Creating the Presidency: Deeds Done in Words.* Chicago: University of Chicago Press, 2008.

Carney, Zoë Hess, and Allison M. Prasch. "'A Journey for Peace': Spatial Metaphors in Nixon's 1972 'Opening to China.'" *Presidential Studies Quarterly* 47, no. 4 (2017): 646–64.

Carpenter, Ronald H. "Frederick Jackson Turner and the Rhetorical Impact of the Frontier Thesis." *Quarterly Journal of Speech* 63, no. 2 (1977): 117–29.

Casey, Edward S. *Getting Back into Place: Toward a Renewed Understanding of the Place-World.* Bloomington: Indiana University Press, 1991.

Casey, Edward S. "Public Memory in Place and Time." In *Framing Public Memory*, edited by Kendall R. Phillips, 17–44. Tuscaloosa: University of Alabama Press, 2004.

Casey, Edward S. *Remembering: A Phenomenological Study.* 2nd ed. Bloomington: Indiana University Press, 2000.

Ceaser, James W., Glen E. Thurow, Jeffrey Tulis, and Joseph M. Bessette. "The Rise of the Rhetorical Presidency." *Presidential Studies Quarterly* 11, no. 2 (1981): 158–71.

Ceccarelli, Leah. "Polysemy: Multiple Meanings in Rhetorical Criticism." *Quarterly Journal of Speech* 84, no. 4 (1998): 395–415.

Chaput, Catherine. "Rhetorical Circulation in Late Capitalism: Neoliberalism and the Overdetermination of Affective Energy." *Philosophy & Rhetoric* 43, no. 1 (2010): 1–25.

Chernus, Ira. *Eisenhower's Atoms for Peace*. East Lansing: Michigan State University Press, 2002.

Citrón, Ralph. "Democracy and Its Limitations." In *The Public Work of Rhetoric: Citizen-Scholars and Civic Engagement*, edited by John M. Ackerman and David J. Coogan, 98–116. Columbia: University of South Carolina Press, 2010.

Clymer, Adam. "The Collapse of a Coalition." *New York Times*, November 5, 1980.

Coe, Kevin, and Rico Neumann. "International Identity in Theory and Practice: The Case of the Modern American Presidency." *Communication Monographs* 78, no. 2 (2011): 139–61.

Cohen, Jeffrey E. "Presidential Attention Focusing in the Global Arena: The Impact of International Travel on Foreign Publics." *Presidential Studies Quarterly* 46, no. 1 (2016): 30–47.

Cooper, John Milton. *Woodrow Wilson: A Biography*. New York: Alfred A. Knopf, 2009.

Cragan, John F. "The Origins and Nature of the Cold War Rhetorical Vision, 1946–1972." In *Applied Communication Research: A Dramatistic Approach*, edited by John F. Cragan and Donald C. Shields, 47–66. Prospect Heights, IL: Waveland Press, 1981.

Cram, E. *Violent Inheritance: Sexuality, Land, and Energy in Making the North American West*. Oakland: University of California Press, 2022.

Crockett, David A. "'The Rhetorical Presidency': Still Standing Tall." *Presidential Studies Quarterly* 39, no. 4 (2009): 932–40.

Cull, Nicholas J. *The Cold War and the United States Information Agency: American Propaganda and Public Diplomacy, 1945–1989*. New York: Cambridge University Press, 2008.

Curtin, Michael. *Redeeming the Wasteland: Television Documentary and Cold War Politics*. New Brunswick, NJ: Rutgers University Press, 1995.

Cushion, Stephen, and Justin Lewis, eds. *The Rise of the 24-Hour News Television: Global Perspectives*. New York: Peter Lang, 2010.

Dallek, Robert. *An Unfinished Life: John F. Kennedy, 1917–1963*. Boston: Little, Brown, 2003.

Darsey, James. "Barack Obama and America's Journey." *Southern Communication Journal* 74, no. 1 (2009): 88–103.

Daum, Andreas W. *Kennedy in Berlin*. Translated by Dona Geyer. New York: Cambridge University Press, 2008.

DeLuca, Kevin Michael. *Image Politics: The New Rhetoric of Environmental Activism*. New York: Routledge, 2005.

DeLuca, Kevin Michael, and Jennifer Peeples. "From Public Sphere to Public Screen: Democracy, Activisim, and the 'Violence' of Seattle." *Critical Studies in Mass Communication* 19, no. 2 (2002): 125–51.

Dilliplane, Susanna. "Race, Rhetoric, and Running for President: Unpacking the Significance of Barack Obama's 'a More Perfect Union' Speech." *Rhetoric & Public Affairs* 15, no. 1 (2012): 127–52.

Divine, Robert A. *Eisenhower and the Cold War*. New York: Oxford University Press, 1981.

Dobbs, Michael. *Six Months in 1945: FDR, Stalin, Churchill, and Truman—from World War to Cold War*. New York: Vintage Books, 2012.

Dolski, Michael R. *D-Day Remembered: The Normandy Landings in American Collective Memory*. Knoxville: University of Tennessee Press, 2016.

Dolski, Michael R. "'Portal of Liberation': D-Day Myth as American Self-Affirmation." In *D-Day in History and Memory*, edited by Michael Dolski, Sam Edwards, and John Buckley. Denton: University of North Texas Press, 2014.

Dorsey, Leroy G. "The Frontier Myth in Presidential Rhetoric: Theodore Roosevelt's Campaign for Conservation." *Western Journal of Communication* 59, no. 1 (1995): 1–19.

Dorsey, Leroy G. "Managing Women's Equality: Theodore Roosevelt, the Frontier Myth, and the Modern Woman." *Rhetoric & Public Affairs* 16, no. 3 (2013): 423–56.

DuBois, W. E. Burghardt. "My Impressions of Woodrow Wilson." *Journal of Negro History* 58, no. 4 (1973): 453–59.

Dudziak, Mary L. *Cold War Civil Rights: Race and the Image of American Democracy.* Princeton, NJ: Princeton University Press, 2000.

Eckwright, Royce E. *United States Air Access to Berlin, 1945–1965: Part I, the Political-Military Background.* Historical Division, Office of Information, US Air Forces in Europe, 1966.

Edbauer, Jenny. "Unframing Models of Public Distribution: From Rhetorical Situation to Rhetorical Ecologies." *Rhetoric Society Quarterly* 35, no. 4 (2005): 5–24.

Edelman, Murray. *Constructing the Political Spectacle.* Chicago: University of Chicago Press, 1988.

Edelman, Murray. *The Symbolic Uses of Politics.* Urbana and Chicago: University of Illinois Press, 1964.

Edwards, George C. "The Bully in the Pulpit." *Presidential Studies Quarterly* 50, no. 2 (2020): 286–324.

Eisenhower, Dwight D. *Waging Peace, 1956–1961: The White House Years.* Garden City, NY: Doubleday, 1965.

Ellis, Richard. *Presidential Travel: The Journey from George Washington to George W. Bush.* Lawrence: University Press of Kansas, 2008.

Ellis, Richard J., ed. *Speaking to the People: The Rhetorical Presidency in Historical Perspective.* Amherst: University of Massachusetts Press, 1998.

Endres, Danielle, and Samantha Senda-Cook. "Location Matters: The Rhetoric of Place in Protest." *Quarterly Journal of Speech* 97, no. 3 (2011): 257–82.

Erickson, Keith V. "Presidential Rhetoric's Visual Turn: Performance Fragments and the Politics of Illusionism." *Communication Monographs* 67, no. 2 (2000): 138–57.

Erman, Sam. *Almost Citizens: Puerto Rico, the U.S. Constitution, and Empires.* Cambridge: Cambridge University Press, 2019.

Fay, Isabel, and Jim A. Kuypers. "Transcending Mysticism and Building Identification through Empowerment of the Rhetorical Agent: John F. Kennedy's Berlin Speeches on June 26, 1963." *Southern Communication Journal* 77, no. 3 (2012): 198–215.

Fessler, Paul. "Ronald Reagan, Address to the National Association of Evangelicals ('Evil Empire Speech') (8 March 1983)." *Voices of Democracy* 2 (2007): 26–49.

Filipink, Richard M. *Dwight Eisenhower and American Foreign Policy during the 1960s: An American Lion in Winter.* Lanham, MD: Lexington Books, 2015.

Finnegan, Cara A., and Jennifer L. Jones Barbour. "Visualizing Public Address." *Rhetoric & Public Affairs* 9, no. 3 (2006): 489–505.

Finnegan, Cara A., and Jiyeon Kang. "'Sighting' the Public: Iconoclasm and Public Sphere Theory." *Quarterly Journal of Speech* 90, no. 4 (2004): 377–402.

Fisher, David E., and Marshall Jon Fisher. *Tube: The Invention of Television.* Washington, DC: Counterpoint, 1996.

Fisher, Walter R. "Romantic Democracy, Ronald Reagan, and Presidential Heroes." *Western Journal of Speech Communication* 46, no. 3 (1982): 299–310.

Foley, Megan. "Time for Epideictic." *Quarterly Journal of Speech* 101, no. 1 (2015): 209–12.

Gaddis, John Lewis. *The Cold War: A New History.* New York: Penguin Press, 2005.

Gaddis, John Lewis. *The United States and the Origins of the Cold War, 1941–1947*. New York: Columbia University Press, 1972.

Gaughan, Anthony. "Woodrow Wilson and the Legacy of the Civil War." *Civil War History* 43, no. 3 (1997): 224–42.

Gilderhus, Mark T. "The Monroe Doctrine: Meanings and Implications." *Presidential Studies Quarterly* 36, no. 1 (2006): 5–16.

Gilmore, Jason. "Translating American Exceptionalism: Comparing Presidential Discourse about the United States at Home and Abroad." *International Journal of Communication* 8 (2014): 2416–37.

Gilmore, Jason, and Charles M. Rowling. "Lighting the Beacon: Presidential Discourse, American Exceptionalism, and Public Diplomacy in Global Contexts." *Presidential Studies Quarterly* 48, no. 2 (2018): 271–91.

Ginzburg, Carlo, John Tedeschi, and Anne C. Tedeschi. "Microhistory: Two or Three Things That I Know about It." *Critical Inquiry* 20, no. 1 (1993): 10–35.

Glantz, David. *The Siege of Leningrad, 1941–44: 900 Days of Terror*. Osceola, WI: Zenith Press, 2001.

Goh, Evelyn. *Constructing the U.S. Rapprochement with China, 1961–1974*. Cambridge: Cambridge University Press, 2005.

Goldsmith, Benjamin E., and Yusaku Horiuchi. "In Search of Soft Power: Does Foreign Public Opinion Matter for Us Foreign Policy?" *World Politics* 64, no. 3 (2012): 555–85.

Goldsmith, Benjamin E., and Yusaku Horiuchi. "Spinning the Globe? U.S. Public Diplomacy and Foreign Public Opinion." *Journal of Politics* 71, no. 3 (2009): 863–75.

Gould, Louis L. *The Modern American Presidency*. Lawrence: University Press of Kansas, 2003.

Grandin, Greg. *Empire's Workshop: Latin America, the United States, and the Rise of New Imperialism*. New York: Metropolitan Books, 2006.

Grandin, Greg. *The End of the Myth*. New York: Henry Holt, 2019.

Grandin, Greg. *The Last Colonial Massacre: Latin America in the Cold War*. Chicago: University of Chicago Press, 2004.

Grathwol, Robert P., and Donita M. Moorhus. *Berlin and the American Military: A Cold War Chronicle*. New York: New York University Press, 1999.

Greene, Ronald Walter. "Rhetorical Pedagogy as a Postal System: Circulating Subjects through Michael Warner's 'Publics and Counterpublics.'" *Quarterly Journal of Speech* 88, no. 4 (2002): 434–43.

Greenstein, Fred I. *The Hidden-Hand Presidency: Eisenhower as Leader*. Baltimore: Johns Hopkins University Press, 1982.

Gronbeck, Bruce E. "The Presidency in the Age of Secondary Orality." In *Beyond the Rhetorical Presidency*, edited by Martin J. Medhurst, 30–49. College Station: Texas A&M University Press, 1996.

Haig, Alexander, Jr., and Charles McCarry. *Inner Circles: How America Changed the World*. New York: Warner Books, 1992.

Halbwachs, Maurice. *On Collective Memory*. Edited by Lewis A. Coser. Chicago: University of Chicago Press, 1992.

Haldeman, H. R. *The Haldeman Diaries: Inside the Nixon White House*. New York: G. P. Putnam's Sons, 1994.

Hamilton, Kevin, and Thomas E. O'Gorman. *Lookout America! The Secret Hollywood Studio at the Heart of the Cold War*. Lebanon, NH: University Press of New England, 2018.

Harrington, Daniel F. *Berlin on the Brink: The Blockade, the Airlift, and the Early Cold War*. Lexington: University Press of Kentucky, 2012.

Hart, Roderick P. "Donald Trump and the Return of the Paranoid Style." *Presidential Studies Quarterly* 50, no. 2 (2020): 348–65.

Hart, Roderick P. *The Sound of Leadership: Presidential Communication in the Modern Age*. Chicago: University of Chicago Press, 1987.

Hart, Roderick P. *Trump and Us: What He Says and Why People Listen*. New York: Cambridge University Press, 2020.

Hartnett, Stephen J. *A World of Turmoil: The United States, China, and Taiwan in the Long Cold War*. East Lansing: Michigan State University Press, 2021.

Hawhee, Debra, and Christa J. Olson. "Pan-Historiography: The Challenges of Writing History across Time and Space." In *Theorizing Histories of Rhetoric*, edited by Michelle Ballif, 90–105. Carbondale: Southern Illinois University Press, 2013.

Haydock, Michael D. *City under Siege: The Berlin Blockade and Airlift, 1948–1949*. Washington, DC: Brassey's, 1999.

Heckscher, August. *Woodrow Wilson*. New York: Charles Scribner's Sons, 1991.

Hinds, Lynn Boyd, and Theodore Otto Windt. *The Cold War as Rhetoric: The Beginnings, 1945–1950*. New York: Praeger, 1991.

Hitchcock, William I. *The Age of Eisenhower: America and the World in the 1950s*. New York: Simon and Schuster, 2018.

Hixon, Walter L. *Parting the Curtain: Propaganda, Culture, and the Cold War, 1945–1961*. New York: St. Martin's Press, 1997.

Hoffman, Karen S. "Visual Persuasion in George W. Bush's Presidency: Cowboy Imagery in Public Discourse." *Congress & the Presidency* 38, no. 3 (2011): 322–43.

Hogan, J. Michael. "Eisenhower and Open Skies: A Case Study in Psychological Warfare." In *Eisenhower's War of Words: Rhetoric and Leadership*, edited by Martin J. Medhurst, 137–56. East Lansing: Michigan State University Press, 1994.

Hogan, J. Michael. *Woodrow Wilson's Western Tour: Rhetoric, Public Opinion, and the League of Nations*. College Station: Texas A&M University Press, 2006.

Houck, Davis W. "Reading the Body in the Text: FDR's 1932 Speech to the Democratic National Convention." *Southern Communication Journal* 63, no. 1 (1997): 20–36.

Hoxie, R. Gordon. "Eisenhower and Presidential Leadership." *Presidential Studies Quarterly* 13, no. 4 (1983): 589–612.

Immerwahr, Daniel. *How to Hide an Empire: A History of the Greater United States*. New York: Farrar, Straus and Giroux, 2019.

Isaacs, Harold R. *Scratches on Our Minds: American Images of China and India*. New York: John Day, 1958.

Jamieson, Kathleen Hall. *Eloquence in an Electronic Age: The Transformation of Political Speechmaking*. New York: Oxford University Press, 1988.

Johnson, Davi. "Martin Luther King Jr.'s 1963 Birmingham Campaign as Image Event." *Rhetoric & Public Affairs* 10, no. 1 (2007): 1–26.

Judt, Tony. *Postwar: A History of Europe since 1945*. New York: Penguin Books, 2005.

Kahl, Mary L., and Michael Leff. "The Rhetoric of War and Remembrance: An Analysis of President Bill Clinton's 1994 D-Day Discourses." *Qualitative Research Reports in Communication* 7 (2006): 15–21.

Kaplan, Amy. *The Anarchy of Empire in the Making of U.S. Culture.* Cambridge. MA: Harvard University Press, 2005.

Kempe, Frederick. *Berlin 1961: Kennedy, Khrushchev, and the Most Dangerous Place on Earth.* New York: Berkley Books, 2011.

Kennan, George F. *Memoirs, 1925–1950.* Boston: Little, Brown, 1967.

Kennedy, David M. *Freedom from Fear: The American People in Depression and War, 1929–1945.* New York: Oxford University Press, 1999.

Kernell, Samuel. *Going Public: New Strategies of Presidential Leadership.* Washington, DC: CQ Press, 1986.

Kiewe, Amos, and Davis W. Houck. *FDR's Body Politics: The Rhetoric of Disability.* College Station: Texas A&M University Press, 2003.

Kissinger, Henry. *On China.* New York: Penguin Press, 2011.

Kissinger, Henry. *White House Years.* Boston: Little, Brown, 1979.

Krugler, David F. *The Voice of America and the Domestic Propaganda Battles, 1945–1953.* Columbia: University of Missouri Press, 2000.

Laracey, Mel. "'The Rhetorical Presidency' Today: How Does It Stand Up?" *Presidential Studies Quarterly* 39, no. 4 (2009): 908–31.

Lee, Benjamin, and Edward LiPuma. "Cultures of Circulation: The Imaginations of Modernity." *Public Culture* 14, no. 1 (2002): 191–213.

Lee, Erika. *At America's Gates: Chinese Immigration during the Exclusion Era, 1882–1943.* Chapel Hill: University of North Carolina Press, 2004.

Lefebvre, Henri. *The Production of Space.* Translated by Donald Nicholson-Smith. Malden, MA: Blackwell Publishing, 1991.

Leff, Michael. "Textual Criticism: The Legacy of G. P. Mohrmann." *Quarterly Journal of Speech* 72, no. 4 (1986): 377–89.

Leuchtenburg, William E. *In the Shadow of FDR: From Harry Truman to Barack Obama.* 4th ed. Ithaca, NY: Cornell University Press, 2009.

Lew-Williams, Beth. *The Chinese Must Go: Violence, Exclusion, and the Making of the Alien in America.* Cambridge, MA: Harvard University Press, 2018.

Lewis, Tiffany. "Winning Woman Suffrage in the Masculine West: Abigail Scott Duniway's Frontier Myth." *Western Journal of Communication* 75, no. 2 (2011): 127–47.

Lewis, William F. "Telling America's Story: Narrative Form and the Reagan Presidency." *Quarterly Journal of Speech* 73, no. 3 (1987): 280–302.

Link, Arthur S. "Woodrow Wilson: The American as Southerner." *Journal of Southern History* 36, no. 1 (1970): 3–17.

Lippmann, Walter. *The Cold War: A Study in American Foreign Policy.* New York: Harper and Brothers, 1947.

Lowenthal, David. "Past Time, Present Place: Landscape and Memory." *Geographical Review* 65, no. 1 (1975): 1–36.

MacDougall, Walter A. *Promised Land, Crusader State: The American Encounter with the World since 1776.* Boston: Houghton Mifflin, 1997.

MacMillan, Margaret. *Nixon and Mao: The Week That Changed the World.* New York: Random House, 2007.

Massey, Doreen. *Space, Place, and Gender.* Minneapolis: University of Minnesota Press, 1994.

McCullough, David. *The Path between the Seas: The Creation of the Panama Canal, 1870–1914.* New York: Simon and Schuster, 1977.

McCullough, David. *Truman*. New York: Simon and Schuster Paperbacks, 1992.

McFarlane, Megan D. "Visualizing the Rhetorical Presidency: Barack Obama in the Situation Room." *Visual Communication Quarterly* 23, no. 1 (2016): 3–13.

McMahon, Robert J. *The Cold War in the Third World*. New York: Oxford University Press, 2013.

Meacham, Jon. *Thomas Jefferson: The Art of Power*. New York: Random House, 2012.

Medhurst, Martin J., ed. *Before the Rhetorical Presidency*. College Station: Texas A&M University Press, 2008.

Medhurst, Martin J. "Eisenhower and the Crusade for Freedom: The Rhetorical Origins of a Cold War Campaign." *Presidential Studies Quarterly* 27, no. 4 (1997): 646–61.

Medhurst, Martin J. "A Tale of Two Constructs: The Rhetorical Presidency versus Presidential Rhetoric." In *Beyond the Rhetorical Presidency*, edited by Martin J. Medhurst, xi–xxv. College Station: Texas A&M University Press, 1996.

Medhurst, Martin J. "Text and Context in the 1952 Presidential Campaign: Eisenhower's 'I Shall Go to Korea' Speech." *Presidential Studies Quarterly* 30, no. 3 (2000): 464–84.

Medhurst, Martin J. "Writing Speeches for Ronald Reagan: An Interview with Tony Dolan." *Rhetoric & Public Affairs* 1, no. 2 (1998): 245–56.

Medhurst, Martin J., and H. W. Brands, eds. *Critical Reflections on the Cold War: Linking Rhetoric and History*. College Station: Texas A&M University Press, 2000.

Medhurst, Martin J., Robert L. Ivie, Philip Wander, and Robert L. Scott. *Cold War Rhetoric: Strategy, Metaphor, and Ideology*. East Lansing: Michigan State University Press, 1990.

Mee, Charles L. *Meeting at Potsdam*. New York: M. Evans, 1975.

Meese, Edwin. *With Reagan: The Inside Story*. Washington, DC: Regnery Gateway, 1992.

Mercieca, Jennifer R. *Demagogue for President: The Rhetorical Genius of Donald Trump*. College Station: Texas A&M University Press, 2020.

Miller, Roger G. *To Save a City: The Berlin Airlift, 1948–1949*. College Station: Texas A&M University Press, 2000.

Miscamble, Wilson D. *From Roosevelt to Truman: Potsdam, Hiroshima, and the Cold War*. New York: Cambridge University Press, 2007.

Morreale, Joanne. *A New Beginning: A Textual Frame Analysis of the Political Campaign Film*. Albany: State University of New York Press, 1991.

Morris, Edmund. *Theodore Rex*. New York: Random House, 2001.

Murphy, Chad. "The Evolution of the Modern Rhetorical Presidency: A Critical Response." *Presidential Studies Quarterly* 38, no. 2 (2008): 300–307.

Murphy, John M. *John F. Kennedy and the Liberal Persuasion*. East Lansing: Michigan State University Press, 2019.

Neiberg, Michael S. *Potsdam: The End of World War II and the Remaking of Europe*. New York: Basic Books, 2015.

Newman, Robert P. "Lethal Rhetoric: The Selling of the China Myths." *Quarterly Journal of Speech* 61, no. 2 (1975): 113–28.

Nixon, Richard. "Asia after Viet Nam." *Foreign Affairs* 46, no. 1 (1967): 111–25.

Nixon, Richard. *RN: The Memoirs of Richard Nixon, Volume 2*. New York: Warner Books, 1979.

Noonan, Peggy. *What I Saw at the Revolution: A Political Life in the Reagan Era*. New York: Random House, 1990.

Nora, Pierre. *Realms of Memory: Rethinking the French Past*. New York: Columbia University Press, 1996.

O'Donnell, Kenneth P., David F. Powers, and Joe McCarthy. *"Johnny, We Hardly Knew Ye": Memories of John Fitzgerald Kennedy*. Boston: Little, Brown, 1970.

Office of Public Services, Bureau of Public Affairs. *Berlin—1961*. Washington, DC: US Government Printing Office, August 1961.

O'Gorman, Ned. "Eisenhower and the American Sublime." *Quarterly Journal of Speech* 94, no. 1 (2008): 44–72.

O'Gorman, Ned. *Spirits of the Cold War: Contesting Worldviews in the Classical Age of American Security Strategy*. East Lansing: Michigan State University Press, 2012.

Olson, Christa J. "'But in Regard to These (the American) Continents': U.S. National Rhetorics and the Figure of Latin America." *Rhetoric Society Quarterly* 45, no. 3 (2015): 264–77.

Olson, Christa J. *Constitutive Visions: Indigeneity and Commonplaces of National Identity in Republican Ecuador*. University Park: Pennsylvania State University Press, 2014.

Olson, Christa J. "Performing Embodiable Topoi: Strategic Indegeneity and the Incorporation of Ecuadorian National Identity." *Quarterly Journal of Speech* 96, no. 3 (2010): 300–23.

Olson, Lester C. "Pictorial Representations of British America Resisting Rape: Rhetorical Re-Circulation of a Print Series Portraying the Boston Port Bill of 1774." *Rhetoric & Public Affairs* 12, no. 1 (2009): 1–35.

Osgood, Kenneth. *Total Cold War: Eisenhower's Secret Propaganda Battle at Home and Abroad*. Lawrence: University Press of Kansas, 2006.

Ó Tuathail, Gearóid, and John Agnew. "Geopolitics and Discourse: Practical Geopolitical Reasoning in American Foreign Policy." *Political Geography* 11, no. 2 (1992): 190–204.

Parker, Jason C. *Hearts, Minds, Voices: US Cold War Public Diplomacy and the Formation of the Third World*. New York: Oxford University Press, 2016.

Parrish, Thomas. *Berlin in the Balance, 1945–1949: The Blockade, the Airlift, and the First Major Battle of the Cold War*. Reading, MA: Addison-Wesley, 1998.

Parry-Giles, Shawn J. "'Camouflaged' Propaganda: The Truman and Eisenhower Administrations' Covert Manipulation of News." *Western Journal of Communication* 60, no. 2 (1996): 146–67.

Parry-Giles, Shawn J. "The Eisenhower Administration's Conceptualization of the USIA: The Development of Overt and Covert Propaganda Strategies." *Presidential Studies Quarterly* 24, no. 2 (1994): 263–76.

Parry-Giles, Shawn J. *The Rhetorical Presidency, Propaganda, and the Cold War, 1945–1955*. Westport, CT: Praeger, 2002.

Perlstein, Rick. *Nixonland: The Rise of a President and the Fracturing of America*. New York: Scribner, 2008.

Pietrusza, David. Harry S. Truman's Speech at the 1948 Democratic National Convention—Harry S. Truman (July 15, 1948). National Recording Preservation Plan, Library of Congress, https://www.loc.gov/static/programs/national-recording-preservation-board/documents/Truman.pdf.

Pietrusza, David. *1948: Harry Truman's Improbable Victory and the Year That Transformed America*. New York: Union Square Press, 2011.

Plischke, Margarete. "Teaching the Berliner." *American Heritage* 48, no. 4 (1997): 26–27.

Prasch, Allison M. "Obama in Selma: Deixis, Rhetorical Vision, and the 'True Meaning of America.'" *Quarterly Journal of Speech* 105, no. 1 (2019): 42–67.

Prasch, Allison M. "Reagan at Pointe du Hoc: Deictic Epideictic and the Persuasive Power of 'Bringing before the Eyes.'" *Rhetoric & Public Affairs* 18, no. 2 (2015): 247–76.

Prasch, Allison M. "The Rise of the Global Rhetorical Presidency." *Presidential Studies Quarterly* 50, no. 2 (2021): 327–56.

Prasch, Allison M. "A Tale of Two Presidencies: Trump and Biden on the National Mall." *Quarterly Journal of Speech* 107, no. 4 (2021): 472–79.

Prasch, Allison M. "Toward a Rhetorical Theory of Deixis." *Quarterly Journal of Speech* 102, no. 2 (2016): 166–93.

Prasch, Allison M., and Julia Scatliff O'Grady. "Saluting the 'Skutnik': Special Guests, the First Lady's Box, and the Generic Evolution of the State of the Union Address." *Rhetoric & Public Affairs* 20, no. 4 (2017): 571–604.

Prasch, Allison M., and Mary E. Stuckey. "'An Empire for Liberty': Reassessing US Presidential Foreign Policy Rhetoric." *Quarterly Journal of Speech* 108, no. 4 (2022): forthcoming.

Rabe, Stephen G. "The Caribbean Triangle: Betancourt, Castro, and Trujillo and U.S. Foreign Policy, 1958–1963." *Diplomatic History* 20, no. 1 (1996): 55–78.

Rabe, Stephen G. *Eisenhower and Latin America: The Foreign Policy of Anticommunism.* Chapel Hill and London: University of North Carolina Press, 1988.

Reagan, Ronald. *An American Life.* New York: Simon and Schuster, 1990.

Reagan, Ronald. *Speaking My Mind.* New York: Simon and Schuster, 1989.

Rose, Richard. *The Postmodern President: The White House Meets the World.* Chatham, NJ: Chatham House Publishers, 1988.

Rosenberg, Victor. *Soviet-American Relations, 1953–1960: Diplomacy and Cultural Exchange during the Eisenhower Presidency.* Jefferson, NC: McFarland, 2005.

Rowland, Robert C., and John M. Jones. "One Dream: Barack Obama, Race, and the American Dream." *Rhetoric & Public Affairs* 14, no. 1 (2011): 125–54.

Rowland, Robert C., and John M. Jones. "Reagan at the Brandenburg Gate: Moral Clarity Tempered by Pragmatism." *Rhetoric & Public Affairs* 9, no. 1 (2006): 21–50.

Rowland, Robert C., and John M. Jones. *Reagan at Westminster: Foreshadowing the End of the Cold War.* College Station: Texas A&M University Press, 2010.

Rubin, Bernard. *Political Television.* Belmont, CA: Wadsworth Publishing, 1967.

Said, Edward W. *Orientalism.* New York: Pantheon Books, 1978.

Saunt, Claudio. *Unworthy Republic: The Dispossession of Native Americans and the Road to Indian Territory.* New York: W. W. Norton, 2020.

Scacco, Joshua M., and Kevin Coe. *The Ubiquitous Presidency: Presidential Communication and Digital Democracy in Tumultuous Times.* New York: Oxford University Press, 2021.

Scacco, Joshua M., and Kevin Coe. "The Ubiquitous Presidency: Toward a New Paradigm for Studying Presidential Communication." *International Journal of Communication* 10 (2016): 2014–37.

Schenoni, Luis L., and Scott Mainwaring. "U.S. Hegemony and Regime Change in Latin America." *Democratization* 26, no. 2 (2019): 269–87.

Schiappa, Edward E. *The Beginnings of Rhetorical Theory in Classical Greece.* New Haven, CT: Yale University Press, 1999.

Schlesinger, Arthur M. *A Thousand Days: John F. Kennedy in the White House.* Boston: Houghton Mifflin, 1965.

Schlesinger, Robert. *White House Ghosts: Presidents and Their Speechwriters.* New York: Simon and Schuster, 2008.

Schulten, Susan. *The Geographical Imagination in America, 1880–1950.* Chicago: University of Chicago Press, 2001.

Schwoch, James. *Global TV: New Media and the Cold War, 1946–69.* Urbana: University of Illinois Press, 2009.

Sexton, Jay. *The Monroe Doctrine: Empire and Nation in Nineteenth-Century America.* New York: Hill and Wang, 2011.

Sheeler, Kristina Horn, and Karrin Vasby Anderson. *Woman President: Confronting Postfeminist Political Culture.* College Station: Texas A&M University Press, 2013.

Shirer, William L. *The Rise and Fall of the Third Reich: A History of Nazi Germany.* New York: Simon and Schuster, 1960.

Shome, Raka. "Space Matters: The Power and Practice of Space." *Communication Theory* 13, no. 1 (2003): 39–56.

Shome, Raka, and Radha Hegde. "Culture, Communication, and the Challenge of Globalization." *Critical Studies in Media Communication* 19, no. 2 (2002): 172–89.

Shulman, Holly Cowan. *The Voice of America: Propaganda and Democracy, 1941–1945.* Madison: University of Wisconsin Press, 1990.

Silvestri, Vito N. *Becoming JFK: A Profile in Communication.* Greenwood, CT: Praeger, 2000.

Slotkin, Richard. *The Fatal Environment: The Myth of the Frontier in the Age of Industrialization, 1800–1890.* New York: Atheneum, 1985.

Slotkin, Richard. *Gunfighter Nation: The Myth of the Frontier in Twentieth-Century America.* New York: Atheneum, 1992.

Slotkin, Richard. *Regeneration through Violence: The Mythology of the American Frontier, 1600–1860.* Middleton, CT: Wesleyan University Press, 1973.

Smith, Craig Allen. "Mistereagan's Neighborhood: Rhetoric and National Unity." *Southern Speech Communication Journal* 52, no. 3 (1987): 219–39.

Smith-Rosenberg, Carroll. *This Violent Empire: The Birth of an American National Identity* Chapel Hill: Omohundro Institute and the University of North Carolina Press, 2012.

Sorenson, Ted. *Counselor: A Life at the Edge of History.* New York: HarperCollins Publishers, 2008.

Sorenson, Ted. *Kennedy.* New York: Harper and Row, Publishers, 1965.

Sosna, Morton. "The South in the Saddle: Racial Politics during the Wilson Years." *Wisconsin Magazine of History* 54, no. 1 (1970): 30–49.

Spear, Joseph C. *Presidents and the Press: The Nixon Legacy.* Cambridge, MA: MIT Press, 1984.

Spragens, William C. *The Presidency and the Mass Media in the Age of Television.* Lanham, MD: University Press of America, 1979.

Steger, Manfred B. *The Rise of the Global Imaginary: Political Ideologies from the French Revolution to the Global War on Terror.* Oxford: Oxford University Press, 2008.

Strober, Gerald S., and Deborah H. Strober. *"Let Us Begin Anew": An Oral History of the Kennedy Presidency.* New York: HarperCollins Publishers, 1993.

Stuckey, Mary E. "Competing Foreign Policy Visions: Rhetorical Hybrids after the Cold War." *Western Journal of Communication* 59, no. 3 (1995): 214–27.

Stuckey, Mary E. *The Good Neighbor: Franklin D. Roosevelt and the Rhetoric of American Power.* East Lansing: Michigan State University Press, 2013.

Stuckey, Mary E. *Playing the Game: The Presidential Rhetoric of Ronald Reagan.* New York: Praeger, 1990.

Stuckey, Mary E. "'The Power of the Presidency to Hurt': The Indecorous Rhetoric of Donald J. Trump and the Rhetorical Norms of Democracy." *Presidential Studies Quarterly* 50, no. 2 (2020): 366–91.

Stuckey, Mary E. *The President as Interpreter-in-Chief*. Chatham, NJ: Chatham House Publishers, 1991.

Stuckey, Mary E. "Rethinking the Rhetorical Presidency and Presidential Rhetoric." *Review of Communication* 10, no. 1 (2010): 38–52.

Stuckey, Mary E. *Slipping the Surly Bonds: Reagan's* Challenger *Address*. College Station: Texas A&M University Press, 2006.

Stuckey, Mary E., and Fred J. Antczak. "The Rhetorical Presidency: Deepening Vision, Widening Exchange." *Communication Yearbook* 21 (1998): 405–42.

Stuckey, Mary E., and John M. Murphy. "By Any Other Name: Rhetorical Colonialism in North America." *American Indian Culture and Research Journal* 25, no. 4 (2001): 73–98.

Takaki, Ronald. *A Different Mirror: A History of Multicultural America*. Rev. ed. New York: Back Bay Books, 2008.

Taylor, Charles. *Modern Social Imaginaries*. Durham, NC: Duke University Press, 2004.

Terkel, Studs. *"The Good War": An Oral History of World War II*. New York: New Press, 2011.

Terrill, Robert E. *Double-Consciousness and the Rhetoric of Barack Obama*. Columbia: University of South Carolina Press, 2015.

Thomas, Helen. *Dateline: White House*. New York: Macmillan Publishing, 1975.

Thomas, Helen. *Front Row at the White House: My Life and Times*. New York: Simon and Schuster, 1999.

Tomonaga, Masao. "The Atomic Bombings of Hiroshima and Nagasaki: A Summary of the Human Consequences, 1945–2018, and Lessons for *Homo sapiens* to End the Nuclear Weapon Age." *Journal for Peace and Nuclear Disarmament* 2, no. 2 (2019): 491–517.

Trani, Eugene P. "Woodrow Wilson, China, and the Missionaries, 1913–1921." *Journal of Presbyterian History* 49, no. 4 (1971): 328–51.

Truman, Harry S. *Off the Record: The Private Papers of Harry S. Truman*. Edited by Robert H. Ferrell. New York: Harper and Row, 1980.

Tuan, Yi-Fu. *Space and Place: The Perspective of Experience*. Minneapolis: University of Minnesota Press, 1977.

Tudda, Chris. *Cold War Summits: A History from Potsdam to Malta*. London: Bloomsbury Academic, 2015.

Tudda, Chris. *A Cold War Turning Point: Nixon and China, 1969–1972*. Baton Rouge: Lousiana State University Press, 2012.

Tulis, Jeffrey K. *The Rhetorical Presidency*. Princeton, NJ: Princeton University Press, 1987.

Turner, Frederick Jackson. *Frontier in American History*. New York: Henry Holt, 1920.

Turner, Oliver. *American Images of China: Identity, Power, Policy*. London: Routledge, 2014.

Venator-Santiago, Charles R. *Puerto Rico and the Origins of US Global Empires: The Disembodied Shade*. New York: Routledge, 2015.

Walker, Jeffrey. *Rhetoric and Poetics in Antiquity*. Oxford: Oxford University Press, 2000.

Walworth, Arthur. *America's Moment: 1918*. New York: W. W. Norton, 1977.

Walzer, Michael. *Just and Unjust Wars: A Moral Argument with Historical Illustrations*. New York: Basic Books, 2006.

Warner, Michael. *Publics and Counterpublics*. Cambridge: Zone Books, 2002.

Westad, Odd Arne. *The Global Cold War: Third World Interventions and the Making of Our Times*. Cambridge: University of Cambridge, 2007.

Wood, Gordon S. *Empire of Liberty: A History of the Early Republic, 1789–1815*. New York: Oxford University Press, 2009.

Yang, Michelle Murray. "President Nixon's Speeches and Toasts during His 1972 Trip to China: A Study in Diplomatic Rhetoric." *Rhetoric & Public Affairs* 14, no. 1 (2011): 1–44.

Zarefsky, David. "Four Senses of Rhetorical History." In *Doing Rhetorical History*, edited by Kathleen J. Turner, 19–32. Tuscaloosa: University of Alabama Press, 1998.

Zarefsky, David. *Lyndon Johnson, Vietnam, and the Presidency: The Speech of March 31, 1968*. College Station: Texas A&M University Press, 2021.

Zhai, Qiang. *China and the Vietnam Wars, 1950–1975*. Chapel Hill: University of North Carolina Press, 2000.

Index

Page numbers in italics refer to figures.